Cultures of Multiple Fathers

Florida A&M University, Tallahassee
Florida Atlantic University, Boca Raton
Florida Gulf Coast University, Ft. Myers
Florida International University, Miami
Florida State University, Tallahassee
University of Central Florida, Orlando
University of Florida, Gainesville
University of North Florida, Jacksonville
University of South Florida, Tampa
University of West Florida, Pensacola

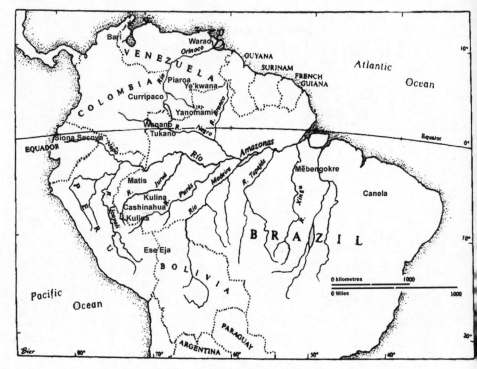

Lowland South America

Cultures of Multiple Fathers

The Theory and Practice of Partible Paternity in Lowland South America

Edited by Stephen Beckerman and Paul Valentine

University Press of Florida

Gainesville · Tallahassee · Tampa · Boca Raton · Pensacola
Orlando · Miami · Jacksonville · Ft. Myers

07 06 05 04 03 02   6 5 4 3 2 1

Cultures of multiple fathers: the theory and practice of partible paternity
in lowland South America / edited by Stephen Beckerman and Paul Valentine.
p. cm.
Includes bibliographical references and index.
ISBN 0-8130-2456-0 (alk. paper)
1. Indians of South America—Kinship. 2. Indians of South America—Sexual behavior.
3. Paternity. 4. Conception. I. Beckerman, Stephen, 1942–. II. Valentine, Paul.
F2230.1.K5 C85 2002
306.7'089'98—dc21   2001034781

The University Press of Florida is the scholarly publishing agency for the State University
System of Florida, comprising Florida A&M University, Florida Atlantic University, Florida
Gulf Coast University, Florida International University, Florida State University, University
of Central Florida, University of Florida, University of North Florida, University of South
Florida, and University of West Florida.

University Press of Florida
15 Northwest 15th Street
Gainesville, FL 32611–2079
http://www.upf.com

Contents

List of Figures and Tables   vii

Introduction: The Concept of Partible Paternity among Native South
   Americans   1
   Stephen Beckerman and Paul Valentine

Part I

1. The Dilemmas of Co-Paternity in Cashinahua Society   14
   Kenneth M. Kensinger

2. The Barí Partible Paternity Project, Phase One   27
   *Stephen Beckerman, Roberto Lizarralde, Manuel Lizarralde, Jie Bai, Carol
   Ballew, Sissel Schroeder, Dina Dajani, Lisa Walkup, Mayhsin Hsiung,
   Nikole Rawlins, and Michelle Palermo*

3. Partible Paternity and Multiple Maternity among the Kulina   42
   Donald Pollock

4. A Story of Unspontaneous Generation: Yanomami Male Co-Procreation
   and the Theory of Substances   62
   Catherine Alès

Part II

5. Canela "Other Fathers": Partible Paternity and Its Changing
   Practices   86
   William H. Crocker

6. Multiple Paternity among the Mẽbengokre (Kayapó, Jê) of Central
   Brazil   105
   Vanessa Lea

7. Several Fathers in One's Cap: Polyandrous Conception among the Panoan Matis (Amazonas, Brazil)   123
   Philippe Erikson

8. Partible Parentage and Social Networks among the Ese Eja   137
   Daniela M. Peluso and James S. Boster

9. Fathering in the Northwest Amazon of Brazil: Competition, Monopoly, and Partition   160
   Janet M. Chernela

Part III

10. Fathers that Never Exist: Exclusion of the Role of Shared Father among the Curripaco of the Northwest Amazon   178
    Paul Valentine

11. A Comparative Analysis of Paternity among the Piaroa and the Ye'kwana of the Guayana Region of Venezuela   192
    Alexánder Mansutti Rodríguez and Nalúa Silva Monterrey

12. Paternal Uncertainty and Ritual Kinship among the Warao   210
    H. Dieter Heinen and Werner Wilbert

13. Sexual Theory, Behavior, and Paternity among the Siona and Secoya Indians of Eastern Ecuador   221
    William T. Vickers

Bibliography   247
Contributors   269
Index   273

Figures and Tables

Frontispiece. Lowland South America

Fig. 6.1. Residential patterns of Mẽtyktire children 107

Fig. 7.1. Matis classificatory kinship (male ego) 125

Fig. 7.2. Matis classificatory kinship (female ego) 126

Fig. 7.3. Conflict between Matis names and roles 132

Fig. 8.1. Network diagram of Ese Eja sexual relationships 152

Fig. 8.2. Network diagram of Ese Eja parent-child links 153

Table 1.1. Cashinahua moieties and marriage sections 15

Table 4.1. Yanomami single and co-fathered births per sex 75

Table 4.2. Yanomami co-fathered births per sex and male marital status 76

Table 6.1. Residential patterns of Mẽtyktire children 108

Table 8.1. Matrix of Ese Eja sexual relationships 151

Introduction

The Concept of Partible Paternity among Native South Americans

Stephen Beckerman and Paul Valentine

The Doctrine

Inhabitants of the modern Western world are well aware that each child has one biological father and one only. We know that, in sexually reproducing organisms, only one sperm fertilizes the egg, and we know this rule holds for people as well as penguins. The doctrine of single paternity, as a folk belief, goes so far back in Western history and is so extended through our social and legal institutions that it is difficult for us to imagine that anyone could entertain any other view of biological paternity. Nowhere in all the begats of the Bible do we find any hint that a child might have more than one father. Aristotle (1992, 53–54) offers no suggestion that a human child might have multiple fathers—although he does hold out that possibility for birds. The Law of the Twelve Tables, the oldest surviving codification of Roman law (451 B.C.), clearly assumes that a child is the product of a single biological father:

The Twelve Tables of Roman Law (451 B.C.)

1. Monstrous or deformed offspring shall be put to death

2. The father shall, during his whole life, have only and absolute power over his legitimate children. He may imprison the son, or scourge him, or work him in the fields in fetters, or put him to death, even if the son has held the highest office of state. He may also sell the son.

3. But if the father sells a son for the third time, the son shall be free of the father.

4. A child born within ten (lunar) months shall be judged a legitimate offspring of the deceased husband. (Harvey 1986)

It is a bit chastening to realize that conclusive *scientific* evidence for singular paternity, for what we can call the One Sperm, One Fertilization Doctrine, is only a little over a century old. Gregor Mendel obtained experimental evidence around 1870 that a single pollen grain introduced into an ovule produced a well-developed seed. In 1879, Hermann Fol published evidence of experimentation and microscopic observation demonstrating that in animals "[f]ertilization is always effected by a single spermatozoon" (Mayr 1982, 666).

Before the end of the nineteenth century, although Western law and custom assumed that each child had a single biological father, that premise was simply a folk belief, resting on other folk beliefs about how babies are made and what the mother and the father contribute—beliefs that seem quaint to us now. Nevertheless, fanciful as these ideas may appear in detail, they had the effect of getting it right insofar as the big question. Biological paternity is singular. Fertilization is a unitary event and copulations after the moment of conception do not contribute anything to the developing fetus. Each child does have only one biological father.

This happy coincidence of folk doctrine and biological reality within our own intellectual tradition has not been without its unfortunate consequences. It has made it easy for us to presume that our folk beliefs concerning fertilization, conception, and fetal development must be everyone's folk beliefs, inevitable and universal. The presumption has channeled and perhaps constrained our thinking about both the biological and the social aspects of paternity. As the articles in this volume demonstrate, other peoples have started from different premises. In this introduction we treat first the biological and then the social-anthropological implications of our faith in the One Sperm, One Fertilization Doctrine; then we discuss the articles themselves. Under each rubric we point out the objections to our Western belief posed by the articles gathered in the volume.

Biology

Most modern scenarios for human evolution invoke paternity certainty as one of the elements leading from African hominids to modern *Homo sapiens*, along with the sexual division of labor, food sharing, lengthy juvenile dependency, and continuous sexual receptivity. The idea is roughly that men provision women and their children with foods that the women cannot obtain on their own, because they are burdened with dependent children. Men are willing to share their food because the women, faithful to their mates, provide the men with a high degree of paternity certainty. When a man brings his game home to his woman, he can reliably assume that the children it feeds are his own (Alexander and Noonan 1979; cf. Washburn and Lancaster 1968.) This scenario, now two decades old, is sometimes called the Standard Model of Human Evolution. It remains the dominant version of the story of the evolution of food sharing and the human family. For instance, in a recent text on human evolution R. Boyd and J. Silk discuss *Homo erectus:* "Prolonged dependence of infants and the reduction of sexual dimorphism may be linked. Females may have had difficulty providing food for themselves and their dependent young. If *H. erectus* hunted regularly, males might have been able to provide high-quality food for their mates and offspring. Monogamy would have increased the males' confidence in paternity and favored paternal investment" (1997, 435). When roughly similar arguments are made for nonhuman animals with biparental care, such as many birds, the male provisioning behavior is presumed to be invoked by proximate cues that indicate a high probability of paternity. There is no need to raise the issue of awareness of how babies are made. However, when the Standard Model is summoned for human beings, then lurking somewhere behind the model is the notion that the men in question are more or less conscious adherents of the One Sperm, One Fertilization Doctrine.

Versions of the Standard Model, with its implicit reliance on the One Sperm, One Fertilization Doctrine, are apparently behind statements in two recent books touching on human nature that take our common Western view of paternity as universal. Steven Pinker, for instance, writes in *How the Mind Works:* "Sexual jealousy is found in all cultures. . . . In most societies, some women readily share a husband, but in no society do men readily share a wife. A woman having sex with another man is *always* a threat to the man's genetic interests, because it might fool him into working for a competitor's genes" (1997, 488–90; italics Pinker's). Even more recently, Edward O. Wilson, in *Consilience,* argues that evolutionary theory predicts that "[t]he optimum sexual instinct of men, to put the matter in the now familiar formula of popular literature, is to be assertive and ruttish, while that of women is to be coy and selective. . . . And in courtship, men are predicted to stress exclusive sexual access and guarantees of paternity, while women consistently emphasize commitment of resources and material security" (1998, 170).

These views of universal human nature, as well as the male-female bargain behind the Standard Model of Human Evolution, are called into question by decades of ethnographic research among tribal peoples in lowland South America. Some of the older work is cited in this introductory essay. Recent findings, particularly those directed to the issues raised here, are reported in this volume. This work, old and new, has made two relevant findings about a substantial number of lowland South American societies. First, the people of these societies have a different doctrine of paternity, one that allows for a child to have several different biological fathers. Second, these people act on that doctrine in such as way as to confute such statements as Pinker's that "in no society do men readily share a wife."

In addition to the societies discussed in this volume, there are quite a few other societies in lowland South America where the idea that paternity is partible, that more than one man can contribute to the formation and development of a fetus, has been reported. These societies are dispersed over much of the continent, and represent many different languages and language families.

For instance, among the Mehinaku of Brazil, speakers of a language in the Arawak family, Thomas Gregor found two theories of conception: "Both theories assert that one sexual act is insufficient to conceive a child. Rather, the infant is formed through repeated acts of intercourse. Since all but three of the village women are involved in extramarital affairs, the semen of the mother's husband may form only a portion of the infant. . . . Joint paternity is further recognized at birth when the putative fathers of the baby honor attenuated versions of the couvade and accept some of the obligations of in-laws when the child grows up and gets married" (1985, 84).

The existence of these ideas is not a recent discovery. Jules Henry clearly encountered the concept of joint or partible paternity among speakers of a language in the Gê family when he worked among the Xocleng (previously known as the Kaingang) in 1933, although he may not have fully recognized what he found:

> "Klendó's daughter, Pathó, is my child," said Vomblé. "How do you know," said I, "since Klendó also lay with her mother?" "Well, when two men lie with a woman they just call her child their child." But not only do men feel that their mistress's children are their children, but people whose mothers have had intercourse with the same man, whether as lover or husband, regard one another as siblings. (1941, 45)

Also in Brazil, but to the north of the Mehinaku and Xocleng, and in a different language family, Eduardo Viveiros de Castro records that among the

Tupi-Guaraní-speaking Araweté, "it is difficult to find someone who has only one recognized genitor" because "more than one inseminator can cooperate . . . or take turns in producing a child. . . . The ideal number of genitors seems to be two or three" (1992, 142, 180).

The Tapirapé are another group of Tupi-Guaran-speaking Brazilian Indians, living hundreds of kilometers to the south of the Araweté. Charles Wagley reports that among them "intercourse had to continue during pregnancy, but it did not need to be with the same male. All men, however, who had intercourse with a woman during her pregnancy were considered the genitors, not merely the sociological fathers of the child. It thus often happened that a child had two or three or more genitors" (1977, 134).

Still further to the south, another society of people speaking a Tupi-Guaraní language, the Aché of Paraguay, have similar ideas:

A man (or men) who was frequently having intercourse with a woman at the time when 'her blood ceased to be found' is considered to be the real father of her child. . . . These primary fathers are most likely to be the ones who take on a serious parenting role. . . . Secondary fathers are also generally acknowledged and can play an important role in the subsequent care of a child. . . . Secondary fathers include all those men who had sexual intercourse with a woman during the year prior to giving birth (including during pregnancy) and the man who is married to a woman when her child is born. (Hill and Hurtado 1996, 249–50)

Thousands of kilometers to the north, J. Hurault writes of the Wayana, Carib speakers of French Guyana: "Selon la croyance des Wayana . . . le mari et l'amant ont tous deux contribué à la conception de l'enfant" (According to the belief of the Wayana . . . the husband and the lover have both contributed to the conception of the child) (1965, 53).

West and south of the Wayana, A. Ramos and B. Albert report on the Sanumá of Brazil, who speak one of the four Yanomama dialects: "According to the ideology of conception, a woman may have intercourse with more than one man around the time she becomes pregnant and all these men are said to contribute to the formation of the fetus" (1977, 77).

In addition to these published cases, Robert Carneiro writes that "the Kuikuru [of Brazil; speakers of a Cariban language] have that concept as well, and they believe that the more men a woman has sexual relations with during pregnancy the better. That way, *fagi*, a spirit sculptor who enters a pregnant woman's uterus, can have more semen to work with in building up and giving shape to the fetus. This explains perfectly reasonably, for them, how it is that a child can have several biological fathers" (pers. comm., February 20, 1998). The baker's dozen of additional cases reported in this volume can be added to the above examples.

If these beliefs were found in only a tribe or two, one might be tempted to write them off as no more than ethnographic curiosities, or even maladaptive delusions, destructive cultural mistakes of the same stripe as the millenarian movements that sometimes persuade peoples—and not just tribal peoples—to abandon their homes and crops to await the end of the world or the coming of a paradisiacal age when all want and injustice is going to be supernaturally rectified. There are clearly some cases in which cultural beliefs promote biologically self-destructive behaviors. Even if the belief in partible paternity were confined to several tribes in a single cultural tradition, one might be able to make a plausible argument that this doctrine is a sort of ideological aberration or pathology.

However, the frequency and distribution of the idea of partible paternity shows that the doctrine is common throughout an entire continent; and that it is found among peoples whose cultural traditions diverged millennia ago, as evidenced by the fact that they live thousands of kilometers apart, speak unrelated languages, and show no indication of having been in contact with each other for many centuries. It is difficult to come to any conclusion except that partible paternity is an ancient folk belief capable of supporting effective families, families that provide satisfactory paternal care of children and manage the successful rearing of children to adulthood. The distributional evidence argues that it is possible to build a biologically and socially competent society—a society whose members do a perfectly adequate job of reproducing themselves and their social relations—with a culture that incorporates a belief in partible paternity.

Indeed, this argument from the geographical distribution of the belief in South America is strengthened by the tantalizing indications in the literature that a belief in partible paternity is not confined to South America, but crops up in other parts of the world as well. A decade and a half ago, Counts and Counts published a report on the ideology of the Lusi of West New Britain Province, Papua New Guinea:[1] "The notion that the foetus grows as a result of multiple acts of intercourse seems to prevail, for the Lusi—even the young people who assert that only one act is required—generally agree that it is possible for a person to have more than one father" (1983, 49). All these findings seem all the more expectable in the light of recent calculations by Wyckoff, Wang, and Wu (2000), which are compatible with the proposition that a good deal of human evolution may have been marked by a reproductive pattern in which semen from multiple mates may have been present at the same time in the female reproductive tract. Indeed, even in the present day there is reason to inquire whether belief in partible paternity may not provide some advantages that are lacking in cultures whose theories of conception are limited to plain-vanilla single paternity. There are a couple of ethnographic cases in South America where we can explore this claim, although we cannot test it directly among all the peoples who profess a belief in partible paternity.

Among the Canela, for instance, virtually every child has several fathers, as reported here by Crocker; and that universality of multiple fatherhood is closely approached, it seems, among the Mehinaku, the Araweté, and possibly the Matis (as described here by Erikson.) In some other societies—the Curripaco, for instance, treated here by Paul Valentine—multiple fatherhood is recognized as a *biological* possibility but is negated on the level of social fatherhood. Only one man can be the pater, the social father, of a child, and other men who have had sex with the mother are not accorded any paternal recognition, nor any rights over nor responsibilities for the child. Among the people of these societies, there is no possibility of comparing people who have multiple fathers with those who do not.

However, there are some societies in the middle range, where many but by no means all children have multiple fathers. In these societies we can begin to look at the advantages that multiple paternity may give to the child and the mother by comparing, among the same people, cases where children have more than one father with cases where children do not. The two societies where we have sufficient data to start to examine these issues are the Aché of Paraguay (Tupi-Guaraní speakers) and the Barí of Venezuela (Chibchan speakers.) Let us look first at advantages that may accrue to the child.

Among the hunting and gathering Aché, Hill and Hurtado report: "The results of logistic regression show that highest survivorship of children may be attained for children with one primary and one secondary father. . . . Our best estimate of the shape of the relationship between age-specific mortality and number of fathers suggests an intermediate number of fathers is optimal for child survival. Those children with one primary and one secondary father show the highest survival in our data set, and one secondary father is also the most common number reported during our reproductive interviews" (1996, 444). Hill has kindly made available some of his unpublished data, which show that in a sample of 227 children born over 10 years ago, 70% of those with only a primary father survived to age 10, while 85% of those who had both a primary and a single secondary father survived to age 10. The difference is significant at p < .01 with a simple chi square test, one tail. Similar comparisons have also been made among the horticultural Barí. There, Beckerman, Lizarralde, Lizarralde, et al. (1998; this volume) again found a survival advantage for children with a secondary father, as detailed in their article in this volume.

How and why can it be that children whose mother has a lover during her pregnancy actually survive better than children whose mother is faithful to her husband? There seem to be two kinds of services that these lovers qua secondary fathers can provide and two people they can provide them to. These men can contribute food (male food: fish and game), either to the mother on behalf of the child, or to the child directly; and they can bestow protection, again either to the mother on behalf of the child, or to the child directly. The papers in this volume provide a number of examples of extra provisioning of children with fish and game, either directly or through the mother or another member of her household (Alès, Beckerman et al., Kensinger, Pollock).

There are no manifest examples in this volume of protective efforts by secondary fathers, although the issue is alluded to in passing by a few of the authors. Hill and Hurtado report that deliberate killing of children was an issue among the Aché, particularly the killing of children whose mother's husband was dead or divorced from the mother. Among the Aché, Hill and Hurtado (1996, 438) suggest that children with secondary fathers might have been somewhat protected from this danger, although the effect did not reach statistical significance in their sample.

Social Anthropology

In addition to sociobiological questions of reproduction and survival, the research reported here bears on central issues in traditional social anthropology. When Malinowski titled a prewar essay "Parenthood: The Basis of Social Structure" (1930b), he was only giving a lapidary formulation to a conviction that went back to the very beginnings of the discipline. As Malinowski himself put it: "The most important moral and legal rule concerning the physiological side of kinship is that no child should be brought into the world without a man—and one man at that—assuming the role of sociological father, that is, guardian and protector, the male link between the child and the rest of the community" (1930b, 137).

From the molecule of mother, single sociological father, and legitimate child, he argued, grew the extended family, the clan, the kinship terminology, and so forth; his title was indeed a summary of his argument. A single father assigned to each child was presumed to be not only universal, but a condition for the development of the rest of human society.

Although Malinowski's theoretical adversary, Radcliffe-Brown (1950), writing just after the war, was careful to note and ratify the ancient distinction between the 'genitor' (biological father) of a child and its 'pater' (social father), he too presumed that only one man could hold the former position and only one man at a time could take the latter. For both these scholars, a child's place in the social world was influenced by its social father—all-importantly if the society were patrilineal, weakly if it were matrilineal, to an intermediate degree if it were cognatic.

In early French structuralism, the place of the single social father appears to have been less explicit, although Lévi-Strauss's original discussion of the origins of marriage exchange in *Les Structures élémentaires de la parenté* (1949) appeared to presume that although several brothers might direct the disposition of their sister in marriage, only one father took that decisive role.

Later discussions of kinship theory (e.g., Schneider 1984), while often discoursing on the application of the kin term for 'father' to many men, usually did not link this plural application of the label to an ideology of conception that allowed for a belief in biological plurality.

Major Themes in This Volume

Although the authors represented in this book approach its topic from several theoretical perspectives, a number of widely shared themes and correlations emerge from a comparative reading of their essays. Nearly as interesting as these relationships is the lack of correlation of some obvious features of culture with the variability found in the presence and particulars of the idea of partible paternity.

Thus, all the societies treated here cultivate manioc and plantains as their staple crops, and fish and hunt for the protein fraction of the diet. Although some of these peoples do far more fishing than hunting, and others vice versa, we have found no relationship between the relative importance of fishing or hunting and the presence or importance of partible paternity. There does not appear to be a relationship between settlement size or population density or any other purely demographic parameter, and the manifestation of partible paternity; nor does there appear to be any interesting geographical ordering of the appearance or absence of partible paternity, beyond the trivial observation that neighbors somewhat resemble each other. Indeed, arguing strongly against the likelihood of correlating the ethnographic presentation of partible paternity with any other cultural feature is the fact that it has been found to be both present (Arvelo-Jiménez 1971, 1974; Heinen and Wilbert, this volume) and absent (Mansutti and Silva, this volume) among different groups of Ye'kwana, a finding that suggests it to be a cultural trait of considerable lability. Nevertheless, a few provocative trends and commonalities do emerge from a comparative reading of the essays presented here.

One such commonality concerns ideas about conception and gestation. Woman's role in conception and the development of the fetus is widely denied among the cultures considered here; the mother is generally considered as the receptacle in which the fetus grows. Some version of this view is reported for the Cashinahua, Kulina, Yanomami, Canela, Matis, Ese Eja, and Curripaco, although Alès makes the point that Yanomami practice stresses the importance of siblings being from the same mother. With respect to the social anthropology of these peoples, Alès observes that, in the context of a belief in partible paternity, this emphasis on the male role in conception and gestation tends to undermine the strength of the patrilineage, because children with multiple fathers are potential members of different patrilineages. This paradox appears to constitute a real social problem for the Yanomami, Curripaco, and Wanano.

Frequently, pregnancy is viewed as a matter of degree, not clearly distinguished from gestation. For the Kulina, for instance, all sexually active women are a little pregnant. Over time, as Pollock reports, semen accumulates in the womb, a fetus is formed, further acts of intercourse follow, and additional semen causes the fetus to grow more. Only when semen accretion reaches a certain level is pregnancy irreversible.

Lea reports somewhat similar ideas among the Mẽbengokre, where there is "neither a notion of fertilization nor of subsequent 'natural' growth; rather the fetus is built up gradually, somewhat like a snowball." Like notions are found among the Yanomami, Curripaco, and Ese Eja. The Barí believe, in contrast, that a single copulation is sufficient to conceive a child, but that the fetus must be anointed repeatedly with semen in order to grow strong and healthy. It follows from these ideas that men in these societies often assert that creating a baby is hard work. Alès reports that Yanomami men say that they expend much energy to make a baby, and become thin from the effort.

Another widespread feature is the negotiability of secondary fatherhood, even where it is recognized as a biological possibility. In general, the mother asserts (or conceals) the identity of the secondary father(s) and the candidate secondary fathers accept or deny the assertion. These assertions and acceptances (and public opinion as to the truth) may change over time and with circumstance. This widespread bargaining brings up the issue of who controls reproduction, and leads to more interesting trends emerging from these essays.

Pollock, building on work by Shapiro (1974) and Århem (1981), suggests an intriguing polarity of "contexts for the reproduction of social life," with an emphasis on marriage and affinity at one end and siblingship at the other. He suggests that partible paternity is most prominent, and most important in child welfare, in societies close to the latter pole.

Another way of looking at this issue is to interpret the polarity as a competition between men and women over whose reproductive interests will dominate social life. In small egalitarian horticultural societies such as the ones considered here, women's reproductive interests are best served if mate choice is a non-binding, female decision; if there is a network of multiple females to aid or substitute for a woman in her mothering responsibilities; if male support for a woman and her children comes from multiple men; and if a woman is shielded from the effects of male sexual jealousy. Male reproductive interests, contrariwise, are best served by male control over female sexual behavior, promoting paternity certainty and elevated reproductive success for the more powerful males. This profile implies that men choose their own or their sons' wives, and their daughters' husbands; that marriage is a lifetime commitment and extramarital affairs by women are severely sanctioned; and that this state of affairs is maintained by disallowing women reliable female support networks, or male support other than that of the husband and his primary male consanguines.

It is obvious that neither sex can ever fully win this contest, yet there are situations that give the advantage to one or the other. Where women clearly have the upper hand, uxorilocal residence predominates; women's husbands are often chosen for them by their mothers, or they choose their own husbands; when a woman's husband dies, his children tend to be brought up by their mother, her brothers, and her new husband; women have broad sexual freedom both before and after marriage; the idea of partible paternity is prominent, with women having wide latitude in choosing the secondary fathers of their children; women usually make no secret of the identity of these secondary fathers; and the ideology of partible paternity defuses to some extent potential conflicts between male rivals—antagonisms that are seldom helpful to a woman's reproductive interests in the long run. The Barí, Canela, Cashinahua, Ese Eja, Kulina, Matis, Mẽbengokre, and perhaps some groups of Ye'kwana fit this description to a greater or lesser extent.

Where men clearly dominate, patrilineality and virilocality are the order of the day; women's husbands are typically chosen by their male relatives; women's sexual activity is policed and sanctioned by men; partible paternity, if it is admitted at all as a biological possibility, tends to be rare and focused on the husband's brothers as the only acceptable secondary fathers of a woman's children. When a woman's husband dies, her children tend to be brought up by her husband's patri-kin, while she may remain unmarried if she is not accepted as a wife by one of the dead husband's brothers; women often conceal the identity of the secondary fathers of their children; and male sexual jealousy constitutes an ongoing potential danger to women. The Curripaco, the Siona-Secoya, and the Wanano are reasonably close to this pole, while the Yanomami are a bit further away, but still nearer this pole than its opposite.

The Piaroa, with their uxorilocal residence pattern and "marked bias to patrilateral filiation" (see chap. 11, this volume), combined with collective food distribution and an ideology that stresses male restraint in sexual activity, appear to be a society in which the battle of the sexes has reached something of a draw, with neither sex's reproductive interests having the upper hand. The Ye'kwana, described by Mansutti and Silva, may be in a similar standoff, more or less equidistant from the poles.

Finally, the Warao, with their robust uxorilocality and fragile marriages until several children have been born, combined with considerable male sexual jealousy, appear to be somewhat closer to the pole at which female reproductive interests dominate (although not as close as the large cluster of societies identified three paragraphs above) despite the weak evidence for a concept of partible paternity.

Organization

The essays in this book are divided into three sections. The first section collects chapters dealing with societies where the concept of partible paternity is present and where the authors make a case that practices associated with the concept have a beneficial effect on the survival of children with multiple fathers. In this section are chapters by Kenneth Kensinger on the Cashinahua, Donald Pollock on the Kulina, Catherine Alès on the Yanomami, and Stephen Beckerman et al. on the Barí.

The second section assembles articles dealing with societies where the concept of partible paternity is found, but where the authors argue that no benefits accrue to the children who have multiple fathers. Here are articles by Philippe Erikson on the Matis, Daniela Peluso and James Boster on the Ese Eja, and Lea on the Mēbengokre. Here also are found two marginal cases: William Crocker writing on the Canela and Janet Chernela discussing the Wanano are effectively on the fence as to whether the institution of partible paternity does (or did) convey significant benefits to children with more than one ascribed genitor, benefits that would not have been obtained without the mother having an affair around the time of her pregnancy. That two such experienced ethnographers should find the issue to be so subtle is an indication of the magnitude of additional research needed.

The third section gathers articles dealing with societies either where the concept of partible paternity is absent or dubious (Dieter Heinen and Werner Wilbert on the Warao, Alexánder Mansutti and Nalúa Silva on the Piaroa and Ye'kwana, and William Vickers on the Siona-Secoya); or where partible paternity exists as a conceptual possibility, but is suppressed on the level of social relations, because only a single social father or the social father and his brother are recognized for each child (Valentine on the Curripaco.) In this third section the authors describe the social institutions that take over the provisioning and protecting functions that in the first group of societies are augmented by the actions of multiple fathers.

Editors' note: The editors thank the contributors for their unfailing cooperation in the preparation of this volume. Their efforts have made its preparation a pleasure. We also thank Sam Scott-Burge for her preparation of the map and diagrams.

Note

1. This reference, as well as one of the South American citations (Henry 1941), is due to Robert Carneiro, who with his customary perspicacity began collecting references to indigenous theories of conception decades ago.

PART I

1

The Dilemmas of Co-Paternity in Cashinahua Society

Kenneth M. Kensinger

For the Cashinahua of the Rio Curanja in southeastern Peru, the identity of a child's mother is certain; it is the woman from whose body the baby emerges, but the identity of the father is less certain.[1] They believe that the fetus is formed in the mother's womb out of semen placed there in the process of sexual intercourse. Any man who has sex with a woman around the time she becomes pregnant or during her pregnancy potentially shares in the paternity of the resulting child. Although marital fidelity is stated as the norm and encouraged, especially by the older men and women, extramarital sex is widespread, at least if one is to believe the rampant female gossip. Both men and women are free to engage in premarital and extramarital sex as long as the affair is carried out discreetly, so that the spouses of the adulterers are not aware of it. Or, if they are aware, they are not put in a position of having to acknowledge their spouses' infidelity publicly. Despite the frequency of women's gossip and speculation about the sex lives of others and the fact that secrecy is virtually impossible, public acknowledgment of extramarital sexual activity is infrequent. Therefore, when a child is born, the mother's husband is socially recognized as its father. When deciding whether to acknowledge that the child has more than one father, or has a father other than the mother's husband, the parties involved consider a multiplicity of factors, including the motivations of both the mother and the potential father(s), the social and economic circumstances of the parties involved, and Cashinahua standards for marital and extramarital sexual behavior. In this essay, I examine the factors a man takes into consideration when he decides to acknowledge or deny publicly being the father of a child. I also look at what is at stake if a woman asserts that her husband is not the father of her child or that he shares paternity with one or more other males.

The Social Context

Moieties and marriage sections provide the framework for defining appropriate marital and nonmarital sexual relationships in Cashinahua society (see table 1.1). There are two male moieties, Inubake and Duabake, and two female moieties, Inanibake or Banubake.[2] The moieties are subdivided into alternating generation groups that function as marriage sections: Inubake and Inanibake are subdivided into Awabake and Kanabake; Duabake and Banubake are subdivided into Yawabake and Dunubake. Proper marriages involve the exchange of spouses between Awabake and Yawabake and between Kanabake and Dunubake. Members of one's own marriage section are classified as one's siblings and thus inappropriate sex partners. The members of the linked marriage section are classified as one's spouses and potential spouses, thus marital, premarital, and extramarital sexual relationships between opposite sex members are defined as appropriate. Members of the other pair of linked marriage sections are classified as parents, parents-in-law, children, or children-in-law and thus are not appropriate sex or marriage partners.

Moiety and marriage section membership automatically provides a significant part of each individual's social identity if, and only if, the sexual activity that produced the child was appropriate with reference to the marriage section identities of the mother and father(s). Under normal circumstances, a man is a member of the moiety of his father and the marriage section of his paternal grandfather; a woman is a member of the moiety of her father's sister and the marriage section of her maternal grandmother. Reclassification of the moiety and marriage section membership of the offspring, particularly that of females, are made if the mother's marriage violated the moiety and/or marriage section rules.[3] This can become an important factor when deciding whether or not to recognize shared paternity.

Although moieties and marriage sections define appropriateness of marriage and sex partners, set the limits for the use of kinship terminology, and provide an essential ingredient in the definition of the social self, they do not

Table 1.1. Cashinahua moieties and marriage sections

	Moiety 1 M = inubake F = inanibake	Moiety 2 M = duabake F = banubake
Marriage Section A	awabake	yawabake
Marriage Section B	kanabake	dunubake

serve as the basis for organizing the social and economic activities of daily life. They function as social groups only in the context of ritual performances. Kinship, family, and place of residence provide the other major sources of an individual's social identity and are the basis for organizing the ongoing life of the community. Although all Cashinahua are by definition one's kin (*nabu*) only certain kin have relevance for an individual, namely those to and with whom one has primary obligations. They are encompassed in three overlapping social groups. The first is *en nabibu*, my primary consanguineal and affinal kin.[4] The second is *en nabukuin*, my extended family, including the primary consanguineal and affinal kin of en nabibu. And the third is *en nabukayabi*, the network of kin included in the two other categories plus village coresidents with whom one has regular and frequent social interaction and economic cooperation.

Finally, there are the residential groups: *habe nun hiwemiski* (those with whom we live), namely the household, *hiwe*, and *mae* (the village). In traditional villages these entities were isomorphic, that is, the household and the village were one and the same; all villages are now composed of two or more households. Although a slight majority of households now consist of a single nuclear family, the uxorilocal extended family, including a woman (with or without her husband), her daughters with their husbands and children, and unmarried sons, is considered the most economically secure form of household. Furthermore, most women express a strong preference for uxorilocal residence because it strengthens their position in the ongoing battle of the sexes. A variant of this is a cluster of houses surrounding the mother's house in which some of her married daughters live with their nuclear families, but where for all practical purposes the cluster functions as a single economic unit.

The Economic Context

A husband is expected to support his wife/wives and children through building and maintaining a house, hunting, fishing, making gardens, and obtaining the trade goods now considered essential for living well. He also has obligations of economic support toward his wife's parents whether or not he is living uxorilocally. The success of his marriage often depends more on keeping his mother-in-law satisfied through his economic activities than satisfying his wife. Of greatest importance is a steady supply of meat into the household. His ability to fulfill his economic obligations depends in some part on the support and collaboration of other kinsmen, particularly his brothers and brothers-in-law.

A wife, in addition to having primary responsibility for child care, contributes her share to the well-being of the household through harvesting crops from the garden, gathering firewood, preparing food, collecting, carding and spinning cotton, weaving hammocks, and making ceramic cooking pots and bowls. If she lives in an extended family household, she shares many of these tasks with the coresident females of the household. If not, she works in collaboration with one or more of the other women from nearby households at those tasks that require her to leave the village clearing, namely harvesting garden produce and gathering firewood. Women, especially younger, sexually desirable women rarely, if ever, leave the village unaccompanied by other women. As a couple ages, their economic well-being is enhanced by, and in some cases requires, the assistance of their children, particularly their daughters and sons-in-law. Thus, although Cashinahua couples often express a preference for boys, who will become hunters, they consider daughters essential for their future economic well-being since it is daughters who attract husbands (i.e., sons-in-law). Furthermore, they cannot rely on having sons in residence since the expectation of uxorilocal postmarital residence will in all probability remove the sons from their parents' household.

The Sexuality Context

The frequency and intensity of extramarital sexual activity tends to be highly variable, depending largely on the libidos of the participants. Some men rarely, if ever, engage in it while others are highly predatory. Most women, according to my informants, rarely find such encounters pleasurable because they are furtive and quickly completed. Women say that most men are only concerned about getting their release and not in satisfying their partners. A few men gain reputations as considerate lovers and consequently are more successful at recruiting sex partners. The most frequent reason men give for engaging in extramarital sex is the unavailability of their wives due to pregnancy or to postpartum or menstruation taboos; women cite either dissatisfaction with their husband's sexual performance or the excitement of being desired.

The choice of an extramarital sex partner ideally is subject to the same constraints as the choice of a marriage partner; partners are usually chosen from the marriage section linked with one's own. However, as with marriage, violations carried out with discretion are largely met with indifference except when they involve persons who are primary kin/affines to each other, that is, those who are one's nabukuin, including one's actual brother or sister, mother or father, mother-in-law or father-in-law, son or daughter, son-in-law or daughter-in-law. Many wives tend to be tolerant of their husbands' philandering so long as the gifts given to the lovers do not negatively effect the economy of the household, particularly the supply of meat. Some women told me with a degree of satisfaction that their husbands were less demanding for sex when getting sexual relief from a lover. Men tend to be less understanding of extramarital sexual activity by their wives but are constrained from making a public issue of it since wives who are sexually satisfied by their husbands are less likely to succumb to the advances of other males. Lest it appear that only males take the initiative in extramarital affairs, it should be noted that women are just as free as men to instigate them; few do, however.

Unmarried males and females are free to engage in premarital sex. However, until a man has established his reputation as a successful hunter, he is not likely to attract married or unmarried female partners, who expect gifts in exchange for their sexual favors. A man rarely hands these gifts to his lover directly; he usually sends them to her by one of his younger relatives, frequently by a younger sister. Single women tend to prefer beads, soap, perfumes, and other trade goods; married women prefer meat since its presence in the house is less likely to arouse the suspicions of, or lead to confrontations with, their husbands. The major constraint against extramarital sex on the part of both husbands and wives is the tensions that may develop between them arising from the knowledge of their spouse's infidelity, whether or not it is openly acknowledged. Often of greater concern is the attitude of the wife's mother to her son-in-law's indiscretions. She may agitate for dissolution of the marriage and his expulsion from the household. It should be noted that most divorces are instigated by mothers-in-law who are unhappy with their sons-in-law for a variety of reasons. The most common reason is that she considers him lazy or an unsatisfactory provisioner of the household—more often than not that he is an unsuccessful hunter. Almost as frequently cited, however, is the son-in-law's attitude; he doesn't show the respect due his mother-in-law.

To Acknowledge or Not to Acknowledge Shared Paternity

Given this background, we are now in a position to examine the dilemmas created by shared paternity. Why does a man publicly admit or deny being the father or co-father of a child? What motivates a woman publicly to acknowledge her sexual involvement with a man or men other than her husband? And finally, what are the disadvantages of public recognition that a child has more than one father as a result of its mother's having had sexual relations with more than one man just before or during her pregnancy?

Social Considerations

Although the mother's husband is considered to be the father of her child, he must publicly acknowledge paternity by observing a series of food taboos and restricting his activities following the birth of the child; most specifically, he must refrain from hunting until the umbilicus has dried and fallen off. These restrictions also apply to co-fathers. A man's compliance indicates his willingness to be recognized publicly as a "real" father of the child. Public acknowledgment of shared paternity means that his past extramarital affair can no longer be hidden from his wife and kin, nor can they ignore it.

Although sexual activity is the subject of gossip and joking, specific occurrences of it often are not given public recognition, allowing spouses and close kin of an adulterous couple to ignore their sexual indiscretions unless they become too blatant. Public acknowledgment of shared paternity, however, has the potential to create or intensify social rifts within and between families. Such conflicts are the frequent consequences of tensions and jealousies instigated or aggravated by marital infidelity and if not resolved, may lead to public quarrels resulting in village fissioning. Alternatively, acknowledgment of shared paternity and acting on it may alleviate these tensions because the co-father has accepted the responsibilities fatherhood places upon him.

An important but less frequently discussed consideration in deciding whether or not to acknowledge co-paternity publicly is the impact it can have on the child's social identity. If the co-fathers are all members of the appropriate marriage section the outcome is negligible since all the males of that group are already classified as father and will be addressed as such by the child. In such cases the impact of acknowledged co-paternity is largely economic. If a co-father has no sons by his wife or wives, however, he may decide to play a significant role in the socialization of the acknowledged son. For a male, having sons is important because it is his sons who provide him with namesakes, namely his sons' sons, and thus with social perpetuity. If, on the other hand, he has no daughters by his wife, he and his wife may treat a daughter he has co-fathered as a member of their household, hoping that when she marries she and her husband will take up residence with them, an outcome only possible if the girl is not her mother's only daughter. Coresident daughters and sons-in-law are a kind of social security for a couple in their old age.

If, however, a co-father is a member of the wrong marriage section or moiety, social recognition of his role in paternity can create uncertainty about the moiety and marriage section to which the child should belong. This problem is resolved when the child is named; a boy's namesake is normally his paternal grandfather, a girl's namesake is her maternal grandmother or her paternal grandfather's sister, often one and the same person. It should be noted that in addition to providing the child a name, the namesake often becomes the child's mentor and guardian, looking out for his or her well-being. The name both determines and serves as an indicator of the child's moiety and marriage section identity. This identity may not be permanent, however. I have a case in my field notes in which a young man wanted to marry a girl. Her father objected because he, the prospective husband, was a member of the wrong marriage section. At that point his maternal grandmother reminded the girl's father and the entire community that young man's co-father (not previously publicly acknowledged) was a member of the appropriate marriage section. After the prospective husband changed his name, moiety, and marriage section membership, her father agreed to the marriage. This was a most unusual case because males are reluctant to change their names and consequently their moiety and marriage membership. Several informants told me that if his father had still been alive the prospective husband would not have been able to do this. Two years later this marriage ended in divorce and the husband reassumed his prior name and marriage section and moiety membership. I have four cases in my field notes of women whose mothers married men, their primary fathers, in violation of the moiety and marriage section rules but whose co-fathers were members of the appropriate marriage sections or moieties. In all four cases the women considered the mothers' husbands to be their primary fathers in terms of economic support but they derived their names and social identities as members of the moieties and marriage sections through their co-fathers.

Economic Considerations

When a woman contemplates asking a man other than her husband to publicly acknowledge shared paternity, she must consider the economic consequences. First, her husband may divorce her, leaving her without economic support. He is unlikely to do so unless he already has another wife or there is another woman who is ready and willing to marry him; he is just as dependent on his wife's economic services as she is on his. A woman is usually reluctant to risk divorce unless her lover is willing to take her as a second wife or leave his present wife to marry her, both unlikely possibilities. Second, if her husband is not a good provider, particularly if he is not a successful hunter, she may decide that it is better to make public that her lover is the co-father of the child so as to assure an enhanced supply of meat for her household. Although she has been receiving small gifts of meat surreptitiously following each sexual encounter, public recognition of the co-father increases the chances of his supplying meat to her household on a regular basis, whether or not their affair continues. Several women told me that they took the risk of public recognition of their adulterous relationship because the added supply of meat would improve their supply of breast milk, thus making the child stronger and healthier. A woman is often encouraged in this decision by her mother, who wishes to enhance the meat supply of her household.

The economic considerations for a man are related but somewhat different. First, before acknowledging co-paternity he must consider the impact that postpartum taboos, most specifically the restrictions on his hunting, will have on the economic well-being of his primary family, particularly his mother-in-law's response to the reduced supply of meat. Second, such acknowledgment places him under obligation for future economic support for the child and its mother, although not to the same extent as if he were married to the mother. In the 1990s, there was an expectation that, in addition to meat, a man will also provide clothing and other trade goods for the child, thus increasing his economic obligations.

Both men and women often consider the potential to initiate or enhance relationships with primary kin of the lover, hence broadening their network of friends (*haibu*),[5] with whom they can collaborate in joint economic activities (e.g., hunting, clearing and burning for new gardens). This option becomes significant when an individual has few primary kin or affines within the village.

Sexual Considerations

How frequently individuals choose to engage in extramarital sex varies widely depending on a range of factors and differs between women and men. The reason women take lovers seems more to be the satisfaction derived from being the object of desire rather than a high libido; based on the reports of men it appears that few women gain gratification from the sexual activity itself.[6] Younger women with few or no children are apt to have more lovers because they are more often the objects of men's desires. Most men say that young women have tighter vaginas and thus are more satisfying sex partners. Some men, especially those most sexually active, disagree, saying that the more sexually experienced women are more active and aggressive during the sex act and thus more gratifying.

Women with nursing babies are not supposed to participate in any sexual activity for up to a year after the birth of a child; this prohibition is the most common reason men give to justify their adulterous affairs. Women with many children have few lovers, mainly because they do not want to risk another pregnancy. Although the reason most frequently given by both men and women for a wife to have an affair is to get even with an adulterous husband, she rarely responds this way but is more likely to retaliate by refusing to have sex with him.

More men than women engage in extramarital sex, but there is a wide range of variability among men. All my male informants acknowledged having premarital sex and most admitted to having sex with women other than their wife or wives. One man with four wives claimed to be having extramarital affairs with nine women concurrently. Men with high sex drives and ambition tend to have more sex partners or at least try to have more. Those with the greatest number of lovers tend to be the best hunters or are men who have reputations for being considerate of the sexual needs of their partners. Because most extramarital sex tends to be quickly completed or furtive, a lover who is concerned about satisfying his partner's sexual needs, and not just his own, is highly desirable. A man with a reputation for impregnating women is rejected as a lover by women who do not wish to risk another pregnancy but is sought out by those who have been unable to conceive. A man who has only sons by his wife is desirable as a sex partner by a woman wanting a son. The same applies to a man with only daughters and a woman who wants a daughter.

An unrepentant and blatant philanderer whose behavior becomes socially disruptive is often expelled from the village, allowing peace, at least overtly, to be restored. A promiscuous female is ostracized by the women and is often abandoned by her husband but is not exiled.

Shared Paternity: What Is to Be Gained?

If gossip is to be believed, most men are, in fact, co-fathers. Nevertheless, between 1955 and 1997 only seven men were publicly recognized to share paternity with the socially recognized fathers. Given the potential for social disruption caused by public acknowledgment, as opposed to public awareness, of extramarital sex and the increased economic obligations entailed, why would a man choose to be named as a co-father?

First, if a man has an active libido and wants to maximize his chances of success, his acknowledgment of paternity establishes his virility, which, combined with a reputation as a caring lover, enhances his chances for success in his sexual pursuits. Second, his acknowledgment shows him to be a responsible individual; he accepts the economic obligations of fatherhood. A man who engages in extramarital sex without accepting any of the attendant obligations is called *shishi*, a raccoon (i.e., a thief). Third, and probably most important, co-fatherhood expands his primary social group, his nabibu, the social group within which the obligations of mutual support and cooperation are most effective. A large and harmonious nabibu is the clearest indicator of a man's success as a man.

Discussion

What are the ethnological lessons to be learned from the Cashinahua? We see that nonmarital and extramarital sex has social implications and potential consequences; it is not simply a private act involving a man and a woman. Few Cashinahua women are sexually inexperienced when they marry, shortly before or after the onset of menses. A girl who gains a reputation of being promiscuous, however, lessens her chances of attracting a husband rather than lovers, thus placing at risk her economic future as well as that of her family. Lovers' gifts are trivial in comparison to the economic contributions of a coresident husband. From a lover she can expect a few trinkets, items of clothing, or choice morsels of meat. Her husband, on the other hand, will build her a house. Annually he will clear and burn a forest plot, where he will plant a garden. He will also clear and plant a peanut garden on a sandbar along the river at the onset of each dry season. He will hunt and fish regularly, supplying the household with a steady supply of meat and fish. And finally, he will produce whatever goods are necessary to exchange with the Peruvian shopkeepers in Esperanza for the clothing, pots and pans, metal tools, and other items that have become a necessary part of Cashinahua daily existence.

Furthermore, a woman's marriage creates a network of social relationships that has both social and economic consequences. When she marries, she and her husband will reside in the household of her mother, where she will continue to cooperate with her mother and other female coresidents in the daily economic chores. As children are born and her responsibilities increase, a woman depends on the assistance of her kinswomen, particularly her mother, to look out for her children while she goes to the garden along with other women to harvest manioc, bananas, plantains, and other crops. She shares cooking chores with the other women of her household. Social ties to her husband's family or to other households within the village (or both) enlarge the network of women with whom she can cooperate in these tasks. They also enhance her chances of receiving a share of the meat distributed when a man from another household shoots a large animal like a tapir or a wild pig, no small consideration since meat is the sin qua non of a Cashinahua meal.

In Cashinahua society, a single adult female is an anomaly, an unmarried woman with young children is inconceivable. A widow who does not remarry is the responsibility of her children, particularly her married daughters. In most cases she continues to dominate the uxorilocal household of which she has been the focal female until old age limits her activities. At that time her daughter, or on occasion her daughter-in-law, will have assumed the focal female role within the household.

An unmarried man is expected to be more adventurous sexually than a single woman, even promiscuous. However, if he wants a particular woman to agree to marry him, it behooves him to confine his sexual activity to her, lest she or her parents, particularly her mother, question the seriousness of his intent. Marriage involves shifting his economic obligations from the household of his parents to that of his parents-in-law, although he may continue to make contributions of meat to his parents and sisters. While marital fidelity is not required or even expected, philandering, particularly if it is not carried out with discretion, places great stresses on his relationship with his wife and opens him to criticism and censure from his mother-in-law. He soon learns that it is easier to please his wife than his mother-in-law, who ultimately has more to say about the durability of his marriage than his wife. He not only continues to work cooperatively with his own brothers but also is expected to work collaboratively with his wife's brothers, particularly in the making of new gardens. Although his marriage adds a new set of obligations, it also provides him with additional males to call on to assist him in his work.

For the Cashinahua, marriage is not primarily a joining of a man and a woman in a sexual relationship, although it is that. It is, rather, the nexus of a series of social and economic relationships that determine a couple's well-being.

In the absence of DNA analysis nonmarital and extramarital sex can create a problem in establishing the social identity of any child born to a woman who has had multiple sex partners at the time she becomes pregnant. The Cashinahua belief that a child is the product of the accumulation of semen implanted in the uterus of the mother during intercourse (her womb is merely the container within which the fetus grows) means that paternity must be established in order to determine the moiety and marriage section of the child. The man (or in the case of shared paternity, the men) who observes the postpartum restrictions on food consumption and physical activities is acknowledged to be a boy's father and the boy becomes a member of his father's moiety and his father's father's marriage section. On this both male and female informants agree, but they disagree on the source of a girl's social identity. Men say that their daughters are members of the moiety of the girl's father's sister, and the marriage section of the girl's father's father's sister and thus it is essential to establish the paternity of a girl. Women argue that their daughters are members of the moiety and marriage section of their mother's mother (who incidentally is often simultaneously the girl's father's father's sister). Thus, from the women's point of view, identifying a girl's father is not required to establish her social identity. However, a man must acknowledge paternity of a daughter by observing postpartum taboos if she is to have the social and economic support necessary for her future well-being. Furthermore, although establishing a child's moiety and marriage section membership may have limited consequences for the child's daily life, it has serious implications for the child's future choices of appropriate marital and sex partners.

From an ethnological perspective nonmarital and extramarital sexual activity is not fundamentally a moral issue. For the Cashinahua, sexual activity with a partner other than one's spouse is not defined as immoral. It becomes an issue only when and if it becomes socially disruptive or when one or both of the parties in a sexual relationship fail to fulfill their social and economic obligations to kin, especially to their spouses and children.

Thus, the philanderer's dilemma is not whether he has behaved morally or immorally but what will be the social and economic consequences of his acknowledging paternity of a child by a woman who is not his wife. The social consequences may include rupturing valued social relationships, or establishing new relationships, or strengthening already existing relationships. The economic consequences are the increased obligations of support for his child and its mother, a not inconsiderable consequence if he already has a wife or wives and children.

Notes

1. This essay is based on extensive conversations with both male and female informants during 84 months of residence with them between 1955 and 1968 and another 12 months during 1993–94 and 1997. Males readily discussed with me sexual matters, real and imagined, but generally refrained from talking about the sexual activities of specific other males. Females were always ready to give me the latest gossip about ongoing or past affairs and were not reluctant to name the parties; however, they refused to discuss their own sexual activities with me.

2. Males usually consider the female moieties to be part of the male moieties (i.e., that Inanibake are part of Inubake and that Banubake are part of Duabake). Women reject this view, citing their separate roles during ritual activities.

3. I stated in a previous publication (Kensinger 1995, 112–13) that an inappropriate marriage did not affect the moiety membership of a male (he would be a member of his father's moiety and the marriage section of his father's father), but that the moiety and marriage section membership of all females had to be adjusted. Evaluation of data gathered during my 1993–94 fieldwork leads me to believe that adjustments may be made for males as well. A person's moiety and marriage section membership may be negotiable both at the time of birth and at a later date.

4. These include F, M, B, Z, S, D, FF, FM, MM, SS, SD, DD, DS, H, HF, HM, BW (female ego), ZH (male ego). The affinal notations are used here as an analytical convenience. The Cashinahua do not make the distinction between affinal and consanguineal kin. All other Cashinahua are considered kin; some are marriageable and some are not. Instead of the affinal notation, it would perhaps be more consistent with Cashinahua thinking to use the following: H = FZS/MBS, W = FZD/MBD, HF = MB, HM-FZ, WF = MB, WM = FZ, BW = FZD/MBD (female ego), ZH = FZS/MBS (male ego).

5. The term *haibu* (vocative *haibun*) is generally used in lieu of kin terms when speaking about or addressing a person who is not a primary kinsman. It implies a social relationship closer than would be expected with a nonprimary kinsman.

6. For a discussion of Cashinahua sexuality, see Kensinger (1995, 75–82).

2

The Barí Partible Paternity Project, Phase One

Stephen Beckerman, Roberto Lizarralde, Manuel Lizarralde, Jie Bai,
Carol Ballew, Sissel Schroeder, Dina Dajani, Lisa Walkup, Mayhsin Hsiung,
Nikole Rawlins, and Michelle Palermo

The Barí Partible Paternity Project (BPPP) is an exploration among the Barí of Venezuela of the notion, widespread in lowland South America, that a child can have more than one biological father. Among the Barí, this belief in partible paternity reveals itself most notably in a common practice whereby a married woman takes a lover during pregnancy, thus providing the resulting child with a "secondary father" in addition to the mother's husband. A previous report from the BPPP (Beckerman et al. 1998) demonstrated a statistically significant advantage in survivorship for children with secondary fathers over other children with only a single father. In this chapter we examine secondary fatherhood among the Venezuelan Barí in greater detail and with more sophisticated statistical methods, and explore the conditions under which it occurs. We also look into the particulars of its consequences for child survivorship.

The phenomenon of partible paternity is of general anthropological interest for the light it throws on presumed cultural universals in sex roles, sexual behavior, and the relations between the sexes. The erroneous idea that paternity certainty is a ubiquitous concern among *Homo sapiens* has a lengthy history, briefly sketched in the introduction to this volume. Current research is revealing the less than universal distribution of a preoccupation with identifying the one true genitor of every child. Among the many cultures in which paternity is conceived in such a way as to make the identification of a single male as the unique genitor of a child a moot issue, the Barí are currently the people among whom partible paternity has received the most anthropological attention.

Ethnographic Background

Although the Barí speak a Chibchan language, related to those formerly spoken in the highland northern Andes, they live in the lowland tropical rain forest, in the southwesternmost lobe of the Maracaibo Basin. Their land lies on both sides of the border between Colombia and Venezuela. They accepted a modern peaceful contact only in July 1960 (Lizarralde and Beckerman 1982). For the century and a half before that date they had been at war with all their neighbors.

In common with many of the peoples of the lowland tropical forest, the Barí lived, in the times before and just after modern peaceful contact, in villages composed of a single communal dwelling, a longhouse usually inhabited by 50 ± 20 people. The longhouse was constructed in the middle of a garden whose main crop was manioc, the dietary staple. As among many of the other native peoples of tropical South America, the Barí obtained the protein in their diet by fishing and hunting, the former more important than the latter; 75% of animal flesh came from fish (Beckerman 1983, 1991).

As pointed out by Dufour (1992, 1994), a manioc-based diet, supplemented by fish and game, is usually ample for adult males, but may be marginal for small children, because the low nutrient density of manioc may not allow the packing of enough food into a child's gut to provide adequate nutrition. Similar problems may arise for pregnant and lactating women. Maintaining a steady supply of a sufficient level of animal protein and fat is important to avoid protein-calorie and micronutrient malnutrition.

The traditional Barí sexual division of labor was far-reaching. Men cleared the fields and planted the first crop; both men and women weeded and cultivated, with women taking the lead role; women did almost all harvesting and all cooking. Women also participated in fishing, building one of the pair of weirs that were used in spear fishing between double weirs, the most profitable way that the Barí obtained animal protein. During fishing expeditions, women guzzled for crabs and slow-moving fish (groping under logs and stones with exquisite slowness until with a quick grab they seized their prey) and usually got a few grams of animal flesh by these efforts. The actual spearing of fish, however, provided the vast majority of the fishing catch, and was a male monopoly, with the fish belonging to the man who speared them. Hunting was exclusively male.

As a result of the sexual division of labor in subsistence, it was sufficiently difficult to make a living without a partner of the opposite sex that single adults typically lived with their parents, or, if the opposite-sex parent were dead, with a married sibling, until acquiring a spouse.

Insofar as social organization, although each longhouse group of Barí had a core of people who were closely related, there were no descent groups among them, or any other kinds of corporate kin groups aside from the hearth group. The hearth group was usually a nuclear to small extended family. It hung its hammocks in a particular section of the periphery of the longhouse and cooked its pooled food at its own hearth. The most common form of hearth group was made up of a married couple, their junior children, and often the husband(s) of the recently married daughter(s.) Elderly parents of any member might also belong, as might unmarried siblings. At times two married adult siblings, with their spouses and children, formed a single hearth group for a few years. Unrelated single individuals sometimes attached themselves to a hearth group for one reason or another.

The hearth group was the social and economic molecule of Barí life, the unit of production and consumption. There was no larger group to substitute for or oversee its tasks of food production and consumption. Gifts of food from the senior male member of one hearth group to one or more members of another did sometimes occur, but were irregular, and were accomplished with the utmost discretion, making it very difficult in ethnographic work to discern who gave food to whom.

The magnitude of the hearth group's role in feeding its members, and the importance of the male component of the diet in that role, was piercingly articulated by a dying man during one of the postcontact epidemics of the 1960s (Lizarralde and Beckerman 1982). His last words to his daughter were a desolate, "Who will hunt for you now?"

Distribution of food within the hearth group took place both formally and informally. Breakfast was the major meal. It took place well after dawn, when the young men of the hearth group returned from their first-light hunting and scouting jaunt into the forest. The wife of the senior man of the group set out one or two heliconia leaves in the hearth group's section of the longhouse periphery. On them she piled a steaming mound of just-cooked manioc chunks and another mound of boiled or smoked fish or game. All members of the hearth group gathered around the leaf, children sitting among the adults. The senior man of the hearth group pushed a chunk of manioc and a fish, or a piece of game, to everyone sitting around the leaf. After a group member had finished these first bits, he could take additional manioc and meat from the piles without waiting to be served. Mealtimes were quiet; it was impolite to talk while eating.

The only other communal meal was dinner, after dark. In protocol, it was much the same as breakfast, but was a smaller meal. If there were a shortage of fish and game, the animal protein was saved for the next morning's breakfast.

Women did all the cooking and had both vegetable and animal foods in their possession from the time they entered the house until they reached the heliconia leaf. On a number of occasions, SB and RL saw a woman take a snack (e.g., part of a small bird, a bit of smoked fish) from one of her food baskets and give it to one of her small children between meals.

A longhouse group was typically composed of about a dozen hearth groups. Relations among them were friendly (their senior male heads were often brothers or brothers-in-law), but each hearth group in effect ran its own separate economy, and longhouse-wide meat sharing was limited to occasional large animals usually hunted collectively by all men in the longhouse, such as tapir and peccary.

The weakness of ascribed kin obligations outside the hearth group is illustrated by a remarkably truncated set of kin terms. In effect, the Barí had a Dravidian system of terminology reduced to (one eminent anthropologist has suggested reduced below) its bare essentials. The few terms for known relatives were supplemented by the classification of everyone, both known kin and those for whom no genealogical connection was recalled, into two categories, *sagdojira* and *okjibara*. The words translate well as consanguine and affine, respectively. The incest taboo covered all people classed as sagdojira; marriage was only possible with an okjibara.

Each longhouse group of Barí occupied a range in which it simultaneously maintained several—normally two to five—different longhouses, distant one from another by half a day's walk or more. The people of the longhouse group (otherwise here labeled the local group) cycled around their range in rough concord with the seasons—downstream on the major rivers during the dry season to fish, in the uplands during the height of the rainy season to hunt.

A handful of local groups were associated as a territorial group. There were no more than ten such territorial groups in peri-contact times. The exact number in Colombia is unclear; there were four in Venezuela (R. Lizarralde 1991; Lizarralde and Lizarralde 1991). These four territorial groups were roughly similar in size, containing 100 to 250 individuals (R. Lizarralde 1991). The transfer of hearth groups from one longhouse group to another within the territorial group seems to have been fairly common.

There is no evidence of violence between or within territorial or longhouse groups. Indeed, in internal relations, Barí civil life was marked by an avoidance of confrontation at even the verbal level.

Marriage normally took place around age 15 for females and 20 for males. All known patrilineal relatives were sagdojira and were covered by the incest taboo, but matrilineal relatives, even those as close as MB-ZD, were eligible marriage partners. About 15% of men were polygynous at some time in their lives; women married only one husband at a time (Zaldívar, Lizarralde, and Beckerman 1991). Local group endogamy was preferred, but given the small size of the longhouse group, was more often than not impossible. Territorial group endogamy was the fallback preference; it was achieved by most Barí (Lizarralde and Lizarralde 1991).

Uxorilocality was in principle the preferred form of postmarital residence, with the son-in-law joining his father-in-law's hearth group until the new couple had a child or two, at which time they usually formed a hearth group of their own. The uxorilocal preference was far from a rigid prescription, however, and a wide variety of residence choices actually occurred, particularly when the bride had older sisters who were already married or when her parents were elderly.

Remarriage of widows and widowers ideally followed the death of a spouse within a few months. However, there was no levirate or sororate to provide an automatic replacement for a deceased spouse. The survivor had to find a new partner and convince that individual to marry. In a significant number of cases, widows did not remarry for years; some never remarried.

When a Barí widow with children did manage to remarry, our observations suggest that the new husband was typically an exemplary stepfather. Orphans who had lost both parents were usually taken in by one of the mother's sisters or by the grandparents. We know of no cases of orphans beyond infancy who were not incorporated by some hearth group. Infants whose mothers died, however, were usually allowed to die.

The high frequency of widowing and remarriage resulted from a high death rate of reproductive-age adults, due to disease (malaria was endemic) and to chronic war—the ongoing attempts, by the region's landowners, oil companies, and homesteaders, to exterminate the Barí. These criollos sometimes hired bands of professional Indian killers, and sometimes formed such bands themselves. Their most common tactic was to sneak up to a longhouse just before dawn, set it afire, and gun down the occupants as they fled. When the killers found Barí on the trail, before they could reach a longhouse, they opened fire at once.

The most common victims of Indian killers, both on the trail and in the longhouse, were adult male Barí (Beckerman and Lizarralde 1995). As a result of this disparity, as well as the greater exposure of men to other dangers of rain forest life, widows were considerably more common than widowers. Over one-third of the Barí women in our sample were widowed while they had dependent children.

The four different Venezuelan territories experienced different intensities of external violence. The two that were on the frontier of national expansion suffered considerably higher rates of violent death than the other two. These conditions of elevated adult mortality, particularly male mortality, due to disease and warfare, were an important part of the context in which the institution of secondary fatherhood was practiced.

Secondary fatherhood is known from life history interviews with post-reproductive Barí that reveal that most women, both in precontact times and currently, took one or more lovers during at least one of their pregnancies. These lovers were believed to contribute to the development of the fetus and were considered secondary fathers of the eventual child. Women's husbands were usually aware of the lovers, and there is no evidence that the husbands objected. This last feature accords with considerable evidence in our notes attesting to a Barí woman's complete control over her sexual activity, once she had completed her puberty seclusion. Although she needed her parents' assent to marry, an unmarried postpubertal girl might have sex with any okjibara she wanted; and as a married woman, she apparently retained this authority over her own sexual behavior. Our life history interviews contain a number of incidents in which women objected to adultery on the part of their husbands, but none in which men objected to adultery on the part of their wives.

In the great majority of cases, the married woman stated that she took a lover only after she was pregnant. However, further inquiry revealed that the indication of pregnancy used by these women was simply a missed period. In this population, where hard physical labor was the norm, the diet was low in fat, and prolonged nursing of the most recent infant was universal, a missed period was far from infallible as an indicator of pregnancy. Only genetic fingerprinting can be conclusive on this point, but some women who believed themselves to be pregnant may have been made pregnant by the lovers they took, after reaching the conclusion that they were already with child.

When a woman gave birth (in a prepared spot in the forest, usually attended by other women), she typically named all the men who had had intercourse with her during her pregnancy. One of the women attending the birth then returned to the longhouse and announced to each of these men, "You have a child." These secondary fathers had recognized obligations to the child. Importantly, they were supposed to provide gifts of fish and game, and even manioc. Several informants volunteered that when a child with a secondary father reached the age at which it could understand such things, the child's mother pointed out the secondary father to the child, saying, "That man is also your father. He will give you fish. He will give you meat."

The above capsule ethnography outlines the ethnographic context in which the phenomena studied in the current research manifested themselves. In the light of this context, a number of hypotheses were developed.

Overview of Hypotheses

Informing the BPPP was the proposition that "multiple paternity was in effect an insurance policy on a woman's husband, providing an additional male with spousal and parental obligations in case the husband died" (Beckerman, ms.). As the project progressed, and our appreciation of the significance of partible paternity became more intricate, the initial hypotheses derived from this proposition were elaborated and additional hypotheses added. In the rest of this chapter, we reexamine the initial hypotheses, and then treat refinements of and additions to them.

The core of this examination is two pairs of logistic regressions. The first regressions examine the effect of secondary fatherhood on survivorship to age 15. The second regressions explore factors that predict whether or not a woman accepted a secondary father for a given pregnancy.

Field Methods

The current database contains the reproductive histories of 114 postreproductive women and their 916 remembered pregnancies. Additional fieldwork may augment these data, but only by a few percent. (There is a handful of currently excluded reproductive histories for which we are missing only a datum or two for completion, and a few postreproductive women are as yet uninterviewed; but we are approaching the limit of all postreproductive Barí women in Venezuela for whom these data can be obtained.) Field interview methods used in obtaining these data were sketched in Beckerman et al. (1998):

> The portion of the Barí Partible Paternity Project interview protocol relevant here begins with a genealogical inquiry, taking the informant as far back in her ancestry as she can go (usually to her grandparents), and then tracing down from these apical ancestors to identify her aunts, uncles, and first cousins as well as her siblings. Then a marriage and re-

productive history of the informant is recorded, with all pregnancies noted, miscarriages as well as live births. Children still living are identified by name, current residence, and current spouse, if married. Birth dates are known—sometimes to the month, sometimes to the day—for most children born after peaceful contact in June 1960. Birth dates for people born before contact are estimated by a variety of means and assigned a reliability code indicating the probable magnitude of error. The age at death of deceased children born in precontact times is estimated by asking the informant to point out a living child who is of approximately the same age as the dead child, at his or her time of death. Finally, after we have a birth ordered list of all the informant's pregnancies including miscarriages, we go down the list with the informant and ask, for each pregnancy, where the birth or miscarriage took place, and whether there was a secondary father involved in the pregnancy. If there was, we request his identity also. In some cases, women have been able to provide these marriage and reproductive history data for their dead mothers and/or sisters as well as for themselves.

We are aware of the various methodological difficulties associated with using recall data, and with assigning birth dates and ages to people for whom in many cases there is no written record of birth. In particular, since we deal below with survivorship to the age of 15, we are acutely aware of the likely misclassification of some older children who died before contact. Certainly there are errors in the data set. Nevertheless, because the protocol assigns age at death before the presence or absence of a secondary father is ascertained, we have been unable to conceive of any way in which there could be *systematic* errors distorting age at death with respect to the existence or nonexistence of a secondary father for a child. (166; emphasis in original)

To this summary description from our preliminary report (Beckerman et al. 1998), it is germane to add here that other locational data—place of death as well as birth—and cause of death, also formed part of the information elicited for each of a woman's children. We have also added to the database information from Roberto Lizarralde's field notes on the territory in which each mother grew up.

In preliminary workup, the data obtained by this protocol were transferred from the original field notes to standardized forms—one sheet for each person of interest in a woman's reproductive history—on which all individuals were assigned identification numbers. These sheets were grouped by woman, and the data were entered in a Paradox database; that database was analyzed in our preliminary report (Beckerman et al. 1998). Subsequently, all data were checked against the censuses and genealogical notes taken by Roberto Lizarralde during the course of his 40 years of fieldwork with the Barí. Some mistakes and omissions were found. The 111 women in the original sample used in our preliminary report had recalled 897 pregnancies. A year-long project of comparing these interview reports with the records of all of Lizarralde's 53 censuses (51 local censuses of settlements or clusters of settlements; two complete censuses of all Venezuelan Barí) raised that figure to 901. Discrepancies of similar magnitude were revealed with respect to birth dates.

Additional fieldwork following the census comparisons included rechecking in the field with the available women in the preliminary report database, as well as the interviewing of a few additional postreproductive women and their children. The reproductive histories of a few of the original women also had to be removed from our revised database because it was not (yet) possible to ascertain whether their newly discovered children had secondary fathers. The revised database used for the current analysis reflected these deletions and additions. It comprised 114 women and their 916 recalled pregnancies.

General Features of the Database

The database analyzed for this chapter contains information on the postreproductive women for whom we have complete reproductive histories with secondary-father information for each pregnancy. The number of pregnancies per woman varied from 2 to 14; mean number of pregnancies per woman was 8.04; modal number of pregnancies was 10.

Of the 114 women, 77 had at least one pregnancy with a secondary father. Of the 916 pregnancies, 214 involved at least one secondary father.

These proportions have not changed greatly over time. Looking at prevalence by decade, we find the proportion of secondary-father pregnancies remaining at 20–25% from the 1930s until the 1980s, at which point it began to fall slightly.

Analysis

Preliminary analysis of the earlier database revealed an apparent survival advantage to children of pregnancies associated with a secondary father. The initial finding was consistent with

Hypothesis 1: Pregnancies with one or more secondary fathers associated had a lower rate of death before age 15 than pregnancies with only a primary father associated.

To check the earlier result with the more accurate and slightly larger current database, and to see whether some other variable besides the presence of a secondary father could account for the improved survivorship, two logistic regressions were run (full description in Bai 1999).

Because the regular logistic regression model assumes that all responses are independent from each other, an assumption obviously violated in a data set comprised of collections of siblings, each collection born to a single mother, it was necessary to use more sophisticated forms of logistic regression, forms that take into account the within-cluster correlation to be expected among a mother's offspring. The population-averaged model concentrates on the effect of the predictor variables on the population-averaged effect (mean of a group of mothers defined by the sharing of a predictor variable), while the subject-specific model concentrates on the effect of the predictor variables on the specific individual mother.

The first regression employed the population averaged (also called marginal) model using generalized estimation equations (SAS Institute 1998) to model the odds of dying before age 15, given various candidate predictors. The odds of dying are the probability that a child died before 15 divided by the probability that a child survived to 15 and beyond. That is, if p = the probability that a child died before 15, then the odds of dying are $p/(1-p)$.

Of the 916 known pregnancies in the database, 768 provided usable observations for this regression. (The remaining 148 were excluded because they occurred less than 15 years ago or, in a few cases, were dead children whose ages at death are unknown; or because some other predictor, mostly place of birth, was not known for the individual.) Ignoring place of birth for the moment, of the 841 pregnancies occurring more than 15 years ago, 571 resulted in children who survived their fifteenth birthday and 270 did not. Thus the overall odds of dying before 15 in this population were $270/571 = 0.473$, or about 5 to 11.

This model computed the significance of the differences in odds of dying before 15 for various clusters or subpopulations, those clusters being defined by the sharing of a value of a predictor variable. The predictors used were (1) year of birth; (2) serial order of birth; (3) territory in which the mother grew up; (4) territory in which the child was born; (5) whether the child had no secondary father, one secondary father, or more than one secondary fathers; (6) sex of child.

The only predictor from this list with a significant effect on the odds of dying before age 15 was the secondary father variable. Comparing the odds of dying before 15 for a child with one secondary father and a child without any, the ratio was 0.305; p = 0.000. Comparing the odds of dying before 15 for a child with two or more secondary fathers and a child with no secondary father, the odds ratio was 0.632; ns. Comparing the odds of dying before 15 for a child with two or more secondary fathers and a child with one only, the odds ratio was 5.188, p = 0.0001.

A second logistic regression on the odds of dying before 15 used a subject specific (also known as a mixed effect or latent variable) model (Hedeker 1998). This model, which deals not with differences between the means of subpopulations but rather with differences between individuals, produced results similar to those reported above (Bai 1999).

What we found, in short, was that having a single secondary father was associated with a significant advantage in survivorship, but that having two or more secondary fathers was associated with a disadvantage. The first result was predicted on grounds already discussed.

Our ethnographic experience suggested that the second result occurred because women took several secondary fathers per child only when they were unmarried and in distress and were, in effect, supporting themselves by something like prostitution. Such women were likely to be chronically undernourished, as were their children. In fact, a look through the database showed that the correlation of survivorship disadvantage with multiple secondary fathers per child was largely due to a single case, an unmarried woman, probably with a chronic disease, almost all of whose numerous children died.

We concluded that although Hypothesis 1 could not be wholly disconfirmed, it was a simplification of the actual situation. A single secondary father did provide a substantial survivorship advantage, but two or more secondary fathers were an index of spinsterhood and were associated with decreased child survivorship.

For obvious reasons, it was of interest to know whether the survival advantage to pregnancies with a single secondary father resulted from a disproportion in nonviable pregnancies (e.g., miscarriages, stillbirths, and perinatal deaths) between pregnancies with secondary fathers and those without; or from a disproportion in deaths later in childhood between children with secondary fathers and those without; or from both. This set of questions arose from *Hypothesis 2: The lower death rate of pregnancies with secondary fathers was due to the extra care or provisioning (or both) that secondary fathers provided to their secondary children.*

Two additional marginal models were run. The first modeled the response variable *dead at birth* (defined as miscarriage, stillbirth or perinatal [< 1 week] death) and used the following as predictors: (1) whether the child had no secondary father, one secondary father, or more than one secondary fathers; (2) birth year; (3) serial order of birth; (4) mother's original territory; (5) ordinal number of husband (i.e., woman's first husband, second, etc.).

In this analysis, it was not necessary to exclude pregnancies that took place less than 15 years ago; the sample size was 801. Here, the presence of secondary fathers was manifest in the same fashion as in the previous analysis. The odds ratio of being dead at birth between those who had no secondary father and those who had two or more was 1.1879; ns. However, the odds ratio of being dead at birth between those who had one secondary father and those who had none was 0.1758; p = 0.001; and the odds ratio between those who had more than one secondary father and those who had only one was 6.7558; p = 0.0034.

This result was consistent with an advantage to having a single secondary father manifested in pregnancy viability and revealed in survivorship in the prenatal and perinatal period. This advantage was presumably related to extra provisioning with fish and game that the secondary father provided to the mother during the pregnancy. This finding offers a reason that a married woman looking after her reproductive success might accept a man as a lover even though she did not anticipate his long-term support, or even his presence, after the birth of her child. We interpreted the augmented risk of death associated with more than one secondary father, as before, as a result of an association between extra secondary fathers and distressed single mothers.

Also nearly significant in this regression was the serial number of the husband. This result was not surprising, since women with second or third husbands were in general an older subpopulation than the universe of all women, and were presumably more subject on average to age-related causes of fetal wastage.

A parallel population-averaged model was run, using the response variable *dead at 15*, but limiting the population to those children (n = 650) who were born over 15 years ago and who survived the perinatal period. In view of the previous findings, only the presence or absence of one or more secondary fathers was used as a predictor variable here. Comparing the odds of dying before age 15 between these children with no secondary fathers and those with two or more, the odds ratio was 0.9817; ns. However, the odds ratio of dying before 15 between those with one secondary father and those with none was 0.3750; p = 0.0014. The odds ratio between those with more than one secondary father and those with only one was 2.6180; ns.

Thus we found that Hypothesis 2 was largely disconfirmed, and that even though having a secondary father did provide a significant advantage to a child who survived the perinatal period, the major benefit of secondary fatherhood appeared to be in a decrease in fetal wastage, probably due to gifts of food given to the mother by her lover during pregnancy.

The original population-averaged model on the whole set of pregnancies was run again, with variable (5) (whether the child had no secondary father, one secondary father, or more than one secondary fathers) removed and replaced with a summary variable that divided the children into three groups: group 1, those who had a secondary father; group 2, those who did not have a secondary father but had one or more siblings who did; and group 3, those who came from a sibling set in which none of the children had a secondary father.

The result—that group 1 children had the highest survivorship, followed by group 3, with group 2 having the lowest survivorship—also replicated findings of our preliminary report, and provoked the question, How could it be that children without secondary fathers who had siblings who did have secondary fathers could have poorer survival than children from sibling sets where no one had a secondary father? The finding was counterintuitive in that it appeared to us from our ethnographic experience that a Barí woman had considerable independence in allocating food to her children as snacks, if not in formal meals. Surely any fish or game given to her to prepare by a secondary father of one of her children could have found its way to all of them. This paradox was the inspiration for

Hypothesis 3: A woman was more likely to take a secondary father for a particular pregnancy if she had lost a child from a previous pregnancy.

The next set of regressions tested this hypothesis. Again, both population-averaged and cluster-specific models were used, but the response variable in these models was not the odds of dying before 15 but the odds of a child having a secondary father.

Here, the predictor variables were (1) child's year of birth; (2) mother's territory of origin; (3) whether a previous child born to this mother had died before this child was born. The sample having the relevant data for the marginal model comprised 746 pregnancies. All first pregnancies were eliminated from this analysis, for the obvious reason that a first-born child does not have a previous sibling who can die or survive. The odds ratio in the population averaged model regression was 1.913, $p = 0.0076$, meaning that the odds of having a secondary father were almost twice as great for children who had had an older sibling die before they were born than for children all of whose older siblings were alive. In neither this regression, nor any of the others mentioned below, was mother's territory of origin a significant predictor of whether a pregnancy had a secondary father.

When the subject-specific (mixed) model was run on the first set of predictor variables, results were similar, but stronger. The odds ratio for having a secondary father following the death of an older sibling as compared to having all older siblings alive was 2.724, p = 0.0005.

Birth year also had a significant small effect in this analysis. The odds of a pregnancy having a secondary father declined to 0.974 of the odds of the previous year for each subsequent year; p = 0.0063. (For the marginal model, a birth year effect of similar size was detected, but the evidence was weak; p = 0.0801.)

Thus, Hypothesis 3 could not be disconfirmed, and provided at least a partial answer to the riddle of how siblings of children with secondary fathers could have worse survivorship than children from sibling sets with no secondary fathers at all. A possible interpretation of the statistical result is that women who might have been reluctant to take a secondary father for any of their children (women on their way to producing group 3 children) became more likely to produce group 1 children (with secondary fathers) after they had already experienced poor survivorship among their previous children, thus creating a set of group 2 children only after the survivorship of the siblings in this set was already compromised.

Recent fieldwork by Manuel Lizarralde suggested one way women may have thought about these matters. Informants volunteered that when a child became sick, the most effective traditional cure was for the father to blow tobacco smoke over the child's body. Only the father was truly effective in this effort, but secondary fathers counted as well as the primary father. It is easy to imagine a bereaved Barí mother thinking to herself that if she had only provided a secondary father for her dead child, she might have saved him, and vowing to provide that benefit for her next child.

Summary and Conclusions

The findings of our preliminary report were largely verified above, with some modification and elaboration, and set in a more extensive ethnographic framework. The evidence was convincing that possession of a secondary father was associated with a heightened probability that a pregnancy would eventually produce an adult (i.e., age > 15 yrs.) Barí individual.

However, despite our early suggestions that the means of this improved survivorship was gifts of fish and game from the secondary father(s) to the child, it was found above that the larger component of the survivorship advantage took place before birth, and was reflected in lower fetal wastage. In light of this finding, we proposed that this major advantage was due to an improvement in fetal nutrition, due to gifts of fish and game that the secondary father gave to the mother herself with respect to her sexual favors. Improved survivorship after the perinatal period was also significantly elevated among children with secondary fathers, but was a smaller component of the survivorship advantage associated with having a secondary father.

Finally, the mystery of how it could be that the siblings of children with secondary fathers had poorer survivorship than children from sibling sets where no one had a secondary father was illuminated by the discovery that women who had lost a previous child were more likely to take a secondary father for a subsequent pregnancy.

This last finding, with its sharp reminder of the individual loss and pain summarized in these vital statistics, returns this study to the point where it began, in the real lives of Barí women and their children.

Author's note: Fieldwork and analysis for this project was supported by two NSF grants (SBR 9420607, SBR 961510), a Wenner-Gren grant, and multiple Pennsylvania State University faculty support subventions to Stephen Beckerman; and by Connecticut College faculty support to Manuel Lizarralde.

3

Partible Paternity and Multiple Maternity among the Kulina

Donald Pollock

Since about 1970 it has become increasingly clear that members of many indigenous lowland Amazonian communities hold the belief that more than one man can be the biological father of a child. We have tended to treat this fact as an ethnographic curiosity, an almost amusing counterpoint to the familiar Trobriand case in which Malinowski's informants vigorously denied that men—even women's husbands—had any ethnobiological connection to their own children. In the broad sweep of possible conception and gestation beliefs, these Amazonian communities occupy a position implicit in, for example, Leach's 'rethinking' of older forms of anthropological thought, but Amazonia specialists have otherwise been at a loss to offer any compelling reason for the existence and apparently wide distribution of such beliefs.

Stephen Beckerman and his colleagues in the Barí "partible paternity" project have finally raised interesting and theoretically significant questions about the phenomenon of multiple ethnobiological fatherhood—the belief that more than one man is the biological father of a child—in these communities (Beckerman et al. 1998). At the very least they challenge us to think more creatively, and with greater ethnographic precision, about the nature and function of such practices and beliefs.

In this chapter I make a small effort to meet this challenge by examining the ideology and practice of partible paternity among the Kulina Indians of western Brazil. I describe Kulina notions of kinship and reproduction, and suggest first how the cultural logic of partible paternity operates in this community. I focus particular attention on the metaphor of siblingship through which Kulina represent membership in local communities, and the paradox presented when these siblings also form the pool of potential spouses and sex partners. *Partible paternity*—along with what I might call multiple maternity—is one of several expressions of this paradox, one that has potential reproductive significance for children.

The Kulina are an Aruan language–speaking group of perhaps 2,500 individuals living in villages scattered along the major rivers of the Purus-Jurua region of western Amazonia, the majority in Brazil, with a few hundred in several villages in eastern Peru.[1] This chapter is based on fieldwork first conducted among the Kulina living in the village called Maronaua, on the Brazilian upper Purus River near the Peruvian frontier, beginning in 1981. Maronaua was large by traditional standards, with roughly 150 residents in 1981; villages in the past ranged from about 20 to 50 individuals, though some now have as few as 10 individuals, and at least one has grown to as many as 250 individuals over the last 30 years. Maronaua was divided in the late 1980s, when the bulk of the population moved downriver to a former rubber-tapping encampment or *seringal*, the Seringal Sobral. Maronaua now has a population of roughly 100, the Sobral roughly 175. By the mid-1990s they, together with five other Kulina villages and a few villages of other indigenous groups such as the Kashinaua, comprised the Área Indígena Alto Purus.

Kulina are slash-and-burn horticulturalists growing manioc—especially sweet manioc—bananas, plantains, and corn in gardens surrounding the village. These staple vegetable crops are supplemented by a wide variety of seasonal plant foods, most gathered by women. Men provide animal protein through hunting and fishing. Hunting was fairly productive during my first long period of research in Maronaua; most men could count on killing a collared peccary or two for a day's hunting. Other game animals included monkeys, deer, and tapir, and more seasonal species such as armadillo, which emerge from flooded burrows in the rainy season. Fishing was extremely productive in Maronaua; a nearby oxbow lake provided abundant fish—so much so that women would complain when men too often took advantage of easy fishing to avoid the more strenuous hunt for game animals.

Beckerman and his colleagues have considered the Barí notion of partible paternity in the context of nutritional supply and child survival, and so it may be useful here to mention briefly that Kulina nutritional practices resemble those of the Barí in many regards. The Kulina division of labor is well defined: men provide raw meat, and women provide raw vegetables and cooked food. As I have described elsewhere (Pollock 1998), Kulina often describe male-female gender relations as an exchange of raw foods for cooked, and of meat for vegetables. The gendered associations of foods also incorporate a hierarchy of ascribed nutritional needs: Kulina believe that adult men need meat; adult women and children eat relatively more plant foods. This entails that Kulina children, who are often left without animal protein, must frequently make do with boiled manioc or roasted bananas, and consequently many children suffer chronic protein-calorie malnutrition. The nutritional deficits of childhood are exacerbated by epidemics of intestinal parasites, and it is not at all uncommon to see Kulina children with large, distended bellies. Infants are better nourished when they are nursing but, in a pattern seen in many small-scale traditional societies, they develop nutritional deficiencies when they are weaned at about age 2 or 3. I return to this issue later, in a discussion of partible paternity.

Kin and Affines: The Paradox of Marrying Siblings

Kulina organize themselves into a number of named, localized groups called *madiha,* which may be translated for convenience as "people."[2] Madiha groups usually take the names of animals; Maronaua, for example, was the village of the *kurubu madiha,* the "*kurubu* fish people," while a neighboring village downriver is that of the *pitsi madiha,* the "pitsi monkey people." Each madiha is associated with a geographic locale; formerly the several small villages occupying an area comprised the particular madiha. As these smaller traditionally organized villages have coalesced into larger single villages, there has been a corresponding tendency to merge the madiha category and single residential group, and notably to assume that all residents of a village are members of the madiha with which that village as a sociogeographic entity is associated.

The members of any madiha consider themselves to be related by kinship to all others who share the madiha identity, whether or not they reside in the same village. Moreover, the madiha forms the boundary of the extension of kinship; members of other madiha, even those with whom one may use a kin term, are not considered to be kin in this sense. Indeed, members of other madiha groups, particularly those that are geographically remote, are usually considered barely human: either dirty, thieving, sexually loose, or hostile. Further, madiha are conceptually endogamous. A Dravidian kin terminology divides the madiha into kin and affines (or potential affines), and it is from this latter category that an individual finds a lover or spouse. Although marriage with members of other madiha is not prohibited, there is a clear and expressed preference for marriage within the madiha category.[3]

As a conceptually closed social system, the madiha presents the paradox, if I may put it that way, of simultaneously positing cognatic kinship among all its members while requiring that certain categories of these kin be treated as affines or potential affines rather than as kin. The Kulina situation thus resembles that described some years ago in the South American context for the Piaroa (Overing 1972, 1973, 1975) and the Kalapalo (Basso 1970, 1975), raising the question that Overing poses for the former: "What does it mean to be affines with those who are kinsmen?" (1972, 284). The Kulina version of the phenomenon of partible paternity must be understood within the context of this paradox and its implications for marriage, reproduction, and the conduct of social life within a village.

Kulina use the term *wemekute* to translate the Portuguese terms *parente* and *parentesco* ("kin" and "kinship"). The term *wemekute* is composed of a collectivizing prefix attached to the root for 'sibling' (*-kute*), and might be glossed as "we siblings." Indeed, it is through sibling metaphors that Kulina speak of the nature of their social world. In this case, then, the question Overing poses might be phrased more precisely in the Kulina context as: What does it mean to be a spouse to one who is a sibling?

Kulina draw upon two models of madiha organization that focus, on the one hand, on the cognatic kindred character of a village or madiha, and on the other, from the point of view of any individual, on a terminological bifurcation of the madiha into two groups, which I will call by the traditional terms kin and affines.

The first of these models draws upon the metaphor of siblingship to express the obligatory solidarity presumed among madiha members and village coresidents. Kulina do not in this sense conceive of the madiha as linked sets of siblings (cf. Basso 1970, 408), but rather as a field of siblings, all of whom are related equally and in the same degree. This conception was often underscored by my informants, who would make rather insistent statements such as "we are all *real* siblings," using the root *-kute* to describe the madiha as an undifferentiated field of relations that are not in any sense fictitious. In some contexts the concept of wemekute is applied generationally, so that the members of ascending and descending generations form distinct sets of wemekute. But even this generational potential is often submerged, for example in the practice of addressing each of one's children as "older sibling," masking the generational difference.

As a metaphor for social solidarity, the concept of wemekute expresses a complex set of assumptions about proper behavior between individual madiha members. These include obligations to provide political support and mutual assistance, to share food and possessions, and to be "mild" and passive in interaction, in contrast to the 'wildness' (*wadita'i*) of forest animals and hostile non-

Kulina.[4] These obligations find their most complete exemplification in the person of the village headman, who is appropriately conceived to be the senior sibling of the field of siblings comprising the village. Within this *wemekute* framework no division between types of 'kin,' or between kin and affines is accepted as a rationale for behavior that violates these norms (cf. Overing 1972, 283). On the contrary, those who repeatedly fail to act as proper 'siblings' risk charges of witchcraft.

The population of Maronaua, at the time of my first visit in 1981, had in fact coalesced around two groups of siblings: brothers and their in-marrying wives, children, and even parents and parents-in-law.

The harmonious social vista of siblingship is inevitably disrupted by marriage, in particular by the assumption that marriage will take place within the madiha. Kulina kin terminology provides an alternative model of the organization of the social universe, a model that encodes the possibility of marriage through a distinction between those whom ego considers kin, and all others, who are affines or, better, potential affines. This kin terminology establishes on ego's generation an opposition between *okute*, "my siblings," and the affinal categories *owini*, "spouse" or "potential spouses," and *wabo* and *karade*, who are owini's opposite-sex 'siblings,' male and female respectively. On the first ascending generation ego distinguishes parents' same-sex siblings from parents' opposite-sex siblings, yielding four categories: *abi*, which includes father and father's brother; *ami*, which includes mother and mother's sister; *koko*, which includes mother's brother, and *atso*, which includes father's sister. These latter two categories are 'potential affines' and 'spouse givers,' the parents of owini. On the first descending generation, ego again distinguishes own and same-sex sibling's children, *ohakama*, from opposite-sex sibling's children, *ohidubade*, (male) and *ohinumadini* (female), that is, ego's child's potential spouses.

The differentiation of these two models of madiha organization is also expressed in their cultural symbolization. As wemekute, 'siblings,' all members of a madiha are linked by shared 'blood' (*emene*) which remains undiluted, so to speak, by madiha endogamy. A further link to a sociogeographic locale is established by the assumption that all residents in the village of the madiha derive their souls (*tabari*) and flesh (*ime*) from the same source, the local forest's white-lipped peccaries, which are themselves the reincarnated souls of dead madiha members, and the consumption of which forms the flesh of human persons (cf. Pollock 1993).

The differentiation of this field of 'siblings' linked by blood is rationalized according to a separate metaphor that refers to notions of conception and nurturance of children. For the Kulina, conception and the growth of a fetus are the consequence of an accumulation of semen in a woman's womb through repeated acts of sexual intercourse. A fetus is formed entirely of paternal semen, and the pregnant woman makes no material 'biological' contribution to fetal development during this gestational stage. However, at birth the process of infant development becomes an exclusively female task as the baby nurses, and mother's milk becomes, at least conceptually, the exclusive substance nourishing the child. The exclusivity of this maternal contribution is further underscored by the food prohibitions placed on the new parents, prohibitions that essentially restrict the consumption of male substances that would pollute the female nurturing process required for the baby to be formed properly. Milk (*dʒoho*) and semen (*idʒowiri*) are thus closely linked in Kulina thought as comparable female and male substances necessary to create and 'grow' a child; both terms derive from the same root, *dʒo*, which serves as the root of a number of terms referring to digestive processes and products, and semen may even be called *dʒoho tsueni*, "black milk," to relate it to the "white milk" of women.

Semen and milk do not symbolize simply the male and female contributions to the creation of new persons. In addition, semen and milk symbolize relations among kin, when these are opposed to relations with affines, and most narrowly relations with siblings as opposed to relations with spouses and spouses' siblings. Unlike the Kalapalo, who cannot say why some kin are potential spouses (Basso 1975, 209), the Kulina are fairly explicit, and the cultural logic of the system is simple: all persons with whom ego shares either semen or milk (or both), that is, all persons who are 'formed' of the same semen or milk, are "my siblings" (okute) in the kin terminological categorization. Those who have been formed of different semen and milk than ego are placed into the affinal categories of the kin terminology, or more precisely, members of affinal categories are presumed to have been formed of different substances than ego. The prohibition on sexual relations and marriage with a member of a 'kin' category is thus expressed as a "fear" (*noppine*) of mixing the same substance that formed each partner. Any individual's brother and sister become unacceptable sex partners and spouses in this logic because they are formed of the same paternal and maternal substances, while owini (potential spouses) are acceptable because they are formed of different substances. Parenthetically, it is by reference to this substantial logic that members of other madiha may be classified as 'affines' but not wemekute.

Despite the reference to 'blood' as the metaphor of siblingship expressing madiha membership, I interpret this as a symbol of a code for conduct, in contrast to the substantial symbols distinguishing kin and affines. Siblingship in this sense is a mode of interaction among madiha members. In short, the lack of differentiation among wemekute derives from a generalized code for conduct symbolized by a concept of undifferentiated 'blood,' while the opposition between kin and affines (as well as male and female) is symbolized by a concept of differentiated semen and milk. And, ideologically, in terms of the wemekute organization, marriage is preferentially endogamous with a 'sibling,' while in terms of the terminological differentiation of kin and potential affines, marriage is prohibited with a 'sibling.'

The conceptual paradox is perhaps best summarized in the Kulina expression *matsi towi*. The phrase is formed of two terms, *towi*, meaning 'to look for,' and *matsi*, which may mean either 'younger sister' or 'vagina.' The expression is normally a metaphor for looking for sex, or as we might say, "on the make." The phrase is most commonly heard when unmarried teenage boys, who often roam in packs in and around the village, are asked, "What are you doing?" A typical response is a collective, giggling, falsetto shout of matsi towi! The ambiguity of the phrase, and its paradoxical nature, are not lost on Kulina: looking for a sex partner is metaphorically looking for a younger sister. But the sexual behavior engaged in with owini—potential or actual affines—is precisely the behavior prohibited by siblingship, and the two modes of categorizing relations (kin and affines versus 'siblings') are thus closely intertwined despite their otherwise neat separation vis-à-vis the contrasting metaphors of blood and semen/milk.

Århem notes that among the group of South American Indian societies he studied "it seems as if the affinal relationship has to be ideologically concealed or symbolically transformed into a consanguineal relationship" (1981, 294). Similarly, Basso and Overing both propose that among the Kalapalo and Piaroa it is affines who are brought within the sphere of kin, for example by the use of teknonyms, and through marriage with 'distant' kin to bring them closer (e.g., Basso 1975, 221; Overing 1973, 562). My impression is that for Kulina the conceptual task is reversed, that is, it is kin who must be transformed into affines: 'siblings' into spouses.

Phrasing of the Kulina situation in this way is based on two considerations. First, the wemekute model of social organization, which presumes 'sibling' ties among all madiha members, is viewed sociocentrically as a fundamental precondition of relations within madiha. By contrast, affinal relations are viewed egocentrically and have a contingent quality; they emerge principally at marriage, and are only crystallized or objectified through specific marriage alliances. The model of social organization provided by the terminological bifurcation of the social universe into kin and affine encodes a potentiality, in Basso's phrase "affinibility" (1970, 410), which is actualized in varying configurations by marriages, but which remains largely submerged outside of specific alliances. This view is underscored by the claim mentioned earlier, that "we are all real siblings."

In terms of the behavioral correlates of relativity, this entails for Kulina that all madiha members are subject to the same expectations in social interaction, those symbolized by the notion of wemekute, or siblingship, until a specific marriage transforms, for the two spouses, potential affines into actual affines. This transformation of relations from wemekute to 'real' affines is primarily focused on husbands, who move into their wives' households at least until the birth of several children, when they and their wives build separate houses, normally next to, or near, the wife's parents' house. Prior to marriage adolescents do not exhibit markedly different behavior toward their potential affines or vice versa. Of course, sexual liaisons are undertaken between those who classify each other as owini (potential spouse), but in these cases the preexisting relationship between sex partners is masked by speaking of lovers as those "who have come from afar" (wahitani) as if to transform the metaphorical sibling relation into no relation at all, rather than to contradict it through sexual access. Indeed, an adolescent girl who becomes pregnant prior to marriage is said to have been "stolen by a stranger."

At marriage, relations with one's affines—now one's actual affines—become markedly transformed. Marriage ritual initiates these transformations, particularly in the now disappearing practice of whipping affines, especially the immediate household members of the two new spouses. Townsend and Adams (1978) interpret this ritualized whipping as an expression of the hostility inherent between affines among the Peruvian Kulina, and indeed, whipping may well be a formalized and socially acceptable manner in which to express anger or tension. In the present context it is significant as a behavior that would not be tolerated among kin, as opposed to affines, and thus at marriage it marks the transformation of these metaphorical 'siblings' into affines.

Again, the primary focus of these changes is in-marrying men, whose relations with their wives' household members undergo modification. Husbands must exhibit considerable 'shame' (nahidʐoti) in the presence of the wife's mother. Prior to his marriage a man may have addressed his wife's mother by name, but when he moves into her household he strictly avoids using her name when she is within earshot, and indeed, avoids whenever possible even looking at her. In-marrying men also become a major source of labor for the wife's father, and are obligated to assist him beyond the requirements of simple 'siblingship.' The wife's father 'orders' or 'demands' such assistance, most notably without the expectation of reciprocation. In the husband's own generation, he is expected to engage in lewd sexual joking with his wife's sister, emphasizing that they are no longer 'kin' but affines between whom sexual access is not prohibited.

Relations between a man and his wife's brother are particularly significant in this regard. The wabo becomes a "friend," atori, in explicit contrast to a 'kinsman.' Rather than bringing the wife's brother (or sister's husband) 'closer,' marriage in a sense creates a formal distance between the two, who are bound by especially strict rules governing their behavior vis-à-vis one another. For the most part it is this wife's brother who will whip his sister's husband if he fails to behave as a proper husband, again, a form of punishment that would never occur between siblings or 'kin.'

In this regard it may be understood why the Kulina do not employ teknonyms for affines, as do the Kalapalo and Piaroa. Affinity is not masked or hidden among the Kulina, but rather appears to be particularly stressed when 'potential' affines become actual affines. Teknonyms are not required when it is precisely the affinal nature of these transformed kin relations that is being marked. On the contrary, there is a distinct tendency to shift from names to affinal category terms when addressing 'actual' affines.

Following the birth of several children—Kulina normally say three children—a husband and wife establish a new, separate household for their family. This move is particularly critical as it marks a retransformation of affinal relations into 'kin' relations. Although the couple may continue to bear children after this move, in ideological terms their reproductive potential is exhausted or, better, their reproductive task is completed after the birth of these children and the creation of a new household. At this point the husband of the new household begins to relax the formal distance enjoined upon him in his relations with his wife's family members. He returns to using personal names for the wife's mother and father. He is no longer bound by the strong obligation to provide labor and economic assistance to the wife's natal household. He ceases sexual joking with his wife's sister. His wabo, his brother-in-law, is fully wemekute, no longer simply a "friend." In a sense, the distance that characterized his relations to these affines while he resided in their household is, almost paradoxically, closed by his move into a separate household. Although the wife's natal household members remain categorized as 'affines,' the quality of their relationship to her husband reverts to being determined by reference to the wemekute 'siblingship' model of social interaction.

The marriageable or potential affine category owini includes both the father's sister's child (FZC) and the mother's brother's child (MBC). Yet there are few marriage alliances created between these true first cross-cousins, and indeed there is a certain reluctance to establish marriages between first cross-cousins. In the past, when marriages appear to have been arranged by the parents of the spouses with greater frequency than today, such marriages seem to have been more common but usually ended quickly.

Both the earlier and the current marriage patterns may be viewed in the context of this tension between siblingship and affinity. Arranged marriages between the children of brothers-in-law are an aspect of the Kulina notion of *manakoni,* an "exchange" or "payment," a feature of the obligatory reciprocity that characterizes the relations between wabo, wife's brother, and the sister's husband. But the fragility of such marriages in the past, and the rarity of such marriages in the present, derives in large measure from the preexisting close relations between these cross-cousins. Marriage between these cross-cousins inevitably creates a kind of affinal distance that disrupts the close kinlike relations they have enjoyed. Note also that marriages in the past were arranged between young children, even between unborn children, that is, precisely at the stage of the domestic group developmental cycle when brothers-in-law were most strictly bound by the reciprocal obligations of manakoni. At the time of my original research marriages were contracted between prospective spouses themselves, at a point at which their fathers were no longer obligated to observe the reciprocity enjoined upon them as 'actual' affines.

It is also within this framework that the Kulina tactical use of kin terms may be understood. Briefly, the multiple, overlapping kin relations existing within such an endogamous small-scale group present the potential for a selection of alternate terms, normally differing along the axis of 'kin' and 'affine.' Kulina most often elect to use the 'kin' term option whenever possible, both to underscore the closeness of such relations and to avoid the 'distance' implied as a potentiality with 'affines.' The major and most interesting exception to this rule is the village headman who married a woman he had originally classified as 'younger sister' (*matsi*). He was able to reclassify her as owini through another set of relationships, and made a marriage of considerable political expedience.

The interplay of these models of madiha organization emerges as a social process or dialectic that cannot be characterized adequately by simple static contrasts such as 'kin' and 'affine.' The two modes of conceptualizing relations with madiha members certainly coexist, to be referenced in appropriate contexts, as Overing (e.g., 1973, 564) suggests for the comparable models Piaroa hold of their social organization. But more important, Kulina social organization presents a dynamic in which a set of relations exemplifying (and evaluated in terms of) 'siblingship' as a code for conduct are transformed into affinal relations, and which are finally retransformed into metaphorical 'sibling' relations, one might say, when the social consequences of affinity are fulfilled. Townsend and Adams (1978) have described Kulina marriage as a fragile institution, full of conflict. Although I found somewhat greater stability in marriage among the Kulina at Maronaua, it was obvious that the affinal relations actualized at marriage had this tense formality absent in relations between 'potential affines.' Affinity emerges for the Kulina as an uncomfortable phase in a social process or developmental cycle, one that conceptually contradicts the norms of interaction that Kulina presume to characterize 'kinship,' or in a broader sense, humanness or personhood. Throughout, it is 'siblingship' that remains the constant, both as a general model of social interaction and as a field against which affinity becomes marked.

Partible Paternity and Multiple Maternity

I have alluded briefly to Kulina beliefs about the nature of conception and gestation; in this section I describe these in more detail, to highlight the potential for children to have several fathers, and even several mothers. Conception is a process rather than an event for Kulina—not clearly distinguished from gestation—in which semen accumulates in a woman's womb until it reaches a large and dense enough bolus to form a fetus. This process requires numerous acts of sexual intercourse: as Kulina say, men must "work hard" to produce a child, and women make no contribution at this stage to the development of the fetus. At the point at which it is formed, the fetus blocks the passage of menstrual blood from the uterus and menstruation stops. Kulina thus understand every sexually active woman to be at least a little pregnant throughout her adult life; it is only when the semen accumulating in her womb reaches a certain level that the pregnancy is regarded as irreversible, and birth inevitable if not terminated by other means.

The process of conception and gestation, as Kulina understand it, leaves open the possibility that more than one man may contribute to the seminal growth of a fetus, and thus two or more men will be 'fathers' to the child, in the particular sense of genitors possessing a culturally recognized ethnobiological connection to the child. Among the Kulina of Maronaua this possibility was commonly a fact. Men and women often had extramarital sexual affairs, especially as young adults, when they were regarded as physically attractive to the opposite sex and were commencing reproductive life.

Indeed, Kulina regularly practice a public ritual involving extramarital sexual relations, a ritual that has been described as the "order to get [meat]" or the *dutse'e [bani] towi* (cf. Rüf 1972). In this ritual, village women who are "hungry for meat"—or at least ostensibly hungry—go in a group from household to household at dawn, singing to the adult men in each house, "ordering" them to go hunting. At each house, one or more women in the group step forward to bang on the house with a stick; they will serve as the sex partners of the men of the house that night, if they are successful in their hunt. Women in the ritual select their male sex partners from among the sexually permitted category of affines or potential affines, but are not allowed to select their own husband. The men of the village leave collectively to hunt later that morning, and in a prearranged display of male sexual cooperation, agree to meet later in the early evening, near the village, to share the spoils of the hunt, ensuring that every man will have something to exchange for sexual access to his ritual partner. At the end of the day the men return in a group to the village, where the adult women form a large semicircle and sing erotically provocative songs to the men, asking for their "meat." The men drop their catch in a large pile in the middle of the semicircle, often hurling it down with dramatic gestures and smug smiles, after which the women scramble to grab a good-sized portion. After cooking the meat and eating, each woman retires with the man whom she selected as her partner for the sexual tryst. Kulina engage in this ritual with great humor, and perform it regularly.[5]

At the very least, then, it is almost certain that any woman giving birth in this village could identify at least one man with whom she had had sexual intercourse during the rather ambiguous and uncertain period of pregnancy, a period that might begin months before the more obvious signs of pregnancy develop. The dutse'e towi ritual, in addition to other, informal extramarital sexual affairs, nearly guarantees that most, if not all children in the village have more than one 'father.'

Kulina notions of child development also raise the possibility that children may have more than one mother, again in the specific ethnobiological sense of a genitrix who has contributed to the biological development of the child. As I noted earlier, a child at birth is believed to have been formed exclusively of male semen. At this point, the female role commences, and through nursing, mother's milk "completes" the growth of the child. At many times during the period of nursing any number of women might nurse the child. It is particularly common for a group of sisters, who are usually coresident in the household, to share nursing functions; it is not unknown for the mother's mother to allow an infant to nurse, even if the grandmother is no longer lactating, to quiet a crying child whose mother is occupied. When I asked if these women were also "mothers" of the child, in the sense of contributing substance to the child's development, and on the model of partible paternity, my informants replied that this was obviously so: the mother's sister, who is most likely to nurse an infant most often, is even called "other mother," as though the kin term itself encoded the fact of multiple maternity.

At the point of weaning, at roughly two years of age, the child is said to be complete, and acquires the signs of personhood: it is called by name, instead of by the term for 'baby' (nono); it is referred to by gender-specific kin terms rather than by nongendered terms; it is buried formally if it dies at this point; and it is said to have "sense," for example to understand not to crawl into cooking fires or off of the edge of house platforms, and to speak and understand speech at least at a minimal level.

Kulina took the possibility of multiple maternity rather casually, and I suspect that they even regarded it as a sign of the closeness of sisters who form the core of uxorilocal households. Moreover, nursing is a public act in Kulina villages, and the sight of a woman nursing a sister's child was not uncommon. It would be difficult to pretend that such sororal wet nurses were not also "mothers" in the specifically Kulina sense in which they too were making an ethnobiological contribution to the child's development and "completion." I have seen Kulina women nurse baby animals, including several puppies and a capybara, and they jokingly referred to themselves as the "other mothers" of these babies, presumably according to the same logic that renders them mothers to the human infants they nurse.

The possibility, and even certainty, that a newborn child possesses several fathers is much less public, though it is not necessarily hidden. At birth, a newborn infant is felt to be vulnerable to the harmful influences of animal meat, especially the meat of male animals. The parents of the newborn child, like the infant itself, are supposed to eat "milder" foods, particularly boiled manioc and plantains, for a period of one or two weeks. The parents avoid eating the meat of male animals, at least theoretically, for the entire period of infancy, while the child is nursing.[6] "Other" fathers typically observe the most stringent rules enjoining them from eating animal meat for a brief period, but men told me that they did not follow this prohibition for more than a day or two. Indeed, men reported that it could be insulting to the father of a newborn infant for other men to observe these prohibitions in too public a fashion and for too long, as though they were not merely "other" fathers, but possibly the primary father. Nonetheless, Kulina said that it would be inappropriate for a man to be angry if one or two other men observed the simplest food prohibitions surrounding the birth of his child; indeed, observing such prohibitions even in a token manner could be important for the health of the child (Pollock 1996).

Kulina social organization, and the metaphor of siblingship, help to submerge the presence of "other" fathers in the normal behavior of a household. Here I must refer back to Kulina understanding of their own kin terminology. I have noted that, in their own interpretation of the meaning and significance of the kin term for the mother's sister—*ami oni'i*, which may be translated as "other mother"—Kulina told me that the extension of the term *ami* to the mother's sister(s) refers to the fact that the mother's sister nurses the child, and is thus "like" a mother in making this critical ethnobiological contribution to the development of the infant into a full person. Kulina kin terminology assigns a comparable qualification to the father's brother(s), who is called *abi wa'a*, or "other father." Kulina were not completely reluctant to assign the same interpretation to the extension of the term *abi* to the father's brother(s), but were clearly uncomfortable acknowledging in a public way the implication that every father's brother in Maronaua was also a genitor of his brother's children.

I interpret this discomfort as an aspect of the paradox of affinity and siblingship that I discussed earlier. In the siblingship mode of conceptualizing the social universe of the village, Kulina describe a group of brothers and sisters. In the affinity mode of conceptualizing the same social universe, Kulina describe two groups of brothers and sisters who marry each other. These are the groups from who one draws spouses and other, extramarital sex partners: they become one's child's "other fathers" and "other mothers" of kin terminology and partible paternity/multiple maternity, though they are, for same-sex egos, one's brothers and sisters. To put it in simpler terms: if I am a man, my brothers are both potential sex partners of my wife and the "other fathers" to my child, in both the conventional kin terminology and in the ethnobiology of gestation; if I am a woman, my sisters are both potential sex partners of my husband and the "other mothers" to my child, in both the conventional kin terminology and in the ethnobiology of infant development through breast milk.

The cultural logic of kin terminology and partible paternity for the Kulina at Maronaua is perhaps best understood in reference to the recent past, of which it is certainly a reflection. No more than a generation before my first visit to

Maronaua in 1981, Kulina in this community had lived in a single longhouse deep in the forest. The older members of the village remembered the social architecture of the traditional longhouse or *maloca* and described the clusters of sibling groups and extended families around the inside walls of the single large longhouse in the shape of an elongated beehive. The arrangement of households in Maronaua duplicated this domestic pattern, as though some giant had simply lifted up the longhouse, leaving the families behind on the ground, in two long rows of extended families. In the Kulina conception of their recently past social organization—which has the virtue, not of being true, but of tapping directly into their cognitive model of social life—a longhouse was composed of a group of brothers that married a group of sisters. Each woman could draw lovers from among her husband's brothers, and her husband could draw lovers from among his wife's sisters. From the perspective of a child in this longhouse, all men were "fathers," either the primary father, who was husband to the mother, or "other fathers," who were his brothers.

In such a conception of the social landscape, social roles, ethnobiology, and kin terminology are isomorphic, and it makes little difference whether a man has been a sex partner to his brother's wife or not; kin terminology encodes the potential for him to play this role, and to shape his relationship with his brother's child, independently of his actual ethnobiological connection to that child. This social fact makes it difficult to compare cases in which children have more than one ethnobiological father and those in which children have only one ethnobiological father; in both types of cases children have "other fathers" who contribute to their welfare and well-being.

Discussion

The Barí case examined by Beckerman and his colleagues offers the possibility of making just such a comparison, and their data suggest that the survival of children into young adulthood is associated with the possession of multiple fathers. Although Beckerman is unable, of course, to document the specific behaviors that grant this survival advantage, his suggestion that the primary benefit of multiple fathers lies in the possibility of avoiding the most severe nutritional deficiencies seems sound.

As I noted earlier, Kulina children, like their Barí counterparts, are subject to chronic nutritional problems, largely as a consequence of Kulina beliefs about the nature of food (the amount of food rather than its nutritional value) and the nature of persons (attributing to adult men the greatest need for meat). The nutritional deficiencies of childhood are doubtless associated with some level of mortality, but I am unable to develop precise statistics on childhood deaths. Unlike the Barí, who could provide extensive data on pregnancies, births, and deaths, Kulina consistently reported to me that they were unable to recall pregnancies or, especially, the deaths of infants and children. Gregor (pers. comm.) has noted a similar phenomenon among the Mehinaku, suggesting that in some cultures parents experience an emotional trauma from a high rate of infant and childhood mortality that is accompanied by a kind of amnesia in which conscious recollection of dead children is repressed.

However, data on the reproductive histories of Maronaua's women since 1981 suggest that they experience an average of roughly seven pregnancies over their reproductive lifetimes. Among Maronaua's former residents, the number of children who survived into adulthood is a mean of four per mother, so it might not be too inaccurate to estimate the mortality rate of children to be roughly 40%. It is difficult to find a meaningful comparison for this figure. Large Kulina communities have what I might call a sibling density that is high enough to make it fairly certain that most or all children have "other fathers." Many households in large villages have two or more resident adult men, providing a more reliable source of animal protein for the entire household than one man alone can offer.

However, there are several smaller Kulina communities along the Purus River, single extended families that have left larger villages, often for political reasons or to avoid witchcraft accusations. In each case the male household head lives with his wife and only two or three other adults, usually a wife's parent or parents, and in one case two of the wife's sisters. In such cases there is little possibility of "other fathers" within the social sphere, and these families consequently offer an obvious, if highly imperfect, comparison to the population of Maronaua.

My data on these small enclaves, each of which numbers no more than about a dozen people, suggest that infant mortality rates are high, perhaps as high as 60%. The numbers of children are small enough that it is not possible to assign statistical significance to the difference, but it is a large enough difference to be suggestive. At a simple ethnographic level the differences are striking. There is ample ethnographic evidence to demonstrate that the presence of several adult men in a single household ensures a better supply of protein for the children of that household. On the other hand, and since members of a single household tend to eat communally, regardless of how many nuclear families are resident in the household, it is impossible to determine if the lower infant and childhood mortality rates of larger, more socially complex households in Maronaua were due merely to the presence of several adult men, or to the obligation of "other fathers" to share meat with their ethnobiological children, whether in their own household or in other households. At the same time, higher infant and child-hood mortality rates of very small, isolated households may be due merely to the presence of only one adult man in each, to the greater scarcity of game animals in the areas in which these households have been established, or some combination of these and other factors. The Kulina case must remain suggestive rather than conclusive.

Several of the contributors to this volume have emphasized that the social and demographic outcomes of partible paternity identified by Beckerman et al. (1998) might also be achieved through an extension of filial relations to fathers' brothers. For example, among the Siona-Secoya, the father's brothers provide forms of support in a "parental fashion" (Vickers, this volume); even though they do not have sexual access to a child's mother, such men may nonetheless be instrumental in ensuring the child's—and the patrilineage's—survival. This perspective shifts the focus away from the sociobiological function of partible paternity, which is hypothetically to maximize the likelihood of genetic immortality through support of children whom one has a statistical chance of having fathered, to the sociological function of providing for the survival of a patrilineal group.

In the Kulina case it is clear that children take advantage of the presence of other adult men in a household, including a father's brothers and the mother's father, to achieve a better level of nutritional support than children in households with only a single adult man. It is also clear that a child's father's brothers (the paternal uncles) are a source of social and nutritional support even when they are not resident in the child's household but live, as is frequently the case, in the households of wives who are not the "real" sisters of the child's mother. Again, the overlapping categories of "other fathers," which include fathers' brothers as well as ethnobiologically related men, provide most children with a range of adult men who can be called upon for various forms of social support, including food. Such relations are normally mediated through women. A child's mother is the individual most likely to approach her classificatory "sister" to ask for meat or other food items when her own household's supply is low; the classificatory sisters are the wives of a woman's husband's brothers, that is, the wives of her child's "other fathers." At this ethnographic level, it is clear that the presence of individuals in the categories of "other father" and "other mother" offer Kulina children a range of social support options that enhance the support offered by the father or mother alone. Whether such enhanced support is converted to a higher likelihood of survival to adulthood may be difficult to demonstrate empirically, but it would be surprising if this were not the case.

The range of examples discussed in this volume also suggest that the Amazonian communities in question might be ordered along a continuum defined around two poles. At one pole, marriage and affinity are the primary contexts for the reproduction of social life; marriage tends to be monogamous; adultery is rare, is morally stigmatized, or both; and paternity is less likely to be partible. In such communities, which perhaps include the Siona-Secoya, the Wanano, and the Curripaco, the support functions of "other" fathers are provided without necessarily being grounded in claims of ethnobiological connection. Chernela's discussion of the Wanano is instructive in this regard: partible paternity is possible within the Wanano ethnobiological understanding of conception and gestation, but is more likely to be a threat posed by men outside of a child's patriclan: a threat to the social integrity of the community as much as a threat to the ethnobiological integrity of the child.

At the other pole of this continuum, siblingship is the primary context or relationship for the reproduction of social life; marriage is more likely to be polygamous; extramarital sexual relations are more common, or even expected; and paternity is often divided. In such communities, which might include the Barí, the support functions of "other" fathers may be grounded in claims of ethnobiological connection. The Kulina might be placed along this continuum at a point near the Barí poll; siblingship is a relation with considerable moral force, so much so that in the social paradox of marrying one's village co-members, the sibling metaphor is explicit. Better to have sex with 'siblings' than with strangers. And for the Kulina partible paternity, like multiple maternity, is so ubiquitous that it appears to be taken for granted in the kin terminological designation of all of one's father's brothers and male parallel cousins as "other fathers."

More than twenty-five years ago Judith Shapiro proposed that indigenous lowland South American societies could be ordered along just this kind of continuum, one defined by the relative emphasis placed on siblingship and affinity as organizing principles of social solidarity (1974). Århem elaborates this comparative analytic to identify what he terms a "fraternal model of solidarity," through which societies in this broad ethnographic region might be compared, in part, in terms of the extent to which affinal relationships are "ideologically concealed or symbolically transformed" into "consanguineal relationships" (1981, 294). Indeed, whichever analytic constructs are employed, a striking feature of these and other classic analyses (e.g., Basso 1970; Goldman 1963; Overing 1975) is the consistent emphasis placed on the tension between affinity and siblingship as organizing principles or metaphors in many indigenous Amazonian groups.

Like many Amazonian communities, Kulina conceive of themselves as communities of "substance," in which persons are materially fabricated in a variety of ways throughout life. Viveiros de Castro's comment about Xinguano notions of the body is accurate for many lowland societies: "the human body must be submitted periodically to intentional processes of fabrication" (1987, 31; cf. Conklin 1996; McCallum 1996). In such settings, the links of ethnobiological substance that are posited between a child and an "other" father must also be understood in the context of the complex material fabrication of persons in general. For Kulina the substantial constitution of persons includes the eating of meat from animals that embody the spirits of dead relatives, use of hallucinogenic substances such as *ayahuasca,* and other body practices that link members of a community in a variety of "substantial" ways. The support of "other fathers" for a child might be viewed as merely a refraction of the social obligations of this more complex set of material, substantive ties that link all members of a Kulina village, many of which are subsumed under the regnant trope of siblingship. Perhaps the sociobiological function of the practices of partible paternity is most comprehensively supported, in a community with a high level of genetic closure, by precisely these overlapping and extensive beliefs about shared substance and ethnobiological connections, especially as they are translated into the forms of social support that Kulina extend to siblings and siblings' children.

Notes

1. See Adams 1962, 1963, 1976; Townsend and Adams 1978; and Rüf 1972 for information on the Peruvian Kulina. Claire Lorrain (2000) has worked among the Kulina on the Jurua River in Amazonas; her observations on Kulina reproduction in that community are consistent with the material I present here.

2. The term *madiha* may be used in a variety of marked senses to distinguish humans from nonhumans, Indians from non-Indians, Kulina from other Indians, and specific madiha "groups." In this chapter I use the term in this latter, most narrow sense.

3. This situation does not obtain in the Peruvian village of San Bernardo, the site of Summer Institute of Linguistics activity with Kulina for some 30 years. My impression is that with the migration of members of numerous madiha groups to that village, the preference for endogamy has been relaxed. See Townsend and Adams 1978 for a description of marriage in that village.

4. "Other Kulina" (*madiha wa'a*), other Indians, and non-Indians (as well as forest animals), are considered inherently dangerous and fear provoking (*oppinata'i*).

5. The Sharanaua of the Peruvian upper Purus River practice a virtually identical "ritual hunt," according to Siskind (1973). The Sharanaua have borrowed the ritual from the local Kulina; Sharanaua women even sing to men in Kulina when they "order" them to hunt.

6. Kulina at Maronaua did not observe this particular food prohibition after the first week or so following the birth of a child, despite insisting that violating the prohibition would harm the health of the child. I discuss this dilemma—a rule agreed upon by everyone, although no one observes it—in an earlier article (Pollock 1996).

4

A Story of Unspontaneous Generation

Yanomami Male Co-Procreation and the Theory of Substances

Catherine Alès

The generative principles of procreation are among the problems for which societies seek explanations. The most common solutions to this problem can be divided into two categories: those that maintain only one generative principle—male or female—to be active, and those that consider two principles to be necessary. The differences between these two types of theory have long been the subject of studies and debates, starting, we can say, with Hippocrates' discussion and Aristotle's views.[1] Aristotle's statement that only male substances can create a child contrasts with Hippocrates, who hypothesized that male and female substances both have roles in the generative process. Hippocrates' point of view was confirmed at a later date by Galen, helped by the discovery of the ovaries (Musallam 1983, 46).

However, another question of central importance to theories of generation is whether, or not, one coitus is necessary and sufficient for the generation of life. Less attention has been paid to this problem, possibly because it is something that is taken for granted in our present-day state of knowledge. A brief survey of the thought of ancient Greece, Islam (Musallam 1983), and medieval France (Duby 1995) illustrates different views of the phenomenon of procreation, according to which of the two theories of generation is favored,[2] but all appear to conceive of the mechanism taking place within the framework of one sole copulation, which is sufficient for the generation of the embryo. This is not without consequence for the ideas that surround the process of generation, which consider the origin of the masculine generative principle to be unique: in other words, a child can be the result of one, and only one, man.

Nevertheless it corresponds to only one possible way of understanding—as far as it is considered to be involved in reproduction process—paternal generation or procreation. Other societies have different conceptions of the possibilities of engendering life; in particular, there are those that consider the embryo to result from repeated instances of coitus, a widespread feature of Amazonian societies.[3] The difference between a conception in which only one coitus is sufficient, and that in which multiple deposits of semen are necessary to achieve procreation is fundamental: the latter allows for a different construction of paternity—for biological co-paternity.[4] Concepts of biological reproduction thus become crucial if we are to understand paternity in Amazonian societies and, in particular, the presence in several of these societies of shared paternity.

Representations of Procreation

In the case of the Yanomami, the fabrication of the embryo is understood to involve various substances, essentially blood and semen, each related to specific principles of male and female fertility. The principle of female fecundity and of birth corresponds to the blood that women produce periodically during menstruation, and to the blood that is necessary for the expulsion of the child at the moment of birth.

As I have argued elsewhere (Alès 1998), the Yanomami relate the origin of female blood to a mythic history in which Tortoise devours Jaguar. Women reproduce an 'image' of this homicide of ancestral times when they menstruate and this initial principle of fecundity has, equally, to be regularly and ritually reactivated, since it is related to the warring activities conducted by men. The Yanomami thus associate the female blood of fertility with the blood of male revenge assassinations. Although translated by different rituals (see Alès 2001b), cycles of menstruation and child pregnancy, cycles of homicide, together with the cycles of ceremonial festivals involving the ashes of the dead, comprise a whole. They are united by a symbolic relation, crucial to which lies biological reproduction.

If the men participate in the reproduction of the principle of female substances through the homicides they perform, within the framework of this vast symbolic complex, the appearance and disappearance of the female flow of blood is also controlled by male semen. Without the presence of the sperm, the woman would not menstruate. The sperm is, then, a regulator of the periodic flow of menstrual blood, of the obstetric blood that permits birth, and of the return of menstruation after the long period of sexual abstinence following a birth. In this logic, the female blood is bound to the male sperm: menstruation occurs only if sperm is present, that is, through sexual intercourse.

To this male 'double control' of both the principle of female fecundity and of the initiation of female menstruation, there must be added a male representation of the procreation of a child. For this to happen, much time must elapse, repeated sexual relations must take place, and various deposits of sperm are required before the embryo can be totally formed. Gradually, due to the seminal liquid, the embryo starts to form, and its head, body, arms, hands, feet, and legs appear and grow. In this scheme, the woman is a container, a receptacle.

In the empty uterus, first of all the sperm starts to fabricate the placenta, which is like the shell of an egg. This is constructed in a spiral, through the accumulation of spermatic material; the sperm then forms the fetus and causes it to grow. When the man conceives a child, he becomes thin, at the same time that the woman becomes fatter. He does a lot of work and expends much energy, so sexual intercourse is not considered only in terms of entertainment.

However, men become proud when they "make" a child: they like to say of a woman, "I am the one who made her pregnant!" Yanomami society is one in which no distinction is made between sexuality and procreation: each time sexual intercourse takes place, a child is formed. The expressions 'create a child' (*ihiru thai*), and that which we could translate as 'make love' (*wamou;* lit., to eat or to like), are equivalent. The idea is always present that the end result of sexual intercourse is the creation of an embryo.

According to the theory of accumulation of semen, elaborated among Amazonian societies, *the process of fertilization does not coincide with the month in which a woman's periods stop.* The Yanomami think that semen is accumulating and forming the embryo over the spans of months before the cessation of menstruation.

From the perspective of occidental biomedical notions of conception, we are here confronting a problem that is even more difficult for us to comprehend than that a child is formed through the accumulation of sperm; that of the duration of the process of generation. The formation of the embryo begins, in this case, from the moment that a sexual relation is initiated. The cessation of menstruation is not a sign that the embryo is starting to form, but that it has already formed, and is starting to grow. The woman's periods stop when she is already 'completely pregnant.' This means that semen has been accumulated in sufficient quantities to constitute the embryo. During the months of menstruation, the semen makes the periods appear and also causes the embryo to form and grow. The latter is considered to be between 5 and 10 centimeters long at the time the woman's periods stop. During the following months, the deposit of semen allows the fetus to grow, and when it is big enough, sexual relations cease also. In this understanding, Yanomami embryology involves all the flows of semen, the flows of menstrual blood, and the growth of the fetus; the periods of sexual relations, menstruation, and the months of pregnancy all form part of the process of generation.[5]

The theory of the accumulation of semen, or of the repetition of coitus, is not, however, associated with frenetic or uncontrolled sexual practices. The Yanomami do not claim to have an elevated frequency of sexual relations: they avoid, for example, repeated intercourse in a single night. Rather, it is necessary to assemble a certain quantity of generative male substance in order to create material capable of constituting the body of a child, and thus time is necessary in the process of 'making a child.'

The question of time here is very important. Men say they do not like to make love too often: it is better to have intercourse, wait a while, have intercourse again, wait, allow the woman's period to come, make love, wait, make love again, allow time to elapse, wait for the woman's period, and so on. The act of conceiving a child takes several months (three to five months, at least, but it can take up to one, two, or three years). The Yanomami believe that it is not good when a couple make a child too rapidly, since a child that is born too quickly can be damaged, and would not grow correctly.[6] In other words, their practices of controlled sexuality appear totally coherent with the idea of the slow constitution of the fetal substance.

In summary, we have seen that procreation is due, thanks to repeated instances of coitus, to the accumulation of male substance, sperm, which, gradually, forms the embryo and creates the child; the woman, in this case, is a container, and does not participate in the production of material that forms the fetus. Up to this point, this case presents an interesting antithesis to that of the Trobrianders and other Melanesian societies, among whom, as reported by Malinowski (1929), copulation is not the cause of pregnancy: sexual intercourse and seminal substance are not involved, but by contrast, it is the women who have a role in the processes of reproduction through their blood. It is clear that there is another form of dissymmetry here, according to which the child is a product fabricated entirely by men, with the woman being the necessary medium for bringing the created human beings into the world. We can compare her situation with that of a surrogate mother, to use a current idiom for a woman who has received an implanted embryo derived from someone else's egg. Nevertheless, if the process of procreation of the physiological body primarily concerns male substances, the presence of the female contribution becomes apparent in other aspects.

The mother participates in the growth of the fetus by supplying it with nourishment during pregnancy and after birth through the medium of maternal milk. The nutrients transmitted to the fetus in utero depend directly on the food intake of the mother. The food passed on to the child through the medium of the mother, hence, comprises largely (although not totally) products procured by the husband. In an identical manner, the maternal milk is also intimately linked to products controlled by the father.

This last point should be referred to the general pattern of the division of food production in Yanomami society, which is oriented in favor of men. The men hunt, and this provides the most valued and prestigious food, and they also practice horticulture. In what is an effective contrast to the majority of Amazonian societies, horticultural activity among the Yanomami, who prefer to cultivate plantain rather than manioc, is principally a male activity, and one in which females participate to only a limited degree. Both sexes participate in the gathering of wild products, although the male contribution is greater with the men gathering the most important and prestigious products, such as honey and fruits. Both sexes participate in fishing, and here female crab fishing is of high prestige. In effect, the sexual division of food production activities permits men to control the dominant part of food production, and it is generally held that they provide nourishment for the women and their children and enable them to grow (patamaï; lit. to make big). The food-providing role of the man is associated with the idea that children belong to him, as, in a related manner, does his wife.

This economic dominance of men is also related to the more general ties that link the nutrition of the fetus, the production of feminine substances that assure the continued growth of the child, and the masculine substances from which the child is formed. In effect, there is a parallel between the formation of paternal sperm and that of maternal milk, and the prohibitions relating to the consumption of dangerous game animals, which apply to both sexes from preadolescence to the onset of adulthood, are linked to fertility and to the process of generation (cf. Alès 1998). The consumption of these dangerous animals is, hence, directly linked to the thickening of the male and female substances necessary for the formation and growth of the embryo and the child.

At the same time, sperm and milk are key substances for biological reproduction, since they are concerned with the constitution of bodily material. Their production remains, however, dependent on economic activities, hunting among others, that are controlled largely by men. On the other hand, where the form of the child is concerned, we shall see that the female contribution is more balanced, since the mother transmits one of the two sexes of human beings. In effect, if it is men who fabricate the bodies of children, whatever their sex, the gender of the fetus is determined by a model of sexual affiliation: women generate females while men generate males.

From the Yanomami perspective, the transmission of physical and psychological characteristics, and of abilities (competence in economic activities, hardiness or prudence, rhetorical capabilities, song, voice, etc.), like the transmission of sexual identity, follow a scheme of parallel sexual affiliation. Here, I want to emphasize that the origin of inherited characteristics can be bilateral. Grandparents and aunts and uncles from both sides thus transmit characteristics to their descendants according to a sexual affiliation—from man to man or from woman to woman. The point we are interested in is that the co-procreated children have more possibilities of transmitted qualities and characters, as they inherit them from each father's side, than single-fathered children.

Moreover, from the point of view of kinship practice, only identical 'vaginas' can confer 'consanguinity' to all descendants, which highlights that the system is cognatic and bilateral.

It is said of the children of several mothers, that, if these mothers are sisters, they are born from one 'sole vagina,' irrespective of the identity of the father: the sisters may be married to the same husband, or to different men, who may or may not be brothers. The sisters produce 'true' consanguineal siblings, who are *mashi yaï*, 'true' relatives. Hence, it follows that siblings whose mothers are sisters fall into the closest category of identity.

By contrast, two children of the same father by different mothers—who are not sisters—cannot be such 'true' siblings. I would say that this reasoning is nothing more than an extension or logical counterweight to the theory of the accumulation of sperm through the multiplicity of sexual acts, and implicitly, the possible plurality of progenitors: in the face of the lack of certainty over the origin of the embryo with one sole sperm, only uterine affiliation can confer 'true' consanguineal siblingship.

It is in order to have children that are 'true' relatives, mashi yaï, that Yanomami men, who practice polygyny, prefer to be united with different members of the same female sibling set. It is only this institution of sororal polygyny, if possible duplicated by one or more of his brothers, that allows a Yanomami man to produce 'true' consanguineal sons. These sons then constitute a large and strongly bound male sibling set, which is in addition supported by an important female sibling set that can procure allies.

This system is coherent in a society in which social solidarity is exercised primarily as a function of the degree of genealogical and geographical proximity, and in which agnatic nuclei, composed of the father, his brothers, and sons, are the bases on which local units are constructed, and through which conflicts are resolved by the use of force.[7] In summary, nonexclusive sororal polygyny, owing to the character of identity transmitted through women, permits a man to endow his descendants with the appropriate means to engender a strong social unit that aims to secure its own defense and its own biological and social reproduction.

Shared Paternity and Social Practices

It remains for us to examine how the Yanomami representation of procreation is translated into daily life, and, more specifically, which social practices are associated with the representation of shared paternity. In the framework of the theory of the growth of the fetus through the accumulation of sperm, we have seen that it is possible for several progenitors to participate in the formation of the fetus. If the mother has two or several partners, it is supposed that all have contributed to its formation, but, in general, it is recognized that one progenitor predominates, and this man is recognized as the social father of the child. In the case of a woman who is married, the husband of the woman usually becomes the child's social father.

It can be that a Yanomami man will cast doubt on the fact that he has been the only one to supply sperm toward the creation of his children. He will believe that he has conceived them in essence, but that others, usually his brothers or a particular lover, have 'assisted' him (and it can happen that these doubts lead to the wife being rejected). At times a man who has not managed to have children with his wife is 'assisted' in this way. His brothers may conceive a child with his wife in his place, and that can take place, with his consent, in cases of impotence or sterility. The child that is born will be recognized as belonging to the husband, who assumes the role of social father, and who confers his ascription to a social unit upon the child. Generally, a woman's 'friends,'[8] or the biological fathers of her child, are known, and these are supposed to supply food to 'help' the pair, the mother as much as the child, whenever the husband or social father is absent. In many cases, the child knows his 'other' progenitor (it is rare that a child should know his further progenitors when there are more than two) and takes him into account in terms of kinship and alliance practices. In reality, application of kinship terminology does not change when it is the brother of the husband who contributes to, and shares, paternity, which is a common case.

Among the Yanomami, the official father is called the 'elder' or 'greater' (*pata*) father, while the secondary father is termed the 'younger' or 'lesser' (*oshe*) father.⁹ In many cases the husband is considered to be the official father. He is thus the 'elder' father, irrespective of the actual ages of the fathers involved. He fulfills his duties by feeding his child and 'making' it 'grow' (*patamai*), and by ministering to the needs of his wife. On this same theme, it is assumed that the second father will also give food to the mother and infant. However, here there are two possibilities: the first is that the husband knows about the relationship between the wife and the second father, and in this case food can be handed over openly; the second, however, is that the husband has no knowledge of the fact, and the relation of co-paternity is hidden. This means that the official father would become angry if he were to find out, and, in this case, there is no other solution for the secondary father than that he procure food for the mother and child when her husband is absent from the collective house, suitable moments being when the husband goes to hunt or to visit elsewhere for several days.

When the 'younger' father is a brother of the husband, food may circulate openly, but when this is not the case, certain husbands can become enraged. It is not unusual to hear the irritated husband say to his wife: "You will have to ask your man friend to feed you. I don't want to burden myself with this!" The message indicates very clearly that shared procreation is at issue, and that several progenitors have 'helped' (*payeriprai*) in 'assembling' or 'uniting' (*shimou*) the quantity of semen that conceived the fetus.

In fact, it is said of a child of shared conception that he or she is *nikerewë*, 'mixed.' Nevertheless, not all children are 'mixed,' since some women are 'stingy' and refuse to make love with other men; they say they want to create a child with their true husbands. Others, by contrast, accept other men, and express the demand, "Make me a child!" to the man of their preference.

The men are able to say how many women they have 'helped' in the creation of a child. In addition, they count how many times they 'cooperated' during the period of the formation of the fetus: once, three times, five times, they say. One man, for example, told me that he had taken part in the engendering of children with three women—with one of them, he had 'helped' in the creation of two of her children, in which he had 'worked' four times and one time respectively. With each of the other two women he had taken part in the creation of only one child, and had participated five times with each one. He was speaking of the offspring that he recognized apart from those he had had with his own wife. It should be emphasized that, in accordance with a Dravidian-type system of kinship terminology, all these partners—if no incest is committed—fall into the category of 'spouses' and call each other, respectively, 'husband' or 'wife.' In other words, although they are not married, they are united from a terminological point of view through a relationship of potential alliance that authorizes them to have sexual relations. In such a system they already are terminological 'fathers' and 'mothers' for their respective children.

However, a kind of hierarchy is established between the different co-progenitors. The husband is always assumed to have participated to the greatest extent in the conception of the fetus, and the friend, or friends, have only 'helped.' Thus, the husband is officially credited with the predominant part of the engendering of the child.

In reality, only the woman knows who participated, and to what degree, in the conception of her child, and it is she who decides, and who tells her partners, who has contributed most to the formation of the child. In addition, it is no rare thing to hear, in macho conversations between men, a man claim, sometimes maliciously, that it was he who, without the knowledge of the husband, was the principal creator of the child of a certain woman.

From the moment at which a partner is recognized as a father, he has an obligation to minister to the needs of the mother and child. The co-father can assist by giving food products to the mother, but in his case only occasionally. The 'collaborators' (*payeripraïwei*) or 'younger fathers' are differentiated, thus, from the 'true father' (*pë fïï e yaï*), who provides nourishment for his family every day.

The relationship between social and biological parenthood, whether multiple or not, effectively becomes central to this debate. Up to this point, we have seen the grand scheme of the practice of shared paternity, in such a way as it is presented in the general case by the social actors themselves. Specific instances of practice, however, are much more complicated and involve several criteria, which can be combined together. An analysis of the data shows that the problem of co-paternity is very similar to that of children who result solely from extramarital relationships. Extramarital procreation and co-paternity effectively question society in similar ways, and both are handled by the same body of practices, which leads us to relativize the importance of solely biological criteria when considering the concept of paternity.

Two different aspects of paternity must be taken into account when one is speaking of a 'father,' the social and the biological. Co-paternity is accounted for in three distinct ways, each of which has its own logic. 'Elder' and 'younger' paternity can be attributed in such a way that: the elder father (*pata*) is the husband, with the younger father (*oshe*) being the 'nonhusband' co-father (or 'friend'); the elder father (*pata*) is the co-father who has participated quantitatively to the greater degree in the fabrication of the embryo, with the younger father (*oshe*) being he who has contributed less; the elder father (*pata*) was the first to have had sexual intercourse with the mother, and hence was the first to begin the fabrication of the embryo, while the younger father (*oshe*) had sexual intercourse with the mother at a later stage, after the process of the creation of fetal substance had already been initiated. This is irrespective of the number of instances of sexual intercourse: even if he had intercourse with the mother on numerous occasions after the first progenitor, the second partner is still the younger father and it is considered that he has only 'assisted' in the creation of the fetus.

In a similar manner, the attribute *yaï*, which serves to designate the 'true' father, can be applied to the social father, since it is he who feeds and brings up the infant, but it can also be used to refer to the true biological father in cases when he is not the social father. From this last perspective, the social father is referred to as the *puo* or *pëtao* father, the 'mere' father; in other words, he is differentiated from the real father. We shall return to this last point at a later stage.

The diversity of situations that we encounter results from three factors, which, although related to one another, are in some ways independent: these are paternal recognition, paternal economic participation, and the child's knowledge of its paternal affiliation. Hence, it is possible to pick out cases in which: the father either recognizes in public that he has participated in the total or partial fabrication of the child (in conversation he will say, "It's mine!") or he does not recognize his participation; the father or co-father takes charge of the child economically—that is, he provides food for it if he lives nearby—or he does not take charge of it; the child knows that it has a true father or co-father who is not the husband of its mother (its social father) or it does not know. Any combination can appear in practice.

It is when fatherhood is shared between brothers that the fewest problems are presented. Two cases are found here: that of simple biological co-paternity of the child, and that in which the husband assumes social paternity without being considered as a biological father, while his brother, or sometimes two brothers, assume(s) biological paternity.

The secondary father does not really come into the equation if he does not live nearby, and in the case of brothers who are co-fathers, if the secondary father is not the husband and social father. A younger father, if he is a brother of the elder father, does not play any great role in the life of his child. Nevertheless, when the mother is single or has been rejected by her husband for having had 'mixed' or adulterous children, the co-fathers can participate more in economic maintenance, which is linked to the affection and recognition that he gives his child.

The situation of a man who acts like a social father to a child without being its progenitor is very similar to the case of a man who is the social father of a child who participated only partially in its procreation. He is the social father, since he is the husband of the mother, and since the child lives with her, he loves it and feeds it.

Children resulting solely from extramarital relationships are, in effect, brought up by the legitimate husband of the mother if she continues to live with him after the event. A mother may confess that it is only her friend who has contributed to the child, or the fact may be obvious if she has fled into the jungle for various months with him or if the husband happens to have been away on a lengthy visit to a distant community, and she will normally inform the child of the identity of its true father. If he wants to keep his wife, the husband has two alternatives. If he is a coward, he will accept the situation without fighting with his wife to any great extent. If he is more bellicose, he will beat the woman to express his anger, and that will be the end of the matter, since she has paid the price of his anger: at the least she receives a blow that will leave her with a scar. The husband can then care for the child, while the true father, living further away, cannot give it the same care and affection. This point is very important since the social father 'becomes' the yaï father, that is, he is (according to the commentator) referred to as the 'true' father, in the place of the biological father.

Children who have another father who is not their social father are able to take advantage of both sides. When the mother or social father becomes angry with them they will run away or be sent by their mother to the house of the biological father, from where they return when they start to miss their mother and social father. An extramaritally born child can thus get to know its siblings, giving him the possibility of loving them, and the opportunity to say to them that when his father disappears they will all live together.[10]

In the case of a divorce, when a woman is thrown out for having conceived a child completely out of wedlock, she brings up her child with the help of her family, and sometimes with that of the true father. Often, from the moment the mother finds another husband, the grandparents adopt the child and bring it up so that they have company and help as they become older.

The situation of children conceived by an unmarried woman, in cases when the father does not take her for a wife, is very similar to that of the children of a divorced woman. The father, in general, will recognize his child and provides economic assistance, but the child lives with its mother and her family, and is sometimes adopted by the grandparents. They 'keep' it with them, as they do not want to let it go to its father when it grows older.

Finally, the attribution of paternity is more complicated in cases of multiple co-paternity. When there are only two progenitors, one father is the elder and the other is the younger. It is a different case if the mother has had several partners: this can happen if she has repeatedly fled into the jungle with different men or has lived through an episode of multiple relationships. The father of the child will be the man who takes the woman for a wife once the conception of the fetus is already or nearly complete. It is assumed that he has also participated in the fabrication of the child, that is, he assumes the social paternity of the child as the woman's husband.

After the death of her husband, a woman can choose between remaining single and marrying another man. A co-father is always in a good position to marry the mother of his shared child (or children) and to provide for them. Nevertheless, in a similar manner to that in which shared procreation between brothers is tolerated, the brothers of the dead man maintain the relationship of potential 'husbands' toward his widow, and can become enraged should she decide to marry outside their male sibling set. A brother of the deceased can, at a later stage, take the widow for a wife, but if none of the brothers wants to be united with her, it is then possible, with time, for her to make a new life with another man. However, she should not officially take another partner while the ritual treatment of her dead husband's ashes remains incomplete, an obligation that is symmetrical also in the case of a man whose wife has died. It is incumbent on the dead man's brothers to provide food for the widow for the rest of her life, whether or not she later marries within their group. The father and his brothers are obliged to provide for her needs, as they are for those of the children, but this will not occur if they become enraged at the widow fleeing with another man. If the woman prefers to go to a distant community, the brothers can sometimes claim the children, or insist that they remain in their community. In effect, they represent the group to which the sons of the dead man are affiliated socially, and have the right to keep them, since they were raised on the food provided by their father and were also fabricated from his semen.

In any case, a widow who chooses not to marry again is not left completely unprovided for. In addition to the help she can receive from her husband's family, she has at her disposal the force of her own labor, and that of her children, and can count on the solidarity of her own relatives—her brothers and her sisters. Child care is provided not only by the mother and fathers, but by the woman's siblings and by the child's grandparents, who also nourish it and bring it up, so that it in turn will care for the grandparents when they grow older. Apart from this, a woman is always in a position to ask, if she wants, for food from her friends, whether or not these are co-fathers of her children, and these will give food to her if and when they have any available. However, geographic proximity is a very important factor, and a co-father, like a divorced father, who does not live close to his child, only contributes occasionally to its upkeep.

One last point relating to co-paternity is worthy of attention. At times it happens that the theory of procreation by the accumulation of semen is contradicted empirically. There are cases in which certain older women recognize that it is possible to have a child without having repeated sexual intercourse: they are experienced and are able to say with certainty that it is possible to become pregnant following only one copulation. However, faced with this problem, another rationalization quickly comes into play: it is thought that *when women are older they can become pregnant more rapidly.*

It is also interesting to mention the type of response that the Ye'kwana give to the same question. When it is said nowadays, on the basis of medical knowledge, that it is possible to have a child after only one instance of sexual intercourse, it is the older people who say emphatically that this is impossible, and that it is necessary to accumulate.

The Ye'kwana, like the Yanomami, express the idea that all men who have made love with a woman since the birth of her last child participate in the creation of her next child. The semen from each copulation accumulates in her. A woman can have a child when she is living with one man, but if, one year earlier, she was living with another, both are counted equally. The semen is accumulated during the two or three years that elapse between pregnancies, in such a way that three men can be co-fathers.[11] If the woman has a husband, then he is the legitimate father, and the last man to have lived with her is the social father. Any remaining men do not recognize the child, for fear that the husband may abandon the woman. They do not claim the child following death of the husband and thereafter the woman remains alone.

There is a subtle difference between the Ye'kwana and Yanomami situations. According to Ye'kwana women, their additional partners do not recognize their children and do not help the mother with the upkeep of the child at all; she must bring up the child alone. Rather, men laugh at women in this situation: for example, they will say, "The woman must have a vagina full of the milk that men have left there," and similar things that express the denigration to which the women are submitted. This is what Ye'kwana women say, and it does not appear that, when translated into practice, the concept of shared fatherhood is particularly favorable to them.

A Statistical Approach to the Pattern of Co-Procreation

An approach founded on a set of numerical data can provide us with additional information that is indicative of the practice of co-paternity among the Yanomami, while recognizing the fact, as noted above, that the information about this topic cannot be exhaustive or without bias. The following data are based on a sample of 194 progenitors from 15 communities in Central Sierra Parima in Venezuela. At the time of this survey their population was estimated at 480 inhabitants. The sample included only those individuals who had already reproduced at least once. Each adult male and female was asked the number of co-procreated children they had had and with whom, their marital status, and the marital status of their partners. These data were cross-checked with other data sets, including the terminological relation and the degree of genealogical relatedness between the different fathers of a child, their status as primary or secondary fathers, and the possible conflict that resulted from married women's co-generated conceptions (see table 4.1).[12]

The data show that 52% of the progenitors considered (101/194) are reported to have co-fathered children (see table 4.2). This is not a marginal feature, as slightly less than half of the women (43/99) and more than the half of the men (58/95) had given birth to co-fathered children.

Table 4.1. Yanomami single and co-fathered births per sex

Co-procreated children	By women		By men	
	No.	Percent	No.	Percent
0	56	57	37	39
1	30	30	30	32
2	11	11	16	17
3–6	2	2	12	13
Total	99		95	

Table 4.2. Yanomami co-fathered births per sex and male marital status

	Co-procreated children				Male marital status			
	By women		By men		Husband		"Friend"	
	No.	Percent	No.	Percent	No.	Percent	No.	Percent
1	30	70	30	52	13	12	17	16
2	11	26	16	28	17	16	15	14
3	1	2	8	14	6	6	18	17
4	1	2	1	2	1	1	3	3
5	—	—	1	2	2	2	3	3
6	—	—	2	3	6	6	6	6
Total	43		58		45		62	

Percentages are rounded up to the nearest whole number.

Do Men or Women Co-Generate More Children?

Of the individuals who have one co-generated child or more, 43% (43/101) are women and 57% (58/101) are men (see table 4.2). The gap is partly due to the fact that at least two fathers per child are required for only one mother. Nevertheless it might be expected that many more men would be co-fathers than women would be mothers of co-fathered children. This result denotes then that the men involved have a number of co-fathered children significantly superior to that of the women, even though both men and women have more than one co-fathered child, as indicated in the table. This fact has to be understood in the context that men are in many instances involuntary co-fathers, in a situation brought about by their wives. In effect it is important to consider that, unlike women, the men have two possibilities for co-fatherhood, the first when he participates in an extramarital procreation, the second as a husband whose wife has sexual relationships with an another partner.

How Often Do Men and Women Co-Generate Children?

Of those women who have co-generated a child or children, nearly 70% have only one co-generated child, and more than 95% have one or two co-generated children, while less than 5% have three or four co-generated children (table 4.2). There are no cases of women with five or six co-procreated children but there are two occasions where the men are co-fathers six times over; one corresponds to that of a man who occurs twice as a husband and four times as a 'friend,' and the second to that of a man who occurs four times as a husband and twice as a 'friend.' As for the man who is five times a co-father, on two occasions this was at his wife's choice. It can be said then that there is not a great difference between the practices of men and women where the larger numbers of co-procreated children are concerned.

On the other hand, of those men who have co-generated children, only slightly more than 50% have a single co-generated child and nearly 80% have one or two co-procreated children. As the statuses of husband and friend are balanced in the cases of one and two children, we can deduce that the difference in the figures between men and women comes essentially from the fact that the men deal with the children co-generated by their wife or wives. Of the 107 cases where males are co-progenitors, in more than 40% men are in the status of husband.

The category of triple co-fatherhood—that is, having three co-procreated infants—is also important for the men. We can observe that the gap is greater in this category where men have three times more co-generated children as a result of extramarital relationships. Nevertheless, we can assume overall that the most common pattern for a man is to have one or two extramarital co-procreated children, and also to receive one or two, de facto, from his wife or wives. Since this feature only concerns slightly more than half of the reproductive individuals, it can be added that there is a relative tendency for some of the progenitors, both men and women, to be co-progenitors in repeated instances.

How Many Fathers Does a Co-Generated Child Have?

From the perspective of the number of men concerned in co-paternity, the most common model of co-paternity involves only two fathers; this is the case for 88% of children (52/59). Ternary (three fathers) and multiple (four or more) co-paternities occur at a similar rate: 7% (4/59) and 5% (3/59) respectively. These latter cases were reported when four or five names of progenitors were given, but the two more frequent sex partners are referred to as the primary and secondary fathers. They correspond to times when the woman had not succeeded in attaching herself to a designated husband. After a temporary period of relatively unstable sexual life, she can be taken as a spouse by one of the progenitors, who will then be the social father of her child. If the woman is already married, one of the co-progenitors is generally the husband and, even if he is the secondary father, he will assume the social paternity.

Who Co-Generates Children?

The relation between married individuals, unmarried individuals, and the concept of multiple progenitors is subtle. As men get married significantly later than women a lot of co-paternities thus involve bachelors while only a few concern spinsters. Almost 40% of the cases (21/55) involve a bachelor. Of these, two-thirds are direct ('true') brothers (12) and first- (1) or second-degree (1) terminological 'brothers,' and their position as primary or secondary father is nearly equal.

The married women are the mothers of 93% of co-fathered children and the spinsters of 7% of them. Of the spinsters, 36% (4/11) have at least one co-procreated child, as opposed to 44% (39/88) for the married women. This means that spinsters do not particularly seek several fathers to maintain them and their children. In other words, co-paternity is not a strategy favored by single mothers more than having a single father for their children: 29% (4/14) of the children of spinsters are co-procreated, as opposed to 71% (10/14) who are procreated with only one father.

As for married women, nearly a third (32%; 24/76) of the births involve entirely extramarital fathers (21 extramaritally procreated children and 3 extramarital co-procreations) and more than two-thirds (68.42%; 55/76) involve at least one extramarital father (co-procreations that imply both marital [52] and extramarital [3] relationships).

What Proportion of Women Have Had Children during Extramarital Relationships?

Most of the children that have resulted from extramarital relationships (with single paternity) were born to only a small number of women. Four women have nearly half (10/21) of the extramaritally conceived children, of which two women had three children, and two women had two. The actors themselves explain their extramarital births by the fact that their husbands are essentially cowards. Of the 21 extramarital births, in 16 cases the husband did not use violence against the spouse. These are the 10 cases commented upon previously, where the husbands are particularly noncombative (and where in two cases the progenitor is a direct brother of the husband); the three cases where the progenitors of the children are 'brothers' of the husband (two direct brothers and one first degree 'brother'); the two cases where the progenitor is the woman's sister's husband; and the one case where the husband is disabled. Beyond these specific instances, two examples involved a divorce with a woman who was injured and two cases of injuries without a divorce; for one of the cases this information is missing.

This set of data is consistent with the fact that only 5% (3/55) of the co-fathered children of married women are extramaritally conceived:[13] a very large proportion of co-paternities (95%; 52/55) includes the husband as either the primary or the secondary father. Nevertheless it is not always possible to avoid a reaction from the husband. In one case, although paternity was shared by a husband and his direct brother, the woman, a mother of five, was badly hurt by the blows she received from her legitimate husband and was consequently rejected by him.

What Is the Frequency of the Husband Being the Primary or Secondary Father?

Of the 50 children corresponding to a binary (or two fathers) co-paternity, in 30% (15/50) of occurrences the husband is the primary co-father, and in 66% (33/50) it is a 'friend.' In other words, from the global total of all co-paternities (55), it is clearly illustrated that the 'friends' are said twice as often to be primary co-fathers as are the husbands (35/17).

This situation is partially compensated for by the fact that, of the 55 instances of co-paternity, 17 correspond to direct brothers, 4 to terminological 'brothers' of the first degree and 3 of second degree. Interestingly, the figures confirm that in almost 40% of the cases (21/55) co-paternity is shared by a direct or very near 'brother.'

For secondary paternity in binary co-paternity, the figures are slightly different; in 30 of the cases the husband is said to be the secondary father, in 18 it is the 'friends,' and the order is unknown in two instances. The asymmetry that can be noted results from the existence of three binary co-paternities, which are extramarital. Concurrently, this leads to the appearance of a greater occurrence of 'friends' in this position.

In the four registered cases of ternary (three fathers) co-fatherhood, the incidence of the husbands as primary father is equal to the friends' rate (2/2). Finally, in the only case of multiple co-paternity (four or five fathers) that involves a married woman, the primary father is unknown. In this kind of situation the husband, who is also one of the co-progenitors of the child, will in general shoulder the social fatherhood of the child and be considered as the primary father. The one example here corresponds to the first child of a very young woman as the result of her indecisiveness over staying with the man she chose as her husband. Subsequently she had a stable relationship with him.

Conclusion

As far as the Yanomami are concerned, some specific points have to be highlighted. The sperm accumulation theory, on one hand, focuses on male affiliation but, on the other, it does not fit very well with a notion such as patrilineal descent. The co-procreated children can have unrelated co-fathers with different ancestral origins. Apart from the fact that the affiliation is reckoned bilaterally, and the qualities and characters can be bilaterally transmitted, we have seen that they can inherit their qualities from their different fathers. Once the child is a mature adult, he will, during ceremonial dialogues pronounced with distant allied communities, tell of his distinct patrilateral ancestral origins as his matrilateral one. This is why the explanation that the child is basically made up of the male substance is not a good argument in favor of the existence of patrilineages (see Alès 1990, 95): in the case of co-fatherhood, de facto, the two or more fathers could belong to different hypothetical lineages.[14]

Another point concerns the relation between the indigenous theory of pro-creation and polygamy. We have seen that 'true consanguines' (*mashi yai*) are those that come from 'one sole vagina' (*mõri naka*). Rather than men, it is women who confer their identity on siblings. This theory is consistent with the practice of sororal polygyny, in which a man prefers to marry several sisters, in order to avoid any differentiation between his children, and to have children who are 'true brothers and sisters.' In addition, it is consistent with the idea of multiple paternity in the process of procreation: with the male contribution being uncertain, the maximal character of identity is transmitted through women. Nevertheless, there is one further point to emphasize that is connected to the concept of shared procreation: *it is the underlying link that exists between the indigenous theory of procreation and polyandry.*

Among the Yanomami, for example, one can say that the indigenous con-cept of procreation leads to the practice of an informal polyandry. The mother receives food alternately from two different men, both for herself and for her child. When the legitimate husband knows and accepts the participation of an-other man in the paternity of his child, it is tantamount to the denomination of 'unofficial polyandry.' When he does not recognize the other man's participa-tion, then we can speak of 'clandestine polyandry,' for, once the mother has agreed to the degree of participation of the second father, then he will consider this a lifelong obligation and it will be taken into account in the relations main-tained by the child in the social network.

Most of the time this 'unofficial polyandry' is adelphic, since the various fathers are brothers, and more precisely, it is one of his brothers that a man will legitimize with the title of 'younger father.' This occurred in approxi-mately 40% of the cases of co-paternity. When the younger father is not a brother, then secondary paternity is not recognized, and either stays hidden or is denied.

This leads us to deduce a relationship between these practices and the 'offi-cial polyandry' that exists among some groups of Yanomami. In certain parts of Yanomami territory, in the upper Orinoco, for example, an open polyandry is effectively practiced. The second husband can live at an adjacent hearth, if he is a brother, and at a more distant hearth in the communal house, if he is not. He will regularly visit his 'wife' at her hearth and shares the same hearth with her when her principal husband goes hunting or goes on a visit. The woman gives him portions of food daily, and the man gives her the products of his labor. Above all, his offspring are recognized and he provides them with food. The comparison between the two practices allows us to see that, as when polyandry is practiced, we generally find that 'adelphic' co-paternity is the most accepted instance.

All these data lead us to think that, in a society in which a mother can eventually have several progenitors for her child, each woman is effectively polyandrous, in the sense that the germ of this idea is already present in the theory; even in groups where polyandry is not officially recognized, women are in a situation of potential polyandry. The fact that a man can reproduce through the medium of several women is recognized in such a way that there are no theoretical (only practical) limits for him to optimize his possibilities of reproduction. By contrast, whatever the number of partners, or husbands, the woman takes in her reproductive life, she remains limited to her own production of children. Taking into consideration the theory of the accumulation of semen, a woman can always take steps to make the possibility of her own reproduction more certain—in case her legitimate husband does not 'make her a child,' for reasons of sterility or infrequency of sexual relations. In one way, she too can have descendants with several different men; by accumulating 'fathers' for her children, she too can count on several 'husbands' in order to guarantee to her children numerous siblings. It can thus be considered that female fecundity is optimized through the use of multiple progenitors, in the same way that men can practice polygamy.[15] This is also true for men, who in addition to polygyny can also use poly-paternity. Masculine descent is thus doubly optimized.

No idea from demographic politics is alien to Yanomami society. Social actors clearly express their desire to multiply and increase demographically. One of their preoccupations is with incest, which haunts them. The development of larger groups allows greater possibilities for intermarriage, that is, for the possibility of creating unions between partners who are not too closely related: they confess that in certain moments of their history they have found themselves so numerically reduced that they have had to make numerous incestuous unions. In the framework of a Dravidian-type kinship terminology, incest is conceived in relation to the inadequacy of the terminology applied between the two partners, which leads, for example, to two terminological siblings being united.

The politics of birth and desired demographic development are also linked to the search for demographic power in the context of war and of conflict. The capacity of a unit for its own defense (and for attack) is related to its capacity to be self-sufficient in the event of conflict, and is the reason why the Yanomami emphasize the primary importance of building up numerically strong male sibling sets, with the formation of a network of relationships of military solidarity and the formation of alliances coming as a complementary measure. One of the reasons for anger when a Yanomami man is lost in the flower of his youth is that 'his son is left alone.' In reality, there can be two or three children, but the expression signifies that the premature death of the man has not allowed his sons to become numerous, diminishing their capacity for self-sufficiency and their defense potential. Women say that they want to give birth to at least six children—two daughters and four sons. They explain that this is the minimum number of men to ensure that their sons will be able to count on sufficient assistance to defend themselves when fighting.

In this context, the theory of procreation through accumulation of semen can thus be interpreted not only, on one level, as a strategy with material aims (alimentation or protection) to ensure a reserve of possible husbands for widows in a society in which men are exposed to a relatively high risk of meeting an early death (Beckerman and Lizarralde n.d.), but also, on another level, as a more general and fundamental strategy to guarantee the reproduction of human beings, and hence, of the group.

These points of view are different in the sense that it is a group of descendants that is sought rather than partners for alimentary ends. In the case of the Yanomami, it is hoped more that the children will provide a form of social security capable of helping and feeding their parents when these become less productive, than a reserve of husbands who will assist women in the event of the death of a husband.

These considerations lead us to more general conclusions, from two different perspectives. The first concerns the variability in the application of the indigenous theory of procreation. On the basis of a construction that is widespread, which supposes the accumulation of male substance in the process of the formation of the fetus, a variety of practices take place in different cultures. Some recognize multiple paternity, and the different fathers have their own particular role in relation to the child and its mother. By contrast, in others, the additional fathers do not recognize their children and are not responsible for their upbringing and their future, nor are they responsible for the maintenance of the mother.

This demonstrates that, if constructions or representations explain, in part, social practices, which are here matrimonial and parental, and have repercussions in the application of the kinship system, the proposition is not symmetrical, in that it is preferable to avoid explaining representations through practices. The same theory of procreation can lead to a variety of practices or applications, which do not permit us to deduce the representations.

The second point concerns the general implications of the representation of shared fatherhood for kinship. The representation of procreation linked to the potential for multiple paternity cannot but question the studies of kinship that can be undertaken in this kind of society. The notion of brothers and half-brothers, for example, in the analysis of the classification of kin is a relative matter. In effect, two true brothers are supposed to have not only the same father and the same mother, but also the same co-fathers. The same proposition can be applied to the case of half brothers of the same father, but from two different mothers, and, similarly, to two half brothers from the same mother, but of different husbands. Hence, we arrive at a situation of extreme complexity when one takes into account that each individual can have several fathers. Among the Yanomami, however, this permits us to understand in certain cases the variability found by way of the application of kinship terminology between two brothers or half brothers, who might be supposed, in principle, to have the same series of terminological names relating to the remainder of the population.

The indigenous theory of conception demonstrates to us that we should focus on this situation of complexity, a situation that our kinship schemes are still far from understanding, since these are drawn from our ethnocentric vision of genealogical relations, which are based on a representation of biological ties traced for each individual through *one unique mother and one unique father*.[16]

Notes

1. While for Hippocrates (1978) there are two forms of sperm, one female and one male, that participate in the formation of the fetus, for Aristotle (1942) female substances do not contain the principle of embryogenesis. Male sperm, which results from a baking of the blood, brings with it the 'pneuma,' which contains the principle of form, which in turn shapes the material in the woman. This is in opposition to female menstrual blood, which is incapable of being transformed into sperm. The woman, the bearer of the material, is in this case only a receptacle.

2. In both Islamic and medieval thought, women are not considered to be only the receptacles of male seed. Two different kinds of sperm are thought to exist, which participate in conception.

3. Such as the Yanomami (Alès 1998) and their neighbors the Ye'kwana. See also Beckerman and Lizarralde n.d. for the Barí, Crocker and Crocker 1994 for the Canela, and Hill and Kaplan 1988 for the Aché, as well as the authors in this volume.

4. We should bear in mind that, in our modern society, it was only in the nineteenth century that the role of the spermatozoa in fertilization and the equivalent roles of ovum and spermatozoon in the constitution of the fetus became known. As Spallanzani demonstrated the fertilization capacity of the male semen in 1780, Prévost and Dumas in 1824 showed that this capacity lay in the spermatozoa. The penetration of the spermatozoon into the egg was then described by Barry (1843) and others, but the concept of the equivalence of these gametes in the fertilization process was not forthcoming until the works of Van Beneden (1875), O. Hertwig (1876), and Fol (1879) (quoted in Bishop and Walton 1960, 2). Still at present, as Françoise Héritier (1996, 204) has underscored, the actual mechanism of fertilization remains poorly explained.

5. I am considering here only the 'biological' aspects of fertilization: fertilization depends on a symbolic complex that is much wider, encompassing an entire ensemble of social and ritual relations. I have already evoked this ensemble above in considering the relation between menstrual and obstetric blood, and the blood of male homicides.

6. The interval between births in Yanomami society is between two and three years. Couples observe a period of sexual prohibition, lasting between a year and a year and a half, following the birth of a child. This allows the recently born infant to benefit fully from breast-feeding and from the full attention of the mother for an adequate time.

7. For further detail, see Alès 1984, 1990.

8. 'Friend' is the translation of the Yanomami word *nofi*, which is used to designate a sexual mate who is not husband or wife.

9. When referring to a particular child one says: *pë fïi e pata*, his elder father, and *pë fïi e oshe*, his younger father.

10. Communal houses are based around groups of relatives with a father, his wives, and their children. When the father dies, the brothers and their wives continue to live together until there arise conflicts that separate them.

11. Menstruation stops as soon as the fetus is formed, then the man can continue to deposit semen for five or six additional months in order to feed the fetus. Sexual relations cease when the child is fully grown in the uterus.

12. Nonreproductive individuals and those too young to have reached their reproductive potential have not been taken into account. A fraction of the reproductive individuals, mainly the oldest ones, could not be included here, as our conversations would have referred to dead people, a sensitive matter for the Yano-

mami. This number comprises 22 individuals and represents a little over 10% of the total number of progenitors considered. In addition, six male progenitors who had co-fathered children in the considered communities actually belonged to neighboring communities that are not included in the sample.

13. In the three cases concerned here, one woman received injuries without divorce and two of them did not: one corresponds to one of the four women referred to above with a noncombative husband and one where a co-father is a true brother. On the relationship between divorcée and injuries, see Alès 2001a.

14. For a discussion of the problem of using concepts such as unilineal descent or patrilineages among the Yanomami, see Alès 1990.

15. Among the Yanomami polygyny is largely practiced without the intervention of norms or preferences, such as polygamy being restricted to leaders and warriors, whether or not they have taken a life. The fact that women engage in multiple sexual partnerships does not support Chagnon's sociobiological theory of selective reproduction based on his statistics that killers have more wives, and so more children, than other men (Chagnon 1988, 985–92).

16. This therefore can only call into question the assumption that all kinship systems are conceived as if based on our own, supposed universal, genealogical grid. In his critical review of the history of definitions of kinship, Schneider (1984) examines this point and shows that according to classical kinship theory kinship systems are ultimately founded on "natural" biological facts. As Schneider (1968) points out about American kinship, we can see here that the conceptions of substances of sexual intercourse and of procreation, such as semen, milk, and blood, influence the way the notion of kinship perceived in biological terms is culturally constructed and defined.

PART II

5

Canela "Other Fathers"

Partible Paternity and Its Changing Practices

William H. Crocker

The Canela believe in partible paternity. A woman may have sex with many men during a pregnancy, and most of these men are considered "biological" fathers to her fetus. These men were only partly her choices as sex partners, for a man or a group of men may have chosen her even though she was pregnant. At the birth of the baby, she designates these men as her fetus's "other fathers," and they must go into couvade to help make the fetus grow and be healthy. She chooses her pregnancy lovers, or accepts them, for many reasons, including liking them especially well; but she also selects superior economic providers, so her child will inherit their qualities.

The 1,300 Canela Indians live in what is culturally Amazonia. Their village is situated 650 kilometers southeast of the mouth of the Amazon River in savanna woodlands (*cerrados*), not tropical forests. They enjoy the protection of a government reservation near Barra do Corda in the center of the Brazilian state of Maranhão. They speak Gê, which is also the language of the better-known Kayapó and Shavante Indian tribes. Before contact, they grew manioc and other crops in stream-edge gardens.

In 1814, almost two centuries ago, they surrendered to a Brazilian garrison and were later settled on only 5% of their former lands. Before this date, they lived more as semi-migratory hunter-gatherers than as settled agriculturalists, and they were subjected to serious annual losses due to warfare with other Timbira nations, peoples of similar culture. It is believed that the numerous Timbira nations inhabited a region from the center of Piaui State west to the Tocantins River (Hemming 1987, 63, 187).

To understand the extreme extent to which the Canela shared almost everything—possessions, food, sex, and even fatherhood—we must take into account that their outlook and motivations were basically pre-agricultural, when contrasted with settled agriculturalists, and that they had to adapt to losses due to the uncertainties of both food collecting and annual warfare. Most hunter-gatherers lived in extended family bands of 20 to 50 people. An individual married a person from another band with the same culture. In contrast, the Canela before contact lived in one village of 1,000 to 1,500 individuals or more, wherein most adults faced each other almost daily. They found their spouses within this unit. Thus, while the Canela had some agriculture, they were psychologically more like food collectors, though they lived in a very large village.

Ethnographic Background

In this chapter I will focus on providing an understanding of the Canela cultural complex surrounding a child's having several "biological" fathers. To accomplish this, I will seek to clarify Canela beliefs about conception and fetal development to furnish the ethnobiological basis. I will then provide related aspects of the kinship terminological system and the domestic group to portray the social setting. Additionally, I will introduce ecological and demographic factors to trace the broader picture in which partible paternity exists. Finally, I will examine the economic and political roles of men and women to show how they operate within the domestic setting, leaving the "other fathers" outside it, and thereby rendering them somewhat ineffectual. Also, I will discuss how orphans, though on the inside of the domestic structure, are nevertheless often left out of its special benefits.

Conception and Fetal Development

The Canela, like many other Amazonian peoples, believe in partible paternity; they hold that when a pregnant woman has sex, the semen becomes part of the fetus itself. Men, in this way, become "biological" fathers of the baby for life (Crocker 1990, 257). Considering the ethnobiological context of this practice, I do not use the traditional terms *genitor* and *pater* since they do not emphasize the relationships that are correct and emic for the Canela. The man married to a pregnant woman and her lovers, but just those lovers who were designated by her as having had sex with her during her pregnancy, are *all* genitors for the Canela. Nevertheless, the mother's husband (MH) is considered more important to the welfare of the fetus/baby/child than any one of these "other fathers" (OFs) (Crocker and Crocker 1994, 83–87).

The Canela talk casually about physical resemblances between a child and its biological fathers, whether the OFs or the MH. They say that the father whom the child most resembles must have contributed the most semen; that is, he had sex with the pregnant mother (M) more times than the other OFs, and possibly even more times than the MH. However, even if they considered a child more closely resembles one of its OFs, they still give the principal role in strengthening the baby to its MH. This strengthening is carried out through the undertaking of rigorous postpartum "restrictions" (i.e., limitations) on the intake of food and sex (Crocker and Crocker 1994, 108–9). Thus, the restrictions practiced by the MH during his postpartum internment are more extensive than the restrictions maintained by the OFs in their postpartum seclusions in their mother's or their sisters' house. Classificatory fathers (step-, adoptive, FB, FZS, FFBS, etc.) are not included in this ethnobiological concept, so it *is* a precise biological one for the Canela.

The Canela believe that it takes more than one ejaculate, usually about six, to make a woman pregnant, but the ejaculates may come from more than one man, or even from many men, one time each. In the potential case of sequential sex with a pregnant woman (Crocker n.d.), all the men involved should be designated OFs. They believe it is largely semen that creates and builds the fetus, though some women speak of food and female fluids as also being contributing elements, but not significantly so. The Canela have no special term for such fluids, as they do for semen (*hiràà*).[1] Different women use different descriptive terms. Thus, assessing their explanations and considering their use of only descriptive terms for female fluids, I believe that for the Canela the male contribution to making the fetus is essentially total. Apparently, the Shavante (Maybury-Lewis 1967, 63) and the Xikrin-Kayapó (William H. Fisher, pers. comm.) hold the same view that it is only semen that makes the fetus.

I have used *contributing fathers* in some of my publications (e.g., Crocker 1990, 257), because this expression is explanatory, though etic. However, the Canela use the terms *other father* (*hũm nõ:* father other), *other fathers* (*mēhũm nõ:* plural father other), and *father* (*hũm/-tsũũ/päm*). They also use *full/primary father* (*hũm-pey*) and *lesser/secondary father* (*hũm-kahàk*), terms that do not stress the biological aspects that are important to this paper. However, I have elected to use *other father* and *mother's husband*. During the late 1950s, an OF was said to be a *hũm-pey*, but during the late 1970s, young Canela research assistants said he was a *hŭm-kahàk,* which shows the decreasing significance through two decades of the OF in Canela thinking.

The Canela believe that the practice of certain restrictions (*ipiyakri-tsà/ aykri-tsà*) against food and sex keeps pollutants out of the body (Crocker and Crocker 1994, 106–9). These ethnobiological pollutants are inherent in most meat juices, though the extent of pollution varies with the kind of meat and the sex of the animal. Generally, gamier and male meat juices are believed to be more polluted than domestic and female ones. While Canela pollutants can be transferred from one individual to another through contact with sexual fluids, the origin of pollutants is, nevertheless, in foods. The practice of undergoing restrictions against certain foods and sex is a general Canela procedure for an individual to acquire important skills in life, such as fast running, endurance, success in hunting, and a curer's psychic abilities. In the situation we are focusing on, however, restrictions are undertaken by the MH and the OFs to strengthen the baby—to prevent pollutants from reaching him or her through the fathers, since biological parents and their children are believed to exist in one continuous, flow-through blood system.

Thus, if a Canela's body has become polluted, these pollutants are necessarily passed to his or her closest kin—parents, siblings,[2] and children. This is because all these one-kin-link-away relatives (Crocker 1990, 235–36) are believed to have almost identical blood (*kapróô*) so that all their blood is shared, as if they all lived in one blood pool (Crocker and Crocker 1994, 107). Grandparents, grandchildren, maternal uncles, paternal aunts, and cross-sibling nieces and nephews, being two kin links away from the fetus, have sufficiently dissimilar blood so that only nondamaging amounts of pollutants are passed on to them through the one intervening kin person. The OFs are considered biological parents (i.e., one-kin-link-away relatives) so that pollutants are, indeed, passed on from them directly to the babies they have helped to make. Thus, the OFs, the M, and the MH must avoid pollutants for the sake of their baby.

A Canela always has some pollutants from food or sex in his or her blood, but if the person is healthy and strong, these pollutants do no personal harm. However, if a Canela is weak from illness, these pollutants make him or her sicker. A program of rigorous restrictions to prevent additional pollutants from entering the body along with certain foods and sexual fluids may be necessary for recovery. Similarly, if someone in a Canela's pool of shared blood is sick, he or she must undergo restrictions to help this person recover. The parents and "fathers" of a newborn baby must undergo restrictions because such a baby is necessarily so weak that it could die from even a small amount of transferred pollutants. This is the ethnobiological context that must be understood to appreciate the rites and practices involving the OFs and their lifelong relationships with their contributed-to children, their "other children" (OCs: *mẽ ʔkhra ʔnõ:* plural child other). These rites and practices are the pregnant mother's selection of her "other husbands" (OHs); the mother's designation at childbirth of which ones of these OHs are the baby's OFs; the couvade for the M, MH, and OFs; the postpartum rite for the MH and OFs, and the lifelong relationship between the OFs and their OCs.

Whether these postpartum seclusions constitute the traditional couvade is a question. They have nothing to do with the MH or the OFs simulating, or coexperiencing with the M, the postpartum effects of childbirth. They have everything to do with helping to save the newborn baby and making it strong. Thus, the focus of these seclusions is on the "parent"-to-child relationships, not on the "parent"-to-parent ones.

Kinship Terminological System

The Canela kinship terminological system is Crow-III, as defined by Lounsbury (1964, 375–77), or, better still, it is characterized by parallel transmission (Scheffler and Lounsbury 1971, 110). It is not matrilineal but rather is bilateral with a matrilateral emphasis. In the Canela version of this Crow categorization, a grandparent is merged (GP = MB/FZ) with a maternal uncle (MB) or a paternal aunt (FZ) of the first ascending generation. Similarly, a grandchild (GC/DD/SS/DS/SD) (*tàmtswè*) is merged into the first descending generation with a cross-sibling's son (GS = ♀BS/♂ZS) called "nephew" (*tàmtswè/ hapal*) or a cross-sibling's daughter (GD = ♀BD/♂ZD) called "niece" (*tàmtswè/hapal-tswèy*). For example, a grandfather is called "uncle" (*kêt-*) and a granddaughter is called "niece." Consistent with Crow skewing and parallel transmission, a FZD is "aunt" (FZ) (*tùy*) as is her daughter (FZ) and granddaughter (FZ). A FZS is "father" (*hũm/-ntsũũ/päm*) and so is a FZDS and a FZDDS, at least in theory. These matrilines of "aunts" (FZDDD/MFZD/ MMFZDD) are still found among the Canela (supported by matrilocal residence), but these "fathers," though found occasionally in the 1970s, were "uncles" by the 1990s. The Canela did not consider these classificatory fathers to be biological fathers. A ♂MFZS, a ♂MFZDS, and a ♂MFZDDS are "uncles." It should not be necessary to furnish the reciprocals of the above kintypes. The additional Canela terms needed are: mother (*ntsii/nàà*), sister (*tõy*), brother (*tõ*), daughter (*katswèy*), and son (*gamtel*).

The above paragraph treats grandparent, grandchild, and cross-sibling relationships. In contrast, siblings of the same sex are merged. Thus, parallel siblings' children are "children" (*khra*), and these "children" are "siblings" to each other. Because of matrilocal residence, the female descendants of female uterine siblings form matrilines that are preserved down the generations through their being coresidents, or residents in nearby houses, while male uterine siblings are dispersed into different households through marriage so that patrilines are not reinforced. Thus, between two matrilines, each descended from two uterine sisters, females of the same generation, whom we would calculate to be first, second, or even fourth cousins, are likely to call each other "sibling" (*khyê*) unless alternative intervening terminological systems, such as formal friendship and name transmission, prevent these siblingships from being practiced.

Turning to affinal terminological relationships, the Canela distinguish between those born in and those married into a matriline. Thus, for same-sex affines, a woman's brother's wife (♀BW) is an "out" (of matriline) sister-in-law (*wèyyê/tswèyyê*) and a woman's husband's sister (HZ) is an "in" (matriline) sister-in-law (*pree/toktùyyê*). Similarly, a man's sister's husband (♂ZH) is an out-brother-in-law (*piyõyê*) and a man's wife's brother (WB) is an in-brother-in-law (*pree/mpàyyê*). The man married to the senior woman in a matriline has become an in-father-in-law (*preekêt/pàykêt*) by this time for the junior men married into the matriline, out-sons-in-law (*piyõyê*). Moreover, the senior woman in a matriline is an in-mother-in-law (*preekêy*) for the married-in women, out-daughters-in-law (*wèyyê/tswèyyê*). For opposite-sex affines, an out-woman-in-law and her in-father-in-law (*preekêt/khrã?tũmyê*) practice complete avoidance as does an out-son-in-law (*wawè*) with his in-woman-in-law (*pãn/hàtswèyyê*). The same terms are used for the "in" and the "out" woman-in-law.

Following the rule that same-sex siblings are equated, a woman's husband's sister's sister (HZZ) is also her in-sister-in-law, a man's sister's husband's brother (♂ZHB) is also his out-brother-in-law, and a man's mother-in-law's sister (WMZ) is also his in-woman-in-law. However, an out-daughter-in-law has only one in-mother-in-law and an out-son-in-law has only one in-father-in-law, the immediate ones for whom they carry out services.

A woman has a married-to husband (*pyên/pyê*) and several classificatory husbands (*mẽ mpyê-?nõ*). The latter are her husband's brothers (HBs), potentially her aunts' husbands (e.g., ♀FZH, ♀FFZH, ♀FZDH, ♀MFZDDH), and potentially her nieces' husbands (e.g., ♀MBDH, ♀MMBDH, ♀MBDDH).

A man has his married-to wife (*prõ*) and several classificatory wives (*mẽʔprõ-ʔnõ*). These are his wife's sisters (WZs), potentially his uncles' wives (e.g., ♂MBW, ♂MMBW, ♂MFZSW, ♂MFZDSW), potentially his wife's aunts (e.g., WFZ, WFZD, WMFZD), and potentially his wife's nieces (e.g., WBD, WMBD, WMMBD, WMBDD). However, a man rarely has two classificatory wives in the same matriline. If a man has sex, for instance, with his wife's mother's brother's daughter (WMBD), who is structurally her niece (♀BD), the latter's mother (WMBW) would be an avoidance "in-woman-in-law" for the man, and her daughter (WMBDD) would be a "daughter" to him, not a "wife."

The data above demonstrate that a man is potentially equated to his structural uncles (MBs) and nephews (ZSs) and that a woman is potentially equated to her structural aunts (FZs) and nieces (BDs). It is this latter structure, pairs of matrilines in matrilocal residences often four generations deep, that plays a major role in holding the Canela society together. The women in a pair of matrilines descended from uterine *cross*-siblings hold nonadjacent, otherwise unrelated, "across-the-plaza" households together, while the women in a pair of matrilines descended from female, uterine, *same*-sex siblings hold adjacent households together to form arcs of houses along the village circle known as longhouses (*ikhre-lùù*).

A man cannot marry into his own longhouse. He must marry into an unrelated house along the arc of some other longhouse of which there were thirteen in 1971. Through marriage, he connects his natal and marital houses, joining his sisters' matrilines with his wife's and her daughters' matrilines. His sisters' male descendants and his own male descendants cannot marry into each other's matrilines. Thus, a man cannot marry into or have sexual relations with the women in his own longhouse. These women would be "siblings" to him if they were in his generation. Such activities would constitute incest (*to ayplè/to ipiyaplè*). Similarly, he cannot have sexual relations in the houses of the matrilines of his "aunts" or "nieces." Nevertheless, he can have sex with or marry any women with whom he is not a kin, an affine (except his wife's sisters), or a formal friend. The Canela have no marriage prescriptions or preferences (except the sororate). They practiced monogamy until the children of a marriage were grown up. Then divorces were allowed. However, extramarital sex was compulsory in ceremonies and in private life, though such practices were almost lost by the 1990s.

The Canela terminological relationship systems described above are not complete for lack of space and emphasis. Often, only examples are given, so it is assumed that the other relationships of a similar sort and reciprocals can be worked out by the reader from the data given. The first Canela words in the parentheses are third-person terms of reference, and other words are either variations or other basic terms for the same expression. (For a full exposition of the Canela relationship systems, see Crocker 1990, 234–57.)

A Canela village is circular, with the houses facing inward onto a circular boulevard. Across the boulevard, a straight pathway runs from the direction of each house to a circular plaza in the center. Thus, a Canela village, and any Timbira one, looks like a large wagon wheel about 300 meters across. When seen from above, the plaza is the hub, the radial pathways are the spokes, the boulevard is the wheel, and the houses are studs on the outside of the wheel (Crocker and Crocker 1994, 2–3).

The social spine of each house is its matriline of three to four generations. Since the average age of first childbirth was calculated to be 16.5 years in 1970 (Crocker 1984, 91), a woman could be a great grandmother at 70. The locations of these matrilines remain fixed in relation to the rising and setting of the sun from village to village through time. Afterbirths are buried deep in the dirt floors of each house, representing the permanence of a female line's location along and around the boulevard. Before 1940, the Canela used to move their one village to a new location every five to ten years, but with the arrival of federal Indian service personnel and their buildings and services,[3] the village has remained fixed near the federal post and schoolhouse except for one move, during 1969.

The Domestic Group

This village structure reinforces the structure of the Crow terminology or of parallel transmission. Fitting this structure, Canela residence is uxorilocal or even matrilocal, because a man goes to live in his wife's house with her mother and with her mother's sisters and their female descendants until he dies, at least in theory. Thus, large houses may contain several matrilines of closely related females (Crocker 1990, 266–67). The husbands of these phalanxes of women in each house are outsiders, as is reinforced by the kin terminology. For instance, there are two terms of reference for brother-in-law, one for the man who married into the house (δ ZH: *ipiyõyê*) and the other for the man who was born in it (WB: *i?pre*). There are also two terms of similar structure for sisters-in-law. Understanding the operating of this intermeshed kin and village structure enables us to comprehend much of the behavior between the sexes, including partible paternity (Crocker and Crocker 1994, 66–71).

The married-in husbands are responsible for the economic support of their nuclear family and of the household in general. The women being close kin support each other, while the married-in men are unrelated by intent. This is because the women only rarely allow men who are related to each other to marry one of their number.

This domestic arrangement leaves women relatively free to go out for trysts with lovers or for other activities, because their sisters in the same household cover for them. It also puts them in charge of food distribution within households and gives them considerable prestige and respect within the society as a whole. Men, as husbands, are the meat providers and the farm plot workers,[4] but they turn their products over to their wives, the male position being subordinate.

Men, born in the households, marry across and around the village circle. Living away with their wives, they nevertheless dominate their sisters' households during almost daily visits to them. As "uncles," they have the responsibility for running the ceremonial extramarital sex world of the young, but they have lost this role. Thus, it was the less tender-feeling, more distantly related maternal uncles, paternal aunts, and grandparents who ordered the young girls into ceremonial roles in which sequential sex was involved.[5] Parents were too embarrassed and too hindered by feelings to do this. The "uncles" and "aunts" also were the ones who suppressed the jealousy of the young males,[6] which inevitably arose even though custom forbade its expression.

Through the select Elders in the plaza,[7] who are like a senate, the men ran the society, keeping the political and ceremonial systems going and disciplining the young. In contrast, the women had no overarching institution similar to the Elders to express their power, which was limited to their own households. An arc of houses along the village circle related by all female kin links is called a longhouse (*ikhre lùù:* house long). Groups of old Canela women worked together with me in 1971 to identify the female ancestor from which each longhouse's matrilines descended. Nevertheless, these longhouses have no names, no political head persons, and little cohesiveness (Crocker 1990, 240–43).

Major Ecological Factors and History

The Canela were living in a precontact ecology up until about 1750. Then indirect contact through other Timbira nations and direct contact through skirmishes with the pioneers around 1790 transformed their way of life completely. They were decimated in warfare by another Timbira tribe and surrendered to a

Brazilian garrison in 1814 for their safety and survival (Nimuendajú 1946, 31–33). Thus, certain aspects of their ecology that have to be considered here must come from before the 1750s, such as their food collecting, their annual warfare, and their propensity to share. Other aspects of their ecology, yet to be considered, come from after 1840, when they had resettled into peaceful times, such as their forced turning to extensive slash-and-burn agriculture with all of its equipment and to their contacts with backlanders and eventually with urban dwellers.

Aboriginally, they raised various crops such as bitter and sweet manioc, corn, sweet potatoes, yams, peanuts, and squash in small tropical stream-edge gardens cut out of low forests with stone axes and fire, but relied to a far greater extent on hunting and fishing and on gathering fruits, nuts, berries, and roots over a large area, possibly 25,000 square kilometers. Thus, through their worldviews and the personal motivations of individuals, they were adapted to the mobile aspects of collectors in that they valued running, tracking game, fast-moving athletics, and trekking over their vast territory. However, they had little taste for the more stable aspects of farming, such as the patience it takes to prepare large fields through slashing thickets, felling trees, cleaning fields after their burning, and planting crops item after item, and still later, weeding several different times between growing crops. For the Canela, there is something dull and ignominious about the farmer's undramatic, sedentary, repetitious movements in contrast to the hunter's dramatic and swift reactions to fast-moving events. Moreover, from the dashing skills of warfare men could turn more easily to hunting than to farming.

Around 1840 the local ranchers and farmers allowed the Canela to come out from hiding in the hills to settle in peace on a small portion of their former lands that was unoccupied. However, with the loss of 95% of their aboriginal territory (Nimuendajú 1946, 72), they were forced by the lack of sufficient land to forage as food collectors to turn to extensive slash-and-burn farming in the backland Brazilian manner, using machetes, axes, hoes, and other regional equipment. These lands included closed savannas, dry deciduous woods, and tropical growth–bordered streams and swamps.

Since 1938, when the first Indian service family arrived to live adjacent to their village, the Canela have learned to value commercial goods and money, and, increasingly, still more extensive farming. In addition, they learned to raise chickens and pigs, and sometimes goats, and to care for horses and mules. However, during the 1970s they still could not raise cattle because the hunger for meat they too often experienced required them to kill the calf before it could

grow to reproduce. Living for such immediate gratification is more characteristic of food collectors of the savannas than food producers. By the 1990s, certain Canela began to raise small numbers of cattle.

Thus, during the twentieth century, the values of Canela men had been turning from those needed to hunt tapir, deer, emu, boar, paca, agouti, fox, and
other game to those needed to farm better. Nevertheless, the Canela have rarely
accumulated sufficient surpluses to sell on outside markets because of the small
size of their farm plots. A backlander who sells enough on the markets to buy
materials to support his family well puts in from six to eight *linhas,* while one
who barely survives farms only about four. In contrast a larger Canela family
than the usual backlander one put in about two linhas during the 1970s and
three during the 1990s. A linha is a little less than a third of a hectare (about
three-quarters of an acre).

Fishing was not important because of the small size of the streams in the
area occupied by the Canela since about 1838. However, another Timbira tribe
about 55 kilometers west of the Canela, the Apanyekra, lives near the Corda
River, from which significant quantities of sizable fish are caught. Thus, it is
reasonable to believe that before contact and loss of lands, the Canela relied
significantly on fishing.

Increasingly since the 1940s, men have been involved in trade with
backlanders for items such as pigs, chickens, oranges, brown sugar blocks, cane
alcohol, and other goods. The six Indian service salaries since the 1940s and the
farmers' retirement pensions since the 1970s have brought a lot of money into
the Canela economy. Nevertheless, at least since the 1950s, the Canela have
relied on extensive support from the government and other agencies, because
their farm products last only about two-thirds of the year.

Demography

The size of the group living together is important. The Canela, like other
Timbira nations, are endogamous and seldom marry members of other
Timbira peoples, though this occurred according to old tales and happens today, but at less than 5%. Living in groups of a thousand and higher could provide the individual with many potential spouses if the kinship system were
structured to make this possible, and the Canela version of Crow terminology
or parallel transmission does just that. No clans exist to extend kin and affinal
relations throughout the population, nor are there marriage rules to limit who a
person can marry. Thus, ego has as potential spouse any alter of the opposite
sex who is not a consanguineal relative, a formal friend, or a certain category of

affine. These are his "other wives" (*mẽ?prõ ?nõ:* plural wife other)—his OWs—or her "other husbands" (*mẽmpyê ?nõ:* plural husband other)—her OHs. Affairs can be had between distant consanguineals and lesser formal friends, turning them into "other spouses." A person from another Timbira tribe who happens to have no kin or affines among the Canela would be a potential spouse for almost all Canela. Thus, the Canela individual has many potential spouses he or she can choose to marry or have affairs with, and this availability is a factor in the presence of numerous OFs. Among the culturally related Shavante, in contrast, the number of sexually available women for a man is limited by exogamous patrilineal clans, exogamous lineages within the clans, and sororal polygyny (Nancy Flowers, pers. comm.), while among the Canela, no clans, lineages, or sororal polygyny exist to enable such an expansion of kin and affinal relationships.

Husbands Provide Economic Support

The men who have married into the same household form a group usually led by the husband of the oldest active woman of this domestic unit. Such informal groups range from two to six men. They may be joined by men from closely related households. This group of married-in men seldom fish or hunt together except for wild boar, since hunting is basically tracking animals with a dog, which brings down wounded game, a solitary pursuit. In contrast, they usually work together on the farm plots of each other's wives, preparing one farm and then another. Women own the farm plots and every mature woman must have one, married or not. These days, two or more of these husbands may travel together to backland communities, or the town of Barra do Corda, about 65 kilometers to the north, to trade or buy supplies for their household. Whether meat or urban produce, they are basically providing food for their wives, but larger supplies such as a mule's load of oranges or a large sack of rice go directly to the leading wife.

Women Control Food Distribution in a Household

Individual wives turn much of their husbands' supplies over to the leading woman of the household for redistribution. The relationships are flexible and vary with the number of nuclear families in the hearth group and the personalities of the individuals involved. Generally, however, each wife and unmarried mature woman has one or more pots or pans that she uses to boil or fry foods on the three to six rocks of the one fireplace area (*hàwmrõ:* hearth). Thus, all the women in the household, the hearth group, see what the other women are cooking. The contents of the pots may or may not be shared, depending on what they are. Important foods, especially significant amounts of meat, are likely to be cooked in the pot of the senior woman, and then she makes the distribution, sometimes favoring the more cooperative women over the others. However, nobody is left out entirely. Nuclear families eat together in their section of the house, away from their extended family kin of the same hearth group (Crocker and Crocker 1994, 176–78).

In contrast to men, who supply meat and backland or urban produce, women supply crops, making almost daily trips to their farm plots to return with large baskets of foods for daily processing, especially bitter manioc, yams, and sometimes sweet potatoes and squash. Corn, rice, and beans, once harvested during March through May, are stored among the rafters of a house, but usually are consumed early in the year's annual cycle. Thus, the Canela rely more on manioc and yams, which are stored in the ground until needed, but even this supply of staples usually runs out by September or October. Then many households of the tribe disband to work in nuclear family groups on backland farms for food. However, by the 1990s this debasing practice was abandoned because the younger men had put in larger farm plots, though they still experience what they call "half hunger" during this season of the year. There are almost no fat Canela. Fortunately, this season from August through January is when emu eggs, honey, and fruits of many kinds of savanna and forest trees, especially palms, become ready for eating.

Orphaned Children

When a child's father dies, its mother may remarry after a period of mourning of perhaps several months. She is not likely to marry one of the child's OFs. Although this is a possibility, it was never reported as an intended or a preferred arrangement. Pregnant women do not choose lovers with this sort of eventual "insurance" in mind, as among the Barí (Beckerman 1997a). Divorce when children are involved was only very rarely allowed before 1975. The divorcing man's own age class, his uncles, and the Elders' age class all militated to keep him with his children. Upon a man's death, his children remain in the matrix of female kin that they were born into; and while a stepfather may be not as involved with his predecessor's children as their biological father was, these children are likely to be relatively well cared for, because the primary support for a child comes from the women of its domestic group anyway.

When a child's mother dies, the loss is likely to be more serious for the child, depending on its age. Nevertheless, the child is still a member of its household of birth, with several mother's sisters called "mother" to care for it. The household's women try to furnish another one of their own in marriage for the widower to keep him with his children. However, if they do not succeed, which is often the case, the child has partly lost its father as well as its mother, because he moves to another household, whether his sister's or a new wife's.

One woman whose mother had died, and whose father had remarried into another household, reported how her father paid little attention to her while she was growing up and how she had to marry early to a man her foster parents liked, but she did not. She did this because of their pressure on her to bring in more economic support for the family through her future husband. She felt that if she had been their biological daughter, her parents would have had more understanding and not pushed her into a marriage against her desires. There is no doubt in my mind that, while orphans are well cared for by the females of the household they were born in, they nevertheless lose the special attentions that parents are more likely to give their biological children. They receive the basic food with the rest of the family, but not the extra piece of cloth or shirt. Thus, they survive just as well as the nonorphaned children. Two out of six of my special Canela research assistants are orphans. Their early independence may have fostered their abilities to think broadly, express themselves better, and learn to write. In any case, I assess that loss of parents—one or two—could not have been a significant factor in an orphan's health or survival.

Orphans are helped by their OFs to some small extent with occasional presents of food and clothing throughout their lives, but unless they come to live in the same household with an OF, the relationship is only marginally supportive. Again, I do not consider that OFs have significantly affected the health or survival of their OCs.

What keeps being orphaned from becoming a drastic experience, as it can be in certain societies, is the fully expressed Canela value of compassion (*kaplĩn/ kaplĩ*) for any other Canela, whether blind, deaf, dumb, emotionally disturbed, crippled, antisocial, or orphaned. A Canela is always a member of his or her household of birth and has an inalienable right to support there—some food and a place to sleep for an indefinite amount of time. Nobody falls through the social cracks among the Canela. Nevertheless, everybody has to work to contribute to the extent possible, though some get away with a considerable amount of laziness.

How "Other Husbands" Were Selected

I use the past tense here because extramarital sex, once a recreation, had all but disappeared among the Canela by the late 1990s, due to several kinds of outside influences, including missionaries. For the same reasons, young women were no longer selecting OFs for their fetuses. While the practice of occasional trysts continues, procuring OFs during pregnancy is risky. Once an affair is known, as almost always happens in such a close-living community, it makes the child's MH jealous, so he might create trouble. He might even divorce the child's mother these days, which would constitute an economic hardship, since it is the sons-in-law who do most of the work in the fields.

While my background materials on partible paternity come from the 1970s, most of the new data were collected in July and August 1999. My council of Canela research assistants and I invited about 25 middle-aged and old women, known to have had several OHs, to work with us for a morning or a day or more, the length of time depending on the fullness of the individual's experience and verbal abilities. They sat with us alone or in pairs. We also brought in four men singly for half days, and I interviewed two other men alone.

When first questioned about why they chose a certain lover when pregnant, the women usually answered, "I liked him." On further questioning, a woman usually spoke of a young man's dashing ways and appearance, or that he was good at log racing or singing with a gourd rattle. Later, she might have talked about his ability to provide meat, or that he had funds to buy commercial goods. I hardly think that these women were so sophisticated that they felt they had to tell the aesthetic side first to hide ugly materialism. The Canela are more direct than that, and materialism is not ugly for them. Besides, I know that the Canela do fall in love. The sample on this topic is not large enough for quantification, and such a line of questioning would not be reliable here anyway, in my opinion. Nevertheless, I believe I can furnish certain interpretations.

Men approached pregnant women as often as pregnant women approached men. However, when the women informed the men that they were pregnant, the men usually backed off, though some wanted sex anyway. Then a woman would ask a man if he would fulfill the customary restrictions for the health of their baby when it was born. If the man agreed convincingly enough, then she would have sex with him. Thus, it was really the women who were doing the selecting, even when the men had taken the initiative. The exception was when a woman became involved in sequential sex, voluntarily or involuntarily

(Crocker n.d.), which occurred more according to structured custom than to spontaneous male or female individual initiative. Then all the men involved, in theory, had to be named OFs and had to go into couvade.

One woman, who already had several children, sought OFs for her fetus because she claimed her husband's semen was weak. It had produced unhealthy children, she believed; most of them had died. This was the exception, however, as few women spoke of choosing men for the sake of their fetus, and no women spoke of selecting men with the hope of marrying them some day. Before 1975 marriages were unbreakable until all the children had grown up.

Examples of Partible Paternity

Pèèpün, age 73, sat with my Canela research council of four on the afternoon of August 18, 1999. Through sex while pregnant she had provided her first daughter, Patpro, with two OFs who were brothers, Tsààpù and Yaye. Thus, three husbands, including her married-to husband Pàlkô, attended their postpartum rite, their *mẽhà?krẽl*. P said she chose them because she liked them for their handsome faces. Our female research assistant asked P on her own in Canela if it really was, instead, the famously large penis of one of the brothers that had attracted her. P answered negatively. Our female assistant continued by asking whether it was because they were good runners and hunters who could provide meat, but P answered that they were too young at the time, only 15 and 14, to be good hunters. P persisted in the point that she had had sex with them principally for just liking them.

For her last child, a son, P had six OFs. The first was "very good at running with logs"; the second was "a great runner—a hard, strong runner"; and the third "ran well with logs." The fourth she said she chose "just because I liked him"; the fifth, "just because I liked him, running had nothing to do with it"; and the sixth because "he had good running experience for my baby." My assessment is that P chose her OHs mainly for liking them and secondarily for gaining their strength for her eventual child. She was not thinking of her own support nor of that of her eventual child through meat or money.

My research assistants brought Kõõlõ, age about 42, before our group as the Canela who was best known for having many OFs for her children. For her first child she had five; for her second, five; her third, three; her fourth, five; her fifth, three; and she had additional children without OFs. K designated the OFs of the first three children, and they came to their postpartum rites. However, she identified the OFs of her fourth and fifth children secretly, so they may or may not have carried out their food and sex restrictions properly in the presence of their unknowing wives. The watershed year for this custom going underground was 1981. Of special note is that the pregnant K, during the 1980s, accepted significant amounts of meat *before* sex several times, as she gave into desirous, demanding youths. The custom had been occasional small gifts *after* sex, but the custom was moving on toward prostitution, and this became the practice by the late 1990s.

Interpretations

The Canela ancestors were contacted significantly around 1750, were heavily involved in attacks by posses of ranchers by 1790, and were "pacified" in 1814. Thus, we cannot know much about the precontact activities of the Canela OFs. Between about 1838 and 1938, however, the Canela lived a relatively peaceful and stable existence in their relations with the local backlanders and the city of Barra do Corda political authorities. The data on Canela OFs that I know about from Nimuendajú's time (the 1930s), from my early field research (the late 1950s), and from my recent, focused field research (summer 1999) indicate that it is quite likely that the institution of the OF changed dramatically during these hundred years.

I hypothesize that the relative security of postcontact times diminished the need for the OF's support of his OCs and that the activities of the Canela extramarital system increased, becoming a form of recreation during the hundred years of postpacification peace and limited contact. Thus, the activities of a woman's child's OFs lost their significance, relatively, with the increase in emphasis of the activities of the child's mother with her OHs.

During the 1930s, when the Canela extramarital system was operating fully and their economic system had not become deficient, I understand that a pregnant woman chose OHs for her love life rather than for her own support or for the future support of her fetus. However, she did sometimes think about obtaining superior qualities from her OHs for her future child. I find that some OFs gave food and items of clothing every few months to their OCs, but that such help was more an expression of affection than needed support and that such contributions were not significant in the overall food supply of an OC for raising the probability of its survival. However, for the institution of the OF to be so fully developed, it must have had more to do with the survival of the OC in precontact times than it did during the 1930s or the 1950s.

During the 1990s, pregnant women only rarely chose OHs, and if they have, the relationship is kept a secret, especially from the fetus's father for fear of his jealousy and a potential divorce. Beliefs about the need for food and sex restrictions to enhance the growth of the baby still persist, but are being practiced less seriously and quite clandestinely by the few young OFs that are being designated. Older OFs, designated before the 1980s, continue to treat their OCs openly.

I assess that the Canela will continue to maintain their belief in partible paternity for decades to come: that the Canela will continue to believe that when a man contributes semen to his classificatory wife's fetus, he will become an ethnobiological father to the fetus. Nevertheless, the Canela will seldom carry out this belief in practice. Clandestine affairs will occur occasionally, but out-of-marriage, ethnobiological fathers made in this way will seldom be socially recognized and will even more rarely maintain the earlier practices carried out for the health of their ethnobiological children.

Notes

1. The orthography used herein is phonemic and is the same as in Crocker 1990 (9–10) and Crocker and Crocker 1994 (189–90), except for the use of /ä/ for the nasalized /a/ and /ü/ for the nasalized /ù/.

2. Siblings are usually considered to be ego's MCs and therefore two links away from ego, but the Canela believe them to be just one link away, like parents and children.

3. I use the generic term *Indian service* (*service* not capitalized) for the two federal organs that have regulated the relations between Brazilian nationals and their indigenous populations that are still living together in a tribal state of existence. These organs are the Indian Protection Service (SPI), during and before 1968, and the National Foundation of the Indian (FUNAI), during and after that date. I use the generic expression, rather than the Brazilian terms, to diffuse the existing feelings about these branches of the federal government.

4. Current Canela fields for producing crops are more like the fields of the Brazilian backlanders than like the Canela aboriginal fields, which were small and included many vegetables but no rice. The current fields include large stretches of rice and bitter manioc, but few vegetables. Thus, it seems accurate to call the aboriginal Canela fields gardens, their current fields farm plots, and the Brazilian ones farms.

5. Sequential sex occurs in several ceremonial festival-pageants, among tribal work groups, and on some other occasions. Designated women, usually those without babies to care for, allow groups of men to have sex with them sequentially. The women serve the tribe this way, since they are not contributing children.

6. Sex jealousy is thought by many anthropologists to be culturally determined. If this were the case, in a society like the Canela in which extramarital sex was not only condoned but required, sex jealousy would not exist. However, sex jealousy

did exist and had to be suppressed even before outside influences began to interfere with the extramarital sex practices. Thus sex jealousy could not be culturally determined, but may be determined at some psychological or psycho-physiological level.

7. The expression *Elders* is capitalized to differentiate it from being understood as the older men of the tribe. The Elders are a special group of older men, those of the oldest age class of the Lower age class moiety, known as the Prokhãmmã.

6

Multiple Paternity among the Mẽbengokre (Kayapó, Jê) of Central Brazil

Vanessa Lea

The Mẽbengokre, better known as the Kayapó, inhabit areas of transition between tropical forest and savanna in central Brazil, with over a dozen villages
located in the states of Mato Grosso and Pará. This chapter is based on fieldwork carried out between 1978 and 1995 with the Mẽtyktire subgroup. They
presently reside in two villages near the state boundary of Mato Grosso and
Pará. One village, with a population of 205 people in 1994, is located in an area
of transition between savanna and forest, on the banks of the Xingu River,
guaranteeing an abundant supply of fish (besides game). The other village,
with a population of 337 people in 1995, is located inland, in an area long inhabited by this Amerindian people, in the heart of the savanna, where meat from
herds of two species of wild pigs constitutes the main source of protein, besides the less abundant tapir, armadillos, monkeys, birds, land and river turtles,
and the occasional fish.

The Mẽbengokre have a uterine ideology that automatically allocates individuals as members of their mother's house. Matri-houses are exogamous
units that transcend the boundaries of any one village. Besides occupying a
specific portion of the village circle, in relation to the sun's trajectory from
east to west, matri-houses are characterized by a distinctive stock of heritable
names and prerogatives.[1] The most outstanding aspect of paternity in
Mẽbengokre society is that it is linked to the vicarious transmission of affinity,
a question to which we will return in due course. As discussed in various
chapters in this book, it is a common belief in lowland South America that
whoever engages in sexual relations with a woman during the course of her

pregnancy is considered to contribute toward the formation of the fetus, engendering the phenomenon of multiple paternity. In the Mēbengokre case, it is the fact that one inherits formal friends from one's genitor, together with the fact that physical well-being is dependent on a person's relation to his or her parents and siblings, that act as deterrents against multiple paternity in the classical sense alluded to above.

When a person is ill, especially a small child, his or her parents and siblings must abstain from eating a series of food items, including all meat and fish, from fear of worsening the state of the sick person or even bringing about his or her death. The Mēbengokre recognize the possibility of an individual having two or more genitors, but in practice it is uncommon. When a newborn infant with various genitors dies, this is taken as a self-fulfilling prophecy of the danger of having various fathers, because it may be impossible to contact all of them when their offspring is ill, to ensure that the necessary food restrictions are adhered to. A genitor who, for example, eats beef on a journey to the city, not knowing that his child is ill, can inadvertently kill it. I came across the case of a child described as having four genitors in one census, while in a later census the same child was described as having one father. It seems as if a series of hypotheses are discarded during the course of time, depending, for example, on the respective fathers recognizing their role, the efficacy of the fathers respecting food taboos, physical likeness, and so on. A few people are considered to have two fathers, or sometimes it is uncertain which of two men engendered a child, but this applies to a minority of cases.

Multiple paternity is an important phenomenon in Mēbengokre society—more in line with the way this expression is used in modern Western society, where it refers to a sequence of a mother's husbands (or lovers) during the course of her child's upbringing. A Mēbengokre village is formed by a large circle of houses facing onto an open plaza or patio, with a men's house (a kind of male clubhouse) standing at the center. At first glance, the majority of households are formed by various nuclear families, linked by two or more sisters, living together with elder relatives, forming extended matri-uxorilocal families. When this scenario is investigated with greater care, it becomes apparent that despite the preponderance of married couples and children, or married daughters, sons-in-law, and grandchildren (DC),[2] numerous older children were begotten by ex-spouses or lovers of the wife, with only the younger siblings being attributed to the current husband. Only widowers take children from a former marriage to a present one, and in all cases of this type, only one child continued to live with the father and his latest wife for any extended period.[3]

Few men or women have all their children with one partner (be it spouse or lover), due to both a high divorce rate and a high mortality rate. Twenty percent of children do not reside with their genitor, despite having only one, living instead either with the divorced or single mother, or with her latest husband (see table 6.1, fig. 6.1). When a woman separates from her husband, at her initiative or his, she remains with her children whether or not she remarries.[4] There is nothing 'natural' about this arrangement, for despite the tendency for children to remain with their mother upon divorce in the Euro-American world, this is not the case for all Amerindian peoples of lowland South America. A recent study of the Kaiowá (Pereira 1999)—Tupi-Guaraní speakers of southern Mato Grosso—stresses that children tend to remain neither with their mother nor their father when their parents are divorced, as this is seen as an impediment to their parents consolidating a new marriage. They go to live with their maternal grandparents or, alternatively, with the woman who assisted their mother to give birth, but in this latter case they become second-class citizens, overburdened with domestic chores. In the case of the patrilineal Kaingang, Southern Jê, children are most likely to be handed over to their paternal grandmother in the case of divorce, and they may later live with their father if he remarries (Veiga 1994, 2000).

Due to the prevalence of matri-uxorilocality among the Mẽbengokre, it is the men who leave the wife's house when they separate and generally even when they are widowed. Marriage entails simply moving in with a woman, an arrangement that is consolidated cumulatively with the birth of children. Separa-

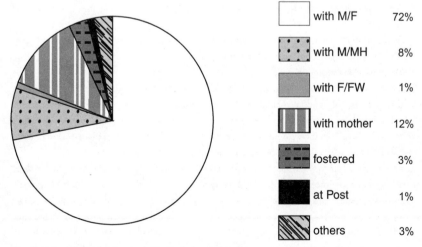

with M/F	72%
with M/MH	8%
with F/FW	1%
with mother	12%
fostered	3%
at Post	1%
others	3%

Fig. 6.1. Residential patterns of Mẽtyktire children

Table 6.1. Residential patterns of Mẽtyktire children

Year[a]	Children[b]	M/F[c]	M/MH[d]	F/FW[e]	Sum[f]	M[g]	No M[h]	Foster[i]	Post[j]	Other[k]
1978	64	50	3	1	54	8	3	0	0	2
1979	75	54	3	2	59	7	3	3	3	3
1982	90	68	6	1	75	8	1	3	4	0
1987	198	140	22	3	165	25	7	8	0	0
1994–95	286	201	23	3	227	35	15	10	0	14
Total	713	513	57	10	580	83	29	24	7	19

a. Year of censuses. (All censuses were undertaken personally.)

b. Total number of Mẽtyktire children. The category includes childless unmarried adolescents, including a few who have had miscarriages or have had a child that did not survive. It excludes those with spouses (with or without offspring). The census data from 1978, 1979, and 1981–82 are based exclusively on the village of Kretire. By 1987 the population of that village had joined with the remaining Mẽtyktire from the village of Jarina. In 1994–95 they had split into two groups again, but the data from the two new villages (which continue to exist) are shown together (facilitating comparison with the 1987 data, for the whole of the Mẽtyktire subgroup of Mẽbengokre).

c. Children who reside with their mother and their father.

d. Children who reside with their mother and their mother's husband (who is not the child's father).

e. Children who reside with their father and his wife (who is not the child's mother, after the death of the latter).

f. The sum of children who live with their parents, mother and mother's husband, or father and father's wife.

g. Children who live with their mother, with neither their father nor a mother's husband; in other words, these are children with no father figure.

h. Children whose mother has died.

i. Children who are fostered out, usually to grandparents. They are still considered to be children of their parents, unlike adopted children, who are considered children of their adoptive parents.

j. Male adolescents residing at the post temporarily, until they marry and move to their wife's house. Whether or not their parents are alive is irrelevant to this category; in former times these youths would reside in the men's house until they married and fathered a child.

k. This residual category partially overlaps with the data in the foster-children column, except that some male adolescents now live with relatives other than their parents (such as mother's sister or stepsister) until they marry, rather than at the post. This column also includes people living with relatives unspecified genealogically, orphans, and those in temporary arrangements. The 1994–95 data include two pairs of children living with their sister(s), after losing their mother, and five siblings who have lost both parents living with the mother's sister ('M'), her husband, and the mother's mother.

tion or divorce occurs when a man moves out or is thrown out by his wife or mother-in-law. Neither separated nor widowed men return to live in their natal homes, together with their sisters (though a married man may sometimes spend a period living with his sisters); instead they tend to install themselves in the men's house for a brief period, until they remarry, thereby acquiring a new home. Tension ensues when a man abandons a wife and children for another woman. In one such case, the newly formed couple left the village for an indefinite period. In another case, a mother-in-law accused the ex-father-in-law of her daughter's husband of having 'ruined' her own husband and grandson with sorcery. From a Euro-American perspective these individuals suffered from a degenerative disease.

Some spouses tolerate their partners having a child with a lover, without this being considered a case for divorce. I knew of two men whose wife's child by a lover was incorporated into their sibling group without discrimination. In a similar case, a woman received meat from the husband of a daughter born to her husband's lover. Another woman, whose rival had shown jealousy, failed to give garden produce to her lover's wife, despite having had a child with him. It was explained to me that the correct procedure would be to give food to the lover's wife. In two cases that I was able to observe at close hand, the genitors had nothing whatever to do with the child born to their lover. Both children were brought up by these women on their own, and subsequently by the husband of each of them. The ex-lover would be unable to send meat or fish to his child without this signaling the continuation of a relation with the child's mother.

Janet Siskind's (1973) analysis of meat being exchanged for sex continues to merit discussion. Gow (1989) has refined this notion, for the issue is more subtle. Men and women cater for the gendered desire of the opposite sex, without a one-to-one exchange being involved. The Mẽbengokre represent men as desirous of sex and women of meat, although men also value meat, and women are not indifferent to sex. To the extent that hunting is a male monopoly, meat can only be obtained via a man. The men depend on marriage more than the women, for it not only guarantees access to garden produce, but also to a home of one's own. For women, home is taken for granted; it is ascribed by birth and is lifelong, and when there are no men around they are able to survive by consuming their garden produce.

Fatherhood, Conception, and Fetal Development

It was difficult to broach the question of conception with the Mẽbengokre, for most people were incredulous that I should need to ask about it. One man finally explained to me that when a woman has sexual relations the semen accumulates inside her, gradually forming the fetus.[5] People are unanimous in insisting that a series of sexual relations is necessary to form the fetus, and it was explicitly denied that a single act of sexual intercourse could result in pregnancy. I asked one woman if her child had been begotten by a lover, as someone had mentioned to me. She denied the fact, declaring that the lover in question was "only a bit of a lover."[6] It is difficult to know where this imaginary dividing line lies between who is a bit of a lover and who is sufficiently a lover to become a genitor. Nevertheless, this means that the Mẽbengokre eliminate a small but incalculable percentage of men from the role of genitor who would be characterized as such from the Euro-American perspective. Hence not only do the Mẽbengokre differ from Western society because they believe that more than one man can fabricate a fetus but, more importantly, a proportion of men who would be regarded as genitors from a genetic standpoint are not recognized as such by the Mẽbengokre because they engaged in sexual relations only once or a few times with the future mother.

Ethnographic studies of the Mẽbengokre mention ceremonial sex in pairs, especially between members of different age categories, for example, between adolescent men and women who have children, or vice versa.[7] Turner (1966, 221–22, 234–35) mentions sequential sex (between one woman and various men) on certain ceremonial occasions, a practice that still occurred at the time of my fieldwork.[8] Bamberger (1974) and Dreyfus (1963) mention punitive rape. Dreyfus (1963, 58) was told that the men could resort to punitive rape if a woman dared to gossip about having had sexual relations with a married man, or if a young woman was too reticent, in general terms, about having sexual relations. She noted that husbands of pregnant wives and of those with newborn babies had extramarital affairs. Men used to return to live in the men's house until a child was weaned. Nowadays they remain in the wife's house, but sleep separately, in a hammock, facilitating nightly sorties after lovers. One woman told me of a ceremonial occasion when a wife takes the arm of her husband's lover. Such lovers are chosen from among unmarried mothers, divorced or widowed women. He can hunt for her and spend the night with her. The female lover reciprocates, sending food to the wife. It was always stressed to me that neither the husband nor the wife should show jealousy when their spouse engages in ceremonial sex. Turner (1966, 222) mentions that on certain occasions the older women can volunteer their services whereas it is compulsory for childless girls. He also mentions (1966, 235) that the mothers of initiates present food to the women who have had ritual intercourse with their sons. Ceremonial sexual practices tend to obliterate any question of male infertility, for if a husband fails to impregnate his wife, then sooner or later some other man will do so.

I asked one man if, as somebody had mentioned to me, he was the father of an unmarried mother's child. He replied that he did not yet know. On another occasion, I asked him how a man knows whether he is the genitor if the woman in question has had various lovers. He replied that if the husband follows the prescribed food prohibitions when the child is ill, and despite this the child dies, then he knows that it was not his child.

Collecting genealogies among the Mẽbengokre uncovered the question of 'pseudo children' (*krô'aj kra*) (i.e., children engendered by lovers but who were brought up as if they were the mother's husband's children, hence his pseudo offspring). Various women requested me to censure information contained in genealogies, intended for use in the schools, concerning the true paternity of their children, asking me to note their husband as the father. I suspect that the figures showing the number of children resident with their mother and father are still overestimated, for the more intimate with a family I became, the more I discovered about the complexity of the composition of domestic groups (see table 6.1). The couple with whom I lived during my last phase of fieldwork exemplified this tendency. The man had married a widow and treated her daughter by a former lover the same way as his own children by this same woman. The girl referred to in this example was about seven and did not realize that her mother's husband was not her father. Supposedly she will later be informed who her real father is, to prevent her from marrying a close relative of the genitor. This illustrates that, for the Mẽbengokre, the identification of the genitor is not of supreme importance, except for defining one's formal friends and for contributing to one's well-being in the case of illness. Some children, whose accused genitors denied responsibility, ended up acquiring the formal friends of their mother's husband or even of the mother's father.

Initially, it seemed to me that a Mẽbengokre woman was regarded merely as the receptacle of the fetus. However, after reflecting on Bamberger's extensive list (1967) of food taboos that pertain to pregnant people, it now seems that although it is semen that forms the body, the mother has an important role in ensuring a well-formed fetus by avoiding a series of foods that could harm it, or lead to difficulties at the time of giving birth. The category of pregnant person (*mẽtujarô;* lit., 'people with protuberant bellies') applies equally to men and to women, and men should likewise observe a series of taboos during gestation and in the postpartum period to avoid endangering the newborn baby. This phenomenon has been labeled couvade in the literature (e.g., Rival 1998; Rivière 1974) and is widespread in lowland South America. My data reveal various accusations of men described as having "killed" their newborn baby by firing a gun, not aimed at the baby but off in the forest. When a baby or child dies, it is the mother who appears to blame herself to the extent that she practices self-flagellation, cutting the top of her head open with blows from a machete, and repeatedly throwing herself backward to the ground until a close relative intervenes to stop her.

Marilyn Strathern (1995a, b),[9] in a stimulating reflection on paternity, notes, in a discussion of a previous article by Delaney (1986), that the Euro-American view of each parent contributing 50% to the fetus is uncommon both across the globe and in historical time. A man may be credited with the creative act of engendering the fetus, or he may be held responsible for nurturing its growth, as in the case of the Trobriands, where the fetus is engendered by ancestral spirits. In the Mẽbengokre case, one man initiates the process, but a series of other men may then consolidate the growth of the fetus. There appears to be neither a notion of fertilization nor of subsequent 'natural' growth; rather the fetus is built up gradually, somewhat like a snowball. In the Xingu area in general (including Amerindian peoples of diverse language families), the men describe themselves in smug tones of self-abnegation as "working very hard" in order to make a child. (See Descola 1986 for a discussion of work envisaged as physical exertion.)

It was commonplace in the anthropological literature, until recently, to view the establishment of paternity as more problematic than that of maternity. There could be no doubt about the identification of the genitrix before the invention of surrogate mothers, although before the invention of DNA tests it was not always possible to identify the genitor. For the Mẽbengokre, paternity is not an area of doxa;[10] there is not always consensus concerning the allocation of responsibility. Consequently, there are some individuals with no father (for at least a certain phase of their life), and others whose mothers point out a certain man as their genitor while the man in question denies responsibility. It is sometimes said, in a derogatory tone, that a certain child is "everybody's" (implicitly referring to a specific age category). It is a hyperbole, synonymous with "nobody's child." I came across two cases of women who refused to identify the father of their child to their coresidents in the village. It was unclear whether such attitudes were temporary or permanent. There was even a woman who claimed that one of her children had no genitor whatsoever; it had been engendered by root medicine. Later I discovered that the genitor had been a lover who belonged to the matri-house of the woman concerned, a rare case of sexual relations with a member of one's matri-house.

On a day-to-day basis, a good father is a mother's husband who ensures that a child does not go hungry for protein. The Mẽbengokre refer to such men as those who "take the child around with them" (*óba*), in the sense of those who rear the child. This implies that one can become the father of a child by nurturing it. A person will always express gratitude and respect for the man who helped to bring him or her up, regardless of whether that person is the genitor or not. This provides an analogy with the Peruvian Piro as described by Gow (1991). They treat kinship as something that is constructed through the process of nurturance. In the Mẽbengokre case, it would be interesting to know whether the importance of the mother's husband illustrates their recognition of the fact that kinship can be socially constructed, or whether they believe that the family constitutes a community of bodily substance. Da Matta (1976) affirms that, in the Apinayé case, a couple is taken as intermingling their substance through sexual intercourse. It would be relevant to know whether MHs tend to observe food prohibitions for their wife's children when the latter are ill. Unfortunately I did not inquire into this question.

Since the mid-1980s, there has been an attempt to resurrect an association between matrilineality and low probabilities of paternity.[11] According to the marital history of numerous mature Mẽbengokre women, it used to be common for young girls of seven or so to marry adult men. Such husbands slept with their young wives without engaging in sexual relations until the girls reached puberty. This arrangement seems to indicate a valorization of virginity, which in turn implies some guarantee of paternity, once the husbands were able to consummate the marriage.

A point shared by much of the bibliography consulted for this chapter is that acceptance of the paternal role depends almost exclusively on the conviction that one is the biological father of a child. The underlying assumption appears to be that the modern Western notion of paternity is metonymical. One is only a father to the extent that a child is an extension of the self. The Nuer, according to Evans-Pritchard (1992), represent the opposite pole of thinking, in so far as the father is the man who provided bridewealth, regardless of whether or not he is the genitor. According to Radcliffe-Brown, a similar view may once have been held in Europe; he cites an early English saying: "whoso boleth my kyne, ewere calf is mine" (1950, 4). The Mẽbengokre have a multifaceted view of paternity. A child can have one or more genitors, but a further avenue to fatherhood is nurturance. It is as if there were two complementary stages to paternity: first, a fetus must be constructed, resulting in the birth of a small baby; second, this baby has to be nourished in order to attain adulthood. Different 'fathers' can be responsible for these separate stages.

Domestic Life and the Circulation of Food

The cognatic kindred of each individual forms a hierarchical structure, indicating which relatives ego can appeal to in order to acquire the necessary food for satisfying his or her hunger. The orphan is a paradigm of misfortune, especially a motherless child who lacks someone to paint and decorate it. Being fatherless is less serious. The genitor can be substituted by the mother's husband, a series of mother's lovers, by the mother's sister's husband ('F'), the mother's father, the husband of the mother's sister's daughter, or even the mother's brothers (real or classificatory), as the providers of protein, one of the key contributions of the adult male. A careful examination of the composition of Mēbengokre domestic groups over nearly two decades (recorded by me in 119 diagrams) revealed considerable variety, when focusing on the issue of hunters per household. This tallies with an already held impressionistic view that quality of life is to a large extent determined by the vagaries of demography. Larger households, especially those with a balanced population of males and females, benefit from having various adult men who take turns hunting, and various women who fetch garden produce while leaving behind a girl or old woman to look after the small children, who can thereby remain at home while their parents are out at work.

Besides the circulation of food within a house, there is also widespread circulation of food between houses. When a hunter arrives back at the village with game, he hands it over to his wife. Upon arrival from a fishing trip, a man leaves the fish in the canoe whither his wife goes to clean it, at the riverside. Subsequent distribution of meat and fish is in the hands of the women. They are expected, sanctioned by the risk of accusations of stinginess, to send raw portions to the house of their husband's mother and sisters whenever there is more than the wife and her children require for immediate consumption. Despite each married woman having her own garden to tend, sweet potatoes, maize, bananas, watermelon, and other crops mature more quickly in one garden than in another, and one woman's entire crop tends to mature in a short time, so there is too great a yield for consumption by the immediate family of the garden's owner. Consequently, there is widespread redistribution of these products from one house to another, especially between a woman and her husband's mother and sisters, but also between sisters, whether or not they reside in separate houses, and to brothers and other relatives, depending on the quantity of food available.[12]

It is only on ceremonial occasions, after large-scale collective hunting expeditions, that a man cuts up raw game and distributes it to the women. On these occasions, the women collect the hereditary cuts that their brothers have the right to eat, and take them home to cook. The brothers return to their maternal home to eat the traditional Jê meat pies, made of manioc flour filled with meat, cooked in banana leaves in stone or earth ovens, which are located outside each house.

The bond between brothers and sisters is lifelong, especially when they transmit their names to each other's children, as they ideally do.[13] Genitors and name givers are conceived as being mutually exclusive categories. The genitor produces the fetus with his semen, while the name giver transforms it into a person. Melatti (1979, 78) has aptly referred to this process as onomastic incest, compensating the fact that men must leave their natal home in order to marry. This is reminiscent of the bond between a Trobriander brother and sister, described by Strathern (1995b), as complementing in asexual terms the relation between a husband and wife. This must be emphasized in order to understand that what Euro-Americans envisage as 'paternity' encompasses, in Mẽbengokre society, certain aspects of the bond between brother and sister. Genitors produce bodily substance, but that raw material is transformed into a person through naming and the transmission of ancestral prerogatives. Men store their ceremonial adornments at the house of their mother and sisters. During the course of rituals they often return home to be painted and decorated. In one sense, organic substance does not constitute the essence of a Mẽbengokre person, for that rots away after death. Names and heritable prerogatives transcend the infinite cycle of life and death, lent out and returned to uterine lines that trace their continuity through fixed location in a specific matrihouse (which may be represented by two or more dwellings) within the village circle.

Men who have sexual relations with unmarried women, without providing them with game afterward, are criticized by the Mẽbengokre as 'stealing' (ô aki) them. A chief told me that he disapproved when men have extraconjugal affairs with husbandless women with children, without providing them with food. Sex is represented as a service that women provide to men and for which they are entitled to recompense.[14] Nowadays, Western goods such as beads, soap, and industrialized tobacco are the standard payment for extramarital sexual relations. It could be argued that the exchange of meat for sex is incorporated into marriage itself, and inadvertently this facilitates multiple paternity in the sense of children depending for survival, not on their genitors, but on their MH or any other man who temporarily (or sporadically) fills the role of meat giver. Children depend on their mothers for food and benefit indirectly from their sexual relations, be it with their genitors or any other men.

Thiel (1994) has argued that ritualized meat sharing among hunters and gatherers allows men to feed children they suspect are theirs without being overt. In line with the metonymical view of paternity referred to above, I regard this view as naive. From my experience of the Mẽbengokre, there is no guarantee that men who beget children are preoccupied with feeding them, as there is no guarantee that they will recognize them as their own children, whether they are so or not. It has been demonstrated that the allocation of responsibility is socially constructed and not an objective fact. Sexual relations are prolific in Mẽbengokre society (as Crocker and Crocker [1994] have described for the Canela), and women who refuse sex too often are labeled as stingy. From a Euro-American standpoint there is maximization of genetic circulation. If children were to depend on their genitors for food, this would render them vulnerable if their father died. In the past, the men used to travel on lengthy warfare expeditions, besides extended hunting or gathering trips. Nowadays, leaders travel to other villages and to the city, both for trading purposes and to defend the interests of their communities. Sexual intercourse is on a par with game, in terms of infinite demand and replenishment, one regulating the supply of the other throughout the community.

Formal Friendship

The genitor, besides being essential to the organic well-being of his child, is also the vehicle of its formal friends (of both sexes), inherited patrilaterally. The institution of formal friendship has been widely treated in the ethnographic literature concerning the Jê. Formal friends play an important role in all rites of passage. The senior member of a pair of formal friends (the age difference being the equivalent of parent and child) accompanies the junior friend, assisting him/her to enter and leave ritual states.[15]

The patrilateral inheritance of formal friends implies the existence of patrilines, traced back only as far as the dead patrilateral relatives remembered by the eldest living people. The notion of submerged patrilineages has been bombarded with criticism in the anthropological literature. However, in the Mẽbengokre case, submerged patrilines is an apt designation. Paternity, through the attribution of formal friends, is indirectly associated with the ideal form of marriage, characterized by a mother choosing one of her own formal friends (inherited through her father) as her son-in-law. She selects a formal friend of the appropriate age, that is, someone slightly older than her daughter. It is frowned upon to marry a formal friend. When a woman does this, she stagnates a source of virtual spouses for her daughters, that is, the mother's formal friends. This discovery of a category of virtual or ideal spouses amongst the Mẽbengokre approximates them to the Dravidianate societies of Amazonia. In societies with Dravidian terminologies, Viveiros de Castro (1993) distinguishes virtual spouses, cross-cousins for example, from potential spouses, distant cognates and noncognates.[16] For the Mẽbengokre, prior to the association of formal friendship with the inheritance of affinity (albeit indirectly), it was enigmatic why the Jê should constitute a stronghold, impervious to notions of matrimonial alliance, within an encompassing Dravidian landscape.

Patrilines are nebulous because they are neither localized nor legitimized by myths, as are names and prerogatives. One does not belong to a patriline in any sense that could be interpreted as implying a notion of double descent.[17] It was found easy to construct extensive genealogies relating to matri-houses but not to patrilines. Many of the formal friends of the population with whom research was carried out were located in distant villages with which there was only sporadic contact.

For the Mẽbengokre, formal friends are neither relatives nor nonrelatives. As one woman explained to me, they are different from nonrelatives because the relation between opposite-sex formal friends is characterized by avoidance, shame, or respect (*piaam*), as exists between mother-in-law and son-in-law. Consequently, when a woman chooses a formal friend as a son-in-law, her relationship with him is unaltered. It is said that one can become blind upon pronouncing the name of a formal friend, indicating a mystical component in formal friendship.

Mentors for Young Boys

Those familiar with the writing of Terence Turner (1966, 1979) may be surprised that the pseudo father (*bam kaàk*) has not been considered in the foregoing discussion. The reason for this is that, first, he is more of a mentor or tutor than a 'substitute' father, and second, the tradition of sending boys off to live in the men's house has fallen into disuse. Vestiges of this practice were found in the late 1970s, when adolescent males lived at the post, 100 meters or so from the main village. This also explains two cases, found in the 1994–95 data, of boys living with a stepsister or mother's sister as a transitionary phase, in preparation for leaving the maternal home for good. The elder male mentors used to teach boys handicrafts, hunting, and medicinal knowledge. Nowadays, the elders constantly complain that the young are bedazzled by the 'white man's' world, being more interested in learning how to operate the radio, drive a tractor, and read and write, than how to become a shaman, sing war songs, or learn about herbal medicines.

A boy's mentor, in the men's house, was recruited from among his classificatory fathers. When a child is born, all the men who are real or classificatory brothers of the father, such as parallel cousins, paint themselves in a specific style, attesting to their relationship of shared brotherhood. Upon the occasion of the birth of a man's first child, he and his brothers, besides being specially painted for the occasion, use long ceremonial poles (known as *pute*) with which they sit outside the men's house during the course of the short rite that marks this event.

The Kin Terminology

The Mẽbengokre kinship terminology has consensually been classified as Omaha, although it lacks the sexual asymmetry described by Héritier (1981) for the African Samo terminology that she analyzes. The Mẽbengokre manifest abhorrence at the mere suggestion of cross-cousin marriage. In accordance with the terminology, which ignores the generational principle, there are many oblique marriages. The avoidance or suppression of affinity is a classical theme from Northern Amazonia and the Guiana region. In my view, formal friendship is a mechanism for suppressing existing ties, both consanguineal and affinal, thereby facilitating new marriages. The use of kinship terms among all members of a village expresses a code of sociality. It does not preclude recognition of the distinction between close genealogical relatives (who cannot easily be reclassified) and the more distant classificatory ones who shade into the category of nonrelatives.

Mẽbengokre social organization can best be described as a type of Venn diagram, with a strong matrilineal dimension, represented by the matrihouses envisaged as moral persons, submerged patrilines (reminiscent of, but not to be confused with double descent), and (universally recognized) cognatic kindreds. Research since the mid-1980s on the Dravidian societies of Amazonia, where the number of marriages with close relatives is proportionately small, in terms of the ideal of endogamy within the local group, and research on those with a Crow-Omaha terminology, where cross-cousin marriage is prohibited, is tending to narrow the gap between them (e.g., Houseman and White 1998).

Environmental Transformation and Its Impact on the Ecology of the Region

The last two to three decades have witnessed striking and seemingly irreversible effects on the Amazon region and the surrounding savanna. In the 1970s, the Brazilian military dictatorship paved the way for the opening up of the forest with road construction and fiscal incentives to develop cattle breeding in the region. The roads facilitated colonization, gold prospecting, and the lumber trade. Different Mẽbengokre areas have been diversely affected by these developments, the logging industry presently posing the greatest threat; it is most intense precisely in the region of the Mẽtyktire with whom most of my research has been concentrated. Year by year, the game supply becomes increasingly depleted as the stranglehold tightens on the Mẽbengokre and other lowland Amerindians, surrounded by cattle ranches and timber merchants, with a yellowish-gray strip of smoke, produced by forest fires, observable by plane at the end of the dry season, dividing the villages below and the blue sky above.[18] The rivers are also becoming increasingly polluted, although the drinking water available to the Mẽbengokre of the Gorotire area, from the Fresco River in which they also fish, east of the Xingu River, had been poisoned with mercury as far back as the early 1980s (Lea 1984).

The land inhabited by the Mẽtyktire is contiguous to the Xingu Park. Nowadays these areas resemble an oasis in the desert when viewed from a plane; they are surrounded by dusty towns, scorched pastures dotted with cattle, and the odd tree trunk that has survived deforestation. Even the remaining forest is scarred by gold prospectors, who leave behind them clearings and muddy pools of stagnant water. A vicious circle is produced, with the Mẽbengokre and other indigenous peoples increasingly dependent on firearms for hunting, in order to maintain a sufficient supply of meat; game is diminishing in quantity and is located increasingly further afield. On the other hand, the belligerence of the Mẽbengokre, along with a number of other factors, has guaranteed them land roughly equivalent to the area of Scotland (Turner 1993, 114), allowing them to enjoy one of the best current land-to-population ratios of any Amerindian society within Brazil.

From the 1970s to the 1990s, many Brazilian Amerindian peoples experienced demographic growth as they gradually built up resistance to newly encountered illnesses and received meager health assistance, such as vaccination programs organized by the federal government. In the late 1990s, with the dismantling of the state—due to the triumph of neoliberalism and the increase in malaria, tuberculosis, and sexually transmitted diseases (including the first cases of AIDS in the neighboring Mēbengokre area, east of the Xingu River), following in the wake of deforestation and gold prospecting—there was little cause for optimism. On the other hand, the dire prognostications concerning acculturation, in the 1950s and even later, proved not only exaggerated but also deleterious to the interests of the Amerindian population, disseminating the opinion within Brazil and elsewhere, that they were condemned to assimilation into national society, resulting in cultural annihilation. Ecological consciousness within Brazil has been gradually increasing since the early 1980s. One can only hope that it will soon be strong enough to turn the tide of ecological destruction of the Amazon and the surrounding region.

Author's note: I thank the CNPq for research carried out between 1978 and 1982, the FINEP for a field trip made in 1987, and the Wenner-Gren Foundation for fieldwork carried out in 1994–95. I thank the FAPESP for funding my participation in the symposium held in Quito, and the other participants for their comments, suggestions, and for the stimulating atmosphere of our brief encounter. I thank Paul Henley and Suely Kofes for putting me on the right track, and Cambridge University Computing Services for assistance with Excel (during the revision of the manuscript).

Notes

1. For further details see Lea 1995a.
2. The standard notation is used to designate kin: F = father; 'F' = classificatory father; DC = daughter's children; MH = mother's husband, and so on.
3. A detailed analysis of the composition of Mēbengokre (Kayapó) households is forthcoming as the chapter of a book (Lea, in press).
4. In only one case was there a man who raised his children when his wife left him for another man. The wife had lost her mother and lived with her father's latest wife. The abandoned father of the children earned a wage as a National Foundation of the Indian (FUNAI) worker and married a woman from another Amerindian people. All three factors may have influenced the specificity of this case.

5. *Prõ nhi ojkwa, irà akupron, kra nhipetx* (lit., "wife sexual intercourse repeatedly, semen gathers, child is made").

6. *Krô'aj mied ngri* (lit., "pseudo husband (= lover) little").

7. Crocker and Crocker (1994) have written about the question of serial sexual relations in various ceremonial situations among the Canela, a related Jê society. It appears to me that when a woman has sexual relations with various men, on the one night, during the course of a ceremony, this is not taken to entail the possibility of becoming pregnant. However, I am not entirely sure, as I did not inquire about this. Contrary evidence is suggested by a narrative concerning a historic event that led to the separation of the Gorotire and the Ireamrayre (ancestral groups of the Mēbengokre). During a fight, the men of one group had sexual relations with the women of the opposite group, leading to the impregnation of both young girls and older women.

8. It generally involved women of the category *kwatỳj* (FZ, MM, FM) of children honored in naming ceremonies.

9. I thank Marilyn Strathern for having made available to me the original version, from 1992, as yet unpublished in English. This article was first published in Italian (1995a) and republished in Portuguese (1995b).

10. Bourdieu (1977, 164–71 and passim) opposes doxa to orthodoxy and heterodoxy. It comprises the world of the self-evident, unanimous, "taken for granted" (164)—a "world which has no place for *opinion*" (167, emphasis in original).

11. According to Hartung, "In some cultures extramarital sex is not highly restricted for women, and in most of those cultures, men transfer wealth to their sisters' sons (matrilineal inheritance). Inheritance to sisters' sons ensures a man's biological relatedness to his heirs, and matrilineal inheritance has been posited as a male accommodation to cuckoldry—a paternity strategy at least since the 15th century" (1985, 661). This view entirely overlooks the fact that the modern genetic definition of paternity is not universally acknowledged. Hartung writes as if Western notions of paternity were shared by all cultures.

12. My disagreement with T. Turner (1979) on this point stems from over a year of working closely with the women and being involved in the daily chores of fetching and distributing garden produce, food in general, water, and firewood.

13. The intricacies of name transmission are dealt with in Lea 1992.

14. It is difficult to put this into words in English. What is involved is a notion of reciprocity, not monetary payment.

15. A wider discussion of formal friendship can be found in Lea 1995b.

16. Viveiros de Castro (1993, 167) includes formal friends in the category of potential spouses. In light of my findings, I include formal friends in the category of virtual spouses—that is, for female ego, her mother's formal friend. Potential spouses, for men and women, are comprised of nonrelatives (*mēkàtàb* or *mēbajtem*).

17. The inheritance of formal friendship is vaguely reminiscent of the Ashanti, with their matri-clans and spiritual element (*ntoro*) inherited from the father, described by Rattray (1923), and later by Fortes (1950).

18. The smoke as seen from the air was particularly striking on my trip to the Mẽbengokre village of Kubẽkàkre, Southern Pará, in August 1998.

7

Several Fathers in One's Cap

Polyandrous Conception among the Panoan Matis (Amazonas, Brazil)

Philippe Erikson

Contemporary Matis Society

Because of the devastating pre- and postcontact epidemics that affected them in the late 1970s, the Matis, Panoan speakers of the Javari basin (Amazonas, Brazil), were both very few in number and, for the most part, very young when I first met them in 1984. Out of 109 people recorded in my February 1986 census (Erikson 1996, 141), only one male and six females were age 40 and above, in striking contrast with the 65 children estimated to be 14 or younger (38 boys, but only 27 girls). Nearly all the elders had died during the epidemics and most people had been either orphaned or widowed.

As generally occurs in similar situations (Adams and Price 1994), the Matis have seen their population more than double in the ten years following its demographic nadir. They are now nearly 240. The population crisis has thus slightly eased, but at the cost of increased imbalance in favor of youth. This critical situation, the result of a series of tragic historical accidents, has had serious implications on various aspects of Matis social life, including many of those discussed in this volume, such as the composition of the domestic group, the fate of fatherless children, marriage arrangements, and even kinship terminology.

After the latest outburst of epidemics, in the late seventies, the survivors from the five previously existing villages resettled in just two longhouses, separated only by a two-hour walk (CEDI 1982). One was relatively small and of fairly homogeneous composition: a leader, his brother, a few in-laws and many children. It conformed with the precontact residential pattern. The other longhouse, by contrast, comprised the remnants of the four other previous entities, regardless of their kinship ties. The result of unusual arrangements made to adjust to depopulation, it was cemented by the medical care provided by Brazilian civil servants (FUNAI), rather than by the usual sociological criteria. Many Matis complained that this composite nature led to unusual (and hardly bearable) levels of tension and strife.

Just as they lacked the right people to live with, so did many Matis lack prospective spouses. In order to compensate for this lack of legitimate partners, many were forced to resort to unorthodox marriages, especially of the oblique type (FZ/BS or ZD/MB), which were previously forbidden due to the Kariera nature of Matis terminology (displayed in figures 7.1 and 7.2). Such matrimonial adjustments are still considered wrong, but many would have been deemed even more incestuous had a semantic twist not been inflicted on the nomenclature. Providing they were younger than ego and did not belong to their own mother's generation, women of the "sister's daughter/mother's sister" (ZD/MZ) class, whom a man would have traditionally lumped together in the same category as mother (*tita utsi*, other mother), were turned marriageable by a simple linguistic trick that shunted the cross-parallel divide. These women have been assimilated with their brothers, being now called *piak*, a term formerly used, man speaking, only for younger male children (or parents) of sisters and male cross-cousins (Erikson 1996, chap. 7). Some women therefore became marriageable by being considered more like a female version of a sister's son rather than a classificatory mother.

As I have argued elsewhere (Erikson, in press), many shamanic and ritual practices were also discarded as a consequence of the epidemics, for fear of possible drawbacks, especially a resurgence of disease. Because it was considered too dangerous, the use of tobacco, hallucinogens, red pepper, frog poison injections, and many other stimulants was abandoned, as were the ceremonial planting of corn and subsequent initiation rituals. On the positive side, being so few people in a fairly remote area, the Matis enjoy a remarkable abundance of land and game. Even with so many children to feed, the Matis eat large quantities of peccary, tapir, or monkey meat just about every day (Erikson 1988). Hunting is said to be much more collective than it previously was, and because so many people now live in one sociologically heterogeneous longhouse, where meals are taken collectively (by men at least) at the center, the distribution of cooked meat is probably much more systematic now than it ever was. Public

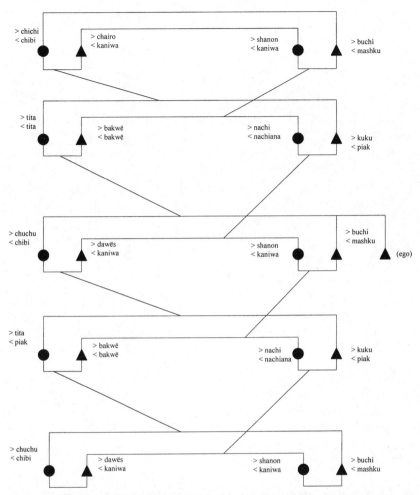

Fig. 7.1. Matis classificatory kinship (male ego) (> senior to ego; <junior to ego)

communal meals are certainly advantageous for orphans and widows, who stand a much better chance of receiving a share than if each household ate on its own.

In other words, Matis society has too few longhouses, too many orphans, and too much meat to be truly representative of Amazonian social life in general, or even of "traditional" Matis social life. The dire crisis they have recently been through makes it difficult to determine the influence of a single factor, namely partible paternity, on children's survival odds. Yet, many of the underlying structural principles are still there to be observed, and their consequences can be deduced if not observed.

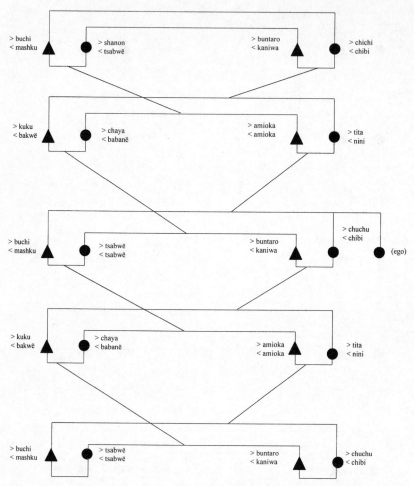

Fig. 7.2. Matis classificatory kinship (female ego) (> senior to ego; <junior to ego)

Polyandrous Conception in Amazonia and among the Matis

In lowland South America, belief in partible paternity, or polyandrous conception, as I would prefer to call it, is widespread.[1] Babies frequently can (and
sometimes even must) have several male genitors. In some cases, like those described among the Tupian Arawété (Viveiros de Castro 1993) or the Carib
Arara (Teixeira-Pinto 1997), ceremonial friendship relationships are numerous
and systematically associated with wife sharing. In other cases, as among the
Matis, brothers commonly (and very openly) share the sexual favors of each
other's wives. Such intimate associations obviously contribute to a generaliza-
tion of polyandric conception.

The part played by mothers in the physical elaboration of the fetus is often minimized, even among people with strong uxorilocal traditions, such as the Shipibo (Eakin, Lauriault, and Boonstra 1980, 96). Whenever women are, half-reluctantly, believed to physically contribute to the fetus, they are often left with the least "substantial" elements: perishable flesh and blood as opposed to durable bones among the Barasana, for instance (C. Hugh-Jones 1979, 115–16). The prevalence of these androcentric theories of conception is discussed by Abelove (1978, 51), who comments that many Amazonian lexicons consequently establish a systematic link between sexuality and procreation, a fact also recently elaborated upon by Rival (1998). Indeed, to use a monetary metaphor, if sperm is stocked until there is enough to produce a baby, male orgasms appear more like contributions to a savings account rather than like the purchase of a lottery ticket (such as we "conceive" it).

From Margaret Mead (1935) we have the well-known statement that fathers are a biological necessity, but a social accident. The frequent denial of the mother's physical contribution to the fetus among Amazonian peoples makes one wonder if the proposal should not be reversed for lowland South America: mothers are a biological necessity (at least as a recipient) but a social mystery, whose physical relationship with their children is something to be constructed (often through nursing) and accounted for. This is neatly assessed by Alès (1998, 295–96), who reminds us that the Yanomami ideology of purely male conception of the fetus dilutes rather than reinforces the importance of paternity, and therefore paradoxically puts a much stronger onus on uterine ascendance for the definition of full siblinghood, for instance.[2]

With respect to the Matis, the idea that a fetus results from the accumulation of several men's sperm is not only present but even seems to be reflected in the kinship terminology. At the very least, a humorous alternative to the ordinary designation of "brothers" (*buchi* or *mashku,* depending on relative age) is *ebutamute,* which translates something like "he with whom I co-procreate." Another possible terminological adjustment to the belief in polyandrous conception might also be seen in the fact that Matis nomenclature tends to treat ego's father's kin category as indivisible. As shown by figures 7.1 and 7.2, the terms used for the kin type that includes brother's son and father's brother, *amioka* (BS, FB, etc., female speaking) and *bakwë* (BS, FB, etc., male speaking), are the only ones to systematically disregard relative age considerations, by contrast with all others, which are split in two to account for such distinctions. This makes the father's category more "generic" than any other, which might be relevant to the present discussion, since it implies that a man will systematically use the term *bakwë*, which literally means "child," to call all the (male) children of all his female cross-cousins, as if all men could consider all (male) children of their potential spouses as being their own. Admittedly, the term *bakwë* is of reciprocal use, which impedes interpreting it too literally as a terminological adjustment to collegial paternity. The lexical unity of father's kintype results from strict virilocality associated with the very classificatory nature of a Kariera kinship system, at least as much as it reflects polyandrous conception. Yet, one cannot but notice that whereas other kintypes are totally partitioned according to relative age (alternate terms depending on whether alter is junior or senior to ego), the category FB/BS is only partly divided by the fact that some of its members are singled out as biological fathers, in which case they are called *mama* instead of *amioka* or *bakwë*. A further distinction may be established between *mama kimo* (principal father) and *mama utsi* (secondary father).

Ordinary Extramarital Sex

Plural paternity, among the Matis, is more than a mere theoretical possibility, and not only in cases of polyandrous marriage arrangements (not as common as polygynous ones, but nonetheless possible). Even for monogamous couples, extramarital sex is not only widely practiced and usually tolerated: in many respects, it also appears mandatory. Married or not, one has a moral duty to respond to the sexual advances of opposite-sex cross-cousins (real or classificatory), under pains of being labeled "stingy of one's genitals," a breach of Matis ethics far more serious than plain infidelity.[3] A young man once came to hide in my house, in order to get away from his mother's brother's daughter whose passes he feared he couldn't decently reject if she ever found him.

I have often heard of brothers asking permission to sleep with each other's wives, just as I have heard (among the Chacobo, another Panoan people) a man telling about the sexual outlet he had found while he and his wife were following postpartum sexual restrictions: he simply asked her if he could respond to another woman's advances, and she agreed. In Amazonia, cheating on your spouse is sometimes deemed wrong (Dean 1998), and jealousy does exist (Camargo 1999), but this is far from meaning that openly having several extramarital sex partners will systematically bring social or moral reprobation. Goody's suggestion (1956) that incest and adultery are but two facets of the generic category "sexual offenses" does not hold for lowland South America. The only time I heard a Matis man arguing with a classificatory brother about sleeping with his wife, he was not complaining about the act itself, but rather about its happening too often! The extent to which such sexual permissiveness is correlated with the disappearance of the elder generation during the epidemics is open to speculation.

The Matis show very little secrecy about their sexual activity. I have heard a man very matter-of-factly discussing the zoophilic practices his father had resorted to for lack of female cross-cousins, then candidly claiming he finally got so tired of having sex with dead monkeys and tree sloths that he decided to raid the neighboring Korubo and steal a girl to be his wife! FUNAI employees state that when they first met them, people would openly make love in crowded longhouses at night, despite the light provided by log fires. (However dim such light may be, Matis longhouses are devoid of any kind of inner walls.) Most intercourse seems to take place in the secrecy of the forest, on a bed of leaves, but even then, couples get away in search of intimacy rather than concealment. Road signs (sticks closing the path) are sometimes planted on the pathway, indicating the direction in which the couple has gone to. Passersby, who can all "read" footsteps and know exactly who is out there, are thus informed of what is going on, and asked to pass discreetly the other way. Most do, except of course very young children, whose conversations and playful imitations of copulation clearly indicate how knowledgeable they are, as early as four or five years old.

The question of what percentage of heterosexual activity takes place outside of matrimony is one to which I do not have the answer. But I do know the Matis had, until fairly recently, partnerships between men who shared sexual access to a woman even though only one of them was considered her husband. Among the Matis, however, rather than occurring between ceremonial friends, such bonds united people who were already related, as father and son. This was because little girls formerly went to live with their prospective father-in-law at a very early age, having usually been promised in marriage to one of their mother's brother's sons soon after birth.[4] The girl's maternal uncle was supposed to raise her until she was old enough to marry his son, and sexual intercourse before puberty was considered a means to make young girls grow. In a Kariera system, in which legitimate sex was strictly forbidden between people of alternate generations, this was technically incestuous, but apparently was usually accepted as part of the girl's education. Premarital avuncular sex explains why so many children, especially among firstborns, prefer to trace their kinship ties exclusively on the maternal sides. For instance, if a man and his ZD have sex, the resulting offspring might hesitate between considering him as a father or as a maternal uncle, but the woman will obviously be his or her mother rather than his or her female cross-cousin. Polyandrous conception, especially in cases where the social system is as straitjacketed as the Matis one is, can lead to a kind of dissolution of fatherhood rather than to its reinforcement by duplication.

Ceremonial Extramarital Sex

One context in which extramarital sex appears legitimate, and even compulsory, is during major ceremonies such as tattooing festivals. In native South America, the initial stages of important rituals commonly imply a strict separation of the sexes; men are out hunting or fishing while women stay behind brewing manioc or maize beer. Quite understandably, a large amount of sexual activity therefore takes place after the two groups reunite, that is, during the height of the party. Most (if not all) of it is extramarital and this is often presented as an essential component of the ritual. The usually roughish games that occur then and that have sometimes been presented as the ritual manifestation of sexual antagonism (Siskind 1973), might be better be interpreted as ritualized foreplay (Menget 1984). Sex, in many Amazonian societies, is used as a bonding mechanism (Crocker and Crocker 1994), especially during rituals. What would ordinarily be "illegitimate" couples are temporarily legitimized in such contexts, as a way of reaffirming global solidarity at the expense of self-contained domestic units. Attention to this function of ritual sexual communism as a public denial of selfish enclosure was acknowledged as early as 1906 by Mauss and Beuchat (1950, 447), and often confirmed in recent Amazonian ethnography. Among the Warao, for instance, Wilbert (1985, 158) describes times during which ordinary affinal ties are suspended and replaced by ritual relations known as *mamuse*. Husbands then swap wives and everyone is free to have sex with whomever he or she pleases. Such mamuse relationships are deemed honorable and are considered to have a fortifying influence on the women's progeny.

The Matis are no exception to this pattern of institutionalized periodic compulsory infidelity. One of their major rituals is quite explicitly centered around uniting both genders as groups, at the expense of couples. During the corn festival, in which youngsters are tattooed (Erikson 1990), one of the most spectacular episodes very obviously mimics collective reproductive activity. All the women, armed with stinging nettles, group in front of the longhouse entrance (*shokwë;* lit., "the house's vulva") trying to bar its access from the men, who, one at a time, try to force entrance head first, until after a long struggle one finally succeeds in passing. The women then step back and let the men enter in one single file, holding ears of corn. This, of course, is merely symbolically sexual, and has little impact on the actual conception of children. Yet, later stages of the tattooing festival imply actual intercourse in the forest, and relevant to our discussion here is the fact that there is a strict ban on lovemaking with your regular partners. The Matis claim that in such circumstances, having sex with your "real wife" (*awin kimo*) or even teasing your "real cross-cousins" (*shanon kimo, kaniwa kimo* or *awin kimo*) with nettles, would induce very dire consequences, possibly even death. In times of ritual activity, sex is necessarily extramarital.

Toward a Sex-Free Definition of Amerindian Kinship

Unsurprisingly then, nearly all Matis, when asked about their genealogy, acknowledge having several emically biological fathers. Yet, this said, it must be stressed that ethno-physiological considerations are not the only ones at stake in the Matis definition of fatherhood. There is also a sociological definition of fatherhood, induced by the Kariera nature of the kinship system and according to which all members of father's kin class are ego's father, which implies many kinds of obligations. In that respect, it must be stressed that when it comes to defining kinship ties, relationships deriving from naming practices have absolute priority over any other considerations, such as genealogical connections (Erikson 1993). When conflicts arise between the two modes of reckoning, sharing a name has precedence over sharing physical substances. The following case study offers a particularly striking example of the importance of this phenomenon (see fig. 7.3).

Here we have a child, called Binan Wasa, who was born from his mother's previous oblique union with her mother's brother (a common occurrence among the Matis), and thus has conflicting patri- and matri-lateral genealogical ties. His mother's actual partner, who happens to also bear the name Binan Wasa, is, sociologically speaking, in a position to be the child's social father (pater). I have no information as to whether or not he can also be considered one of his biological fathers (genitor), but it is an obvious possibility since sex with the mother is obviously an option open to him. On a day-to-day basis, the older Binan Wasa raises and feeds the younger one, acting, seeming, and probably feeling, as if he were his father. His full brothers (Kwini and Iba) treat the child according to matrilateral links, therefore calling him *bakwë* (brother's child). Considering all this, senior Binan Wasa should appear, at the very least, as junior's foster or surrogate, if not real, father. Yet, because onomastic ties, among the Matis, have absolute priority over any other kind of links, he must consider his "near-son" as a true brother. On account of their identical names,

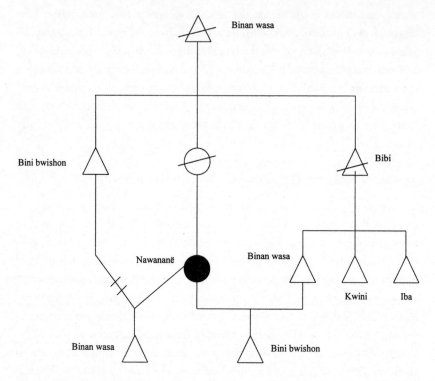

Fig. 7.3. Conflict between Matis names and roles

the two Binan Wasa call each other *buchi* (older brother) and *mashku* (younger brother).

For people such as the Matis (but I believe this is true for most Panoans and probably many Gê peoples as well), a feeling of a common substance (and the subsequent sharing obligation) can be grounded on nonbiologically defined factors. Relationships based on such "immaterial" links as the sharing of a same name or such and such a body ornament can also create obligations, just as binding as those derived from what Westerners would describe as kinship-proper. Partible paternity is but one aspect of a very generalized Amerindian tendency to expand kinship ties well beyond the range of nuclear or even ex-tended families that are based on biological links. This we might label expan-sive kinship, and DeMallie clearly shows that it is far from being restricted to Latin America: "the [nineteenth-century] Sioux recognized the biological basis for procreation; however, it was not the defining criterion for kinship. Biologi-cal relationship was only one of the several ways of becoming related in Sioux culture, and there is no evidence that it was accorded primacy or preeminence in the definition of relatedness either in theory or in daily life" (1994, 135). Being a father, among native North and South Americans, is not something that ultimately rests upon a single factor resulting from genital activity. It is also based on ritual action, commensalism, body paints, seclusion, name giving and sharing, and many other assets that contribute to what Seeger, Da Matta, and Viveiros de Castro (1979), in a landmark paper, have defined as the ongoing production of being and the gradual construction of kinship characteristic of native South Americans. Obviously, recognition of kinship ties does have an influence on food distribution patterns, but what I question is that such recognition is presented as being fundamentally based on physical (polyandrous) conception.

Conclusions

With respect to the practical implications of partible paternity, I must admit I do not share the unilateral optimism of Beckerman et al. (1998) about its adaptive nature. There are several reasons for this. In the first place, many ethnographic reports stress that whereas having several fathers is a necessity, having too many might prove harmful. Gregor, discussing how the Mehinaku envision the tragic fate of a woman subjected to collective rape, reports: "She sickens and dies, she gives birth to twins (in itself a horrendous event) or in one instance an 'oversized' baby that was killed as soon as it was born 'because it had too many fathers'" (1990, 489). Elsewhere, Gregor states: "Just as too little sexual activity is insufficient for conception, too much is also undesirable. A promiscuous woman risks having a child that is 'too large,' or twins" (1985, 89). Other instances in which semen overload is presented as harmful, rather than beneficial, to the baby, can be found in Butt 1975, Goldman 1963 (166), or McCallum 1994, among others. The notion of twins as a kind of penalty for overdiversified sexual activity has also been commented upon by Lévi-Strauss (1991, 89–90).

In other cases, even among people extremely lax on sexual matters, like the Matis, men sometimes put children's lives in danger *because* they are another man's product. In one case I witnessed, an angry young man threw his baby son in the river, after a quarrel with his wife and one of her lovers. The child was saved, but obviously partible paternity almost cost him his life. Such cases might be widespread. Chagnon, for instance, reports that "a man will (in some cases) order his wife to abort if he suspects that somebody else conceived the child" (1968, 75). Murphy and Murphy similarly note: "Illegitimate children are commonly destroyed at birth, as are twins and children with serious birth defects" (1974, 101). The often dire effects of paternal jealousy sometimes even make their way into the mythology. Stolze Lima (1995) tells of a founding father among the Juruna who refuses to provide for his third son because he has other biological fathers.

Regarding meat distribution, Beckerman et al. (1998) argue that the fate of children is somehow positively correlated with the number of co-fathers who will provide for them. This might be true in some cases, but at least four factors induce me to take this with a grain of salt. In the first place, let us recall that the obligation to provide meat for a child does not necessarily rest on actual physiological ties only. There might therefore be mechanisms allowing children to benefit from "extra meat" provided by "extra kinship" independently from polyandrous conception.

Second, it might just happen, as I have seen among the Matis, that those women who have the most lovers (and whose children will therefore have the greatest number of fathers) do so precisely because they are widowed and are going through a critical phase of their lives. Therefore, their children might have several providers (who are in fact providing for their lovers, rather than for their children), but at the expense of a steady, regular provider. I have no quantified data, but in my experience, such children are rather less well fed than the average. Given the abundance that reigns among the Matis, this does not seem critical, but widows, no matter how many lovers they have, tend to spend more time than married women searching for palm fruits and other substitutes for meat.[5]

My third point derives from the fact that, among the Matis at least, some of the meat that is most systematically shared (namely the larger mammals, such as peccary and especially tapir) happens to be tabooed for very young children. I have vivid memories of a two- to three-year-old toddler bursting out of the longhouse where everyone else was eating, walking straight up to me, and whining indignantly: *awat peama, eobi,* "I haven't eaten any tapir." He was too young, according to the Matis food code, to receive even the slightest piece of such potent meat. Even if sharing were indeed increased on account of seminal ties (a fact that I doubt as far as the Matis are concerned), it would therefore only be really beneficial for children above the age of three or four.

Finally, I wish to stress that what seems advantageous from one child's point of view might have exactly the opposite consequences when looked at from another child's point of view. After all, the meat that will be directly or indirectly given by his co-genitor to one child living in a separate household might also be considered as taken away from his other children, particularly those of the wife or wives he lives with. To state it differently, belief in partible paternity might seem unadaptive from the viewpoint of men, whose protein collection, following the model, could be seen as dispersed by such belief for the benefit of children who are likely to be genetically unrelated to them. Sociobiologically speaking, this is unsound and leads one to wonder if it makes sense for a cultural trait to be deemed adaptive from female ego's perspective but not from male ego's.

Another point worth pondering has to do with social organization. I for one find it difficult to accept that cultural traits are selected by evolutionary pressure the way biological ones are. Yet those defending this idea with regard to a possible correlation between partible paternity and added protein for youngsters are left with the following puzzle: partible paternity usually unites real or classificatory brothers, and yet most Amazonian peoples are somehow uxorilocal, thus dispersing potential co-fathers.

All in all, I am not entirely convinced that meat distribution patterns are the major issue with respect to the implications of partible paternity. What is really at stake with polyandrous conception might not be what it entices you to feed to others, but rather what it prohibits you from eating yourself. The issue might not be which child will eat such and such a cut of meat, but rather which adult will (or will not) refrain from such and such a cut of meat. From an emic point of view, fatherhood is defined (or at least reinforced) by adherence to couvade prohibitions (which by the way diminish the amount of meat available since they impede hunting). This is probably more important as a defining criterion of Amazonian fatherhood than the reshuffling of distribution patterns it might entail. By choosing to respect (or not to respect) the postpartum food taboos generally imposed on fathers throughout the Amazon basin, men are making a statement about their allegiance to such and such a woman, showing a willingness to assume responsibilities for children, proving they are mature enough to care for their offspring, and this is to some extent independent of mechanical factors such as having had sex with the mother. I am therefore inclined to conclude that partible paternity is neither advantageous nor disadvantageous as such. Having more than one allegedly biological father might be beneficial to some children in some circumstances, but it might just as well be detrimental to others in different contexts.

Notes

1. Although I will be using the term *partible paternity* in this paper in order to stay in key with the other participants, I only do so reluctantly because it seems to imply that paternity is fundamentally one, its basic unity only being accidentally transgressed (hence partible). Partible paternity is far from being a South American specialty. In fact, a European version seems to exist under the label telegony, a belief according to which a woman's previous sexual experiences might inform her matrix in such a way as to influence her future offspring, independent of who their father might subsequently be. Such folk beliefs are by no means "remote" and "exotic." They account for the extreme severity with which sexual unions between so-called Semites and so-called Aryans were repressed by Nazi law a generation ago (Terray 1996), and even today are probably not unrelated to the horrendous zeal with which rape was systematically applied by all parties during the Bosnian wars (Nahoum-Grappe 1996).

2. Considered in a wider perspective, native South American theories of conception might give women a more important role than it seems. Our tendency to interpret conception in purely physiological terms probably leads to overemphasizing the importance of semen. But what about substances such as milk, which is sometimes considered a female equivalent of semen and is also believed to contribute to the child's body, albeit after birth? Furthermore, semen itself is sometimes seen as ultimately derived from female agency (and saliva), via the ingestion of the beer men need to drink to be able to produce semen (McCallum 1994).

3. For a more detailed discussion of Matis ethics, see Erikson 1996 (chap. 15).

4. The particular importance of maternal uncles in the upbringing of children also has another consequence regarding the partible paternity debate: The "safety net" of orphaned children, especially girls, is less likely to reside in secondary fathers than in maternal uncles. As a matter of fact, the former's importance is such that, among the neighboring Matses (closely related to the Matis), even non-orphaned newborn girls are reported to risk being cast off—that is, thrown in an animal hole or strangled—if no potential father-in-law has spoken for her and accepted a share of the responsibility for raising her (Fields and Merrifield 1980, 4). In the case of boys, judging from my experience among the Matis, orphans tend to be taken care of by their *tita utsi* ("other mothers"; women of the mother's sister category) rather than by secondary fathers.

5. On palm fruits as a common Amazonian substitute for meat, see Beckerman 1977.

8

Partible Parentage and Social Networks among the Ese Eja

Daniela M. Peluso and James S. Boster

Among the Ese Eja, both paternity and maternity are partible. Like many of the societies discussed in this volume, the Ese Eja attribute partial paternity of children to a woman's extramarital sex partners.[1] In addition, maternity is partible through the practice of adoption. Here, we review how Ese Eja beliefs about reproduction, marriage, child rearing, and kinship affect their understanding of the parent-child bond. We examine the social consequences of their different ways of reckoning parent-child relationships. We also explore the structure of the sexual network among the married adults of one community. We argue that while both motherhood and fatherhood are partible, only paternity is ambiguous. This weakens the patriline, makes moiety assignment uncertain, and strengthens female control over reproduction and social relationships. Despite the constraints it imposes on possible marriage partners, individuals use the multiplicity of parenthood to define their identity, expand their social networks, and position themselves politically. The structure of the sexual network is sparse but complex: the number of partners does not appear to be determined by factors such as size of kin networks, physical attractiveness, or productive capacity.

Ethnographic Background

The Ese Eja are a lowland Amazonian group of about 1,200 individuals who live in several communities along the Beni, Madre de Dios, Sonene, and Tambopata Rivers, in the border regions of Pando, Bolivia, and Madre de Dios, Peru.[2] The Ese Eja language belongs to the Tacana language family, which is part of the Macro-Pano-Takana language group.

The Ese Eja are divided into two patrimoieties that, until recently, were exogamous:[3] *icha* could only marry *kaka* and vice versa. Though no longer exogamous, moiety membership is still patrilineally transmitted and is associated
with distinct personalities and physiognomies.[4] At present, no rights to resources are inherited with moiety membership. Ese Eja also regard themselves
as composed of three geographically and dialectically distinct groups that have
a long history of warfare and intermarriage.

Most Ese Eja reside uxorilocally.[5] These households consist of a married
couple, their unmarried daughters, unmarried sons, married daughters and
sons-in-law, grandchildren, adopted children, and maternal grandparents. This
pattern allows the maintenance of female residential lineages. Thus women are
surrounded by significantly more of their kin than are men.

Ese Eja kinship terminology is a variant of the Dravidian system. This bifurcate merging system divides the mother's from the father's line and merges
the mother with her sisters, and the father with his brothers. As discussed below, the practice of adoption and the attribution of partible paternity further
complicate the reckoning of kinship.[6]

Marriage and the Household Economy

Ese Eja recognize marriage (*ejame'iñaki*, or *hamatijawiaki*) as a basic social
relationship that all individuals seek to attain and maintain. Marriage sanctions sexual intimacy, establishes responsibility for children, and organizes
economic production and cooperation. Only a few high-status men marry
polygynously.[7] However, extramarital affairs are common: About three-
quarters of married adults are reported to have had extramarital sexual relationships. For the duration of the affair, the man is expected to present his
partner with small gifts of meat, fish, or trade goods, especially colored
thread.[8] If the affairs are carried out discreetly, for a short term, and without
diverting substantial resources from the household, they usually do not dis-
rupt the marriage. Spouses who display jealousy are criticized as *kia'nawe*
(stingy). Ideally, one should enact the Ese Eja ethic of sharing by displaying
indifference toward a spouse's extramarital affairs. However, despite these
norms of generosity, these relationships can be the subject of gossip and a
source of irritation to the neglected spouse. Although these relationships
tend not to be discussed in the presence of the spouse, the existence of these
nonmarital relationships appears to be a matter of general knowledge and
interest, including by the spouse, and may even be declared by the mother in
the choice of names for children. On at least one occasion, the husband, on

overhearing the wife's discussion with Peluso, reminded her of one of the secondary fathers.

Until recently, avuncular marriage was preferred: men married their *boyase* (sister's daughter) and women married their *toto* (mother's brother). It is now disapproved of as *memoo* (incest), probably due to Christian influence. While marriages are still occasionally arranged, younger people commonly express a preference for marrying someone they are in love with (*jahahibakiani*). They define attraction as being a combination of *kia'bame* (beauty) and *epeeji* (friendship). Individuals' skills appear to have little to do with the estimation of their attractiveness: Men say that women can always learn how to cook and women say that men can always learn how to hunt and work hard. The opposite sex is divided into *wapa* (marriageable) and *wapa pojiama* (nonmarriageable).[9] Parents, children (all direct ancestors and descendants), same-sex siblings of parents, and parallel cousins are all wapa pojiama. As discussed above, the category recently has been extended to include parents' cross-sex siblings. Sex with wapa pojiama is memoo and can be the cause of illness, especially skin pigmentation problems. Although sexual affairs between wapa pojiama occur, marriages do not.

The division of labor in mature marriages sustains the household as the basic unit of economic production, subsistence, and exchange. Men are responsible for building houses and clearing gardens, while the work of planting and harvesting the garden is shared by men and women. Women are responsible for child care and weaving. Hunting with guns and bows and arrows is exclusively by men; women occasionally opportunistically catch small mammals using sticks or machetes. Men usually skin and quarter large animals, and women process small prey. Both men and women fish, although again they employ different technologies, each targeting different species, according to the season. Men fish with bow and arrow, harpoons, hook and line, and nets, while women grab fish in shallow pools during the dry season. While men collect and pound fish poison into the streams, women help gather the stunned fish (Alexiades 1999).[10] When more than enough meat or fish are caught to feed the household, it is usually shared among extended kin. Often, a small crowd congregates as the animal is skinned and quartered. The hunter or his wife may either distribute pieces to their kin at that time or may instruct a child to take a piece to a particular household.[11] In general, meat is provided to the household by men and distributed within and among households by women.

Marriages are considered established when a couple begins to have children and to work well together in their gardens. Smooth collaboration is both a source of marital satisfaction and a sign of friendship and harmony. Both men and women comment that it is good when a spouse is an epeeji (friend). In good marriages, interdependency and complementarity are expected to develop over time. The couple starts their cooperation by establishing small gardens, usually while they are still living with the wife's parents. By the time they have several children, they are usually able to provide for them as well as contribute to the general household. When a couple decides to build their own house, it is usually close to the woman's parents' household, adding to a residential cluster.

Theories of Conception

Like other Amazonian groups, the Ese Eja hold the view that a child is formed by the accumulation of *ema'i* (semen) from successive copulations following the last pregnancy, including those from sexual affairs. Beckerman et al. (1998) describe the most typical Amazonian practice of secondary fatherhood as one in which the mother-to-be enlists extramarital partners to help form the fetus only after she is judged to be pregnant with her husband's child. In contrast, Ese Eja women are not concerned with pregnancy when arranging their sexual relations. This raises the probability that occasionally the secondary father is indeed the biological father. The Ese Eja term for pregnancy, *o'ejipoanahe*, literally means 'to have continued to make one' (*oe:* one; *ji:* something one does continually or habitually; *po:* to make; *nahe:* [past tense]). Hence, their concept of conception refers to the continuous habitual sexual activity of forming a fetus. The infant is formed in the *eyone* (uterus), an expandable container that grows and swells through repeated intercourse and ejaculation of sperm. Failure to conceive may be attributed to either the barrenness of the woman or the sterility of the man. Barrenness is regarded as the result of having a uterus that is inflexible and small while sterility is a result of having sperm that is *piaja* (rotten).

Using this theory of conception, many children are regarded as having more than one father. Following Beckerman et al. (1998), we refer to the additional fathers beyond the woman's husband as *secondary fathers* and to the paternity as *partible*. Hence, a mother's onetime extramarital liaison will lead to the child being only a little bit like a secondary father. For instance, a female acquaintance once complained about how unreasonable it was that her husband's ex-wife's child should visit and expect to be fed: "She was only three months pregnant when they split up, therefore the child was more formed by [her new husband] than by my husband!"

A child's resemblance to the mother's husband is not usually sufficient to reassure him that the child is his responsibility. In many cases of suspected partible paternity, the mother's husband claims not to perceive the resemblance. One neighbor's son, who was given up for adoption because of his partible paternity, looked to the ethnographer as almost identical to his mother's husband. When asked if he thought that the child looked like him, he replied, "only a little bit—that's because there was not a lot [of his own sperm], it all gets mixed together.'" Even when a child, rejected by the mother's husband and given up for adoption, grows up to be *oyahayo* (just like him), the man often remains indifferent to the child.

Though the above examples show that a man has some choice in recognizing a wife's child as his own responsibility, women exercise a great degree of control over the degree of paternity attributed to particular men through their discussions of their own and others' sexual encounters, as discussed below.

Cultural Models of Parenting

For the Ese Eja, the growth of a child is not a spontaneous process but one that requires intentional action. Children do not grow the way trees grow (*powaani*), or hair grows (*kwashaani*), or a river grows (*jawekiani*). Trees, hair, and rivers all grow on their own without the intervention of human intent. Children grow the way that crops grow (*tiiani*);[12] they need to be tended, protected, and cultivated. The term reflects the importance to the Ese Eja of active nurturance and caregiving in raising children, an activity joined by older siblings and other household members.

Ese Eja recognize a variety of possible parent-child relationships. These include the relationship between: a woman and a child she has given birth to (birth mother); between a man and a child his wife gives birth to (birth father); between a man and a child an extramarital sex partner gives birth to (secondary father); between an adult and a child they have adopted (adoptive parent); between an adult and a child of the adult's same-sex sibling (classificatory parent); between a woman and a child of a co-wife in a polygynous household (polygynous mother);[13] between adults and the children of a spouse from a previous marriage (stepparent); between adults and children in another household for whom they take partial responsibility for child care (shared parent);[14] and between adults and a child they raise who has been left without an immediate family due to the sudden deaths of the child's former caregivers or other unusual circumstances (foster parents).[15] Because these categories can overlap each other or other kinship categories (e.g., classificatory and polygynous mother, foster parent, and grandmother), the variety of potential parents gives rise to a great deal of flexibility in providing care for children. Of course, the multiplicity and flexibility of the categories also allows a certain amount of manipulation of the categories, depending on context and the goals of the actors involved.

Adoption

Just as Ese Eja beliefs about conception allow for the recognition of multiple fathers, the practice of *wojani* (adoption) allows for the recognition of multiple mothers who may share in the raising of and caring for children.[16] Adoption is extremely common in Ese Eja communities. As in much of the rest of lowland Amazonia and many other parts of the world, couples frequently choose adoption when they are unable to conceive or when family sex ratios are skewed. However, among the Ese Eja, adoption is not limited to these prototypical situations.[17] Most households include adults who were adopted or raised with adopted siblings. For example, in one small Ese Eja community of 43 adults, 21 were adopted, 16 had adopted children, and 9 had given children for adoption by other families. These figures represent a lower bound; other larger communities have higher rates of adoption.

Ese Eja couples are expected to give away their first two children; the first child should be given to the wife's parents and the second child to the husband's parents. Frequently, however, the wife's mother receives both of the first two children. Given the preference for uxorilocal residence after marriage, this practice often does not result in the separation of the birth mother and the child. Adoptive mother, birth mother, and child all remain in the birth mother's natal household or residential cluster.

Children are regarded as bringing vitality, joy, and meaning to an Ese Eja household. A household without children is incomplete and *kia'eno* (sad). Couples explain that they give their children to their parents for adoption so that "they have someone to raise," so that "they will not be alone," or because "they need someone to help them." These are also the reasons grandparents offer for their desire to raise their children's children. Thus, children replace themselves in their parents' households with their own children. This is regarded as a favor and an expression of gratitude to their parents. In effect, menopause and old age are not a barrier to continuously raising one's own children—social practices overcome reproductive limitations. Stack (1974) has described a similar pattern of adoption of firstborn children to matrilineal kin in African-American communities, one that Draper and Keith (1992) have interpreted as an adaptation to early loss of fertility due to various health problems, including high blood pressure.

Other reasons prompting people to give their children up for adoption include single motherhood, remarriage, indiscreet partible paternity, and close birth spacing. Usually children remain with widowed or single mothers, to be raised with the help of a stepfather when she remarries. She may also choose to give children up for adoption, especially if she is raising only one small child. Alternatively, she may share the children with her family, especially if she has many children. The choice among these possibilities may be partly determined by the mother's chances for remarriage: Sharing with family the care of a number of children is an option pursued by older women who are less likely candidates for remarriage. In general, the mother decides who will receive children that are given up for adoption. Only when a woman abandons her husband and children is their fate his decision.

The partible paternity of a child is another reason for giving it up for adoption: The smaller the proportion of paternity attributed to the mother's husband, the greater the chance that the child will be given up. In one community, 14 of the 27 children reported to have secondary fathers were given up for adoption, while only 6 of 46 children without secondary fathers were given up (52% vs. 13%; $\chi^2 = 12.9$, p < 0.001). Some mothers' husbands insist on strict exclusivity. For instance, one girl explained why she is the only one of her parents' eight children that was not adopted out: "I am the only one who is purely [my father's], the rest are mixed. He didn't want to raise the others." Other cases verge on infanticide: "[The boy] was mostly made up of [an Ese Eja man from a neighboring village] and so [his mother's husband] tried to throw him in the river when he was born. That's when [the child's mother] gave him to her [father's brother's son] to raise." Again, though the husband may be most important in the choice to give up the child, it is the wife who chooses who will adopt it. She usually gives the child to her own family since neither the husband nor his kin recognize it. Close birth spacing is also a motive for giving children up for adoption. In this circumstance, parents are often concerned that they will be unable to meet the diet and behavioral restrictions of parenthood or provide adequate breast-feeding, with deleterious consequences for the child's health.

Ese Eja families generally treat birth and adopted children equally. Children call their birth and adoptive parents *nai* (mother) and icha/kaka ([father's moiety affiliation]). Although there are terms in Ese Eja for adopted children (*etiimee*) and for adoptive parents (*etiimeeji*),[18] these terms are not used in everyday conversation and their existence does not reflect any differential treatment of birth and adoptive children.

Networks of Relatedness

Partible paternity and adoption have important economic, reproductive, and political effects on networks of relatedness. As argued above, Ese Eja notions of partible paternity multiply the number of father-child ties, weaken the relationship between mother's husband and child, and greatly complicate the reckoning of kinship.

The notion of partible paternity diffuses men's responsibilities for children. While a man cannot be certain that any child is exclusively his own, he is also assured that if he has had sex with a woman since her last pregnancy even once any resulting child is at least partially his.[19] His proportion of paternity depends on his share of sexual access to the woman, considering both the number of times they have had sex and the number of other partners (besides the husband) she has. The fewer partners the woman has, the fewer sex acts are needed to establish substantial partible paternity. Husbands tend to be more concerned about their proportion of paternity than are extramarital sex partners.

Men rarely refer to their partible children as *ebakwa* (their own children);[20] it is mainly women who assert the relationship between children and their partible fathers. For example, one might refer to a child as *kewamehocanahe* (conceived secretly) or as Wisibiyahiya (the contraband child of a person named Wisibi). The Ese Eja use of the Spanish term *contrabando* (contraband) to refer to partible children reflects the illicit and secretive quality of the affair and the notion that another man's child is being smuggled into the household.[21]

Ese Eja birth mothers do not make the sort of definitive public announcement of the paternities of their children described for other Amazonian groups, such as the Canela (Crocker and Crocker 1994), the Barí (Beckerman et al. 1998), or the Mehinaku (Gregor 1977).[22] Among the Ese Eja, the identification of secondary fathers and the judgment of their proportional contributions to paternity does not depend on the public affirmation of one woman, but instead results from the (mainly private) allegations and speculations of many. Mothers are generally the ones who inform children of the identity of secondary fathers and, through their admission or denial of an extramarital affair, have the greatest influence on the child's sense of who the fathers are. However, it is clear that other women can also strongly influence peoples' understandings of their paternities. For example, two neighbors who occasionally called each other 'brother' explained, "The old women say that we are mixed."[23]

It is predominantly women who generate and ratify these stories of paternity and women who most directly negotiate appropriate sexual behavior, as illustrated by the following case. A young woman, Sibí,[24] explained that her father's brother, in addition to being her classificatory father is also considered to be her secondary father. She learned this from her father's (and secondary father's) mother, her paternal grandmother. (Because the grandmother had raised Sibí, she was also Sibí's adoptive mother.) Apparently, Sibí's birth mother had had a long affair with her husband's younger brother. Sibí's paternal grandmother had tried to persuade Sibí's birth mother to stop the affair, warning her that most of her children's paternity should belong to her husband: "Oh, how he would fool around with my mother! This is why I am my uncle's [partible child]. [My siblings] are all of my uncle. . . . My grandmother would ask my mother, 'Why are you having so much sex with my young son? Your baby should be purely of your husband!' This is what my grandmother would say to my mother but my mother did not listen, she continued with my uncle." It is interesting that the grandmother not only advises her granddaughter of her partible paternity but also attempts to control the sexual behavior of her daughter-in-law.

More rarely, it is the secondary father himself who reveals his partible paternity. For example, one older man would occasionally jokingly call a young woman 'daughter.' Eventually she confronted her mother, who confirmed her suspicion that there was some foundation to the joke. Men who are accused of being sterile are often the most vocal about identifying their partible children.[25]

Secondary fathers generally do not contribute much to the raising of their partible children. Unlike the Canela (Crocker and Crocker 1994), Ese Eja secondary fathers do not join birth or adoptive parents in the dietary and sexual restrictions that ensure the health of children. And unlike the Aché (Hill and Hurtado 1996), they generally do not contribute game or fish to their partible children's households. On the rare occasions in which food is shared with the household of partible children, the gift is usually motivated by social relationships other than partible parentage, such as kinship.

Occasionally, when a substantial proportion of paternity is attributed to a particular secondary father, that father may be asked to be generous to his partible child. Usually, this happens only when the secondary father has been the mother's husband during part of her pregnancy. When the secondary father is not generous, a child may be told to take the initiative either by soliciting food whenever the secondary father returns from a successful hunt or by stealing from his gardens.

Conversely, a woman may also make the counterargument that her husband is not responsible for another woman's child because their affair was brief. This is evident in the case described above of the woman who complained that her husband's ex-wife's child came begging for food even though the ex-wife had only been three months pregnant at the time of their separation. However, secondary fatherhood is a more important consideration in discussing the marriage prospects of the child than it is in assessing the parental responsibilities of the secondary father.

One of the most important effects of partible paternity is to limit the child's choice of marriage and sex partners. This is because Ese Eja consider the children of their mother's sex partners as partial or partible siblings. They are wapa pojiama (nonmarriageable). Although they rarely address each other in public as brother or sister, they are sometimes referred to as such in private. A marriage between two such partible siblings constitutes memoo (incest) and is unacceptable. Nevertheless, partible siblings occasionally have sexual affairs. If a pregnancy results, it is usually terminated. It is principally when the proportion of ema'i (semen) contributed by the secondary father is considered to be comparable to that of the mother's husband that the child is advised of the secondary paternity. Occasionally the identity of secondary fathers is not revealed until adulthood, especially when secondary fathers live in distant villages and the chances of incestuous relations with partible siblings are limited. There is more urgency in advising a daughter of the identity of her secondary fathers because she runs the risk of seducing them.

Ese Eja have considerable latitude to either recognize or ignore relationships with others based on partible paternity. Often, the consequence of partible paternity is to weaken kin links through men, because relatives often shun the children of a close kinsman if they do believe he has a substantial share in the paternity of the child. This is clearly revealed when kin who are expected to mourn a death do not. For example, on one occasion, the news came that a baby had died but the sister of the mother's husband did not grieve, explaining, "I have no pity because he was not my brother's real son, he was of another man, he was not purely of my brother. This child was damaged. His chest was squashed in, he was crazy. What could it be? Punishment from God? For this reason, . . . it would be a waste of my time to be sad." A woman's motherhood is never questioned in the same way, for obvious reasons. Together with the preference for uxorilocal residence after marriage, partible paternity weakens the importance of the patriline, makes moiety membership ambiguous, and erodes men's political power.

Partible Paternity and Ethnic Identity

To this point, we have discussed partible paternity in an intracultural context. Yet many affairs involve liaisons of Ese Eja with *deja* (non–Ese Eja) partners.[26] The term *deja* is translated into Spanish as *gente*, which conveys a sense of gentility or higher social status. The category can further be differentiated into *deja nei* (true deja [mestizos]), and *deja oshe* or *ichaji oshe* (white deja, white capuchin monkeys [Europeans]). Similarly, the term *Ese Eja* can also refer to indigenous peoples in general or be modified to specify members of the linguistic group: *Ese Eja nei* (true Ese Eja). An intermediate category is labeled *deja nisho* (false deja [Ese Eja who pretend to be deja]). All these terms contrast with *Iñapari* (wild Indians).[27] Although deja is a broad category, the prototypical referents are mestizos and *ribereños*, people of mixed European and Amerindian ancestry who are native Spanish speakers. Yet despite the fact that deja prototypically refers to non–Ese Eja, in all Ese Eja communities there are some individuals who are simultaneously Ese Eja and deja, whether as a result of marriage or, more commonly, extramarital affairs. Almost always, the relationships unite Ese Eja women with deja men. Previously, most of these relationships were with mestizo employers, laborers, and merchants. Presently, they are most often with state health workers and schoolteachers. Most deja secondary fathers deny paternity and do not assume responsibility for the child even when they do not deny it. This is not true of deja men married to Ese Eja women.

Offspring of Ese Eja and deja are perceived by deja as being Ese Eja. They speak Ese Eja and live in the same way as other members of the community. The main difference lies in their being socialized to perceive themselves as being part deja. Being deja gives these persons a status that is associated with literacy, leadership, and merchant abilities even if these associations do not translate into practical or economic outcomes. While having an Ese Eja secondary father might affect one's social and political relationships within the group, having a deja secondary father affects one's social and ethnic identity and the perception of one's personality. It is not unusual for someone to rationalize the clever act of a child by commenting, "He is deja," and to use it in other circumstances as an explanation for why the same child is "lazy." The dual status of deja and Ese Eja often conveys similarly contradictory attributes, as illustrated by the cases of Eduardo and Silvia.

Eduardo is known to outsiders as Ese Eja and to insiders as both Ese Eja and deja. Known as a *brujo* (sorcerer), he is also a wealthy and powerful merchant. Many Ese Eja work for him and are indebted to him. There are many stories about the people he had taken violent vengeance on, about the powers of sorcery that he has harvested from human skulls, about the many brujos in town that he has employed to harm others for him, and about his unfair business practices. Most of these stories depend on the shared understanding that Eduardo is deja. The affair that his mother had had with a mestizo brujo was well known. From this deja secondary father, Eduardo inherited many of the qualities that make him so controversial, including his use of sorcery and his sharp business skills. Both these traits were in turn linked to his desire for power and revenge.

Silvia is another example of a child of an Ese Eja mother (and father) and a deja secondary father. A beautiful, arrogant, aloof woman, Silvia considers herself better than everyone else in the community. She often lectures her neighbors on the "civilized" way of doing things. To mock Silvia's habit of flaunting her partible deja heritage, her neighbors would describe the sexual act that gave her that status in very graphic terms.[28]

For both Eduardo and Silvia, having a deja secondary father conveys both advantages and disadvantages, both social status and social distance. Toward Eduardo, the distance is mainly expressed as fear, toward Silvia mockery.

The direct emotional and material contributions by secondary fathers to their partible children are negligible regardless of whether they are Ese Eja or deja. Some of the examples cited above indicate that children are more likely to be able to extract resources from Ese Eja secondary fathers than from deja ones. Yet having a deja secondary father often provides tangible benefits. For instance, many of the successful community leaders are part deja. The social attributes associated with being deja, such as literacy, assertiveness, and organizational skills, are all perceived as essential for community leadership and for dealing with the outside deja world.

Adoption not only gives a child a new set of parents and siblings but also reconfigures the entire kin network. Some of these effects are minimal, especially when the adopted child lives in the same household as the birth parents. For example, a brother might be revealed to be a nephew. But some changes are more dramatic, as when a sister-in-law is revealed to be one's birth mother or the neighbor is revealed to be one's birth father. As with notification of the identity of secondary father, adopted children are told of their birth parents in late childhood, in time for them to avoid incestuous relationships.

Once an adopted child has knowledge of the birth parents, the child is expected to form a closer relationship with them while simultaneously maintaining a close relationship (*chipiani*) with the adoptive parents. This does not always happen. Many describe feeling awkward or indifferent to their newly discovered family. Revelation of the identity of the birth parents sometimes exposes the adopted child to an additional set of expectations, as when birth parents ask that the child share meat or wild fruits, or help clear, plant, or harvest fields. The new relationship of the birth parents and the child is a subject of scrutiny and gossip by the rest of the community. The child makes a statement about the importance of the new relationship with the degree of conformance to the new set of demands. Both children raised in the same household as their birth parents and children who are reclaimed by their birth parents upon the death of their adoptive parents tend be closer to them than those who are not.

In Ese Eja adoptions, it is not only parents and children that must readjust to the disclosure of an adoption but entire families. One individual who had been raised by his birth father's father once described how he used to relish the nasty gossip his sister used to share with him about his sister-in-law: "We used to make fun of her together and laugh at her since my sister and she did not get along. I feel very bad about this. The day my [adoptive] father died, [brother's name] came to get me. He told me he was my father. I had really thought that he was my brother. That's also when I found out that my sister was really my aunt and that my sister-in-law who I would treat badly was really my mother! I was very embarrassed."

As in the case of partible paternity, the most dramatic changes are the shifts in who is marriageable. When the birth parents are revealed, suddenly some of the people who were wapa (marriageable) may become wapa pojiama (nonmarriageable). While it is acceptable for a woman to marry her father's sister's son (her cross-cousin), it is forbidden for her to marry her brother. Where it is permissible to have an affair with your brother-in-law, it is unacceptable to have an affair with your father. Choice of a partner in marriage or in an affair must be reconciled with the constraints imposed by relationships by birth, relationships by secondary fatherhood, and relationships by adoption. Of course, often these relationships are the subjects of disagreement, making the reckoning of kinship and potential sex partners even more complicated.

Adoption, like partible paternity, ultimately limits the number of potential marriageable partners but expands the family. The status of wapa pojiama (nonmarriageable) does not change when an adopted child is told who its birth parents are. In other words, if a 'brother' is revealed to be a 'cross-cousin,' he does not suddenly become a candidate for marriage, he remains wapa pojiama. An affair with him would be regarded as memoo (incestuous).

Just as a man's share in paternity does not obligate his kin to recognize their relation to his child even when he is the mother's husband, adoptees can also be ignored by kin. A child might belong to the adoptive parents, but it may not necessarily belong to the whole extended family. For example, when Wini traveled from Peru to a community in Bolivia, he expected to stay with his adoptive father's brother's children (his parallel cousins). But he was surprised: "[The family of my adoptive father's brother] did not welcome me. They are mean. I arrived not knowing where to hang my mosquito net, where to eat. At last [my birth mother's sister] came to take me to her house so I could stay with her family. She knew how to welcome me."

One interesting aspect of this case is the mismatch of the valuations of kinship through birth and adoption. Wini values kinship through adoption over kinship through birth, and in his home community he interacts with his birth parents as neighbors, not as parents. In contrast, the adoptive family clearly do not regard their parallel cousin through adoption as kin while his kin through birth clearly do. The example illustrates how the same kin relationship can be variously interpreted.

Sexual Networks

We now explore the pattern of social ties among the married adults of an Ese Eja community generated through their sexual relationships with both marital and nonmarital sex partners. We also examine how the structure of the sexual network relates to kinship ties and other attributes of individuals. The analysis omits relations of these 22 couples with five unmarried sexually active males and two unmarried sexually active females in this community and all relations with individuals in other communities. The sample is thus composed of an equal number of men and women, all of whom are of a comparable marital status.

Our analysis of the sexual network was guided by a number of questions (and their apparent answers): Is it possible to infer from the pattern of sexual relationships preferential marriage patterns? (no); Does the pattern of nonmarital relationships follow the same preferential marriage patterns? (no); What role does kinship play in the recruitment of sex partners? (little); Does one's personal kinship network help in the acquisition of sex partners? (no).

One might have thought that kinship would play a significant role in determining the number of sexual relationships established by each adult. This assumption might be particularly true for males, such that men with extensive kin networks (particularly through women) might through these women find nonmarital sex partners. This was not the case. If anything, men with substantial numbers of female kin in the community had slightly fewer partners than those with smaller networks (perhaps due to incest prohibitions), though this difference was not statistically significant.

Table 8.1. Matrix of Ese Eja sexual relationships

	a	b	c	d	e	f	g	h	i	j	k	l	m	n	o	p	q	r	s	t	u	v	
A	1	0	0	0	0	1	0	1	0	0	0	0	0	0	0	0	0	0	0	0	0	0	3
B	0	1	0	1	0	0	0	1	1	0	0	0	0	0	0	0	0	0	0	0	0	0	4
C	0	0	1	0	0	0	0	0	0	0	0	0	0	0	0	0	0	0	0	0	0	0	1
D	0	0	0	1	0	0	0	0	0	0	0	0	0	0	0	0	0	0	0	0	0	0	1
E	0	0	0	0	2	0	0	0	0	0	0	0	0	0	0	0	0	0	0	0	0	0	2
F	0	0	0	0	0	2	0	0	0	0	0	0	0	0	0	0	0	0	0	0	0	0	2
G	0	0	0	1	0	0	2	0	0	0	0	0	1	0	0	0	0	0	0	0	0	0	4
H	0	0	0	0	0	0	0	1	0	0	0	0	0	0	0	0	0	0	0	0	0	0	1
I	0	0	0	0	0	0	0	0	1	0	0	0	0	0	0	0	0	0	0	0	0	0	1
J	0	0	0	0	0	0	0	0	0	2	0	0	0	0	0	0	0	0	0	0	0	0	2
K	0	0	0	0	0	0	0	0	0	0	2	0	0	0	0	0	0	0	0	0	0	0	2
L	0	0	1	1	0	0	0	0	0	0	0	1	1	0	0	0	0	0	1	0	0	0	5
M	0	0	0	0	0	0	0	0	0	0	0	0	2	0	0	0	0	0	0	0	0	0	2
N	0	0	0	0	0	0	0	0	0	0	0	0	0	2	0	0	0	0	0	0	0	0	2
O	0	0	0	0	0	0	0	0	0	0	0	0	0	0	1	0	0	0	0	0	0	0	1
P	0	0	0	0	0	0	0	0	0	0	0	0	0	0	0	1	0	0	0	1	0	0	2
Q	0	0	0	0	0	0	0	0	0	0	0	0	0	0	0	0	1	0	0	0	0	0	1
R	0	0	0	0	0	0	0	0	0	0	0	0	0	0	0	0	0	1	0	0	0	0	1
S	0	0	0	0	0	0	0	0	0	0	0	0	0	0	0	0	0	0	2	1	0	0	3
T	0	0	0	0	0	0	0	0	0	0	0	0	0	0	0	0	0	0	0	2	0	0	2
U	0	0	0	0	0	0	0	0	0	0	0	0	0	0	0	0	0	0	0	0	1	0	1
V	0	0	0	1	0	0	0	0	0	0	0	0	0	0	0	0	0	0	0	0	0	1	2
	1	1	2	5	2	3	2	3	2	2	2	1	4	2	1	1	1	1	3	4	1	1	45

Table 8.1 summarizes these sexual relationships. In this matrix, the rows represent men, the columns represent women, and the number in each cell represents the type of relationship (2 for a marital relationship, 1 for a nonmarital sexual relationship, 0 for no sexual relationship).

Figure 8.1 represents the same data in the form of a network diagram. It shows a three-dimensional representation of the main part of the network, with individuals arranged by their proximity to each other in the sexual network. Married couples have been labeled with the letters A through V, with the capital letter used to denote the husband and the lowercase to denote the wife. Thus A is married to a, B is married to b, and so on. This figure omits the six couples who are not connected with the rest of the network: three couples have relations only with each other; the other three are connected to each other but not

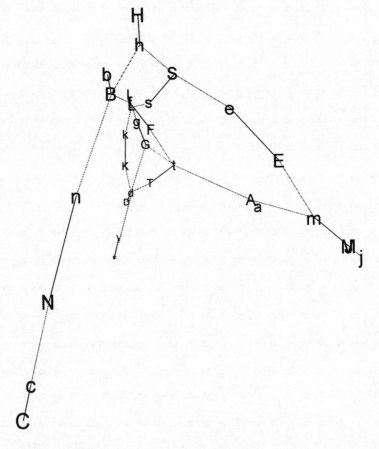

Fig. 8.1. Network diagram of Ese Eja sexual relationships

to the rest of the network. Spouses are connected by heavy (black) lines and extramarital partners by light (gray) lines.

Figure 8.2 shows the pattern of parent-child links, using the same configuration of individuals as in figure 8.1. Because of incest prohibitions, the pattern of kinship relationships does not overlap with the pattern of sexual relationships. It is also evident that the kin ties are much more numerous than the sexual ties and crosscut them, binding distant parts of the sexual network together. Not shown here (because it would make the diagram too confusing) are ties between children and adoptive parents and between children and secondary fathers. Suffice it to say that the total network of relationships is both dense and complex.

The overall structure of the network reflects the fact that not all individuals

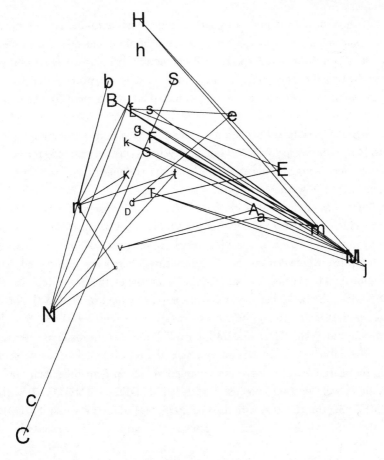

Fig. 8.2. Network diagram of Ese Eja parent-child links

are equally sexually active in it. The network can be described as composed of three spiny projections connecting relatively isolated individuals to a more densely interconnected core group. In the first projection, husband C is connected to wife c, who is connected to husband N, who is connected to wife n, who is connected to husband B, who is connected to wives b, h, and f. In the second projection, wife j is connected to husbands M and J, who are connected to wife m, who is connected to husbands D and A and, through them, to the rest of the group. This pair of couples, M and J, constitute the only set of spouse-exchanging couples—all other relationships were not reciprocated, as discussed below. In the third projection, wife v is connected to husband V, who is connected to wife e, who is connected to husbands K and T. Connections among the core couples (E, K, G, T, F, S, L, H, and B) are too numerous to enumerate.

Because we are examining a subset of individuals with the same number of men as women, the mean number of sexual relations of the men and women is the same: on average one spouse and one nonmarital partner. However, patterns of sexual relationships in other groups lead us to expect greater variance in the number of sex partners among women than among men. For example, in Gregor's sexual ethnography of the Mehinaku (1985), the women had half again as high a standard deviation of sexual contacts as men did, ranging from 0 to 14 in a community with 20 adult men. What is surprising among the Ese Eja is that there is no significant difference in the variance of the number of sex partners had by women and men.

There was no discernible kin-based preference for partners, whether inside or outside of marriage. While preferential cross-cousin marriage may be the norm in many Amazonian societies, very few (less than 20%) of the sexual relationships were between first or second cousins. There were no reported sexual relationships between closer kin. Of the 22 marriages, the closest link was that of S with s, he being her father's matrilateral cross-cousin [FMFSS]. Among nonmarital relationships, the closest links were S with e [MFSS], S with h [MFSS], and T with d [MFSS, MMSS]. In all three cases, the man is the woman's matrilateral cross-cousin. It is interesting that three of these four cases (including the marital case) involve the same individual, S. Four other pairs of sex partners were second cousins [I with i: FMFDDS, FMMDDS; T with t: MMFDSS, MMMDSS; K with d: MMFDDS, MMMDDS; P with i: FMFDDS, FMMDDS]. All the remaining 37 pairs of sex partners had no traceable relationship.

We had hoped to systematically collect judgments of the relative physical attractiveness and work skills of the members of the community. Unfortunately, informants found this task tedious and unpleasant and ultimately the data proved impossible to collect. However, anecdotal evidence suggests that this comparison would not have yielded an explanation of the variation in the number of sex partners. For example, the best hunter in the community had no nonmarital relationships while, at the other extreme, the man with the largest number of sexual relationships was widely perceived as lazy and not particularly physically attractive.

Even though the record is of cumulative lovers acquired, there is no clear cumulative increase in the numbers of lovers reported with age. This could have several possible explanations (a cohort effect, whereby younger individuals have more lovers than earlier cohorts; a memory bias such that older individuals forget or deny more of their partners). However, instead of generational difference or bias in reporting, the most likely explanation is twofold. First, individuals have most of their nonmarital relationships in their youth; second, since the village was founded 20 years ago many of the youthful partners of the older members of the community have been left behind and have been lost to our sample.

Although there was one case of a reciprocal exchange relationship in which a pair of couples exchanged spouses with each other, this was unusual. All 21 of the other nonmarital relationships were not reciprocal. Thus, in general, the nonmarital relationships are not exchanging spouses. It is this nonreciprocity that gives rise to one of the most interesting properties of the sexual network. As suggested by the sparse, filigree quality of figure 8.1, the network is very nearly a minimal spanning tree, connecting most of the adults of the community with relatively few extramarital relationships. A complete minimal spanning tree would require that every married adult has one (and only one) extramarital partner and avoids an affair with his or her spouse's extramarital partner's spouse (no swapping). Although this sort of structure would facilitate the transmission of STDs (which are thankfully rare), it also may help to bind the community together. We do not know for certain whether there is a deliberate avoidance of spouse swapping, but the following case (which occurred after the ethnographic present of this chapter) may be an exception that proves the rule. The young bride of V, v deliberately seduced D, the husband of d, who was having an affair with V, v's husband. She did it to *joder* (Spanish: screw over) d, her husband's extramarital partner. Apparently, this led to the dissolution of v's marriage to V; V subsequently married d, and v left the community. This case may indicate why spouse exchange is avoided; in this case, it led to divorce. Certainly v's description of her seduction of d's former husband, as a means of getting revenge on d, suggests that the seduction was an act of hostility directed toward her rival for her (now former) husband's attention. We need more ethnographic reports of Amazonian sexual networks to determine whether avoidance of spouse exchange is a recurring feature of them.

Conclusions

We have argued that among the Ese Eja, both paternity and maternity are partible, through the institutions of secondary fatherhood and adoption, respectively. By acknowledging secondary fathers, women weaken kin links through males and create ambiguity in the patri-moiety system. Conversely, the practice of adoption strengthens links through women by favoring matrilineal kin as recipients of adopted children. Both secondary fatherhood and adoption limit a child's potential marriage and sex partners but expand the child's social networks. Although there are some economic benefits to having a secondary father, there are greater social and political benefits, especially in the case of secondary deja fathers. No simple explanation accounts for the structure of the sexual network: the number of partners is not determined by factors such as size of kin networks, physical attractiveness, or productive capacity. The real pattern appears to be complex. We hope that future research can illuminate and explain some of this complexity.

Authors' note: A preliminary version of this paper was presented in the session "Paternidad compartida en las tierras bajas de Sudamerica" (Stephen Beckerman and Paul Valentine, organizers) at the 49th International Congress of Americanists, Quito, July 9, 1997. We are profoundly indebted to the Ese Eja for their guidance, kindness, and hospitality. Daniela Peluso's doctoral fieldwork (1993–96) was supported by grants from the Social Science Research Council, Fulbright IIE, the Wenner-Gren Foundation for Anthropological Research, and American Women in Science. She is also grateful to the FENAMAD (Madre de Dios, Peru), CIRABO (Beni, Bolivia), and INRENA (Lima and Madre de Dios, Peru). Special thanks to Miguel Alexiades, Robin Goodman, and Steven Rubenstein for their comments on an earlier draft and to Stephen Beckerman and Paul Valentine for their work in editing this volume. We thank Michael Brown for his original observation that Ese Eja maternity as well as paternity was partible. We also wish to thank Emi Yamamoto Peluso for the translation of Kimura 1983.

Notes

1. The term *secondary father* refers to "partible" (Beckerman et al. 1998) or "multiple" male parents (Gregor 1985). Crocker and Crocker (1994, 83) use the

terms *co-father* and *contributing father* interchangeably to refer to the same concept. Carneiro (n.d.) coined the phrase *multiple paternity*.

2. Ese Eja is the self-denomination and means "true people." The Spanish terms Guarayo and Chama, used for the Ese Eja in Peru and Bolivia respectively, are considered pejorative. At other times, the Ese Eja have been referred to as Chuncho, Tiatinagua, Echoja, Mohino, Moino, Moeno, Mohiño, Pacaguara, and Toromona. As is often the case, these names have been used rather indiscriminately by different authors for different ethnic groups, creating considerable confusion (Alexiades 1999, 84).

3. The Ese Eja are one of several Panoan groups showing evidence of a moiety system, including the Amahuaca (Dole 1979) and the Cashinahua, Capanahua, Matis, Matses, and Sharanahua (Kensinger 1995).

4. Icha are believed to be hairier and better hunters than kaka.

5. In the Tambopata Ese Eja communities uxorilocality is no longer commonly practiced. In other communities, there is considerable variation in postmarital residence.

6. Kin systems also extend into "the world of the dead." The *emanokwana*, spirits of deceased kin, continue to reproduce among themselves and foster new relationships with living kin through participation in emanokwana ceremonies.

7. The practice, never common, appears to be dying out.

8. This expectation is not extended to unmarried adolescent boys having affairs with married women.

9. Also referred to as *we'e* and *we'pojiama* (Kimura 1983; Jack Schoemacher, notes, Cochabamba, Bolivia).

10. While the Ese Eja clearly favor meat over fish, fish provides a more important and regular source of protein in some communities, especially those with higher population densities, where game has been depleted. Up to the last century, Ese Eja subsistence had been more dependent on hunting, with different prey harvested in each season. In the rainy season, men traveled deep into the interior to hunt spider monkeys, while in the dry season, extended families would travel downriver to exploit turtle eggs, bird eggs, and game close to the river. Swiddens were cultivated at different points along the river, providing these foraging groups with a reliable supply of plantains (*plátanos; ejawi*). Although plantains remain the main staple, their cultivation has declined in some communities, due partly to the lack of adequate soils and partly to the growing cultivation of rice as a staple and commercial crop. In short, the ecological changes and market forces following increased sedentarization have prompted a decline in the importance of hunting with greater reliance on fishing, a decline in the importance of plantains with increasing intensive rice cultivation, and a decline in the broad-spectrum gathering of forest products with more focused exploitation of brazil nuts. See Alexiades 1999 for a more detailed description of changes in Ese Eja subsistence practices over the past century.

11. If the hunter has hunted communally, as happens in the case of hunting white-lipped peccaries, he will distribute the meat to those in his hunting party who came home empty-handed.

12. *Tiiani* means to mature or to become old; *-tii* implies "old" when used as a suffix with nouns referring to people (e.g., *eponatii,* old woman; *ettii,* old person).

13. In most cases, polygyny is sororal and polygynous mothers are classificatory mothers also.

14. We use the term *sharing* of children since the Ese Eja use the Spanish word *compartir,* but the term *borrowing* has often been used in the anthropological literature as "an arrangement by which a child is not considered adopted but is temporarily or permanently cared for by a kinsman of the parent" (Geertz 1961, 39–40). This option is often pursued when the original household of the child has become too large or when, as often happens, the grandparents have a special affinity with a particular child.

15. In the cases of shared and foster parentage, the previous categories of relatedness do not change.

16. The core meaning of *wojani* is the same as that of the English term *adoption:* the raising of another person's child as one's own. We use the term *adoption* as a gloss in this core sense without many of the additional connotations associated with the Western concept of legal adoption.

17. The Ese Eja case appears to be a counterexample to the relationship between the rate of adoption and the rate of infertility proposed by Goodenough (1970).

18. *Etiimee* is literally translated as "to cause one to grow old," and *etiimeeji* as "those who cause one to grow old." The terms appear to emphasize the sustaining role of adoptive parents in contrast to the procreative role of birth parents (cf. *tiiani*).

19. This is similar to Canela beliefs (Crocker and Crocker 1994, 85). Usually more than one act is required to establish substantial partible paternity.

20. Kimura (1983) has stated that men refer to their partible children with the terms *eheawa* for males and *eheaji* for females. For Kimura, *eheawa* and *eheaji* refer to the results of the biological act of the procreation of offspring, without implying an emotional attachment to the child, comparable to the English word *spawn.* However, we are unable to confirm this. Perhaps the term *eheawa* was used for such cases since it literally means "to come and father"; but *eheaji* is a word for father, used to refer to another person's father. (Again, one refers to one's own father by his moiety, icha or kaka.)

21. *Contrabando* (alternatively, *contrabarado*) is an idiom in Spanish and Portuguese used in this sense in many other parts of Amazonia (Miguel Pinedo-Vasquez, pers. comm.).

22. As Gregor (1977) notes, the authority of the pregnant woman to assert paternity allows her to choose to deny her involvement with a man she has come to regret having had sex with.

23. These individuals are believed to be "doubly mixed," meaning that both of their mothers had had frequent sexual relations with both fathers. This kind of spouse swapping is reasonably rare.

24. This and all other personal names used in the text are pseudonyms. We

have followed the convention of using Ese Eja pseudonyms for individuals primarily known by their Ese Eja names, and Spanish pseudonyms for individuals primarily known by their Spanish names. Most people have both.

25. In one case, a man has claimed paternity of a child that was born many
years after his wife had left him.

26. See Alexiades 1999 for a discussion of the concept of *deja* and its implications for resource use.

27. Strictly speaking Iñapari refers to an ethnic group, Harakmbut perhaps,
which was effectively wiped out through contact with the nation-state at the turn
of the last century. Ese Eja oral history includes many instances of skirmishes and
other forms of exchange with this group. The Iñapari, in the cultural imagination
of the Ese Eja, represent naked wildness. Hence, they call the Iñapari *los calatos*.

28. They used the Spanish phrase "ha puesto el culo en el aire a la mamá de
Silvia" (he put Silvia's mother's rump in the air).

9

Fathering in the Northwest Amazon of Brazil

Competition, Monopoly, and Partition

Janet M. Chernela

Along the margins of the Uaupés River in Brazil, when a Tukanoan father ritually bathes to mark the birth of his new offspring, he may find other men prac-
ticing the same paternity rite for the same child. Yisido, a Tukano of the Uaupés
River,[1] claimed that this was a common occurrence among his distant Tukano
relatives. From his statement it is impossible to determine the incidence of "co-
fathering." However, in the northwest Amazon of Brazil, shared paternity is a
recognized possibility, albeit an undesirable one.

Speakers of Eastern Tukanoan languages, numbering over 10,000,[2] form one
of the largest remaining coherent indigenous culture complexes in Amazonian
South America. Occupying an area of approximately 150,000 square kilometers at the forested headwater streams of the Rio Negro in Colombia, Brazil,
and Venezuela, this population consists of fifteen or more intermarrying and
linguistically distinct patriclans.

Kenneth Kensinger (1995) refers to "real" society, that is, a notion of society
that includes practical actions and the ideas regarding how practical life is, as
well as ought to be, lived. His approach follows the traditions of Kenneth Pike
and Ward Goodenough, who introduced and developed the concepts "emic"
and "etic." According to this system, emic models are the endogenous taxo-
nomic structures implicit in local speech and action, both conscious and uncon-
scious, while etic concepts are those of the anthropologist. Kensinger points to
the logical and dialectical relationship of the two analytic concepts. "An emic
model," he writes, "cannot be a mere translation or rewording of informants'
statements; nor can it be restricted to such statements. It must be based both on

what they say and on what they do; it must define marriage as opposed to nonmarriage within Cashinahua society and as compared to marriage in American, Nuer, Trobriand, or Japanese society" (1995, 122). The two are in dialectical relationship to one another. Etic categories and concepts, developed by anthropologists, provide the basis for comparison of different cultures, thus contributing to a general science of culture.

In this chapter I present the naturalizing ideology endogenous to notions of birthing and fathering, as well as practices associated with them, among the Eastern Tukanoan speakers of the northwest Amazon. In doing so I reconsider the prevailing assumptions regarding the nuclear family and clan as received from classical Malinowskian social anthropology.

I use the terms *patriclan* and *clan* here, in place of the term *sib*, which has gained currency in contemporary anthropological literature, in order to better juxtapose the present argument with former ones. The terms *sib* and *clan* are synonymous, referring to a kin group whose members assume, but need not demonstrate, descent from a common ancestor. (*Sib* is used only in cases where reckoning is patrilineal, whereas *clan* may be used for both matrilineal and patrilineal systems of reckoning.) In addition to recognizing a kindred based on a putative ancestor, each Tukanoan patriclan is an out-marrying unit, recognized by a distinct language and a name. I will refer to these entities as language groups following Jackson (1974). I use the term *Tukanoan* to refer to any member of the Eastern Tukanoan family of languages and the terms *Tukano*, *Desana*, or *Wanano* to refer to a specific group within that linguistic family.

My example is taken from one of the 15 to 20 linguistically distinct language groups of the region, the Tukanoan Wanano,[3] located along the Uaupés River in Colombia and Brazil.[4] Brazil's 10 Wanano settlements are situated from 3 to 24 kilometers apart along the middle course of the main river,[5] from Jandhu in Brazil to Uarucapury in Colombia.[6] Established settlements contain from 30 to 160 persons. I estimate the total Wanano population in Brazil to number between 500 and 600. When we add the approximately 180 Wanano who live on the southern, Colombian bank of the Uaupés, and the 800 Wanano cited by Waltz (n.d.) as living in the upriver Colombian portion of the Uaupés, the Wanano population totals some 1,500 to 1,600 individuals. This population refers to village composition and therefore includes in-marrying wives who, as we will see, are members of Eastern Tukanoan groups other than Wanano.

Wanano villages are situated on high ground at the river edge. The occupational area is cleared of all vegetation and houses face onto an open plaza. Numerous small trails lead from the residential clearing through the surrounding forest to distant gardens. The Wanano are fishermen and horticulturalists, with fish providing the principal source of protein, and the root crop manioc the principal source of carbohydrates. These items, and the utensils used to gather or process them, are essential to the sharing of resources that occurs informally within a village on a daily basis, and more intermittently and formally among several settlements. Minimal exploitation of resources characterizes day-to-day life; intensive exploitation occurs prior to occasional elaborate exchange ceremonies. The activities are gender-specific, with men fishing and women farming.

Debates Then and Now

In writings on the family that are now considered classic, Bronislaw Malinowski attributes three defining characteristics to the nuclear family: it is a social and biological unit, consisting of a socially defined mother, father, and offspring; a residential unit; and a unit of production and consumption. He explicitly distinguishes the nuclear family from the larger entity known as the clan: "The family is always the domestic institution par excellence. . . . The clan, on the other hand, is never a domestic institution. . . . Bonds of clanship develop . . . out of the primary kinship of the family . . . and play no role in reproduction or childcare." In further contrasting family and clan, he writes, "The clan functions in an entirely different sphere of interests: legal, economic, and above all ceremonial. Once the functional distinction is made between the two modes of grouping, the family and the clan, most of the spurious problems and fictitious explanations dissolve into the speculative mist out of which they were born" (1930a, 22).

In criticizing his predecessors in debates that characterized the British anthropology of the 1930s, Malinowski describes as "absurd" the notion of the clan as a reproductive unit: "These actors are obviously three in number at the beginning—the two parents and their offspring. . . . This unquestionably correct principle has become at the hands of some modern anthropologists the starting point for a new interpretation of Morgan's hypothesis of a primitive communal marriage. Rivers, the most conspicuous modern supporter of Morgan's theories, is fully aware that group-marriage implies group-parenthood. Yet group-parenthood [is] an almost unthinkable hypothesis. . . . All the primitive theories of procreation . . . invariably define parenthood as an individual bond" (23). Moreover, he adds, "This conclusion has led to such capital howlers as that "the clan marries the clan and begets the clan" and that "the clan, like the family, is a reproductive group"(24).

Malinowski's position has prevailed and is now deeply embedded in anthropological definitions and assumptions regarding the family. However, data presented in this chapter and elsewhere in this volume (see also Beckerman et al. 1998) challenge the assumptions made by Malinowski that *sociologically defined* conception could not allow for multiple progenitors, and that fatherhood roles may only reside in a single individual.

The Tukanoan case raises a number of significant questions in this regard. As that case demonstrates, a clan may fulfill many of the criteria relegated by Malinowski to the nuclear family. Among Eastern Tukanoan speakers fatherhood *may* be attributed to more than one man, in theory. In the absence of claims to the contrary, however, the husband of the child's mother is the designated social father. Fatherly behavior is expected of all the males of a local clan toward all the young of the clan. As we will see, the multiple aspects of caretaking, including affection and food getting, are provided by all clansmen. A child's identity, furthermore, is linked to the patriclan, a principle made explicitly manifest when the clan takes precedence over the mother's possession of children in the event of her husband's death. Indeed, it is only in the most individual sense of identity that mother's husband holds a monopoly as pater. Yet, this, too, may be contested, as we will see.

Ethnographic Background

Social Organization: Siblingship

In the northwest Amazon, as I have said, group configuration is organized according to principles of unilineal descent from a common patrilineal ancestor. Individual patriclans are, in turn, connected to one another through a rule of compulsory out-marriage, known in anthropological parlance as exogamy. Intermarriage across linguistically separate patriclans results in an unusually coherent and homogeneous cultural matrix of diverse language groups. The further preference for marriage to a cross-cousin creates a tightly knit network of relationship ties throughout the region.

The Tukanoan system of classification supposes a nested hierarchy of inclusiveness, where the reference point at each level of inclusiveness is a putative named ancestor who emblemizes or stands for his descendants. The living reckon affiliation on the basis of patrilineal descent from a specific totemic ancestor, though this descent is stipulated or putative rather than demonstrated. At each level of inclusiveness a different pivotal ancestor becomes relevant, and thus a different calculus of membership is applied. Starting at the lowest level of inclusiveness, an individual is a member of a local patrilineal descent group,[7] known as "the children of X" where X is the founding ancestor. At a slightly higher level of magnitude all the local descent units of a single language group consider themselves to be descended from a single focal ancestor, and, on that basis, a unified whole. At the highest level of inclusiveness, descendants of ancestral brothers, each the ancestor of a separate language group, consider themselves to be in phratric, or brotherhood, relation to one another. At each level, the name and recognition of a focal, totemic ancestor unites persons into a putative brotherhood.

The term *koroa* reflects the overarching principle of patrilineality applied to any level of social organization. It is used by the Wanano to refer to any of the mentioned descent-ordered, exogamous units, independent of magnitude level. By combining the ancestor's name with the suffix *-pona* (children of) or by adding the affixes denoting persons, *-küro* (masc.) or *-koro* (fem.),[8] the members of a koroa identify themselves to one another and to others as close kin. Referring to one another as *korokü* (male) or *koroka* (female), members of the same koroa signal affectivity and intimacy analogous to the English phrases "peas in a pod" or "birds of a feather." Membership may not move across the koroa of any given level, as affiliation is based solely on one's inherited status as member of a patrilineal descent group, and that membership is exclusive. The notion of koroa thus establishes an in-group with far-reaching ties of solidarity (extending from members of the clan to all members of the language group), and expressed in terms conveying social proximity. The potential for both inclusiveness and exclusiveness is strong.

As one koroa, the Wanano regard themselves as agnates descended from one of the founding ancestors born of the body of an ancestral anaconda. Originating downriver at a site known as Milk Lake, the primordial anaconda is said to have journeyed upriver until its arrival at the Uaupés River. There the supernatural anaconda turned round, and from the segments of its body emerged the first ancestors of each of the localized patriclans of the Uaupés river basin. The dispersion of social groups from the anaconda body represents a socio-topographical order that establishes the relations between spatial orientation, descent, and seniority.

Clan litanies, sung on the occasion of visiting settlements, reify and authorize settlement histories by canonizing ancestral precedence. Based on these chanted histories, each patriclan has a designated location in space, said to be the "sitting-and-breathing" place (*duhisina*) of that group. In the proper placement of a patriline, the realms of the living and the ancestors are bridged as their souls are recycled. It is only through continuity in descent-space that an ancestral spirit may return to the place where the ancestors "sat-and-breathed." (Families may be out of place, but this removal simply reinforces the model of things as they should be and may not always be.) The specificity of placement is regarded as critical and disputes over ancestral rights can lead to violence. The preferred state of *duhisina* (sitting-and-breathing) contrasts with the negatively valued states of wandering (*thinari*) or "mixing" (*sü'sari*),[9] discussed below (and see Chernela 1993, 1988a).

The Wanano recall their dead by name, speak about them at length, and inscribe their memories into a topographical nomenclature. Space functions to represent history, as lithographs and stone formations in the river indicate ancestral events and the "houses" that mark those events. The river as such is an encapsulation of history, a reading of positions and origins, a codex in which are inscribed the signs of history and the rights and relations of the living by virtue of the dead.

Recall that a patriclan—no matter what level of magnitude—is an out-marrying unit, with rules of incest requiring that a person marry into a different patriline than one's own. In the system of kinship nomenclature, patrilineal relatives are identified as kin, whereas matrilateral relations fall within a category that may be translated as "in-law" or "cross-cousin."[10] The implications of this will be clarified below.

The term for father is *pükü*,[11] composed of the morphemes *pük-*, denoting parental (+1) generation, and the gender suffix *-ü*, denoting masculine referent. Terms for father's brothers—*pükübü'ü*, for father's younger brother, and *püküwa'mi*, for father's older brother—combine the noun stem *pükü* for father with affixes that designate the relative ages (seniority) of father and father's brothers. Terms for father's siblings extend to persons of father's generation throughout the language group and are also used for members of different language groups within the same phratry. Father's sister, however, as well as all female Wanano of first ascending generation, is denoted by the very different term *wamanyo*. The term refers to a woman, who, it must be remembered, is likely to become a child's mother-in-law.

A man addresses and refers to the offspring of all male kinsmen ("brothers") in his generation as *makü* (masc.) and *mako* (fem.). These terms, also used in speaking to his own offspring, gloss as own son and daughter. Parallel nephews and nieces are prohibited as marriage partners to ego's children. They will be called "my child" by all the males of the descent group. In contrast, the children of a man's sister, who may never be of his own descent group, are addressed by him as *paka makü/o*, emphasizing their separate identities. These cross-nephews and nieces are the preferred marriage partners for a person's own child. When the rules of restricted exchange are followed, son's wife will be male ego's *paka mako*, and female ego's *papüko*. These terms may also be applied to the children of all Wanano females of ego's generation.

Relatives who are of the same generation and language group refer to one another as siblings, employing *wami/o*, for "older" brother and sister, or *bü'ü/ ba'o*, for "younger" brother and sister. These kinsmen, it may be remembered, are forbidden as marriage partners. The ideal is to marry one's own father's sister's child or mother's brother's child (cross-cousins), who is sometimes the same person. This preferred marriage partner is called *tanyü* (masc.) or *tanyo* (fem.).

Although membership in a clan is acquired at birth, it is institutionalized through various means throughout an individual's lifetime. One of the most important of these is the naming ceremony, at which a child receives a clan ancestral name bequeathed by his father and his father's clan brothers. To a Tukanoan, the bearer of an ancestral name is the "exchange" for that ancestor, his transformation or incarnation in the present. This exchange principle cycles clan names down through the generations, perpetuating a socio-spatial order that is, ideally, replicated in every generation.

One generation of brothers generates another through the name exchange. The male line of men structures descent and generational time, linking descendant with ancestor, present and future with past. Although women participate in synchronic linkages, connecting different descent groups, they are virtually absent from the descent model of reproduction.

Language and Descent

Another prominent means by which clanship is manifest is through speech. At the center of social and political life of the patrilocal village is a monolingual cluster of agnatic kin consisting of males, considered to be brothers, and their children. As sexual relations are forbidden within the extended siblinghood of the language group, spouses must be members of a language group other than one's own (see also C. Hugh-Jones 1979; S. Hugh-Jones 1979; Jackson 1974, 1983; and Sorensen 1967 for similar findings for other Eastern Tukanoan groups).[12] The monolingual fraternal core of the village contrasts poignantly with the speech diversity apparent among in-marrying wives, whose speech points to their outsidedness. They derive from distant locations and speak several different languages. In the context of the settlement into which they have married, wives are considered to be "alien" or "other" (*paye masuno* glosses as 'other' or 'outsider' in Wanano). As speakers of languages other than that of the local descent group in which they reside, married women are said to be "mixers" (*sü'sari mahsa*), or "other people" (*paye mahsa*), pointing to their exclusion from the patriclan at the village core. In the Wanano village of Yapima, in which I conducted fieldwork, the eight in-marrying wives derived from five different language groups, and continued, after their marriages, to speak the languages of their natal villages. The combined practices of patrilineal descent reckoning and virilocal postmarital residence further the solidarity of a resident male brotherhood and exacerbate the social distances of women. Although in-marrying wives may form affective bonds with one another, numerous factors limit their impact as a formal, cohesive, political power. For most women, input into village-level politics takes the form of informal social criticism.

The social position of a wife vis-à-vis the clan settlement into which she has married is most salient when a man dies, for then his children remain with his agnatic kin. A widow who chooses to remarry outside the patriclan of her deceased husband must leave her children in the local descent group to which their deceased father, and they, belong. When, in the course of my fieldwork, a widow attempted to surreptitiously carry off her children to the village of a new husband, the children were captured and returned by the deceased husband's clansmen.

Devaluation of Mother's Language

The most prominent vehicle through which descent identity is produced and reproduced is speech. As a manifestation of descent, linguistic performance is closely monitored with consistency and loyalty to father's language strongly valued.[13] A child is aware of both mother's and father's languages from infancy, but is socialized to speak only father's language.

If a child speaks any language other than father's, he or she is ostracized. One child, raised among his Wanano kin, was thought to be the offspring of a passing Colombian trader. This child was told often that Wanano was *not* his language, and he must not speak it. "You are Colombian," he was told, "and you should speak Colombian." The assumption that the linguistic identity of the father should be that of the child well illustrates the Tukanoan model of paternity, language, and personal and group identity. For Tukanoans, language indexes the paternal tie.

It may then be said that fatherhood, for the Tukano, is constructed through speech—through language-in-use. The child must learn to distinguish the two parental languages and discern which is appropriate to verbalize and which not. In effective linguistic socialization, a child learns to accept the differential values placed on mother's and father's languages and to fear the negative conse-quences of uttering mother's language. Overt instruction provides the child with signals that mother's tongue has no social or public value. As the align-ment of like and unlike self is established in the course of Tukanoan lan-guage acquisition, mother's language and kin, linguistically and emotionally "close," are reconstructed as "distant" and "other"; while father's language and kin, linguistically and emotionally "distant," are reconstructed as "close" and "self."

The Incest Taboo

It will be recalled that members of the same generation refer to one another by one of two terms: sibling, for those who speak the same language and recog-nize the same ancestry, and cross-cousin, for speakers of all other Eastern Tukanoan languages. The terms *brother* and *sister,* applied to members of the same language group, carry the connotation of own group or family. In con-trast, the terms for cross-cousins (Wanano, *tanyü* and *tanyo:* persons of the same generation related through parents of different sexes) carry strong con-notations of "otherness," sexuality, and potential marriage.

When a Desana bachelor confided in me that the young Wanano women in whose village we were both guests, "treated their consanguines as though they were cross-cousins," he implied that the girls did not limit sexual encounters to cross-cousins, as they should have. As a bachelor in the cross-cousin category, and the only available nonincestuous partner to the young Wanano women in the village, his remark must be understood as that of a spurned aspirant.

The strictly maintained incest taboo forbidding marriage or sexual relations with anyone of one's own language group leaves as the only permissible sexual partners members of other language groups—in other words, a speaker's cross-cousins. Indeed, several nuanced usages of the cross-cousin terms con-vey sexual overture. In a local village, the only nonkin—and therefore nonincestuous partners to clan members—are the in-marrying wives of their agnates.

Discretion and Demarcation

On the basis of information conveyed to me by speakers about others, and in a few cases substantiated by the person reported upon, most of the married women I came to know over time had several lovers. These sexual partners were most frequently a woman's husband's brothers and nephews, if only because they resided in the same village. (Relatedly, one of the most common forms of introduction into sexual life for a young man is through his father's brother's wife, who may also be his mother's sister.)

The casual extramarital encounters married women carry out are normally conducted with extreme discretion. "Raw" sex, sex with a partner other than one's spouse, should be kept at a distance from the parameters of the domestic space, within which the monogamous unit is an integral element in the configuration of daily social life. Extramarital liaisons occur without recrimination if they take place with discretion away from the village and among nonincestuous partners.

Remote gardens, dispersed in the forest and accessible only by trails or streams, are regarded as women's domains. Most gardens contain makeshift overhangs or lean-tos to which hammocks can be attached, making convenient trysting places. The spatial demarcation between field and homesite differentiates the official from the unofficial, the legitimate from the casual, the social from the nonsocial. No indication of an affair should be registered publicly. Raw sex is "unseen," an occurrence that occupies a "time out of time."

Perceived Resemblances

Although lovers attempt to keep their meetings covert, "outings" of lovers occur both in informal gossip as well as in public, ceremonial settings where spontaneously composed songs are one form of social commentary. This outing is especially prominent in occasions involving visiting in-law clans, known as po'oa. In the po'oa, comportment moves from "formal" to "informal" (see also Goldman 1963), from ancestral litanies and rhetorical speaking at the outset, to flirtation songs and gossip songs at the close. Potential sexual partners sing openly flirtatious songs in which the repeated refrain, "My cross-cousin," signals sexual innuendo, advance, and, possibly, invitation.

Women's songs to one another frequently disclose everyday social relationships among villagers. In spontaneously composed songs by women performers to women listeners, the names of alleged lovers are revealed and suspicions aired. In the course of a song a woman may point to a perceived resemblance between a child and one of the mother's lovers, inciting a conflict between social pater and other potential biological fathers. For example, a singer may announce that a woman's children resemble one of the woman's lovers. One Desana woman teased that the children of her husband's brothers strongly resembled her adult bachelor son. A Tukano mother sang that her own child resembled another adult male, introducing uncertainties regarding the paternity of her own offspring. More typically, liaisons go unacknowledged. Casting doubt on the paternity of a child is a deliberate, politically motivated attempt to embarrass a woman or her husband.

The Politics of Sex

If the spatial demarcation is breached and distinctions between the official and the unofficial are blurred, humiliation and conflict will likely result. This consequence imbues the act of open infidelity with power. Women can deliberately humiliate and influence husbands through public displays of infidelity. (I never saw the sexes reversed here.) One case that occurred during my presence well exemplifies this. At a large ceremony involving visiting patriclans, a woman and her husband's nephew withdrew from the ritual dance house and met in her house and hammock. The husband easily found the couple, as the wife had left her crying toddler alone in the dance house. On finding wife and nephew together, the husband struck his wife squarely on the jaw. In the heated dialogue that followed, the husband and wife aired their grievances before a crowd of interested spectators now removed from the dance house to witness the commotion. I was among them. Amid the shouting, the wife accused her husband of not fishing enough for herself and her children. The husband beat his wife peremptorily, then turned to the apologetic nephew, whom he excused politely, saying, "I know this is not your fault; it's her way." Shortly after the incident the husband fished for two sleepless days and nights to sponsor a large feast of smoked fish for the villagers. Had the wife simply wished to carry on an affair, she would have followed the rules of discretion. Instead, she used the transgression to openly humiliate her husband.

Relations with illicit lovers are expected to be fleeting. An attraction that persists over time is regarded as dangerous and lovers who are visibly infatuated with one another are ridiculed. Any indication of preoccupation with a sexual partner, such as an open display of sexual attraction, or frequency of meeting, is likely to be interpreted as an indication of sorcery. The choice to make an issue of any liaison is a political one.

The episode of lovers X and Y was still discussed with animation when I first arrived among the Wanano. The infatuation of these two paramours, a young wife and a widower of a patriline other than her husband's, caused a deadly feud between the two local descent groups. Over several years, all local deaths were attributed to the countersorcery of husband and lover and their clan allies. The competition came to an end with the death of the widower-lover, attributed to sorcery by the husband's patriline. The case is important because it points to a critical difference in the way potential paters are regarded. By not recognizing the patriline of the husband or the rights that accrue to it, an outsider as progenitor represents a breach of the intact descent line. The potential ambiguities and conflicts associated with paternal identity are of paramount concern to Tukanoans when a breach of norms associated with sexuality and parenthood extends to nonclan partners. Then, problems of paternal legitimacy pose threats to the integrity of the patriline.

Social Fatherhood

The notion of extramarital sexual relations as inevitable, yet short-lived, is consistent with the contention that a child will likely be the biological offspring of the mother's husband, since according to Wanano models of conception, intrauterine growth is the result of the accumulated semen of numerous sexual encounters. Although the mother carries the infant, the semen of repeated ejaculations is the *materia primae* of the child. Unless challenged, it is presumed that the husband of the mother will be the father-donor of her children. But, in spite of Malinowski's strong denial of the existence of the belief, it is considered possible that other, unofficial, partners made "contributions" to the offspring. In the latter case, all potential progenitors are required to follow the proper paternal ritual procedures.

Paternal Ritual

On the birth of a child, official paternity is ritually signaled through a period of withdrawal, known in the literature as the couvade. The ritual, in which the new father enacts weakness, rests on the belief that in the earliest months of an infant's life father and child are linked in a precarious symbiosis. In order to avoid harm to the infant, Eastern Tukanoan fathers observe a postpartum period of withdrawal, known as *sua nümüne*. During this period, a new father must avoid any activities deemed dangerous to the child. Any strenuous action he performs could adversely affect the infant. As examples of dangerous activities, it is said that a recent father should not lift a heavy object, clear a garden, chop wood, strike an object, build a house or boat, paddle or pull a canoe, fish or hunt. A new father must limit his diet to small amounts of nonmeat foods, such as dry manioc flour. According to some Tukanoan spokespersons on the subject, a man should remain reclined in his hammock during this period of vulnerability, fed and attended by his wife and his mother.

As the father resumes eating, each food item that he takes anew must be blessed in sequence. The first foods are ceremoniously prepared peppers and manioc bread, followed by subsequent starchy vegetables and certain small fish. Meat and large fish are resumed last. The father returns to strenuous tasks gradually and cautiously. The rate at which the father resumes normal activities and foods is determined by the progress of the infant's development. The development is monitored closely and the father will return to abstentions if the child's health shows signs of deteriorating (see also Chernela 1991).

When the period of ritual inactivity is completed, the father is expected to undergo a ceremonial bath in the river. The ceremony invokes the birth of the clan ancestor in the same river. A shaman fumigates and cleanses the new father with protective substances such as cigar smoke and tree resins. The bath marks the end of the seclusion period and the start of the gradual return to ordinary routine by both the wife's husband and any other potential genitors. This bath, a public signaling of fatherhood, was remarked upon earlier as the site where multiple "fathers" might simultaneously discover one another.

The ritual bears close resemblance to the ceremonial seclusion and dietary restrictions observed by a young man entering puberty (S. Hugh-Jones 1979). Now, with the birth of his own child, a male completes his passage to manhood. The abstentions themselves underscore his masculinity, marking as they do the strength that indexes "maleness." At the same time, the enactment establishes the primacy of the male in the role of birth giver. By dramatizing the symbiosis ordinarily attributed to the mother-offspring relation, the father-child relation supersedes the connection between mother and child, establishing father as principal and wife as "other." It also visibly demonstrates the identities and associated responsibilities of all potential progenitors.

Fathering: Fathers, Brothers, and Co-Paternity

In former times, a local patriclan inhabited a single longhouse, with each conjugal couple occupying its own hearth and sleeping area (C. Hugh-Jones 1979; S. Hugh-Jones 1979). Today's villages are comprised of separate households aligned in a manner that corresponds closely to the spatial allocation of the traditional longhouse. Each household may be likened to the hearth compartment occupied by the nuclear families of the longhouse.

Although the nuclear family today constitutes a residential unit, it is not the household that is the unit of production and consumption—a proposition fundamental to Malinowski's distinction of family and clan. Instead, the local descent group or patriclan replaces the nuclear family both as the unit of production and the unit of consumption. Patrilines own specific, named fish traps. The number of appropriate sites is few, depending on village location. Together, brothers of the same local descent group construct, maintain, and harvest fish from several traps. The daily catch is presented to the wives, who boil the fish in pepper broth. Wives also prepare drink and bread from the manioc collected in their gardens. On most days, at dawn and at dusk, the women line up their preparations in the center of the village where the community gathers to eat. Each villager samples each vessel, proceeding along the line of contributions, ceremoniously dipping manioc bread into each household's offering.

Although processes of preserving fish or meat, such as smoking, are used for gift giving and for travel, retaining surpluses of these foods for reasons of any other kind is considered antisocial. A woman who keeps smoked meat or fish in her home would be criticized for her lack of generosity to her fellow villagers. Hiding accumulated food would not only awaken jealousies and cause the hoarder to be the subject of rude gossip, it might also invite and provoke sorcery against her. If a yield is particularly high, it is cooked at once for all present. If the yield is small, or if there is no fish, the wives prepare the same pepper-and-water mixture and serve it in the same manner.

Since there is little variation in a woman's garden production, her own vegetable contribution to the community meal is relatively constant. In contrast, the differentials between the contributions of men are highly variable. Contributions to the group meal are public, and although no comment is made to the provider, both he and his wife are humbled by a poor showing.

One way wives pressure their husbands is through flagrant indiscretion. The wife who carried on a dalliance with her husband's nephew, in her husband's home, likely intended the humiliation. Whatever else her complaints, as her recrimination implies, she found her husband an insufficient provider of food.

As we have seen, Tukanoan clan brothers provide for one another's children as a collective. Through the pooling of the daily catch, each male regularly labors for *all* of the children of a village—his own offspring as well as those of his brothers. Aside from a woman's husband, it is these men who are the likeliest genitors or biological fathers of her children.

Competition and Monopoly

As a result of a broad extension of incest rules and strongly felt preferences, the few marriageable partners available to a Wanano man are the same as those available to his brother, placing brothers in competition for a few eligible cross-cousins. Relations among brothers are therefore ambivalent, as they are expected to show solidarity, yet they are in competition for the same women.

Ambivalence in the brother relationship and its manifestation in the fatherhood ritual is well illustrated in Yisido's account. According to Yisido, when a man enters the ritual bath that marks the end of his seclusion as a new father, he will discover at the river edge several other "brothers" (clan mates) in similar ceremony. The story implies the suspicions among brothers regarding "shared" paternity, and demonstrates the causal link understood to exist between a child's well-being and the behavior of "all" biological contributors, given the model of conception.

Suspicions of shared paternity among clan brothers are paid little attention. Reprisals are rarely taken. The case is different, however, if the biological father is not from father's own patriline. Let us return to two of the earlier episodes to contrast attitudes toward paternal "contribution" by a clan insider versus the paternal agency of a clan outsider. In the case in which a husband discovered his wife in his own home with his paternal nephew, the apologetic nephew was excused. The case of extramarital relations was treated with extreme tolerance and the male completely absolved of any wrongdoing. However, in the affair of a married woman whose lover was a widower of a different patriclan than her husband's, bitter enmity followed. This second example posed two distinct, but related, threats not found in the first case. As a widower, the lover may have been in pursuit of marriage, rather than a passing affair, and might therefore have presented more than a sexual threat. At least as significant, however, is the fact that the lover was not from husband's descent group. This relationship threatened the monopoly of the patriclan over the offspring of its members. A woman whose lovers are members of her husband's patriline does not threaten the prerogative that the wife of a Wanano clan member must bear the offspring of that clan. Outside lovers, however, do threaten the prerogative of the patriline to the coherence and exclusivity of its identity.

Conclusions

Kinship, in general, and fatherhood, in the specific, are social constructions. Speakers of Eastern Tukanoan languages share with members of numerous lowland South American cultures a system of meanings associated with fatherhood that allows for the possibility of shared paternity. In the case of Eastern Tukanoan societies, social recognition of fatherhood is set on course with the birth of the infant and the public, ritual display of fatherhood. In this display, we are told, several males may participate, thus identifying themselves as "partial paters" for the same infant. Fatherhood and filial identity are further constructed through life in the production of talk, as children speak exclusively in the language of father's descent group. In the course of a child's development, fatherhood, language, and clan membership continue as transformations of one another in the formation of the individual as clan member.

Since the writings of Malinowski anthropologists have generally agreed that bonds of affiliation and descent are socially rather than biologically defined. Malinowski argued that for the Trobriand islanders of the 1920s, the nuclear family existed in spite of an absence of conceptualizing the role of father in the physiological processes of reproduction. The link between father and child is not based in biology, he concluded, but rather in the prior condition of father as husband of child's mother. The role of pater, commonly assumed to be natural, is, in fact, social.

The Tukanoan model, however, turns the Trobriand one on its head and is therefore of special interest. For Tukanoan speakers, the role of father is conceptually linked to his role as producer of offspring: a male is father because he (with or without others) creates the offspring by natural means. According to the Tukanoan model of conception, the child is created of male bodily substances that result from a series of sexual acts. The connection, played out in social life, is *represented as biological.* Tukanoan fatherhood, founded in the discourse of biology, and accorded the status of natural processes, may thus be said to be naturalized insofar as it is explained and represented in terms of material, biological input.

Since multiple copulations from several donors can contribute to the same offspring, a potential ambiguity exists. The theoretical naturalization of fatherhood may lead to multiple contenders, to partial progenitors, and to political contest as the "facts" of biological interconnectedness may be constructed, surmised, and otherwise subject to political manipulation and negotiation.

As this chapter has suggested, some forms of paternal partitioning are recognized by the Tukano as interdictions, while others are not. The assumption underlying the patriline is the continuity between generations of fathers and offspring. Upon the death of a man, reproductive rights lie with the patriclan, not the widow.

Where descent is embodied in linkages of generations of males as far back as a putative male ancestor, paternal legitimacy is critical and threats to the continuity of the paternal line are of central concern to men (Chernela 1988b, c, 1997). The power inherent in woman's word to confirm or deny paternal ties is of particular importance in patrilineal systems, such as that of the Wanano, where offspring are de jure members of father's group. Women marry across patrilineal descent groups and provide the links of in-law alliance between different patrilines. The wife mediates relations between husband and offspring, and may at any time crosscut that relationship by revealing information that alters the collective assumptions of father's—and therefore offspring's—identity.

There is thus a tension between the assumption of fatherhood by husband and the knowledge and fear that paternity may be usurped—not by a brother or nephew—but by an outsider, a linguistic and consanguineal "other," creating problems of legitimacy that would threaten the integrity of the patriline. An outsider as progenitor represents a breach of the intact descent line and the rights that accrue to it. The Tukanoan case illustrates the continuing need within social anthropology to carefully distinguish the interrelated concepts of descent, filiation, alliance (marriage), and the identities, activities, and expectations associated with each relationship.

The above discussion has led to a reconsideration of Malinowski's formulation of the family, reproduced over generations as the basis of a modern social anthropology. That which appeared to be a facile dichotomy between the nuclear family and clan appears to be more complex than previously described. Rather than supporting a clear-cut binary division between the individualized pater/family and the community/clan, it is of greater explanatory power to regard these relationships as overlapping and integral.

The data described here counter Malinowski's representation of the nuclear family, with its assumed monopoly on reproductive, productive, and consumptive activities, versus a clan that is ceremonial and juridical. The Eastern Tukanoan case, for example, is but one that shows that many of the specializations assigned by Malinowski to the nuclear family are taken up in practice by the local descent group. Among these is the provision of food. Although prepared in individual households, the daily harvests of the working residents of a village are pooled and redistributed regardless of contribution. It is of interest that these same food providers are also the likeliest genitors of the children of the same settlement and descent group.

Because of a generalized practice of sexual activity with more than one partner—and an ideology that accommodates multiple contributions to offspring—fatherhood, although individual, also extends metaphorically to all males of a clan. As clansmen develop important relationships not only with wife's children but also with the children of their brothers' wives—as "real people ought to live" (Kensinger 1995)—the presumed monopoly on paternity is diminished.

Notes

1. The name of this river appears as Vaupés in Spanish spellings and Uaupés in Luzo-Brazilian spellings.
2. The figure 10,000 is based on the 1987 census figure 14,164, which includes

neighboring Arawakan- and Cariban-speaking groups, compiled by the Centro Ecumenico de Documentaçao e Informaçao (CEDI), Museu Nacional, Rio de Janeiro. It exceeds by 5,000 the estimates of Sorensen (1967) and Jackson (1976). The figure of 150,000 km² is the sum of 90,000 reported by Jackson (1976) for the Colombian Vaupés, and 60,070 km² reported by CEDI for the Brazilian Uaupés basin.

3. The alternate spellings, Uanano and Guanano, are also found in the literature. The Tukanoan name, by which the group identifies itself, is Kotira. I have chosen to use the term Wanano on the basis of convention established in the anthropological literature.

4. All data presented here were collected in Brazil.

5. Hopper (1967, 12) wrongly places the "Wanana" below the mouth of the Tiquie.

6. Since I did not visit the Colombian Wanano settlements, I take the upriver limit of Wanano occupation from the literature.

7. I have used the terms *patriline* and *patrilineal descent group* to refer to a named social unit where membership is based on reckoning descent through the male line. Unlike certain African societies, Eastern Tukanoans do not recall the names of their ancestors, which link contemporary generations with ancestral generations; their lineages are shallow and their founding ancestors are putative. I use the terms *patriline* and *patrilineage,* however, because these best describe the way in which the Wanano and indeed all Eastern Tukanoans view their own descent groups. See Goldman 1957 for a similar position.

8. The orthographic symbol *ü* here represents a high, front rounded vowel, similar to the German umlaut.

9. I have used the orthographic symbol ' to indicate a glottal stop and *h* an aspiration.

10. In all but grandparent and grandchild generations terms, father's relatives are distinguished from mother's, separating one's own patrilineal kin group from mother's relatives.

11. Kin terms are preceded by one of the following possessive pronouns: *yü-* (my), *mü-* (your), or *to-* (his or hers). The gender morphemes *-ü-*, denoting male referent, and *-o*, denoting female referent, are affixed to the stem.

12. The Cubeo (Goldman 1963), Makuna (Århem 1981, 1989), and Arapaço (Chernela 1988b, 1989) are exceptions to the pattern of linguistic exogamy.

13. Exceptions to this rule may be found, as among the Tariano, a former Arawakan-speaking group now speaking Tukano.

PART III

10

Fathers that Never Exist

Exclusion of the Role of Shared Father
among the Curripaco of the Northwest Amazon

Paul Valentine

The notion and practice of partible paternity is common throughout large areas of South America (Beckerman et al. 1998). The social, economic, and ecological conditions that have facilitated the creation and perpetuation of this custom are addressed in this case study of the Curripaco,[1] an Arawak-speaking group who number some 4,500 and who live in the tropical rain forest of the northwest Amazon, on the border between Colombia and Venezuela.

Unlike the Barí (Beckerman et al. 1998) and the Canela (Crocker and Crocker 1994), the Curripaco believe that it is wrong to engage in sexual intercourse before or outside marriage, yet they also believe in partible paternity. They believe if a woman copulates with more than one man then these are all, to a greater or lesser extent (depending on the amount of sexual access they have with her), the biological fathers of her child. This chapter argues that, in the Curripaco case, the notion of partible paternity provides a rationale for clan brothers to share wives and, within a fairly rigid and controlled marriage system, offers individuals some freedom in choice of their sex partners.

Ethnographic Background

Curripaco contact with the whites spans some 250 years of slavery, exploitation, and repression, during which time their way of life has changed radically (Hemming 1978, 1987; Wright 1981). Yet many have maintained significant features of their culture, including their kinship and marriage rules, in addition to their beliefs concerning conception, the couvade, and partible paternity.

The Curripaco inhabit small villages (average population of about 40), situated on the banks of the Içana and Guainía Rivers and their tributaries, ideally with easy access to good fishing sites and terra firme (uplands) for gardens. The palm-thatched, mud-walled, rectangular houses, each with its own hearth, are frequently in line abutting the plaza, and follow the same layout as the traditional, multihearth longhouses they have now displaced.

The Río Negro basin is a notoriously harsh environment. It is one of extremes—extreme humidity, low soil fertility, violent rainstorms, and marked seasonal periods of food scarcity (Holmes 1981, 1985; Moran 1995). The local white population calls the area *rios de hambre*, rivers of hunger. Yet the Curripaco have developed a number of key strategies to cope with this taxing environment. Perhaps one of the most noteworthy is their balancing of two ecozones—the flooded forest and terra firma. Most readily accessible terra firma is located along the upper reaches of the rivers, whereas the flooded forest is situated downstream. Where terra firma is scarce the Curripaco are forced to make gardens at great distance from their settlements and live there in temporary shelters over several months of the year. Those on the higher reaches have ready access to their gardens from their riverine settlements. As is common throughout the region, the staple crop is bitter manioc (Uhl 1980).

The Curripaco hunt and fish. Both are equally important protein sources. The return on fishing is low, highly variable, and to some extent predictable, depending on season and location. The most productive sites are situated near cataracts, lagoons, and flooded forest areas that tend to be located downriver (Chernela 1993; Clark 1982; Moran 1990, 1991). Those who live on the upper reaches frequently make seasonal trips to these sites to take advantage of times of temporary abundance (Matos Arvelo 1912; Wright 1981). The return on hunting is low and only to a small degree predictable, depending on season and location. Game nearly always keeps well clear of village settlements, though sometimes game animals browse in gardens. Only during the dry season, when they come to the water's edge, are they occasionally in easy range of hunters.

Men's and women's activities are clearly delineated and complementary. Working alone or in small groups, the men clear the gardens with axes and machetes, burn the slash, and help in the planting and weeding. The women do most of the year-round gardening tasks and work many hours extracting the cyanide content from manioc tubers to transform them into nonpoisonous foods (Dufour 1983). Women do nearly all the cooking and perform most of the household tasks. Men exclusively hunt, and apart from a very few exceptions do all the fishing. The men fish individually or leave the village in a group, split up at their destination, and return together. Those who own the traps and have access to cataracts and lagoons, and the flooded forest to which fish migrate (Chernela 1993), reap the largest rewards.

Given the low nutrient value of manioc (Dufour 1983, 1994) and the varying and sometimes very low catch returns, both men's and women's contribution to diet are crucial (Holmes 1981, 1985). In one case, a husband and wife and their children (the eldest boy was about 12) inhabited a settlement alone. When the husband died, the widow was advised to migrate; her economic situation was untenable. In another case, a man whose parents were dead and whose brothers had left the region was forced to move from village to village with his young children, all dependent on distant relatives for support. He too was in a very vulnerable position. Given the difficulty of subsisting without a partner, unmarried people usually live with their parents or their married brothers.

On returning from a fishing trip, a man gives his wife his catch. She may then prepare him a meal and he will expect her to serve him manioc bread and other garden produce. Small birds and some smaller cuts of large game are usually consumed by the individual family on the fisherman's or hunter's return, and some of the choicer cuts may be discreetly distributed to other families in the village. Up until the mid-1980s, the meal was cooked in an open or latticework-sided kitchen at the rear of the house, where he sat to eat it. Although this meal was not taken in view of the plaza, it was not eaten in secret. I was told that if there was almost no food in a village, and a father succeeded in obtaining a tiny catch, he was permitted to feed his children secretly.

By far the greater part of the catch is shared at communal meals. Some conjugal families also eat alone secretly, but it is very difficult to estimate the extent of their consumption. The house at the front of the line tends to be bigger than the rest and serves many of the functions of the entrance and central body of a longhouse. Here, in the mornings and evenings, villagers gather to eat a communal meal. Each woman brings from her own hearth a steaming pot of fish or meat soup, if there is any, and manioc bread and a bowl of toasted manioc drink. I have witnessed a village of 21 people eat a meal of half a dozen sparrow-sized birds mashed into a gruel—the only protein coming into the village that day.

At the communal meals men eat first. The bowls of food are put on a table or on the floor. The men stand or squat around, moving back and forth to the food. Each dips his manioc bread into the bowls of soup, scoops up some fish and wanders off, eats, and returns to the bowl. Women and children follow the same procedure but usually sit on the floor and eat after the men.

Failure to share food gives rise to a considerable amount of friction, and the extent of this failure provides a fairly clear index of social cohesion within a village community. Those who do not share are thought either to be stingy or are expressing in a very visible and tangible way their discontent with the village leadership or with the community as a whole (Hill 1983, 1993). The relationship between the several hearths of the separate conjugal families and the pooling of food at the community meals is perceived by the Curripaco as a strategy for sharing out scarce resources. Also, it is a simple paradigm of the unit of production and distribution, and of the local patrilineal descent group, which together with their affinal relatives—primarily the women who marry into the group—form the village community.

Like other northwest Amazon people (Århem 1981; Chernela 1993; Goldman 1963; Jackson 1983), the Curripaco are divided into a number of exogamous patrilineal clans. In the Curripaco case, rivers are divided into clearly defined sections, and each section, including the hunting areas and fruit trees in the forest adjacent to it, is owned by a particular patriclan. Each clan is divided into about five patrilineages that are hierarchically ranked into elder and younger brother lines. The chiefly lineage, the top, is located at the site with the greatest access to natural resources; the younger brother and client lineages are located at progressively less favored sites. Named male ancestors mark the divisions at the clan level, but not at the lower levels of segmentation.

The Curripaco describe this process of lineage segmentation and relocation in myth. According to one version, Inapirrikuli, the trickster-hero, went to Hipana, located on the Aiari River, the 'umbilicus of the world,' and pulled from vagina-shaped holes the grandparents, the first brother and sister of each clan. These ancestors were the founders of the different clans. Inapirrikuli blew tobacco smoke over each brother-sister pair, gave them their totemic clan 'soul' (*iiwaruna*), and as the tobacco smoke entered their bodies, they breathed in, sprung to life, and spoke. He then handed them their trumpets together with other ritual objects and dispatched them to river sections, which their descendants own to this day. The first grandfathers then exchanged their sisters in marriage, and the sons of these unions became the first ancestors of the various patrilineages of each clan. These ancestors then quarreled, disbanded their 'houses,' broke up their communities, and went their separate ways to found new villages, in just the same way, say the Curripaco, as sets of brothers and parallel cousins quarrel and found new settlements today.

Clan and lineage members express and reaffirm their group membership and their common patrilineal descent in a number of ways. Clans and lineages have added to their names a suffix: sons of (*enai*) or grandsons of (*dakenai*). Members of the same clan or patrilineage call themselves *wakitsienape*— brother or parallel cousins, whereas those who are not of their clan or lineage are referred to as 'in-laws' (*warimattairi*) or 'cross-cousins' (*wetinaki*). The distinction between members of one's own clan as opposed to members of others' clans—that is, between kin and affines—is highlighted by using the terms 'our people' (*wanaikikha*) for kin, in contrast to 'other people' (*apada naiki*) for affines or potential affines.

Clan members' common ancestry is putative, not demonstrable. The Curripaco can name their first clan grandfather and their own historical patrilineal grandfathers and great grandfathers, but they can only indicate the birth order of the founder lineages' ancestral 'brothers.' Each clan owns a set of ascribed names that are recycled through the generations, effectively eliminating time from social reproduction.

Clan members also express their group membership in terms of a shared totemic soul that manifests itself as a particular animal in dreams, and in their ownership of clan trumpets, which at key rituals are decorated to depict these animals. At these rituals the men paint themselves to represent these animals. They say they put on the animal's skin, or shirt. Secretly, they refer to the trumpets as their 'grandfathers,' say that their trumpets are their clan or lineage (*nuinaikikha*), and identify the name of the nuinaikikha as those of their trumpet. Trumpets, clan chants, and a shared totemic soul are badges of their common patrilineal identity.

Traditionally, clansmen also owned clearly defined stretches of river and the land adjacent to it. Each river section is called the 'house' of that clan. This ownership takes the form of exclusive rights to utilize the resources of their territory. Clan members who own land are *hwepaitte*, a privileged position, members of other clans are 'visitors' (*nadenda*), and can only hunt or garden there after they have obtained permission from the senior men of the owning clan. The Curripaco recall cases of feuding and shamanic attacks as a consequence of clans and local lineages invading or claiming their neighbors' territory. Even nowadays, villagers who hunt and fish in the river section belonging to another clan will first seek permission from the local headman, and on their return give him a share of their catch. If they overstay their welcome, it leads to bad feeling and accusations of sorcery.

Rights to these traditional homelands are also expressed in religious terms.

In a clan's territory the members, both living and dead, are linked by ties of kinship and by their ownership of sacred land to a particular locale. Part of the territory is sacred land (*iiyarudati*), a place where the ancestral house is located, where clan members' totemic clan soul will go when they die; such an area is out of bounds to hunters and fishermen. It is also believed that visitors are more likely to fall seriously ill in foreign parts. The forest spirits (*yopinai*) are particularly unforgiving to visitors. Not only does each clan collectively control territory, but also supernatural forces add their clout to discourage foreigners who presume to exploit their resources.

To defend their river sections and the adjacent, local lineages traditionally formed alliances with other groups. Although fraught with difficulties, marriage alliances were a way of attempting to neutralize potential enemies. In these circumstances it is not surprising that marriages were not and still are not mere liaisons between two individuals. Often neither partner has much choice in the matter. For instance, one of my Curripaco assistants never spoke to his wife before their marriage. Rather, marriages are political and economic reaffirmations of relations that often stretch back over the generations. They take place between local lineage groups of different clans; they never occur within the clan. Preferred marriage is with the bilateral cross-cousin. However, unlike the Tukanoan groups of the Vaupés (see Chernela, this volume), marriage within the language group is regarded as perfectly proper. Arranged by the men of the older generations, in the past children were often spoken for, women were married off in raids of mock capture, and warfare ensued if symmetrical exchanges between local lineage groups were not honored. Even nowadays, if one local lineage group reneges on a marriage agreement and strikes out and forms new marriage alliances elsewhere, then personal grudges, sorcery accusations and shamanic attacks almost inevitably ensue.

When a marriage takes place, the woman usually leaves her own village to live with her husband in his village. Generally, a village is composed of a local, out-marrying, patrilineal core of men, perhaps a couple of brothers and their sons, together with their unmarried sisters and daughters. Added to this core are the wives, who may be drawn from a number of different clans and have taken up residence in their husbands' village. Each husband-wife unit has its own house and hearth.

Recall that patrilineal relatives are classified as 'kin' and matrilateral relatives fall within a category that can be glossed as 'in-laws' and 'cross-cousins.' This classification is consistent with other features of the Dravidian nomenclature and dovetails with the separate agnatic descent lines. Turning first to the affinal terms, the Curripaco drew my attention to the way the *noli-kikimi* (brother-in-law–father-in-law) pattern repeats itself over the generations. A *noli* (brother-in-law) for ego's father is his son's *kikimi* (father-in-law), and ego's noli is ego's son's kikimi. This pattern is one way the terminology distinguishes affines from kin. For example, if ego's father-in-law marries ego's classificatory mother then their children are ego's cross-cousins. On the other hand, if ego's father-in-law takes his wife from another patriclan, his children are still his cross-cousins. In short, ego's father's classificatory brothers-in-law are ego's fathers-in-law, and ego's brothers-in-law are his son's fathers-in-law. They are all 'other people,' all affines.

In a similar way, in ego's own agnatic line, the *tetemi-padχ* (sibling-FB) pattern repeats itself. As ego's father's *tetemi* (siblings) are ego's *padχ* (FB), so ego's own tetemi are ego's padz. In other words, ego's father's brothers are ego's patrilineal uncles, and ego's brothers are his children's patrilineal uncles. Although the terminology does not imply any rule of descent or lineal exogamy, nevertheless the Curripaco consider significant the repetitive cycles of kin and affinal terms. For them, these terms not only mark 'us' from 'other people,' they also illustrate the way men, not women, provide the crucial link between the generations. Similarly, as has been mentioned, patriclan names are recycled through the generations, thereby identifying a person temporally as well as relationally.

Sexual Strategies, Shared and Forgotten Fathers

The Curripaco do not find it easy to talk about personal sexual matters. A Curripaco cannot ask someone if he or she had intercourse the previous day. Someone who has recently engaged in sexual relations cannot go near an ill person or a shaman for fear of injuring them. Sex cannot be openly talked about. It is impossible, for example, to sample a broad segment of the Curripaco population to find out who is copulating with whom and whose baby is whose. Such information can only be obtained through gossip and by gaining the confidence of a small community.

Strict rules govern sexual behavior. At initiation ceremonies, young people are fasted, whipped, and forced to eat hot peppers. Among the things dinned into initiates, besides the virtues of self-sufficiency and the imperative that 'hunger hurts,' are the sexual rules. They should not engage in sex before marriage, nor with partners other than their spouses during marriage, and if their husbands die, they must either refrain from sexual relations or only marry one of his brothers or close parallel patrilateral cousins of the same patrilineage.

The Curripaco have several views about conception. All accept the possibility of multiple fatherhood. I first came upon the view in 1981, when talking to elderly men now dead. According to this view, when a man first has sex with a woman, the seminal fluid, like fat, flows around the body, stuffing her. When she becomes chubby, the fluid starts to fill the womb, mix with a clot of blood, and, as further intercourse takes place the blood and fluid mix and a fetus is gradually formed. Additional copulations help the growth of a strong and healthy baby. Thus, from the Curripaco perspective fertilization is a process, not an event.

In 1996 I talked on the same subject to a group of Curripaco men, who included a primary school teacher in a Curripaco village. It was clear that the notion of conception had changed somewhat. It now incorporates certain Western ideas, but all agreed that multiple paternity is easily possible. The current view is that the seminal fluid mixes with a clot of blood, that further acts are required, and that a fetus is slowly formed. Once a fetus is formed the woman no longer has her menses and no further acts of intercourse are necessary. The notion that the seminal fluid is like fat, and that repeated acts of sex strengthen the fetus, has been discarded. All agreed, however, that one act of copulation is not enough. To make sure, I asked a group of four or five men the same question that the Crockers (Crocker and Crocker 1994, 85) put to the Canela. If a man had sex once with his wife, then left to do his national service for some nine months and she was looked after by his mother, could she become pregnant? The answer was, "Never." Curripaco men say rather smugly that making a woman pregnant 'is hard work.'

Since several acts of copulation are required, more than one man can contribute to the formation of a fetus. The man with whom the mother has had the most sex, and who therefore contributes the most seminal fluid to the formation of the fetus, is called the 'major father' (*laniri kanetsa*), while the others are the 'lesser fathers' (*laniri panali*). If a woman has sex with various men then she runs the risk that none will recognize the child as his own. The Curripaco say that the child is everybody's, which in effect means nobody's. How do these notions of partible paternity correspond to the strict rules regarding sexual behavior already described?

In fact, what the Curripaco say they do and what they actually do correspond only approximately. In one of the two villages where I have been working over the last three years, there are six women with children. To my knowledge, two have had illegitimate children, two men have been accused of having illegitimate children, and one woman has adopted an illegitimate child. In the other village, there are five women with children. One has had several illegitimate children and another has adopted one. In both villages a pair of brothers are sharing a wife.

What strategies are employed by the Curripaco to maintain marriage alliances and the integrity of their patrilineages while simultaneously enjoying these additional sexual activities? How do men and women at different stages of their lives manipulate their social situations to gain some freedom to select sex partners? One way is to exclude the role of secondary fathers, particularly if they are not brothers. Single people are not supposed to engage in sexual activity—to 'walk out,' as the Curripaco say—but some do. Secret meetings take place in the gardens, near the port, and on canoe journeys when passengers disembark for a few moments. Various euphemisms are employed. A young man will say, 'He carried her yucca basket back from the gardens,' or 'He took her fishing,' and a woman will flirt and ask a youth, 'Would you like to eat with me?' Young men and women, who are in the marriageable category, engage in bawdy talk. In between the jokes and the double entendres, young men like to recount certain myths that recount sex acts. The punch line of one joke that refers to the actions of a character in a myth is 'You can have sex with a woman once and not be discovered, you can have sex twice and not be discovered, but if you have sex three times then people will find out. So let's have it twice!'

Sometimes couples do have sex before marriage and the women become pregnant. These women usually hide their condition for as long as possible. When a woman is discovered, her father and her brothers often hit her to force her to identify her lover or lovers. She may argue that she alone knows who the major father is. In the cases I have recorded, she chooses the most desirable partner—for instance, the younger man, from the larger village (which implies she will have to do less work in the gardens) and who belongs to an ethnic group of higher status than her other lover. The lover can accept the woman's version, or say that since he only had sex with her a couple of times someone else must be the major father. If alliances already exist between the two local lineages, enormous pressure will be put on the young couple to marry. For the Curripaco, biological paternity is negotiable.

If no man accepts responsibility for the pregnancy, then very frequently the woman has to leave the region and live with distant relatives along another river. There she may give birth secretly and kill the baby. I have witnessed a woman starve her illegitimate child to death. She then returns to her home village and picks up the pieces of her life afresh. Nowadays, such acts of infanticide happen much more rarely. The Curripaco are afraid of the intervention of the local authorities and since there is greater access to powdered milk in the traders' stores, more married women, usually close relatives of the pregnant woman, are prepared to adopt the illegitimate children. In the cases I have witnessed, the child has been adopted by the mother's mother or the mother's mother's sister.

If, on the other hand, the young man accepts responsibility for the pregnancy—with support from the parents and the local lineages concerned—then the woman lives with the man and the marriage is gradually cemented. They talk; he says he does not have much to offer her, but that he is prepared to work for her and her father. And she says she is not very good at household tasks, but she is prepared to try. She cooks him some food and then hangs her hammock next to his. Gradually, they become husband and wife.

According to the Curripaco, the mother has a minimal role in the physical elaboration of the fetus. This is neatly commented upon by Erikson (this volume), who reminds us that frequently in lowland South America, "the mothers are a biological necessity (at least as recipients) but a social mystery, whose physical relationship with their children is something to be constructed (often through nursing) and accounted for." Indeed, the Curripaco almost deny the physical contribution of the mother to the fetus. They say that the mother suffers when carrying the baby in her womb, spills blood when it is born, and nurses it, whereas it is the father or fathers who "make" the fetus. It is they who provide the blood, not the mothers. The patrilineage members share a common blood, which symbolically joins them as a group and through the generations. At a birth, for instance, the father fasts to protect himself and his baby, whereas the mother, many Curripaco say, fasts only to protect herself. When a person falls ill, people of the same blood should fast together, whereas affines, even the sick person's own mother, are not obliged to.

At birth, the major father and the mother must enter a fast and seclude themselves within the house and narrow environs of the village. For instance, if the father were to eat large, bloody and fatty game or fish, he would mystically injure himself and his baby. Likewise, the baby would be injured if the father were to use any sharp instrument, such as his ax or machete, or if the mother were to harvest garden produce. Fathers say they undertake the fast because they care for their infants. They and their babies are of 'one blood,' and they recognize that what happens to them will directly affect their offspring. The fast also helps create a closer identity between father and baby, and since the parents undertake the rigor of the fast together, it also helps bring them closer together.

For the Curripaco, marriage is a gradual process; one "has a man or a woman" (*kainukana*), but whether that union precisely occurs is a matter of debate. When a woman comes to hang her hammock next to her man and cook for him, then some younger Curripaco say they are "married" (kainukana). But older informants disagree; they say they are 'married' only when they have demonstrated that they can support and sustain each other. Having a baby, and going through the fast together, cements a marriage. Lesser fathers do not have to fast. As 'they do not think of the baby,' nor want it, nor feel responsible for it, they can do it no harm. By not fasting they relinquish all claims to the major father. They have no place in the marriage.

Couples with newborn babies cannot eat collectively at the village meals because of their special diet, nor can they engage in economic activities. They may have set aside some manioc and flour to tide them over this time, but this is hardly enough. They must rely on kin and affines to provide them with smaller fish and birds to supplement their diet. By fasting, the father is making a public statement. He is saying he is mystically and physically connected to the baby and that his actions will have a direct effect on its well-being. He is calling on his kin and affines to support him, his wife, and baby in this time of need. Indeed, the relatives rally round, visit with presents of food, and give advice and help. In this way the role of the father is reaffirmed and the baby is incorporated into his kin network. Kin of secondary fathers have no special place here.

A case study may illustrate how the Curripaco expect the couvade to draw the married couple into a kin and affinal network. Four years ago, a Curripaco primary school teacher married a Bare woman and went to live and work in her village near the municipal capital. The Bare are a more acculturated people who no longer speak their own Arawakan language or share communal meals. After the birth of their child, the teacher's father-in-law came to visit them only once, advised them (as is the custom), and brought them hardly any food. The husband had to rely on his tiny salary to buy provisions from the village shop. It was this lack of assistance and recognition that persuaded him to apply for transfer to a small, isolated Curripaco village where the couple lives with his kin. The lack of support he received during the couvade highlighted their isolation and his lack of social recognition as a father.

When the child is born it has to be chanted over by a qualified ritual specialist. The baby is given a patrilineal clan name, a clan totemic soul, and special access to ritual objects that belong only to the patrilineage. By chanting over the baby it is incorporated into the patrilineage. Secondary fathers are forgotten. If the baby were to have fathers of different clans, its identity would be indeterminate. The Curripaco say it is as if such a baby were a mixture of species—as if it were both a tapir and a jaguar. A baby of this kind is called a *mapachica*, and a woman who has sex relations with multiple men is scornfully warned by her male patrikin that she is looking for a mapachica. Mapachica is a parasitic plant that resembles mistletoe and is propagated by bird droppings. The Curripaco explain that in the same way these birds leave their droppings promiscuously, so may men have children; that as this plant grows without trunk or roots, so a mapachica child has no trunk—no patrilineage.

But what happens if a woman cohabits with two men of the same patrilineage? Sometimes because of the local demographic situation, or because of the lack of political allies, there is a scarcity of women in a village. Typical Curripaco villages are composed of a patrilineal core of men and their immigrant wives; on occasion there are not enough women to go around. In these circumstances it is not unusual for them to share a wife. This may happen particularly if one of the brothers is physically or mentally inadequate.

Such relationships are accepted, with the proviso that the woman must be willing to participate in the sexual relationship. It does not undermine the social identity of the child because it is a member of its fathers' patrilineage, to which both fathers belong. In one case, after the birth of a baby one brother publicly fasted and refrained from subsistence activities, while the other brother secretly performed the ritual and employed a chanter to bless his food. In another case, both brothers publicly acknowledged the fatherhood of their children by the same wife. In these relationships there is a balance. Each man is sacrificing a degree of paternity certainty, but gaining the support of an additional man for his children. The woman gains because the second husband helps in the gardens, cleaning, weeding and carrying, and brings home fish and game, some of which finds its way into the family pot to feed her and her children. In one such marriage, one of the wife's husbands died suddenly. Gossip has it that he was a victim of sorcery, killed by a rival woman's envy. Her two husbands were maintaining her and their children too well.

But these relationships can be unstable. Brothers do compete for wives, and if one is successful, the others may resent him. In one instance, which is unraveling at the moment, one brother is turning against his sibling in fits of jealousy, throwing scorn on him for being lazy and not finding a woman of his own. He says he would kill him if he were of another clan, but that he respects him because he is his brother, because they share the same blood and they have helped each other in the past. If these drunken brawls continue everyone agrees the village will divide and the brothers separate.

Extramarital sexual relations with clansmen other than the husband's are always secret and may bring serious consequences. Given the virilocal nature of Curripaco residence, they rarely occur on a day-to-day basis. Liaisons most frequently occur at *pudali* ceremonies, and nowadays, at *fiestas patronales* (villages' patron saints' day celebrations). These gatherings involve affines and potential affines coming to a village as guests for several days, reaffirming past ties, bringing gifts, feasting, and drinking (Journet 1995). It is not unknown for couples to slip off into the night when their spouse and kin are drunk. These are times of sexual license, but it is still deemed wrong to engage in such quick trysts; couples should not get caught. It should not become a public matter. What happens if they do depends on the circumstances and the character of the aggrieved partners. Some partners pretend not to be aware of what is going on, others do not. Once discovered, the man may argue that he only had sex with her once, whereas she had had sex with many other men so it is impossible that he could be the major father of any subsequent baby. Anyway it was she who had actively pursued him, and he, being a man, could not resist. She has a similar repertoire of excuses—that she had sex with no one else other than him and then only once and, what is more, he had taken advantage of her drunken condition. Nevertheless, these are moments of high tension and, especially if the affair continues, may lead to divorce.

The Curripaco recall no case of a woman living openly or discreetly with two or more husbands of different clans, whereas they know of a number of unions involving brothers fairly openly sharing a wife. I calculate, based on my knowledge of three villages (inhabited by 18 conjugal families), that about 15% of marriages, for at least some of the time, involve brothers sharing a spouse. From a woman's point of view, committing adultery more than a couple of times with a man from a clan other than her husband's is problematic. If the liaison is discovered, then the husband may divorce her. If he does, he will always take the children and force her to rely on the support of her lover. By entering such a relationship the woman has to calculate the risk of being discovered, the risk of losing her husband's support and access to her children, and the cost of being subject to sorcery attacks that inevitably follow from such a social upheaval. What she gains are a lover, perhaps his support, and the option of starting a new family in a different settlement. Which alternative she chooses depends on the circumstances. Over the last 18 years I have witnessed four such cases, in three of which the women have divorced their husbands to live with their new partner.

From a man's point of view, entering an extramarital relationship has its costs and benefits too. Sexual liaisons at pudali ceremonies, although risky, are not considered 'hard work.' Cheating on your wife regularly, however, brings social and moral reprobation and ridicule—'He has two penises.' Such behavior can also easily lead to threats of violence and sorcery attacks from the husband and his wife and their kin, and the dissolution of his marriage, especially if his wife has a large kin group to support her.

Key to all these extramarital affairs is the status of the children—whether they belong to the patrilineage of the husband or the lover. Husbands should not be cuckolded; wives should not bear children by men of other lineages. If it is thought they do, they should be divorced and expelled from the village. Women are the vehicles by which the patrilineage is recreated over the generations, and this process must not be breached by their sexual affairs.

Not only should children be procreated by the lineage; they should also be brought up by it. Divorced men are expected to keep their children rather than leave them to the mercies of a stepfather and an ex-partner and her kin. Likewise, if a husband dies, the widow is expected to have the children brought up by his kin and to marry one of his 'brothers.' If she does not, the consequences lead to a train of sorcery accusations. In the two cases I heard about, according to gossip, sorcery attacks were directed primarily by 'very angry' fathers-in-law on their daughters-in-law and their new husbands.

Conclusion

The Curripaco present a case in which secondary fatherhood is institutionalized within the cultural ideology of conception and fetal development. Nevertheless, cultural rules operate so as to select a single male as the only recognized social father, and to deny such status to other men who may have copulated with the mother. The exception to this pattern—when two brothers are recognized as sharing paternity of a child—is permitted because paternity shared between brothers does not confuse the child's patrilineage identity.

The Curripaco, then, form a contrast with the Barí, Kulina, Canela, and Matis. Even though they have similar views about how babies are made, the corresponding patterns of social behavior are strikingly different. A belief in partible paternity is compatible with many different ways of arranging for the raising of children.

Note

1. The Curripaco are known by a number of terms. Hill (1983, 1993), for instance, refers to them as the Wakenai, and Wright (1981) calls them Baniwa.

11

A Comparative Analysis of Paternity among the Piaroa and the Ye'kwana of the Guayana Region of Venezuela

Alexánder Mansutti Rodríguez and Nalúa Silva Monterrey

The Piaroa and the Ye'kwana are two indigenous peoples of the Guayana region of Venezuela who, apart from sharing many sociocultural traits characteristic of the subculture found in indigenous societies of the region (Rivière 1984, 2, 4), are neighbors with a long tradition of contacts and trade (Mansutti Rodríguez 1986, 51). In this essay we compare their theories of human conception and gestation, their gender relations, kinship and marriage systems, population distribution, community composition, and control of production and consumption processes. These are all factors that help us understand why the Piaroa and the Ye'kwana do not recognize shared parenting, understood as the socially recognized intervention of two or more genitors.

We collected our field data on the Piaroa between 1984 and 1998. Our data relating specifically to shared paternity we obtained from 1997 to 1998 from Piaroa of the Sipapo and Autana river basins. We collected our Ye'kwana field data between 1987 and 1998 from the Caura river basin dwellers.

The Piaroa: General Ethnography

Also known in the literature as the Wothuja and the Dearua, the Piaroa are an Indian people of the Sáliva language group whose 16,000 members occupy a large area of the Vichada Department in Colombia and the states of Amazonas and Bolívar in Venezuela.[1] Their traditional habitat was around the minor black-water rivers and thickly wooded interfluvial regions of the Sipapo,

Samariapo, Cataniapo, Parguaza, Suapure, and Manapiare river basins. During the last 40 years a rapid process of migration has brought the Piaroa to the edge of the great rivers of the region—the Orinoco and the Ventuari. However, data indicate that they are only recently adapting to these new locations. For instance, many features of their technology are more suited to the resources of the small streams that were their traditional habitat (Mansutti Rodríguez 1988c, 20).

While there has been a marked concentration of population near the Orinoco, the Piaroa traditionally lived scattered in the forest, occupying small village communities (*malocas*) of no more than 30 inhabitants that often associated with other villages to form neighborhoods. Demographic density is approximately 0.25 inhabitants per square kilometer, but this is a result of recent significant demographic growth (Mansutti Rodríguez 1993a, 25). According to the ethnographic literature (Anduze 1974, 32; Codazzi 1940, 46–47, 50; Hitchcock 1948, 168; Overing 1975, 15), density previously did not peak above 0.1 inhabitants per square kilometer.

The Piaroa do not have corporate groups. Rather, they have kin groups called *tjutamu* (of my grandfather) or *anokuotju* (root) with a marked bias toward patrilateral filiation. Such groups do not include ritual associations nor do they carry any obligation for members. Tjutamu or anokuotju are a key indicator of the historic memory of the people, demonstrating the assimilation to Piaroa society of members of other indigenous groups (Mansutti Rodríguez 1993b, 508; Zent 1992, 354). It is said that these groups were linked to specific territories, and that there existed a hierarchy similar to that of the Tukano social organization in the Vaupés region (Århem 1981, 120–21; Chernela 1985, 78–79; S. Hugh-Jones 1993, 108).

The maloca is the center of Piaroa life. Inside family relationships may be constructed in different ways. Nevertheless, there is always an elder man considered master of the house (*itsode'ruwa*). He and his wife are usually accompanied by some married children, usually daughters given the uxorilocal pattern of postmarital residence, and occasionally by one or more brothers or sisters of the senior partnership and the partners of some of the children (Mansutti Rodríguez 1988a, 24, 26; Monod 1987, 63; Overing 1975, 91–95; Zent 1992, 474–75). There are accounts of large malocas where there used to be two or more groups of this type, but they were exceptional and short-lived.

While food may be prepared simultaneously at several hearths in the maloca, its collective distribution always falls to the itsode'ruwa. After praying over the food to divest it of any illness-bearing potential he shares it out. In the Piaroa world, food production is coordinated among all community members. Almost all production is carried out by individuals or small groups. A few exceptional activities, such as fishing with *barbasco* intoxicants, are collective ventures. Food preparation occurs within the nuclear family; its distribution occurs within the collective domain of the village.

Sibling kinship is very strong and is a key network on which today's larger communities are based. Before the introduction of vaccination programs, rates of infant mortality were so high that it was less likely that most of the children of the same maloca survived. Today, however, it is common to find villages where at least two siblings reside together—often the itsode'ruwa, together with his sister, and their respective partners. The bilateral cross-cousins (*chusapo*) marriage pattern converts husbands (*chirekwo*) of a group of sisters (real or classificatory) into "brothers" (*chubuo* or *chijawa*). A sexual relationship between a woman and one of her husband's brothers is not defined as incestuous. However, we have never encountered instances of such liaisons occurring within the domestic group. On the other hand, we have come upon cases of marriage being dissolved because of the man's unfaithfulness or because the woman has abandoned her husband, and even her children, to run off with her lover. But these sexual relations take place only between individuals from different settlements. Sexual relationships with close nonmarriageable relatives are totally prohibited. If they were to occur, it is believed the rule breakers would be punished by ill fortune and the most painful of sanctions. They would be eaten alive by a jaguar or bitten by a snake. Infidelity is always undesirable, but the seriousness of the infraction depends on who it occurs with. Control of feelings is of paramount value to the Piaroa. The masculine archetype is a thin man (who controls his appetite), who is wise (who controls his tongue), who is incapable of exercising physical violence (who controls his strength), and who never falls prey to outbursts of rage or merriment (who controls his emotions). Those who behave in this way are eligible to receive shamanic knowledge and inherit the right to hold a Warime celebration. They become *tjujatju'ruwa*, or masters of people. By contrast the women, being unable to control themselves, cannot become great leaders.

Piaroa Theories of Fertilization: Gestation and Growth of the Fetus

Tjuure is the word the Piaroa use to signify semen.[2] It is associated with the noun *ujura*, used by the Piaroa to designate the power and roar of the jaguar (*Panthera onca*). Thus tjuure translates as "our (masculine) power"; consequently, for the Piaroa semen is a substance of power.

Fertilization, the act of creating new life from life, is viewed in different ways in the Piaroa world. The origin myth of the Piaroa recounts that the semen of the Ofuo'daa, the famous half-tapir (*Tapirus terrestris*) half-anaconda (*Eunectes murinus*), engendered in a quartz vessel—the shamanic metaphor for the uterus—a mythical deer called Buo'ka, who in turn created from his vision a brother and sister, called Wajari and Chejeru (Boglár 1978).

Represented here in the quartz and the semen, shamanism and the material world, are constants of a society that assumes that all things material are an expression of the fertilizing thought of the original creator, Änämäin. These thoughts are seen and materialized by Wajari, thanks to his ability to see the invisible bestowed by wisdom (*akurewa*) and the shamanic tools (*märipa*). These material and magic worlds together explain each of the acts of fertilization and gestation that human beings witness during their lives.

With his shamanism, it is up to Wajari to materialize the known world—a universe already created by Änämäin in the realm of the invisible. The Piaroa have access to that invisible realm via ritual and propitiatory songs that help them conjure from the belly of the mountains the souls of animals and plants they require for their survival. These beings, once released, are fertilized by the shamans with their power of thought so that they multiply (*wejutju*) before being materialized.

Toward the conclusion of Piaroa's origin myth, Wajari goes fishing and models people from the flesh of his catch (Morales et al. 1984, 5). Once he has managed to make human beings they become alive through the power of his thought. In all these processes, magical intervention, via the power of the shaman's tools, allows fertilization and gestation. In every case, it is the power of words and visionary thought that gestates potential new material realities.

Paradoxically, the power of shamanism is limited in the case of fertilization of a woman by a man. The Piaroa conceive of human fertilization as a process belonging to the material world—shamanic power may prevent it, yet is unable to control gestation once it has been initiated. Fertilization is subject to fate because the Piaroa lost the power to initiate it when Wajari, the materializing demiurge, quarreled with Änämäin, the original power of the original times. If Wajari had been more prudent and not quarreled with Änämäin, then the Piaroa could be materialized in the same way as the Ofuo'dau created Buo'ka with their semen, or the master of prayer (*meyeruwa*) materializes animals and plants. They would not have had to leave fertilization and the determination of the sex of their children to fate. As punishment, Änämäin left the process of fertilization and determination of the sex of the offspring to the mercy of factors exogenous to those of the shaman's creative powers.[3] Thus the shaman is able to intervene only to prevent a pregnancy. Once the seed contained in the sperm has established itself he can only help guide the healthy development of the child, but he cannot definitively decide, although he may try, exactly when a woman will become pregnant and what sex the offspring will be.

The word for sexual relations in Piaroa is *itjikuiu*, which means "delivery of child." The Piaroa believe that the man puts a seed into his semen (*tjuure*) that once rooted becomes a child. Once the child is created then growth occurs thanks to the prayer (*meyé*) of pregnancy, which wards off adversity. This prayer calls upon mythical personages whose assistance can ensure the fetus's healthy growth (Oldham 1998, 233). There is no role for the semen other than the semen that provided the original seed, as semen arriving at the uterus after fertilization "do not contribute to strengthen the child." What is discernible is the conjunction between the material fact, "the seed deposited in the man who fertilizes," and "the power of thought and word, represented in the *meyé* which guides the growth of the seed." This view coincides with that of other indigenous groups inhabiting lowland areas, who conceive of the uterus as a receptacle, yet contrasts with others, who conceive of the accumulation of semen as a condition of the fertilization or an indispensable nourishment for the growth of a healthy child (Arvelo-Jiménez 1974, 84; Viveiros de Castro 1992, 179–80; Thomas 1982, 62). The semen as seed undermines the possibility of shared paternity based on semen as a fetus-forming or child-nourishing agent during gestation. In contrast, the recognition of the formational power of prayer (i.e., thought) opens the possibility for the chanter (*meyeruwa*) to be recognized as "gestator" of the fetus. However, the meyeruwa (the master of prayer), who guides the pregnancy, is not considered to possess special abilities that entail shared paternity. This makes sense if we think that in general, the most important shaman in a community tends to be the father or brother of the pregnant woman, neither of whom could possibly be the father of the expected child.

Marriage and Sexual Partnerships

Even when Piaroa gender relationships are kind and understanding, without overt aggression and with the active participation of men and women in domestic matters, they still cannot be defined as equal. Indeed, the most important manifestations of power and authority in Piaroa society are monopolized by men. Warime, the ceremony celebrating the constructive power of the spirit, is a privilege of the mature men and its organization is monopolized by those men who inherit that right. The meyé, the propitiatory and preventive prayers that protect families, cure the sick, and make the earth flourish, are also a male privilege and few women have gained the right to say them. Nor are the shamanic rites (*märipa*) performed by women,[4] as men openly mistrust women's ability to wield such powerful forces and instruments.

This masculine control of power is expressed by the control adult men exercise over their women's movements to other settlements and around the maloca. They also have a monopoly on aggressive shamanism, and give more weight to the male contribution to the development of their children's attributes.

Given the absence of corporate groups and the conceptual impossibility of several men fertilizing one woman at the same time, it might be thought that this would enable socially accepted forms of infidelity. However, although the acceptance of infidelity is theoretically possible, it is not acceptable. The fear of disorder implicit in the loss of control of one's appetites, a defect that men attribute to women and children, acts as a brake upon the social acknowledgment of extramarital relations, always the product of uncontrolled appetites.

The introduction of elements of shared paternity is unthinkable in a society that upholds control of appetite as a standard conferring prestige and authority (Mansutti Rodríguez 1991, 83). Infidelity is not spoken of publicly, it is secret, and when a woman suspects it in a man she has the power to behave similarly in revenge. Either way disclosure always sparks a scandal.

Kinship and Paternity

Being recognized as a pater signifies being acknowledged as a transmitter of culturally defined rights and duties. At the same time, being recognized as a pater is to locate oneself in an ascending line of paters that accounts for one's origin. In the Piaroa case, descent is rarely traced beyond the grandparents.

Piaroa society functions in accordance with the Dravidian model of cognatic kinship but with a significant patrilateral marriage bias. This Dravidian model promotes marriage between bilateral cross-cousins and, in the Piaroa world, matri-uxorilocal postmarital residence (Mansutti Rodríguez and Briceño-Fustec 1993; Overing 1975). Sex, generation, and colaterality are the factors that regulate the structure of the terminology. Formally, the system requires a child to call all men belonging to the genealogical generation of its parents, "father" (*cha-o*), whether they are classified as "father's brother" or "mother's sister's husband." Given that in this generation there are only four large parental groups and that they tend to share the members in equal parts, then it may be presumed that a Piaroa child will call 25% of the total population belonging to its parents' genealogical generation,[5] and 50% of the male members, father, cha-o. In theory, then, a Piaroa child benefits in some way from a form of shared paternity.

However, this system is not always consistent with the system of associated obligations. The language of kinship generates social topologies, which allow us to locate the actors within specific social relationships. These locations contain inherent associative potentials, which may or may not materialize. The strength of the bond depends on social proximity. Those who are close relatives—what the Piaroa call *tjuku chawaruwa*—form a rigid network, but the location and designation of those who are in more distant relationships (*otomena chawaruwa*) depend on the wishes of those involved to develop the potential relationship implicit in the terminology.

The flexibility of Piaroa "hot" kinship (Godelier, Trautmann, and Tjon Sie Fat 1998, 5) is related to the inflexibility of their kinship terminology, which divides the members of society into watertight compartments, rigidly determining potential husbands or allies. This inflexible system is not viable, as the low population density and the disturbances caused by age differences within each generation would lead to the inevitable consequence that, after a few generations, there would not be a partner for each person (Mansutti Rodríguez and Briceño-Fustec 1993, 61). Therefore the "real" or "hot" system, as Godelier and his colleagues call it, generates mechanisms by which a person can be renamed according to the particularities of the circumstances. However, the redefinition of terms, with the aim of broadening the field of potential allies cannot be used to assign more than one genitor to a person.

The Piaroa system, as well as having several alternative methods of finding the most suitable kinship relationship, also has mechanisms that enforce the redefinition of relationship networks where matrimonial links are established. Indeed the most important relationship for the Piaroa is that of marriage. It is so important that once it occurs all other relationships are reordered. Thus, if ego marries his classificatory younger sister (*chijawa*) the marriage alters the existing relationship between the husband and the woman's close relatives. The brothers become brothers-in-law (*chusapo*), and the classificatory parents become parents-in-law (*chimiya* and *chimiyaju*). The wife, who prior to marrying was not a potential wife (*chusapo isaju*) but a younger sister (*chijawa*), now becomes a wife (*chirekwa*). He, without ever being a potential husband (*chusapo*) now becomes a husband (*chirekwo*). This postmarital reordering of kinship relationships could be used to define modes of shared paternity. However, this does not occur. When a man marries a woman with children he is free to take on those obligations associated with the condition of "father" to the children.

Even when in general men accept the responsibilities of fathering the children of another man with the new wife, the treatment of the children depends on the support of the man involved. One female informant told us, "That depends on whether he is a good man or not." We have records of cases when the children of a previous union at the time of a second marriage were given by the mother to the grandparents, either maternal or paternal, for them to bring up. However, this tends to be the exception. Usually the new husband acts as father to his wife's children.

Known and acknowledged paternity is so important in Piaroa society that until a few years ago a child with no known or acknowledged father was destined to die either through infanticide or neglect. We have reference of a case of a child saved by the grandfather; the women wanted to kill the child as it had been conceived by a criollo who, while recognized as the father, was not approved by the women. Once again it is clear that the Piaroa demand a clear paternal relationship—this is an obstacle to the recognition of multiple fertilization and gestation.

In conclusion, the small size of the Piaroa maloca, the control of food distribution by the community patriarch, the keen emphasis on control of the emotions, and the lack of corporate groups, make Piaroa society an infertile ground for the acknowledgment of modes of shared paternity. Among the Piaroa such a practice does not facilitate easier access to food, and it would be limited by the few available men in the village. In the Piaroa case shared paternity does not strengthen patrilineages and has no impact on any particular matrilineage. Finally, the practice would impede the political and ritual advancement of those unable to rein in their sexual appetite.

The Ye'kwana

The Ye'kwana—also known as the Makiritares, Mayongon, or Maionkong— are an ethnic group of the Caribe language family whose population of some 4,000 individuals live scattered along the river basins of the Upper Orinoco, Cuntinamo, Padamo, Cunucunuma, and Ventuari Rivers in Amazonas State and the Caura and Paragua Rivers in Bolivar State, Venezuela. A small population is also found along the Uraricoera River in Brazil.

Catholic missionaries have been present among the Caura Ye'kwana since 1958. Apart from providing education, the mission was also a magnet for the people of the area. This led to less mobility and the creation of high-density permanent settlements. In this region the average village population is 169. The headman (*kajiichana*), who represents authority, leads each village. He makes decisions together with the heads of families and other elders. Previously, the predominant pattern of settlement was one single community dwelling (*churuata*) for the whole village; this only exists today in the smaller settlements.

Each maloca has a center where the unmarried men sleep and where communal food is prepared. On the periphery is a concentric ring formed by compartments occupied by the extended families. The center is called *anna* and the periphery *ösa*. When the villages grow and small neighborhoods are created, the distribution of dwellings reproduces the distribution of the family groups in the ösa of the previous maloca (Silva Monterrey 1992). The community maloca, in the center of a village, where the houses are close together, is like the original anna. It is here the communal meals and celebrations are held. Indeed this communal maloca is also called anna.

Each village, in addition to having a headman, has a cook who is in charge of organizing communal meals and ensuring that there is sufficient food for the men during their daily meals in the central maloca. As and when necessary he requests supplementary food from the other households for the men's table. Despite his title he does not actually cook; rather the women of his family do the cooking. The cook receives any surplus meat from the households, which is distributed generously in the anna for locals and visitors alike. His role as cook is even more important at the community celebrations, as the food and drink are his responsibility.

The food goes first to his house, where the women prepare manioc bread, vegetables, and meats. At communal mealtimes, at least twice daily, the families send the men their food rations. The women eat in the family home together with their children. The women decide which food to send to the anna for the men; the only food that escapes their control is the surplus given directly to the cook by the producers.

The women of a household work closely together in producing and cooking food. They are the mainstay of the Ye'kwana village domestic space. A community is constructed from the dwelling of a father with his wife and unmarried daughters plus the houses of the married daughters and their children. The norm proscribing marriage with the first cross-cousin may mean that several consanguineous brothers marry several consanguineous sisters, but this is not frequent. However, although they might not share close family ties within the group of husbands and co-brothers-in-law, they establish close cooperation and it is common to see them traveling and organizing hunting parties together.

Female fidelity is an important value for the Ye'kwana. A man's philandering may be tolerated, but female infidelity is considered an offense. If a woman's infidelity is discovered she will probably be abandoned and those who are fickle will have trouble finding a husband because, as the men say, Who would want to be responsible for her? This attitude toward women shows how much they are controlled. In the past it was common for women to let their hair grow as a sign of fidelity while their menfolk were away traveling. There are cases where the community, observing the fickle and unfaithful behavior of particular women, obliged them to cut their hair as a punishment. If the husband returned at that time he would easily discover that his wife had been unfaithful without anyone actually having to tell him.

Ye'kwana Theories of Fertilization and Fetus Gestation

For the Ye'kwana sex is an intimate subject. Elderly or very extroverted women may talk about it, but that is unusual. Indeed when the subject is mentioned women lower their heads and the men blush. This was all true in the heterosexual dialogue between the researcher (female) and the male Ye'kwana.

In Ye'kwana mythology Wanadi, the demiurge creator, was not born from a woman but rather was conceived and materialized from tobacco smoke. Then Wanadi created his people from his *wiriki,* the supernatural magic stone encountered in shamanic maracas.

The demon Kajushawa, also known as Odosha, was "born from a woman on his own initiative." Wanadi did not like this and got very angry, saying that from then on problems would occur, "as to be born in such a way was not good."

There are different explanations of how a baby is made. It is held that having sexual relations during pregnancy is positive as this makes the baby's growth more harmonious. The role of the semen as a nutritious element is not clear, however, although it might well be inferred from this practice. It is also considered that during fertilization the baby receives blood from the father and that the mother is merely a receptacle.[6] This is expressed clearly in the Ye'kwana language, as the uterus is called *sichu ewiti* (i.e., the uterus is considered the vessel for the child). The baby is nourished by the food ingested by the mother but there is no elaborate explanation of how and where the baby grows.

It is important to note that blood is almost sacred for these people. It is a source of life but equally of pain and sickness. Blood in any form (menstrual blood, from wounds, etc.) must be avoided. Prohibitions exist; for example, men must not eat animal marrow, especially deer, as the marrow generates blood and bad blood may be passed to the child of a man if he gets a woman pregnant.

From the ethnobiological point of view, a child has just one creator, and men are always referred to as the father of such and such a child: a child always has only one father. While several colleagues (Arvelo-Jiménez 1974; Heinen, pers. comm., 1995) have evidence that in the past the possibility of shared paternity existed, today this is quite inconceivable for the Ye'kwana of the Caura region. According to Arvelo-Jiménez, "the Ye'kwana believe that each sexual act contributes to conception, and consequently they consider that it is a process composed of repeated coitus. The semen accumulates gradually and increases the volume of the content of the uterus until it is completely full. At that moment conception has reached its zenith and the woman is pregnant. They argue that every man who has sexual contact with a woman before she becomes pregnant is considered father and genitor of her next child. Thus many people have more than one parent/genitor. The bones are inherited from the father and the blood from the mother" (1974, 84).

Today in the Caura these ideas have shifted somewhat. This may be due to a variety of influences or just a response to regional variations in understanding the subject. With regard to the belief that fertilization is a process of filling up the uterus, it appears that "people used to think that" but they insist on clarifying that this process should be undertaken preferably just by one man, the husband, the head of the family, and not by several men. If a woman is unfaithful and acknowledges the fact, then the men who were with her immediately before the recognition of the pregnancy are considered potential genitors. The Ye'kwana women are able to recognize a pregnancy in its very early stages, even before regular menstruation ceases. From somatological observation of their nipples changing they can quickly and reliably detect a pregnancy and begin to discuss whether there are doubts as to the parenthood of the baby. The men who have been with a woman before the detection of the pregnancy may openly declare their relationship and assume possible paternity but this does not bring with it any commitment to the mother or child. In this case it is established that the woman assumes responsibility, while the men who were with her before she became pregnant, or else the offended husband (if she is married), have to decide if they are going to raise the child or leave it to the mother. If a man denies a possible paternity, rumors circulate without further repercussions.

In the past, a pregnancy with no defined father was considered to have been engendered by the devil and infanticide may have been invoked. Nowadays, a father may be identified, or if not, it is said that the mother does not wish to name him. This reasoning excludes the devil and saves the child. According to our data it is considered that just one man is the father and it is he who undertakes to raise the child.

We found a notable difference in relation to what Arvelo-Jiménez (1974, 84) asserts regarding the contribution of the parents to the formation of the child. In the Caura the women say that they are simply like a bag and so men have rights over the child as it is via their semen (*ku'ta*) that they fertilize (*yomodetaadü*). It is the men who give their blood to children.[7]

Marriage and Sexual Partnerships

Couples marry or establish partnerships at the age of 15 to 17. The Ye'kwana in general are monogamous, even when polygamy is permitted. It is socially acceptable for people to have premarital relations. The mothers arrange marriages with the approval of the fathers and upon the request and with the consent of those involved. Occasionally, the shamans oblige someone into an unwished-for marriage but this is quite rare.

Married men and women avoid each other in public and tend to be discreet in their behavior as a couple. They are only seen together in the family home, in their gardens, or while traveling. Displays of affection only occur within the domestic environment. Public avoidance is such that the married couples avoid each other even at parties when people dance criollo style; the married men dance with the unwed girls even when their own wives are present. The marriage tie is reaffirmed publicly by the wives taking food to their husbands in the maloca.

At mealtimes the men eat together in the maloca while the women usually eat at home with their children. On those rare occasions when the women eat in the maloca they do so at a separate time from the men. For example, during parties the men eat first and the women at a second shift.

Political power is wielded by the men, who organize community life on the basis of work to be done, trips to be made, and relationships to be established with the surrounding communities. Women have control over the domestic space and garden production. They also organize for community tasks and have their own female leader. She often confers with the male leaders, together establishing priorities for work and other projects.

Women and men have different spheres of power; the women exercise theirs in the local-domestic arena while the men's power extends to the regional and strategic global sphere. Women also have access to symbolic knowledge. There are no women shamans today but we know that there often were in the past. They participate actively in ritual with their own knowledge of magic.

However, having access to certain levels of power does not thereby allow women freedom of movement. Women may not travel alone but must always be accompanied by close male relatives or other female relatives and always with the consent of their husbands or fathers. The feminine ideal is that of a decorous, hard-working, faithful woman who "does not go wandering around all over the place"; they should be home-loving women who apply themselves to their work, their parents, their husband, and if they have them, their children. It is this ideal of modesty that in our view undercuts the possibility of shared paternity.

The masculine ideal is that of a hard-working, cooperative man concerned with looking after his family. Within this ideal, infidelity is disruptive. Women show displeasure at a husband's unfaithfulness, and if it continues against the wife's wishes it can lead to the breakdown of the relationship. The men at any rate tend to be discreet with their peccadilloes although social control is less rigid in their case.

Kinship and Paternity

The Ye'kwana have a Dravidian kinship system. There are no corporate groups and kinship is cognatic with a strong patrilateral tendency. This is clearly demonstrated with children of persons who have married into other ethnic groups, where the Ye'kwana consider that a child belongs to the group of the father. Ye'kwana men assume fathering responsibilities from an early age. The young man looks after his child with the guidance of the parents-in-law, who also support his own continuing development. The Ye'kwana believe that with each new child the cycle of family life is begun once more, as if they were all reborn.

When the child is born, the acknowledged father enters couvade and, like the mother, must adhere to strict food prohibitions. Further, the father and mother must respect a series of compensatory restrictions that guarantee the strong, healthy growth of the child. For example, among other things, the father-genitor with a newborn baby cannot go hunting or play musical instruments.

If the baby falls sick and it is necessary to practice a vengeance rite such as the *woi*, the father-genitor and only he, together with the mother and the biological brothers of the sick person, must comply with a series of restrictions that should lead to the sick person regaining good health.

In other words, genitor paternity implies a series of obligations and restrictions that do not apply to terminological paternity. If the woman is unsure who her child's father is then the possible genitors have no commitment or restriction upon them. Within the domestic group the father-genitor is the main, but not the sole, provider of meat and fish. Occasionally the women fish but this is usually when the husband is absent. If the husband is absent then the mother's father will supply protein to the grandchildren. The unmarried men resident in the paternal house also provide protein to close kin, including the children of their consanguineous siblings. The Ye'kwana have broad networks of cooperation and after a good hunting trip the distribution mechanism will ensure that part of the product will be shared with even distant relatives. The women grow crops, which ensure daily survival at all times given that the men are frequently on the move. Despite this constant traveling, relations between the genitors and their children are very affectionate. Parents are caring and loving with their children especially during infancy. As the children grow the boys become involved in the father's productive activities and the girls work alongside their mothers. While they pass a lot of time separated, the fathers have a close relationship with their daughters, which is strengthened by the custom of matri-uxorilocal residence. As for the boys, once they marry the relationship with the father-genitor and in general with the nuclear family are limited by the restrictions of life within a new family.

In accordance with the Dravidian terminology, ego considers his or her father's brothers "fathers" (*waja*). These other "fathers" have similar obligations and relations with these "sons" and "daughters," even if they are not their own. However, the duties related to postmatrimonial residence in the case of women and economic cooperation occur only in the case of the father-genitor. A classificatory father may have great esteem for his children (his brother's children) and in the absence of the genitor, temporary or not, will establish a relationship of cooperation and help with his brother's progeny when necessary. When the genitor has many siblings there might be little age difference between the eldest children and the classificatory fathers. The relationship between them, therefore, while respectful, is more one of camaraderie.

Paternity for the Ye'kwana of the Caura River then can be summed up thus: (1) paternity is attributed to the person who conceives the child and recognizes the child as his—that is, a single individual recognized as genitor; and (2) social paternity is ascribed to all the individuals that in the Dravidian kinship system fall into the category of "father" (waja)—that is, the father-genitor and his brothers and any husbands of the mother who, given the closed nature of the system, correspond to father's brothers.

Discussion

Both Piaroa and Ye'kwana have Dravidian kinship systems that pave the way for the possibility and the actual occurrence of several men being called "father." This is a formal condition that may facilitate the recognition of shared paternity for a particular ego as long as it involves those men called "father." Equally, both have specific terms for husband/wife—*chirekwo/chirekwa* for the Piaroa and *inño/jinñammo* for the Ye'kwana—which signifies a revision from the basis of the matrimonial tie, of the ego-centered kinship relationship. Both conditions bring flexibility to the kinship system so that the existence of shared paternity is recognized in the language of the family.

Both societies equally conceive of the uterus as a receptacle in which the sperm generates the pregnancy. This belief facilitates a view of the child as a product of the semen contributed by one or several fathers. However, the Piaroa assume that the pregnancy is a product of the rooting in the uterus of the seed of the father's semen, an idea that is expressed in the word for having sex (*itjikuiu;* lit., "delivering the child") and in the metaphor for semen which Krisólogo (1976, 85) found: *chiwiriwi hakua chawa,* or "seed-liquid from the penis." Given that it is a seed that germinates, it is not possible for more than one father to be responsible for fertilization. Indeed the Piaroa say that the semen deposited in the uterus of a pregnant woman in sexual relations after fertilization contributes nothing to the fetus.

The Caura Ye'kwana think differently. They believe that the accumulation of a specific quantity of semen deposited by the man in the uterus during several acts of coitus unleashes the pregnancy and that sex after that can nourish the fetus. It is unclear if this belief implies that they also believe in shared paternity. On the contrary they insist on single paternity. Therefore, we face two options in the Ye'kwana case: either that the Caura Ye'kwana have a different view of paternity from the Ventuari and Upper Orinoco Ye'kwana, or that we have a paradigm shift as regards fertilization and gestation.

Impeding shared paternity in both societies is the food distribution system. We know in the case of the Barí (Beckerman et al. 1998, 166) that those children who have more than one progenitor have greater access to animal protein and thus greater chances of survival. However, in the case of the Piaroa and the Ye'kwana, having more than one father does not make a great difference in terms of access to food, as distribution is collective in both societies and anyway in Piaroa society a responsibility of the itsode'ruwa, who shares it out fairly on the basis of age and sex, while the distribution of food among the Caura Ye'kwana is controlled by the women, who thereby ensure access for themselves and their children. The access of adult men to food is a *sui generis* system ensuring they are provided with food grown by their family as well as access to community surplus. Both societies have a patrilateral bias and thus give more political power to the men. But neither has patrilineal corporate groups whose existence could be strengthened by specific forms of shared paternity, nor does either have inheritance mechanisms that depend on belonging to a kin group.

A common element in both societies, but one whose weight we are unable to ascertain, is that for at least 30 years they have been subject to three Western discourses that may well have influenced their theories of fertilization and paternity: the Christian discourse, the biomedical discourse, and biology as taught in school. However, we believe that if a theory of fertilization and shared paternity were deeply rooted in both societies, then 30 years of systematic Western influence would be insufficient to generate radical change in all the generational groups of the society. Consequently, either there has been insufficient sociological force in the institution and theory of shared paternity in both societies, or the way in which the Caura Ye'kwana perceive shared paternity is a regional variant, different from that of the Ye'kwana of the Upper Orinoco and Ventuari regions. This would explain the similarities and differences of their positions vis-à-vis Arvelo-Jiménez's findings. Further, these regional variants provide a provocative example that neither proximity nor the intensity of the exchange of ideas, goods, and services is a guarantee of homogeneity among Amazonian lowland societies.

Finally, both societies demonstrate extreme rebuttal of infidelity. Among the Piaroa, Anduze (1974, 95, 117) reports infidelity as undesirable. This ethnography was based on research carried out between 1958 and 1967, when the process of sociocultural change was just beginning to speed up. Further, no author we know of has reported the possibility of shared paternity among the Piaroa. This confirms our hypothesis that in the Piaroa cases this institution is unknown. In the Ye'kwana case as we saw, infidelity merits severe reprisals. Therefore we may assert that in both cases it is an undesirable practice that provokes shame and tension, and may lead to divorce. Shared paternity, in the absence of mechanisms to socially legitimate its effects, is not viable even though it may be conceptually possible.

Conclusions

The family is the linchpin of society and at the same time reflects changes in the system. An institution such as shared paternity, which appears on the periphery of kinship and marriage systems as one way to strengthen social institutions like patrilineal corporate groups or which increases some children's survival chances, does not appear to have sufficient strength to become a universal institution in lowland Amazonia. Many societies located there have no type of corporate group and resolve the problem of equitable food distribution along other channels.

Another interesting conclusion brings us to focus on the wide variety of situations extant in these neighboring lowland societies. The Piaroa and the Caura Ye'kwana have very different ideas regarding paternity, fertilization, and gestation; however, both disapprove of shared paternity as the ideal.

Among the Ye'kwana we have encountered a wide range of views on fertility and gestation, a clear example that implies that neither regional proximity, nor the intensity of interchange of ideas, goods, and services are a guarantee of the social and cultural homogeneity among or within lowland Amazonian societies.

Notes

The authors express their gratitude to their informants and to financial agencies that have made this research possible. We also thank the Venezuelan Consejo Nacional de Investigaciones Científicas y Tecnológicas (National Council for Technological and Scientific Research, CONICIT), the Fundación para la Ciencia y la Tecnología de la Región Guayana (Foundation for Science and Technology in the Guayana Region, FUNDACITE-Guayana), the Universidad Nacional Experimental de Guayana (Guayana National Experimental University, UNEG), and the BioGuayana Programme.

1. This figure comes from the reported Piaroa population in the Indigenous Census of 1992 (Venezuela 1993), giving a projected decennial growth rate of 60%.

2. Overing (1986, 147) asserts another term to designate semen (*edeku*), also used to denote excrement and vomit, which would create a certain analogy among the three things. According to our notes (Mansutti 1988b, 66) a cognate from *edeku—edere—*is used to designate vomit, which approximates Overing's argument and also that of Krisólogo (1976, 92) and Krute (1988, 303), who talk of *edo'wah/chedewa,* other possible cognates. In contrast, neither Krisólogo nor I agree with Overing's gloss on the category for semen. Krisólogo says that the term is *chiwiriwi hakua chawa,* which translates literally as "seed-liquid from the pe-

nis" and thus could be viewed more as an allegory than a concept. In the research that I have carried out both on myths and on shamanism and daily life, the category I have encountered for semen, *tjuure,* certainly is very similar to the notion of fertility encountered by Oldham (1998, 237), a graduate student of Overing.

3. Oldham (1998, 232) says that the Piaroa can intervene in the choice of their child's sex. This may be a regional variation on the theme as his informants come from the Paria River, to the north of where we collected our data.

4. However this does not prevent some women from becoming chanters (*meyeruwa*), a specialized shamanic function devoted to propitiatory prayers to prevent or cure illness, to make nature flourish, and to intervene in the most varied aspects of daily life. Presently one of the most powerful Piaroa meyeruwa is a woman living in a small maloca by the Gavilán River, a tributary of the lower Cataniapo. It is still quite exceptional nonetheless. It is even harder for women to employ shamanic functions of a *yuwäwäruwa*, or *soplador* (as the chanter is called in criollo Spanish) for these are shamans in charge of using the *märipa* or more aggressive sorcery. There is no evidence of any woman ever becoming a yuwäwäruwa.

5. A genealogical generation is that integrated by all the individuals named with the kinship terms of the same terminological generation. Thus all individuals named *cha-o, cha-ju, chimiya,* and *chimiyaju*—the four terms that cover G + 1—are members of the genealogical generation of ego's parents, whatever his or her age.

6. During the presentation of a draft of this article, as a paper at the Congress of Americanists, Catherine Alès commented that in her research in Amazonas State, Venezuela, she had found that the Ye'kwana believed that the blood was provided by the mother.

7. Note that Arvelo-Jiménez says that the blood is given by the mother and not the father. In relation to the bones (*ye'jö*) Ye'kwana have no clear explanation.

12

Paternal Uncertainty and Ritual Kinship among the Warao

H. Dieter Heinen and Werner Wilbert

Reliable ethnographic information pertaining to traditional Warao beliefs about paternity, conception, and childbirth does not extend beyond the 1950s. To complicate matters, since 1980 many Warao communities have undergone profound culture change, rendering certain native customs inconsequential vestiges of the past. Although this general situation could seriously skew our findings, we believe that, with few exceptions, the elderly of our target population grew up under what might be considered traditional social conditions. Accordingly, the ethnographic present of this paper applies to Warao culture of the early twentieth century, attested through longitudinal fieldwork since 1966 (Heinen) and 1983 (Wilbert), respectively. The data presented in this chapter were mostly obtained among the Winikina subgroup of the lower central Orinoco delta. It remains to be seen how applicable they are to Warao society as a whole.

Ecological and Social Environments

The Warao habitat comprises primarily the wetlands of the Orinoco delta and, secondarily, adjacent territories in Venezuela and Guyana. Ecologically, the primary region can be divided into an upper and a lower delta. During the principal rainy season, the water of the Orinoco main stem overflows its banks, inundating the upper delta for several months at a time. In the lower delta this annual event is less dramatic, owing to the diffusionary effect of its distributaries and secondary channels. In contrast, the hydrodynamics of the lower delta is mainly governed by tidal flooding.

The lower delta is a vast swampland with mangrove forests extending far inland along the banks of its nonfunctional distributaries. The region is crisscrossed by major distributaries and interconnecting secondary channels. The myriad of islands formed by this network of rivers feature pronounced levees and extensive groves of moriche palm (*Mauritia flexuosa*), or morichals, that particularly in the southeastern delta reach from the riverbanks far into the island interiors. Perhaps the only areas qualifying as terra firma are the Amacuro region, south of the delta, and stretches along the Sierra de la Paloma, west of the Gulf of Paria in the state of Sucre.[1]

The Warao are of Chibchan affiliation and descendants of ancient marshland foragers and fishermen whose presence in the Orinoco delta predates the arrival of Cariban and Arawakan farmers by several thousand years. The largely inaccessible territory served its aboriginal occupants as an effective refuge from Western encroachment. However, rather than existing here in virtual isolation, the Warao took part in a vast and multiethnic trade network that operated until early colonial times. Functioning as a system of regional subsistence specializations, the network facilitated the exchange, among others, of fish and game for horticultural products. Modern Warao, numbering approximately 29,000 individuals, concentrate in the lower central and particularly the southeastern sectors of the lower delta, between the Arawao (Araguao) and Wirinoko (Río Grande del Orinoco) Rivers.

Generally speaking, the Warao inhabit two main social environments. One of these prevails in the northwestern delta, where a cofferdam constructed on the Manamo distributary has profoundly altered the hydrodynamics of the region.[2] The intrusion of brackish water forced hundreds of Warao to relocate further upriver. This placed them into the distinctly different ecological niches occupied by the criollos near Tucupita, the state capital, where they began adapting to cattle ranching and urban life (García Castro and Heinen n.d.). The second social environment of Warao is found mainly in the central delta, where communities continue as "morichaleros" (gatherers of moriche sago, and true marshland dwellers). In the sixteenth century Sir Walter Raleigh identified the ancestors of these people as Waraweete, "true Warao."[3]

Because all Warao speak the same language, they were long considered culturally homogeneous. However, closer scrutiny revealed them as a composite of diversely specialized regional groups. Some were nonagricultural fishermen and foragers who, until the 1950s, depended on moriche sago as their staff of life. Others were farmers who cultivated various tubers, including manioc and taro. Still others, like the Siawani, specialized in the construction of seaworthy dugout canoes in which they navigated the Caribbean.

Composition of Domestic Groups

Contemporary settlements that occupy a large area have spawned a number of misconceptions regarding Warao domestic groups and marriage patterns. However, large settlements were found to actually consist of multiple dwelling clusters, symbolically separated from one another by a few meters of vacant land.[4] Each cluster corresponds to a domestic group (or band) that formerly frequented the morichals as a differentiated social unit. Although Warao domestic groups are clearly exogamous, marriages between members of such groups in multicluster villages have given the erroneous impression of domestic-group endogamy. Endogamy is indeed practiced by the Warao, but at the level of agglomeration (or subtribe),[5] comprising several clusters of villages with a combined population of 600 to 800 (Heinen, Salas, and Layrisse 1980, 49–50).

Warao society is fairly consistently and permanently uxorilocal with a strong uterine bias suggestive of matrilineality (J. Wilbert 1958). However, communities build around a nucleus of denotative and classificatory sisters (bilateral female cousins) who play a critical role in raising and enculturating their children, including orphans. Exceptions to matrilocal residence are mostly based on rules pertaining to the absence of functional parents-in-law[6] and polygynous marriages in which the daughter of the first wife's brother becomes an "assistant" (*tekoro*) to her paternal aunt. Despite their relative stability, however, domestic groups do pass through a cycle of growth, consolidation, and dispersal (Heinen 1972).

Because sons-in-law are often subjected to great social hardship,[7] young men prefer to marry as close to home as possible. They also try marrying into the same village as one or more of their kinsmen, so as to assemble several of their male relatives within a group of otherwise unrelated or unknown co-brothers-in-law (*aharayaba*). This practice sometimes results in communities such as on the middle Sakobana distributary, where most inmarried men come from the same village. As among other matrilocal Guayanan societies, Warao sons-in-law are poorly assimilated by affinal kinship and considered *awaraowituana*, "not true relatives."[8] Despite the prevailing Hawaiian terminology at the G-0 level, siblings are differentiated as *dakobo witu* (B, ws) and *dakoi witu* (Z, ms), "proper brothers and sisters." They are much concerned about accidentally marrying a half sibling, particularly because the dakobo witu or dakoi witu via the father's line are *naminakomoni*, "impossible to know" or recognize and because malformation of children is ascribed to someone who unwittingly marries a half sister.

The domestic group is headed by the parents-in-law, the "old mother-in-law" (*dabai*) playing a key role in the redistribution of fish and game supplied by the couple's sons-in-law (*dawatuma*). The Winikina and related agglomerations observe strict mother-in-law avoidance. To communicate with his sons-in-law, a father-in-law (*arahi*) asks his oldest daughter to relay a message to her husband. Being the principal son-in-law (*dawa awahabara*), the husband conveys to the team of co-brothers-in-law (*aharayaba*) the old man's wishes.

Initially unstable, Warao marriages tend to consolidate following the birth of two or three children. The principal reason for a marriage breaking up is the death of one of the spouses. Normally, if the husband dies, his widow joins one of her sisters to become a second wife to her former brother-in-law. In these situations the first wife, regardless of whether she is younger or older than the second, remains the "owner of the house" (*hanoko arotu*), while the second wife accepts the status of assistant (*tekoro*). If the woman dies, the widower is likely to marry into another village, leaving his children in the care of their maternal relatives. Accounts of orphan neglect notwithstanding, the local group provides protection for all its offspring, and the Warao orphan (*dawana*) has several relatives to take care of him or her. Among them is the maternal grandfather, referred to as *aidatu* and known as "the one who makes (the child) grow up." The stepmother (*danitaha*) will become a *dabai mohoka* (spare mother-in-law) to the future spouse of the child.

Conception and Childbirth: Blood, Semen, and Gestation

Warao beliefs about blood and semen and their connection with intercourse and gestation are apt to confuse Western observers. Up to and including the generation of Winikina born in the 1940s, the idea of "blood vitality" played an important role in the selection of marriage partners. According to traditional medical theory, blood is an essence common to all life. It is a finite bodily component that determines a person's physical strength and reproductive prowess.

The concept of blood as a common life essence is articulated in Warao notions of cosmogonic origins, when Earth Mother (*hobahi arani*) in a mainly aquatic world, gave birth to human males. Subsequently, her blood mingled with fluvial waters, coagulated, and formed a living womb as seen in the peat bogs of the lower delta. From this womb the "tree people" (*arboreal flora*) of the delta were born. They share their ancestral mother's blood in the form of aromatic essences that women herbalists use to maintain their people's health and vitality (W. Wilbert n.d.).

The theory of a finite allotment of personal blood as a determinant of bodily strength is partly predicated on the correlation between unchecked hemorrhaging and death. A severely wounded person runs out of blood just as a tree, stripped of its bark, dries up. Another element of the limited personal allotment of blood theory rests on the superiority of male brawn over female muscle strength. Women are physically weaker than men because repeated blood loss through menstruation and childbirth debilitates them. There is no notion of the body's capacity to generate new blood.

The fact that women bear healthy children despite reiterated reproductive bleeding, probably prompted the distinction between "blood vitality," as manifested in physical strength, and "blood integrity," as indicated by resistance to disease. The latter is largely determined by diet. Upon ingestion, proper food becomes soft and "nourishes" the blood, keeping it red and fluid. Improper diet compromises the integrity of blood, leading to progressive deterioration of health and increased susceptibility to disease.

The notion that the strength of blood can vary from person to person is of utmost importance to traditional reproductive theory. Reminiscent of the gestation process through the mingling of water and blood in Earth Mother's womb, the human fetus is thought to result from the mingling of semen and blood in a woman's womb. However, conception is possible only if the male's blood (capable of generating potent semen) matches in strength the blood of the woman (Kalka 1995, 103ff.). The blood of neither partner must be stronger or weaker, lest the fetus suffer such ill effects as deformities, low height-weight ratios, spontaneous abortion, or stillbirth. Should the blood of one consort "work" less hard than the blood of the other, it manifests in an anemic pallor of the weaker partner.

Thus while blood compatibility of sexual partners is prerequisite to human reproduction, it is the father's semen that initiates a pregnancy and nourishes the fetus. But although mothers may engage in additional sexual activity for no other reason than to further the in utero development of their baby, there is no evidence that semen from multiple genitors constitutes a fundamental requisite of fetal gestation. This contrasts with many reports of partible paternity from numerous other lowland South American groups, especially Carib speakers

(Arvelo-Jiménez 1971, 93; Dole 1984, 49; Thomas 1982, 63; see also Rivière 1969, 62–63; for a partial exception see Basso 1973, 75–76). Variations of this practice have been reported from groups like the Gê, Tukano, and Tupi (Århem 1981, 178; Viveiros de Castro 1992, 179–81, 360 n3–4, 374 n11; Crocker 1984, 71, 90; Goldman 1963, 166; C. Hugh-Jones 1979, 15–16, 221; Jackson 1983, 188–89; Murphy and Murphy 1974, 102; Wagley 1977, 133–35).

As for the Warao, the desirability of multiple semen acquisition during pregnancy has its counterindications, which suggests that contributions of semen from genitor fathers can have negative effects on the fetus. Some fetuses are said to be unable to cope with an abundance of disparate semen and develop into cantankerous children and misfits. Others supposedly fail to reconcile the formal differences of contributing pater and genitor donors. When born, such children do not resemble the woman's husband and may be rejected by him or worse (J. Wilbert, pers. comm.). In any case, while Warao maternity is always unequivocal, paternity is ambiguous. Nevertheless, after the birth of a child, husbands usually submit to practices reminiscent of couvade. But whether these are remnants of a once more fully developed Warao institution is hard to say.

Ritual Kinship

Warao men do not condone sexual relations between their wives and other men. They are quite jealous of their spouses and demand the convocation of the assembly of villagers (*monikata*) to air and resolve cases of infidelity (see also Briggs 1996). Extramarital children are disapprovingly referred to as *dimamana*, "of two fathers," unless they are the product of a union to which the husband consents. If a man falls seriously ill, for example, he may agree to his wife having sex with his brother (or cousin). Children resulting from such unions enjoy the same social status as children born to regular couples. Seriously ill or infertile men may also invite a brother or a cousin to take his wife as a partner during the *habi sanuka* dance of the "little rattles," a fertility ceremony of pan-Guayana distribution.[9] If the couple in question agrees to this arrangement, the woman becomes the man's *amuse*. They dance together during the day of the ritual and have sex during the night. The following day, the genitor offers the husband a gift *horo amoara*, in "payment of the skin." In the event that a child is conceived during habi sanuka, the woman's husband is attributed the status of *dimawitu* (true father) while the genitor accepts functioning as *dima mohoka* (spare father). Thus, rather than disgracing sterile males, Warao society provides an institutionalized mechanism of circumventing the dysfunctional effects of infertility. In fact, the genitor and the woman's husband often become lifelong friends, and the genitor may provide for his ritual wife's child or children until he marries into another village.[10]

A woman in labor is assisted by a midwife/godmother (of the newborn), who helps deliver and bathe the infant. The woman is either referred to as *akobukatu*, "the one who lifts up the child" or as *anabukatu*, "the one who severs the umbilical cord." In ritual context, the godmother is called *hoaratu* (*hoharatu*), indicating that she is the one who bathed the infant (*horosimo*, "rosy skin") at birth and severed its umbilical cord. In turn, the child will be known throughout his or her life as her *hoarabita* (*hoharabita*), "the one she bathed."

Adolescent girls establish another kind of ritual kinship with "godparents" (including one woman and up to five men) who conduct the rite de passage associated with the onset of the young women's first menses. They refer to these adults respectively as *ahotarani/hotu arani*, "blood-mother" and *ahotarima/hotu arima*, "blood-fathers" (Heinen 1988, 634; Kalka 1995, 77; Suárez 1968, 207). Godparents cannot be close relatives of the initiate. Furthermore, initiates enter into a speaking avoidance relationship with their godfathers, similar to that existing between a son-in-law (*dawa*) and his mother-in-law (*dabai*). In this case they refer to each other as *mahotuarima*, "my blood-father" and *mahotukatida*, "my blood-daughter."

At menarche, a girl is secluded until bleeding subsides. She covers her face with both hands (*moho mahaya*) and is taken to a wooden bench or a prepared tree trunk, where she is bathed. Her hair is cut close to the scalp and her head anointed with *mobosimo atoi* (annatto, or onoto), a red pigment obtained from the crushed seeds of the small tree *Bixa orellana*. The rite de passage from girl (*anibaka*) to nubile young woman (*iboma*) is held in greater esteem than the marriage rite. However, the iboma is not considered marriageable until her hair has grown long again. Some time after the conclusion of the ritual her father or husband offers sago tortillas to the "true blood-father" (*ahotarimawitu*) and his assistants. Normally, the "godfathers" respond as a group by offering a gift of money or brightly colored and highly coveted glass beads.

Same-Sex Relatives and Shared Paternity

Warao relatives of the same sex and generation are called *kayaba*, "our common offshoot," whereas relatives of the opposite sex are called *kayabayana*, "not of a common offshoot." This clearly demonstrates that the Warao hold that the sexes are fundamentally different.[11]

There is an interesting term for "children of several fathers," namely, *kayabauka*, "child of our shoot, our generation." Barral (1979, 256) translates this into Spanish as *hijo de puta* (child of a whore), a recent expression used by acculturated Warao, implying promiscuity on the part of the mother. Although the Warao do employ this negative denotation in marginal cases, the term *kayabauka* is generally used in the positive sense of its literal translation.

Warao communities tend to have numerous sets of half siblings. From a man's perspective, the firstborn of any father is called *nibora anoboto iwarawara*, even if his wife was a former widow with children of her own. If he wishes to be more specific, he refers to his firstborn with the former widow as *kwasikamo iwarawara*, "the first from a given point in time." However, if the widow is only recently pregnant and he sleeps with her before the infant is born, the child will be the man's half son or daughter because two fathers were involved in its gestation; one deceased and one living. A Winikina shaman, Antonio Lorenzano, explained the latter situation, taking the case of José Ramírez as an example. José Ramírez was an old *wisidatu*-shaman who was killed by a jaguar. He left behind a second spouse of his polygynous marriage, whose son, Silvano, was now regarded as *asibi Ramire auka*, "the half son" of Ramírez (Heinen, Wilbert, and Rivero 1998).

Tamaha Silvano *hakotai,*
Silvano *hakotai, tai Ramire auka.*

As far as Silvano is concerned,
this Silvano is the son of Ramírez.

Anihima, oko waraya anihima.
Kwarea hakó, waniku hisaka ekorakore, tai nisanae.

[The woman didn't have her] period. We call it the *anihima.*
At the end of a month, when the month ended,
[Antonio Pacheco] got married to her.

Eku hisaba warakore, warisaba aibuae.
Sibane Ramire auka.
Tai sibane . . . sibane.

To tell you exactly, the man copulated with a pregnant woman.
It's half the son of Ramírez.
He is half and half.

Tai diawarae.
Nokabaya, amaseke ama mauka arani.
Taisi ariatuka . . . wabae.

He was born.
Some time went by and now the mother of my son was born.
The next one died.

Taisi ariatuka, Josefina Pacheco, Santiago *atida.*
Tai ariatuka. No araimahayana.
Araimahakate dibu ha.
Oko kasabasabaya ariatuka.

Then came Josefina Pacheco, the wife of [my maternal nephew] Santiago.
She is the "next one," *ariatuka.* Not *araimaha.*
To really express the "next one" we have a word.
We here say *ariatuka.*

Tamaha tai kwasikamo iwarawara,
kwasikamo iwarawara.

The first [child with a widow] we call *kwasikamo iwarawara,*
the first from a certain date on.

Matida hakotai, tekoro, kwasikamo iwarawara,[12]
taisi ariatuka Santiago *atida.*

Regarding my [second] wife, the *tekoro,* she is *kwasikamo iwarawara,*
("the first child of Petra with Antonio Pacheco");
the next one is the wife of Santiago.

Tuatane tanae, maraisa.
That's how it was, friend.

Summary

According to traditional Warao beliefs, conception is effected by the mingling, in utero, of a woman's blood with the blood (semen) of a man, always if blood is abundant in both individuals and is of compatible strength. While semen triggers conception and continued intercourse benefits the fetus, multiple paternity is not required for successful fetal gestation.

Partible paternity occurs under extraordinary physical, social, and marital conditions. A physically impaired man, sick or infertile, approves that his wife engage in ritual wife sharing with one of his denotative or classificatory brothers to procure a child. Convention assigns to the husband the status of pater and to his "brother" the status of genitor. Extraordinary social conditions occur when pregnant mothers choose to engage in additional sexual activity in order to strengthen the fetus through the semen of multiple genitors. Special marital conditions prevail when a man marries a recently pregnant widow and copulates with her. The resulting child is recognized as the offspring of both the deceased and the living fathers.

Conclusions

Traditional domestic groups of Warao society are composed of 25 to 55 individuals of whom no more than one-fourth are reproductive women. Adding to this the fact that agglomerations experience a preadolescent mortality between 47% and 50% (Layrisse, Salas, and Heinen 1980, 66; J. Wilbert 1980, 29), it is obvious that a high fertility rate is imperative to group survival. Infertility in men and women has, therefore, grave long-term consequences for the family and the group in which it occurs. To mitigate the seriousness of male sterility, the Warao instituted the habi sanuka ritual, which permits a genitor to substitute for an infertile husband. Multiple fatherhood is recognized in such cases by differentiating between "spare" and "true" fathers. But the biological roles in this wife-sharing arrangement are culturally inverted by openly assigning the status of genitor to the former and the status of pater to the latter. This switch saves face, creates a family, and guarantees the married couple's and their group's future. Warao men are extremely jealous of their wives and would hardly agree to wife sharing were it not to provide an altogether satisfactory solution to a serious social and biological dilemma. We therefore submit that the institutionalization of multiple fatherhood for the sake of optimum fecundity of women through ritual wife sharing was the cardinal objective of the habi sanuka ceremony early in the twentieth century.

Notes

1. There is a small contingent of "morichaleros" (*daunarao, hobahi arao*) in the federal states of Sucre and Monagas as well. They are Warao with only rudimentary dugout canoes. Here, horticulture is practiced by specialized Warao and by Warao contingents living among the descendants of Carib-speaking farmers like the Pariagoto (Guayano).

2. Built in the mid-sixties to reclaim large tracts of land from the western delta, the floodgates of the dam closed in 1967. In addition a paved highway was constructed that connected Tucupita, now the capital of Delta Amacuro State, with the terra firma of Monagas State for the first time.

3. In 1595 the English explorer Sir Walter Raleigh and his lieutenant, Lawrence Keymis, ascended the western branch of the Orinoco delta and met with the Waraoan-speaking Siawani.

4. Such clusters are governed by a captain (*kabitana*), a public prosecutor (*bisikari*) or policeman (*borisia*), and a speaker (*dibatu*).

5. We follow here Peter Rivière (1984), who proposed substituting *subtribe* with *agglomeration*.

6. Parents of the bride "functioning" as heads of household. Sometimes, at the time of marriage, the bride's household of orientation has been disrupted because her mother has died.

7. A son-in-law is subjected to hard labor, required as he is to provide for his own nuclear family and for the larger domestic unit under the tutelage of his "mother-in-law." Sons-in-law are commonly obliged to render bride service for the lifetime of their wives and need to prove themselves as able providers and laborers lest they be sent away by their wives' parents.

8. This leads to the designation, in Cariban languages, of slaves or servants as *poitos,* "sons-in-law" (not the other way round). In the Pemon area of Kamarata a son-in-law is *poitorü.*

9. Pemon: *parishara* (Heinen, field notes, 1997); Ye'kwana: *wasaiy hadï* (*wasai jadü* in present Ye'kwana spelling) (Heinen field notes, 1982).

10. In Warao, gifts of food and other goods that the genitor may surreptitiously give his child or children are called *yaribu.*

11. If *kayaba* is a collective term for a group of same-sex, same-age (parallel *and* cross) relatives among the Warao, it seems to exclude implicitly the formation of a group of brothers (parallel cousins) that could lay claim to a marriageable cross-cousin, which among the Ye'kwana is the defining unit of multiple fatherhood.

12. Lina is the first daughter of Antonio Pacheco and the second wife of Antonio Lorenzano, mother of his son Florentino.

13

Sexual Theory, Behavior, and Paternity among the Siona and Secoya Indians of Eastern Ecuador

William T. Vickers

This volume is based on the premise that "a substantial number of lowland South American societies . . . have a . . . doctrine of paternity . . . that allows for a child to have several different biological fathers" (Beckerman and Valentine, this volume). Further, a team of researchers from the Barí Partible Paternity Project (BPPP) have presented data indicating that for the Barí people of western Venezuela there is "a statistically significant advantage in survivorship for children with secondary fathers over other children with only a single father" (Beckerman et al., this volume). The mechanism proposed to explain this advantage in survivorship is that "secondary fathers" provide their putative offspring with incremental supplies of fish and game, which ensures a higher and more regular intake of dietary protein for these children (Beckerman et al. 1998:167).

From the theoretical perspective of evolutionary ecology it would make sense for such a culturally recognized secondary father to contribute to the welfare of his putative child if there were a reasonable probability that the child was his progeny, since this would enhance the representation and survival of his genes in the next generation. In cases where the mother has had multiple sex partners, there is a chance that the secondary father is the biological progenitor of the child (his precise chance would depend on the number of males who had intercourse with the mother, and their relative frequency of intercourse with her). As noted, observations from the Barí suggest that "secondary fathers" do contribute to the welfare of their putative children, thus conferring on them a higher survival rate (Beckerman 1997b; Beckerman et al. 1998; Beckerman et al., this volume; M. Lizarralde 1997; R. Lizarralde 1997). This finding is a nice dovetailing of field data and theory.

However, we should not assume that this model of "paternity uncertainty" and social recognition of secondary fathers is a general pattern in lowland South American Indian cultures unless more extensive comparative research reveals this to be true. Also, the question of whether such secondary fathers actually make significant contributions to the welfare and survivability of their putative offspring must be carefully evaluated.

Several conditions must obtain if the recognition of secondary fathers is to become an accepted cultural practice and confer greater survivorship on children. First, women must have easy access to multiple sex partners. Second, the societies in which the women live must be tolerant of extramarital affairs, so that one or more men can be socially recognized as secondary fathers. Third, the secondary fathers must take an interest in their putative offspring and contribute to their material well-being.

The purpose of this chapter is to describe and discuss the reproductive theories and behaviors of the Siona and Secoya Indians of northeastern Ecuador in light of these issues. I will argue that few Siona and Secoya births involve paternity uncertainty because the prevailing theory of reproduction recognizes only one male as the genitor of a child. Further, in most cases paternity is socially acknowledged via a formal couvade ritual in which the father "recuperates" from the ordeal of the birthing process and takes ritual baths to purify himself.

I also will argue that most Siona and Secoya women do not have multiple sex partners immediately before and during their pregnancies. In part, this assumption is based on the fact that Siona-Secoya settlements are highly dispersed and women have limited access to males who are not members of their extended families and households. But it is also based in Siona-Secoya theories about human sexuality, reproduction, and fetal development. The Siona-Secoya believe "excess" sexual behavior is risky for men, women, and the fetus, and it is seen as especially dangerous to shamans and other users of *yahé* (a hallucinogenic potion made from a woody vine, *Banisteriopsis caapi*). And, in traditional Siona-Secoya society, yahé ceremonies were communal and most men and women participated in them.

As Monique Borgerhoff Mulder (1992, 340) has noted, human reproductive decisions may involve quite different strategies depending on the "socioecological conditions" in which people live. In the Siona-Secoya case the evidence suggests that most adults have opted for a strategy of investing in parental effort and offspring quality rather than mating effort and offspring quantity (Alexander and Borgia 1979; Lessels 1991).

The People and the Setting

The Siona and Secoya of Ecuador are closely related peoples who speak mutually intelligible dialects that belong to the western branch of the Tukanoan language family. From the sixteenth through the eighteenth centuries the Spanish referred to both groups as members of the "Encabellado Nation" (Chantre y Herrera 1901). In the nineteenth and early twentieth centuries both were referred to as Piojé (Simson 1879, 1886; Tessmann 1930). However, the proper term of self-referral in the native dialects was and is Pāĩ (Secoya) or Bāĩ (Siona), meaning "people." Julian Steward (1949) estimates that the Encabellado population numbered about 16,000 at the time of European contact.

The ancestral homeland of the Encabellado covered 82,000 square kilometers along the Aguarico River and the north bank of the Napo, below the mouth of the Aguarico. To the north their territory was bounded by the Putumayo and San Miguel Rivers. The estimated population density within the Encabellado homeland was 0.2 persons per square kilometer (Steward 1949). This ancestral territory is now divided by the international borders of Ecuador, Peru, and Colombia, and small populations of Encabellado descendants are found in all three countries (their total number probably does not exceed 2,500 individuals).

This chapter focuses on the modern Siona and Secoya residing along the Aguarico River and its tributaries in northeastern Ecuador. The most important distinction between these two groups is their accounts of their places of origin. The ancestors of the Siona lived on the Aguarico River and its tributaries (other Siona of Colombia live along the Putumayo River and its tributaries). The Secoya, in contrast, trace their roots to the north bank of the Napo River, below the mouth of the Aguarico (including northern tributaries of the Napo such as the Wahoya, or Santa María River). This ancestral Secoya homeland is located in Peru.

Regardless, the ancestors of the modern Siona and Secoya of Ecuador were close neighbors who shared common linguistic and cultural traditions, and both groups have interacted and intermarried for centuries. Early Spanish explorers and Jesuit missionaries simply considered their dispersed settlements to be local communities of Encabellado, and not separate ethnic groups.

The Siona and Secoya languages and cultures of today are very similar in most respects, although there are some slight differences in vocabulary and in the pronunciation of words. Due to intermarriage, many of their settlements in Ecuador have both Siona and Secoya residents, and many individuals have both Siona and Secoya ancestry (Vickers 1989b). For these reasons I sometimes use the hyphenated term *Siona-Secoya* to refer to the general and shared traits of these peoples.

In recent years other anthropologists have questioned the Siona-Secoya designation and have suggested that there are significant differences between the two cultures (e.g., Cipolletti 1988, 13–14; Moya 1992, 71–74). María Susana Cipolletti bases her argument on perceived differences in myths collected from different individuals and on the statements of some native informants who identify themselves as either Siona or Secoya and stress their separateness from the other group. In my view, the observed differences in myths represent individual and intracultural variation rather than intercultural variation. Put simply, each shaman or individual has a slightly different version of the shared oral tradition, as one might expect in a culture whose literature is spoken and performed, rather than written down in a canonical document such as the Bible.

Further, the perceived political antagonisms between some Siona and Secoya families reflect the age-old essence of the culture, which has always stressed the autonomy of individual households and settlements, and mistrust of one's neighbors. This is a common trait among Amazonian peoples and it is often based on sorcery accusations between villages as well as the desire of communities to maintain control over their local resources. In my view the modern Siona and Secoya are both the descendants of the seventeenth- and eighteenth-century "Encabellado Nation" and share their cultural and linguistic traditions. They are also related through marriage and frequently live in the same settlements. Hence I believe the Siona-Secoya designation is appropriate when speaking of traits they share.

Environmental Conditions and Resources

The Aguarico River region is classified as Tropical Wet Forest in the Holdridge Life Zone system. The predominant vegetation is dense forest, with trees ranging from 24 to 45 meters (80–150 ft.) in height, large woody climbers, and numerous epiphytes and buttressed trees. Other plant associations include areas of secondary growth developing from old garden and settlement sites, communities of plants that are characteristic of floodplains and riverbanks, hilltop communities, and liana associations. The average elevation of the region is 250 meters (823 ft.) above sea level. From the air the landscape appears generally flat, although there are occasional hills and some relief is noticeable at ground level.

The climate corresponds to Köppen's Af or Tropical Wet, with no month drier than 60 millimeters of rainfall. The mean annual rainfall is 3,375 millimeters (132 in.). The "dry season" runs from December through February, and the "wet season" from March through July. Temperatures are remarkably stable throughout the year, with a mean daily high of 31°C (88°F) and a mean daily low of 21°C (70°F).

There are a variety of soil types within the Aguarico basin, including some that are very good by Amazonian standards. This is because the Aguarico is a white-water river that deposits Andean sediments along both sides of its course. The best soils were formed by alluvial deposits over an ancient clay bed and consist of volcanic matter mixed with sand and pebbles. These soils, which are technically classified as Vitrandepts and Dystrandepts, are loose, well drained, and relatively fertile (MAG/ORSTOM 1980).

The Cuyabeno River is a northern tributary of the Aguarico and is a black-water river, which carries few suspended solids. The region it flows through is characterized by ancient depressions that were excavated by river action and that are now partially refilled by decanted clays and organic residuals. The hydromorphic soils of these low, swampy areas are not suitable for cultivation in their natural waterlogged state. However, there are a few alluvial dikes along the Cuyabeno with sufficient elevation to allow cultivation. About 11% of the study area consists of rounded hills that are composed of highly weathered and compacted red-clay soils (oxic dystropepts). These soils have high levels of aluminum compounds and less agricultural potential.

The fauna of the region represent the typical genera found throughout Amazonia, although there is a higher than usual rate of species endemism, perhaps because this area of the Amazon basin may have been a rain forest refuge during warm and dry periods of the Pleistocene (Meggers 1975). The Siona-Secoya consider about a hundred species of animals to be edible, but many of these are smaller game and birds that are rarely taken. A longitudinal study of their hunting from 1973 through 1982 recorded kills of 48 species (Vickers 1991). As in all of Amazonia, the fish fauna is amazingly diverse, with thousands of species represented. The Siona-Secoya catch and consume about 70 of these species.

The Settlement Pattern and the Composition of Domestic Groups

Siona-Secoya settlements tend to be small, dispersed, and impermanent. Traditional Encabellado settlements were somewhat hidden away on the tributaries of the Aguarico and Napo Rivers for defensive purposes. In the seventeenth and eighteenth centuries the Jesuits attempted to relocate these communities to *reducciones* (mission villages) on the banks of the larger Aguarico and Napo Rivers to ease the problems of transportation and communication. Despite some initial success, this effort eventually failed (Vickers 1983). Today many Siona and Secoya settlements remain on the tributaries, although there are three villages along the Aguarico River in Ecuador (Biaña, San Pablo, and Si'ekoya).

In the past each Encabellado community was associated with a particular tributary or section of the larger rivers, and these local territories averaged 1,150 square kilometers. When people relocated their settlements they typically did so within their local territories. This pattern is still evident among the modern Siona and Secoya, although pressures from plantation owners and enticements from missionaries have produced a few long-range migrations in the twentieth century (as in the early 1940s and mid-1970s, when some Secoya families moved from Peru to Ecuador).

In order to understand Siona-Secoya settlement patterns, we must consider their forms of household organization. The traditional household consisted of an extended family residing in a "big house" (*hai wi'e*). Such houses had an oval floor plan and earthen floors (they were similar to the types known as longhouses in the anthropological literature and *malocas* in Colombia). The extended family consisted of a man, his wife, their married and unmarried offspring, and their spouses and children. Patrilocality was the modal, but not exclusive, residence pattern in such households. The longhouse functioned as a unit of economic production and consumption. However, each married woman within the house maintained her own hearth and did her own cooking, although she often shared food and prepared beverages (generically known as *kono*) with other residents of the longhouse. The hammocks of her husband and unmarried children were arranged around her hearth. Big houses of this sort are rarely seen in Siona-Secoya settlements today, although extended family living and sharing often persist in residential arrangements (described below).

The simplest form of household today is the conjugal-nuclear household, which also functions as the most basic unit of economic production and consumption. This consists of a husband, wife, and their children, who inhabit a single house (*wi'e*). This more "modern" thatched house is elevated on posts and has floors made from split palm trunks (even more recent innovations include corrugated metal roofing and floors made from wooden boards). Such households may be found singly along rivers, but more commonly they are part of a small cluster of houses whose members form an extended family.

Hence the modern variant of the extended family household is a cluster of houses in which the married offspring and their children reside in separate dwellings located adjacent to the parents' dwelling. As in the past, patrilocality is the modal, but not exclusive, residence pattern. These extended household clusters also function as broader units of production and consumption (one step removed from the conjugal-nuclear units that comprise them). Small Siona and Secoya settlements typically consist of a single cluster of houses that shelter an extended family.

Larger villages (*dadipï*) usually consist of a number of house clusters (extended families) arranged in a line settlement along a river. Such large villages are usually the result of missionary or school influence and tend to be unstable. Villages do not function as units of production or consumption. In terms of kinship, the various extended family house clusters in a village may be unrelated, or may be more distantly related than the parent-offspring ties found within the house clusters. The populations of villages range from about 50 to 160 individuals, but they fluctuate as households join or relocate through time.

Although Siona-Secoya house architecture has changed over the years, the modal pattern of residence is still some form of extended family living arrangement. As noted, this may be constituted by a few houses of related kinspeople in a single small settlement, or by a cluster of houses within a larger village.

Regardless of the settlement type, Siona and Secoya families tend to relocate their houses at irregular intervals ranging from five to twenty years in duration. Multiple factors influence these decisions, including both environmental and social conditions (Vickers 1989a, 58). Among the environmental conditions are the availability of garden land, flora, and fauna, the incidence of pests and disease, and the deterioration of houses. Social factors such as everyday tensions and disputes, sorcery accusations, and the death of a family member also provoke relocations.

The Subsistence Economy

The Siona-Secoya subsistence economy is based on slash-and-burn cultivation, hunting, fishing, and collecting. In a 1973–75 dietary survey in the village of San Pablo on the Aguarico River (Vickers 1989a) gardens provided 72.0% of the caloric intake, hunting 18.6%, fishing 2.0%, and wild plant foods 3.7% (3.7% of the calories came from purchased foods). However, hunting and fishing were very important as they provided 81.5% of the dietary protein (18.5% came from plant foods). The relative contributions of different foods varies by location and season. For example, along the Cuyabeno River fishing surpasses hunting in importance year-round, whereas along the Aguarico it is most important during the dry season.

Siona-Secoya gardens are made in both primary and secondary growth during the dry season, and the debris is burned (unless rains catch the cultivator unawares). Ninety-five percent of gardens are polycropped and the most diverse gardens have over 60 varieties of cultivars. The most important staples are 15 varieties of manioc (*Manihot esculenta*), 15 varieties of plantains and bananas (*Musa* x *paradisiaca*), and 9 of maize (*Zea mays*). Many other tubers, tropical fruit trees, palms, condiments, and medicinal and utilitarian plants complete the garden inventory (Vickers and Plowman 1984). Households typically have three or four gardens of different ages and in different stages of production (because different cultivars mature at different rates). Garden labor is shared by all members of the household, save infants. Men do the heavier work of slashing and felling, while men, women, and children cooperate in planting, weeding, and harvesting. The laborious tasks of manioc harvesting and processing, however, are done primarily by women.

Among the Siona-Secoya most hunting is done by men. Women occasionally assist in the collection of turtle eggs, or catch a tortoise along a jungle trail, but they rarely hunt in the systematic and intensive way that men do. Female respondents state, "Hunting is for men," and, "The forest is the place of the men and our place is in the village." Boys learn about hunting by listening to the accounts of the men and by playing at hunting around the village and in gardens. As they enter adolescence they sometimes accompany adult hunters, but rarely attempt serious hunting before the age of 15 or 16. However, they are expected to demonstrate their hunting abilities prior to marriage. A young man with a reputation for being lazy and not being able to hunt and clear gardens has difficulty finding a wife, for most marriages are arranged between sets of parents who inquire about the skills of the prospective bride and groom. Hunting, like gardening and cooking, is seen as an essential component of domestic life and economics.

When Siona-Secoya hunters search for game they walk briskly along forest trails, pausing only briefly to check for signs of animals. When animals are encountered and a decision is made to pursue them, the chase is as immediate and energetic as conditions allow (some animals must be approached quietly). Hunters return to the village with the same brisk pace, even when carrying carcasses of heavier game such as white-lipped and collared peccaries (*Tayassu pecari* and *T. tajacu*). Hunting is a purposive activity intended to provision households with meat, while economizing on the time and energy expended by the hunter. Hunters seek to carry a substantial load of meat back to their households so that they need not hunt again for several days or even a week or more. Once a hunter reaches the limits of what he can carry (about 50 kg.), he rarely pursues additional game (unless traveling by canoe, when more weight can be accommodated). The largest game animal, the tapir (*Tapirus terrestris*), may weigh in excess of 200 kilograms, so it is cut into sections and transported by several individuals (a solitary hunter who kills a tapir carries a portion of the animal back to the village and then returns to the kill site with helpers to finish the job).

My 1973–82 study (Vickers 1991) of Siona-Secoya hunters indicated that they were proficient, with a mean yield of 2.1 kilograms of meat (butchered weight) per man-hour of hunting (or 16.2 kg. butchered weight per man-day). In a sample of 802 man-days of hunting recorded in the 1,150-square-kilometer territory around San Pablo, only 117 (15%) resulted in no kill. The mean number of kills per man-day of hunting was 1.6 animals.

In contrast to hunting, fishing is practiced by almost everyone (save infants). Still, men invest more hours in fishing than women and children do. In the 1970s fishing yields along the Aguarico River averaged 1.0 kilogram per hour, with most fishing occurring during the dry season when the Aguarico's waters were lower and less turbid. In contrast, fishing along the black-water Cuyabeno averaged 0.7 kilograms per hour, but was practiced throughout the year.

Although wild plant foods contributed only 3.7% of the calories in my 1973–75 diet survey, they become more important during periods of migration and scarcity (when people do not have access to established gardens). Many collected plants are important as medicines and others provide materials for crafts, construction, and ritual use (Vickers 1994). Both men and women forage for wild plant resources.

The Provision and Sharing of Foods

As in all cultures, Siona and Secoya cuisine is not just food. Meanings are associated with different food items and reflect the overall values and structure of the society (Farb and Armelagos 1983). For the Siona-Secoya both manioc bread (*'ãõ*) and beverages (konó) are key symbolic foods that have strong female associations. They are made by women and represent their contributions to the complete meal. The serving of konó to visitors and family members represents the woman's hospitality and duty to her family. Women are judged on how well they meet these cultural expectations, and lose status with kin and community if they fall short. Such women are typically described as "lazy" or "irresponsible," and their husbands are pitied as living "deprived lives" in "bad marriages." Secoya respondents also describe several instances in which husbands beat their wives because they were not served konó when they returned from hunting. Indeed, in 1980 one Siona man hacked his wife to death with a machete because she served konó too slowly.

Conversely, it is the man's responsibility to do the heavy work in clearing gardens and he must supply meat through hunting and most of the fish (as noted, women sometimes fish, but rarely hunt). A man who clears gardens that are too small, or who hunts infrequently or in a desultory manner is likewise criticized and seen as a "poor provider." Meat and fish (*wa'i*) are the primary male contributions to the complete meal.

Siona-Secoya meals are constructed according to a simple formula:

starchy staple (*'ãõ*) + meat or fish (wa'i) + beverage (konó)

It must be noted that *'ãõ* has several levels of meaning. At its broadest level of contrast it means "food." A more specific meaning is "meal." The most specific meaning of *'ãõ* is "manioc bread." A meal that contains manioc bread, meat or fish, and a beverage is considered complete and satisfying. A meal that lacks one of these components is considered unsatisfactory. However, it is acceptable to have a meal without manioc bread as long as there is another starchy staple to fill its niche in the "complete meal" (e.g., boiled manioc or plantains).

The fundamental meal structure of *'ãõ* + *wa'i* + *konó* thus symbolizes the complementarity of female and male contributions and responsibilities within the household economy. Indeed, the Siona and Secoya state that "a man or woman cannot live alone." The occasional middle-aged bachelor or spinster must remain attached to his or her parents' household because neither can maintain a satisfactory home and diet without a partner of the opposite sex. Widows, widowers, and abandoned spouses who are not living in extended households must depend on their opposite-sex children to help them out. If they have no children who are capable of such assistance they may attach themselves to the households of kin. Otherwise, their only option is to "visit" other households with the hope of receiving invitations to join in meals or gifts of food to take back to their houses. However, such people soon earn the ridicule of their fellow villagers (this is expressed more through backbiting than direct confrontation).

As discussed earlier, Siona-Secoya households may consist of a single conjugal-nuclear family, but more typically they consist of extended families (residing in the traditional longhouse or its modern variant, the household cluster). But even within the extended family household each married woman maintains her own hearth and does her own cooking. When her husband returns from hunting or fishing he typically gives the fish or game to his wife for cleaning and cooking. If the kill or catch is very small it may not be shared beyond the conjugal-nuclear unit (regardless of their residential arrangements).

More typically, the kill or catch is not so meager, and the wife or husband shares portions of the meat or fish with other members of the extended household (even when they reside in separate houses within the household cluster). If the hunter has made a large kill (such as a white-lipped peccary) the meat distribution is even wider, including portions that go to more distant kin and friends in other houses (a child is often sent to deliver these gifts). When a tapir (the largest terrestrial mammal) is killed each household in the settlement receives a portion.

This pattern of sharing can be seen as a set of concentric circles. At the center is the basic conjugal-nuclear unit, followed by the extended household, then more distant kin and friends, and finally the village. Sharing when there is sufficient meat or fish is functional because it establishes bonds of reciprocity and because the Siona-Secoya have limited means of preserving large quantities of meat and fish (smoking is the most common method, but it is effective for only about a week).

While some anthropologists (e.g., Siskind 1973) have described Amazonian societies in which men give gifts of meat to their female lovers and thus "trade meat for sex," I have been unable to discern such a pattern among the Siona-Secoya. If such exchanges occur they must be infrequent and furtive. Elsewhere in this chapter I argue that the rate of adultery among the Siona-Secoya appears to be low due to a number of factors, including their concepts of human sexuality and reproduction, their dispersed settlement pattern, and their organization of the household and daily activities (which are not conducive to clandestine liaisons). If I am correct in these interpretations, "meat for sex" exchanges outside of marriage should be rare.

The Dangers of Sex

The cornerstone of Siona-Secoya religion and intellectual life is a rather unim-
pressive-looking vine known as yahé. Its scientific name is *Banisteriopsis caapi*
and it belongs to the Malpighiaceae family. Yahé is important in Siona-Secoya
thought because it is used to make a sacred potion that contains several psychoactive alkaloid compounds (Schultes and Hofmann 1980). This potion is consumed in communal ceremonies and allows shamans and other Siona-Secoya to
transcend their everyday sensory experience and "know" the universe of their
many spirits and demons. The visions experienced through yahé have contributed greatly to the Siona-Secoya worldview and give meaning to almost all
areas of their lives, including their views of human sexuality.

The traditional leaders of the Siona-Secoya are male shamans who are
known as *yahé unkuki* ("drinkers of yahé"). These men serve as religious sa-
vants and political counselors for the various Siona and Secoya communities.
Their leadership is based on influence rather than authority. A man is recognized as a shaman and drinker of yahé only after completing an arduous ap-
prenticeship under the guidance of a senior shaman and gaining the respect of
his community through demonstrated competence in conducting yahé ceremonies, singing yahé songs, and curing illnesses. The Siona-Secoya literally believe that the health and well-being of their communities depend on the competence of their shamans.

Until the missionization and modernization of recent decades, most Siona-
Secoya boys aspired to become shamans and almost all drank yahé from childhood in ceremonies presided over by shamans. However, shamanic training
requires great dedication and devotion to ascetic principles that involve fasting,
consumption of large amounts of the yahé potion and preparations based on
other psychoactive plants, and sexual abstinence. Hence most aspirants
dropped out of their apprenticeships and only a select few achieved full
shamanic status.

Regardless of their deficiencies in shamanic training, most men continued
their participation in communal yahé ceremonies and drank the hallucinogenic
potion throughout their lives. Equally important, their shared worldview was
yahé inspired and constantly reinforced by shamanic interpretations of everyday events, including weather conditions, hunting success, the behavior of
people and animals, and illness and death.

Women and girls also participated in yahé ceremonies but could not become
shamans, although some were known for their expertise as herbalists and inter-

preters of dreams. The exclusion of women from formal shamanic training was absolute, and was based on beliefs about the dangers of menstruation and menstrual blood. In the Siona-Secoya worldview, menstruation is an "illness" of women, and male contact with menstrual blood can lead to life-threatening conditions such as anemia (*mini hu'iñe*) and severe hemorrhaging from the nose. This danger is seen as being particularly acute for shamans and other male drinkers of yahé, and several days of abstinence from sexual relations precede each yahé ceremony. Further, menstruating women are isolated in special huts until their period passes, and may not cook for their families, nor use utensils and bowls that are touched by others (they keep a separate set of bowls and utensils in their menstruation huts).

In a broader sense, most aspects of female sexuality are also tinged with danger. For example, female blood is shed during childbirth, and both wife and husband must endure days of ritual bathing with warm water and *Inga* leaves to purify themselves. It is also believed that a man who has "too much" sexual intercourse with his wife will be a poor hunter. I will give other examples to illustrate this point later in this chapter, but my main purpose here is to establish the fact that there are important relationships between the Siona-Secoya use of yahé, their worldview, their theory of sexuality, and their actual sexual behavior.

Ideal Constructs of Sex and Reproduction

Contrary to the expectations of many people, the sexual behavior of indigenous peoples is not always characterized by uninhibited expression or promiscuity. Among the Siona-Secoya sexual expression is restrained by a system of belief in which many aspects of human sexuality are viewed as dangerous. This does not mean that the Siona-Secoya are afraid of sex per se, but rather that certain taboos influence their sexual behavior. As in all cultures there are some discrepancies between ideal and real behavior, and I consider these in the sections that follow.

Courtship and Marriage

Courtship is a formal process in Siona-Secoya society. Little boys and girls sometimes play in mixed groups, but after the age of nine or ten a girl's parents discourage her from playing or socializing with boys or young men and instruct her to stay near her house and assist her mother. From this age to marriage girls are expected to help with cooking, gardening, fetching water, and washing clothes. In effect, the girl is entering a cloistered period that does not end until she marries.

The traditional puberty ceremony for girls was quite elaborate (Vickers 1976, 227–30), and was conducted at their first menses. A special hut was constructed where the girl was confined for several weeks and attended only by her mother. Because menstrual blood is considered "unclean," the girl bathed daily by scraping her skin with *Inga* leaves that had been warmed in hot water. Used leaves were not discarded, but were placed on a growing pile to prove she was complying with the purification ritual. When she left the hut to urinate or defecate she had to walk on a special path constructed with wooden poles so she would not bleed on the ground and contaminate the village.

Before the girl's final emergence from the hut she received instruction from her mother: "After coming out of the hut you can't play with children or act like a little girl. You can't run . . . you have to walk slowly and without smiling. When people visit you must serve *chicha* (a native beverage) without smiling, and answer politely. You are a different person now." Her father gave her similar advice: "Now you are a woman. You can't play with boys as before, and you must walk with much respect and greet older persons. When you visit another house you must sit in one place and not gossip. We are not going to tell you these things again. We speak once and you must remember our advice." While the tradition of isolating girls during the puberty ritual is fading, they still receive instruction from their parents.

If a bachelor is interested in a girl as a potential wife he dresses in his finest garments and makes social calls to her household. Normally the youth will converse with the men of the house on topics such as hunting and fishing, perhaps to demonstrate his manliness and seriousness as a hunter and provider. The girl does not participate in this conversation, but may peek at the men from another part of the house as she goes about her chores.

Marriages are arranged by the parents of the prospective bride and groom. They conduct negotiations in which the merits of the young man and woman are alternately questioned and defended. The parents' main concerns are whether the prospective son- or daughter-in-law has demonstrated sufficient maturity as evidenced by his or her performance of appropriate work activities. For young men these include hunting, fishing, and clearing gardens, and for young women cooking, harvesting manioc, and making manioc bread ('ãõ).

The vast majority of Siona-Secoya marriages are monogamous. In 27 years of research among the Siona-Secoya, I have recorded only one incidence of polygyny. This was in a case in Peru in which one man had two wives. The divorce rate is also quite low, although divorce is easily obtained (a husband or wife simply leaves his or her spouse). A large majority of the Siona-Secoya marry for life. From 1973 to 1990 I recorded information on 115 marriages (including older and younger couples). Only 10 of these marriages ended in divorce (9%). There were two additional cases in which husbands allegedly killed their wives.

In ideal Siona-Secoya culture men should not be overly interested in sex because of the danger that menstrual blood will contaminate them, make them sick, and possibly kill them. It is also believed that excessive sexual intercourse inhibits their comprehension of yahé visions, weakens them, throws off their aim when hunting, and makes their wives suffer. The ideal men, the shamans, should show very little interest in sex because they aspire to a higher and more intellectual comprehension of nature and the universe through yahé.

Men think of sexual intercourse (yo 'oye) as "using the woman." A man who "uses" his wife too much is thought to be unappreciative of her "suffering" during pregnancy and childbirth. As one male respondent stated, "A woman suffers a great deal and her husband must respect her and not use her too much."

Women, in turn, should be cloistered as girls in the care of their mothers and should be chaste at marriage. They should be shy in sexual matters with their husbands and never initiate sexual relations nor be aggressive during the sex act. If husband and wife engage in sex at home (usually at night), they try to be as quiet and inconspicuous as possible. Other times they may have sex while foraging together in the forest. After intercourse, a woman must bathe before cooking or serving food to others. Shamans, in particular, can "sense" when a woman has not bathed after sex, and will refuse her offerings of food and drink.

During their menstrual periods women desist from cooking and are isolated in a special hut lest their blood contaminate others. They should not walk around the village because their blood might drip on the ground where others step. One shaman, with obvious revulsion, told me he did not like to visit the village of San Pablo because many women lived there and he could "see" their menstrual blood on the ground.

Kissing between the sexes is tabooed (even during sexual intercourse) and is viewed as a demonstration of "insanity." When asked if a husband and wife may kiss, one respondent said, "They don't kiss, even when the husband returns from a long trip. They are afraid to kiss. When he greets her, he embraces her . . . it is an expression of affection. A mother and father may kiss infants, but not others. Chara and Mecias [two Siona men] saw Orville Johnson [an American missionary] kiss his wife María in Limoncocha . . . it shocked them very much. When María spoke to them they turned their heads away because it was something shameful to them." Likewise, men and women should not hold hands, although children and adults of the same sex may do so.

Conception, Pregnancy, Fetal Development, and Birth

According to my Siona and Secoya respondents, a human fetus and the resulting child grow from the semen of a single genitor. As one Secoya male explained, "The man gives everything that becomes the child. Everything goes from the man to the woman. The child is not formed by the woman." I then asked him how sterility might be accounted for. His response was, "The man is defective. He can't give [semen]." This respondent insisted that the Secoya have no concept of the female contributing an ovum to the reproductive process.

Regardless, there is clearly a recognition among the Siona-Secoya that some women are too old or otherwise unable to bear children. Female infertility is considered a legitimate reason for divorce, and in one reported case it was the motive for the murder of a wife who had faked two pregnancies and two miscarriages before her husband discovered her trickery. However, there is no concept of female infertility as a consequence of the normal biological process of menopause. Instead, it is strongly held that older women do not bear children because they have been "cured" of menstruation and child bearing by a shaman.

For women who have not received the shaman's "cure," the cessation of menstruation is recognized as the beginning of a pregnancy. No formal announcement is made, but the fact that the woman doesn't go to the menstruation hut or bathe with warm water and *Inga* leaves reveals her condition to the village.

Pregnancy is a period of caution for both the wife and her husband. Many taboos must be followed if the well-being of the fetus and the mother are to be assured. At the onset of pregnancy a husband and wife abstain from sexual relations because it is believed that the penis can injure the fetus. It is also believed that a man can kill the fetus if he lays his legs across the pregnant woman's body or disturbs her too much. So the husband and wife sleep apart (or with a space between them).

Most pregnancy rules and taboos are based on belief in imitative or contagious principles. For example, a husband must not repair holes in his canoe with pitch because it will cause the infant to "stick" in the uterus. Similarly, the husband and wife must not recline opposite one another in the same hammock or the fetus will reverse in the uterus and present a difficult breech (feet-first) delivery. If the mother paints her body with *genipa* (a dark blue dye from the evergreen *Genipa americana*) the infant will have birthmarks. When the woman engages in a task or bathes she must finish quickly so that her baby will have a quick birth.

The principle of contagion also governs dietary taboos during pregnancy. The mother cannot eat sticky fruits because it will cause the infant to stick in the uterus. If the mother eats tapir meat the infant will have a big head, and if she consumes peccary it will have clubbed feet. The eating of twin fruits (e.g., bananas) will cause twins to be born.

Although the pregnant woman continues to cook, she must touch only those wares that belong to her household. She can visit around the village, but is not allowed to accept refreshment from the utensils of others. Usually she carries a calabash and hides it near the house she plans to visit; if she is offered food or drink she will excuse herself for a moment and fetch it. If she has forgotten to bring a calabash, her hostess may look around the house for an old one that can be burned after use, or the visitor simply may drink from a folded leaf.

A woman seeks a private spot away from the house to give birth. It is believed that the other children of the household will fall ill if the birth takes place in the house. The husband assists by going to the chosen place and constructing a temporary shelter. He also carries a hammock and water to the site, but does not stay to witness the birth.

When the birth is imminent the woman goes to the shelter accompanied by one or more older women who will assist her. The hammock is doubled and tied to one of the rafters of the shelter. The woman gives birth in a squatting position and pulls on the hammock to support herself. After the delivery one of the midwives cuts the umbilical cord with a blade of *Pariana* grass and ties the stump with a string made from *Astrocaryum* palm fiber. The mother digs a shallow hole beside the place of birth and buries the placenta in it. One of the female helpers touches a hot coal to a chunk of incense (made from plant resins) to produce fragrant smoke. This is blown over the buried placenta to frighten away demons. After bathing the infant, the mother returns to the house.

Postpartum Isolation and the Couvade

When the mother and newborn infant return the husband quickly constructs a screened-off area within the house by sticking palm fronds into the earthen floor. The mother and child are isolated within this partition. The husband then observes a period of ritual rest (which anthropologists term the couvade) until the infant's umbilical stump dries and drops off. He passes this time by "recuperating" in a hammock hung just outside the screened area. Thus he is symbolically united with the burden of childbirth and asserts his paternity of the child.

Both the mother and the father are believed to be contaminated by the vaginal blood that was spilled during the childbirth (even though the husband was not present at the moment of birth). Each day they bathe in warm water and scrub their skin with *Inga* leaves to purify themselves. Again, this action by the man is symbolic of his paternity.

When the infant's umbilical stump drops off it is buried beneath the house and the father resumes his normal activities. The mother and child remain isolated until the mother's postpartum vaginal discharge ceases (about one month). Ideally, the husband does not resume sexual relations with his wife until she indicates she is ready.

The Spacing of Births

According to Siona-Secoya belief, a woman should not have too many children and her births should be well spaced. Many respondents say three or four children are ideal. Two reasons are given: "We don't want the woman to suffer," and, "We don't want the mother to work too hard." Ideally, a woman should give birth at intervals no closer than four to six years, when the preceding child "is big enough to fish alone and the mother doesn't have to watch him too closely," or "when the child can swim and walk alone," or "when the child has all its teeth."

In 1974 there were three Siona mothers in the village of Shushufindi who had small children born at close intervals. When other women saw these infants and small children clinging to their mothers they made sarcastic remarks among themselves, such as "We aren't opossums to live like that!"

The Siona-Secoya attempt to space births by a variety of contraceptive techniques, including postpartum abstinence from sexual relations. As mentioned earlier, a husband should not resume intercourse with his wife following a birth until she indicates her willingness. This period of abstinence extends through the postpartum isolation of the mother and child, and may continue for a year or longer. In the words of one man, "one to three years . . . you put up with it until she answers that you can use her. You don't try to overcome her. Having the baby was a big task. We endure this hardship to conserve the woman."

Interestingly, the Siona-Secoya ideal of spacing births is very similar to the observed four-year mean birth intervals of !Kung foragers of the Kalahari Desert in southern Africa (Blurton Jones and Sibley 1978). Borgerhoff Mulder notes, "Extensive evidence from human populations that offspring survivorship is poor when births are closely spaced (Hobcraft, McDonald, and Rutstein 1983; Knodel 1978) indicates that parental care in these first years of life enhances offspring survival. . . . !Kung women, by spacing their offspring at 4-year intervals, maximize the number of offspring surviving to 10 years (the age beyond which mortality is very low in this population)" (1992, 345–46).

Transgressions

Adultery is probably a cultural universal, although the frequency of its expression and attitudes toward it vary across cultures. Adultery occurs in Siona-Secoya society, but my field data suggest it involves a minority of Siona-Secoya adults and is less frequent than in many other societies. When it occurs, and is discovered, it typically results in marital crises and may lead to divorce.

While I do not have quantitative data on adultery rates in Siona-Secoya communities, I have heard gossip and backbiting related to adultery. The Siona and Secoya live in small settlements and little behavior escapes their notice, especially when it presents a recurring pattern. Very few Siona and Secoya men have reputations as womanizers (*nomiyïkï;* lit., "user of women"). Those who do have low social standing within the community. One Secoya male in particular is ridiculed because of his womanizing tendencies and has been given the pejorative nickname *wa'so* after the acouchi, a small rodent (*Myoprocta acouchy*). Such mockery is a severe sanction in this village-level society, and most men attempt to avoid it by living within the boundaries of acceptable behavior.

I know of two cases of divorce that resulted from women having extramarital affairs. In both cases the women subsequently married their lovers and these second marriages have proved stable. However, both affairs caused great consternation and stigmatized their participants in the eyes of the community. These affairs and their aftermaths are discussed in the published autobiography of a Secoya man (Piaguaje 1990).

One could argue that the observed stigma of adultery in Siona-Secoya society derives from the influence of Protestant missionaries from the Summer Institute of Linguistics between 1955 and 1985. However, as I have shown in this chapter, Siona-Secoya beliefs about sex, reproduction, and marriage have deep roots in the traditional culture and worldview. For example, the beliefs about contamination by menstrual and birth-related blood are closely intertwined with the traditional female puberty ritual, the couvade, and the taboos associated with shamanic training and the yahé ritual. All these rituals are indigenous and have nothing to do with missionary influence.

Other factors also reduce the opportunities for extramarital affairs in Siona-Secoya society. A woman's access to potential sex partners depends on a number of factors, including the prevailing settlement pattern, residential arrangements, and the organization of the household and daily activities.

While many lowland peoples of South America live in nucleated villages, others have more dispersed households, including those with widely scattered longhouses, or malocas, that shelter extended families. This is the traditional pattern of the Siona and Secoya, whose traditional maloca-style house is called the *hai wi'e* ("big house"). The Siona-Secoya pattern of scattered settlements reduces a woman's access to men who are not members of her immediate household and family.

Additionally, Siona and Secoya women are rarely unattended. Most of their waking hours are spent cooking or doing domestic chores around the house or in nearby gardens, and they are usually accompanied by other women or children. When they venture farther from their households they usually travel with their husbands and children (as on foraging expeditions or when visiting other settlements). In short, dalliances with males other than their husbands are complicated by both the physical separation of settlements and the fact that women are rarely unescorted when they leave their own homes. Of course, such factors do not completely eliminate adultery, but they complicate it and make extramarital liaisons more difficult to arrange.

Multiple "Fathers" through the Patrilineage

Siona kinship terminology is of the Omaha type, and is patrilineal, bifurcate merging, and has age-grading prefixes in the first ascending (parental) generation (Vickers 1976, 171–78). Within the patrilineage it recognizes "father" (*ha'ki*), "older father" (*ai ha'ki*), and "younger father" (*si ha'ki*). "Older fathers" are the father's older brothers, and "younger fathers" are the father's younger brothers. Grandfathers are termed *ñekwï*. Secoya kinship terminology is quite similar to Siona terminology (Vickers 1976, 178–79), but both father's older and younger brothers are termed *pikï yohe*. This term signifies "father's brother" (or paternal uncle). In both the Siona and Secoya systems all of father's brothers are members of the same patrilineage or sib. In contrast, both the Siona and Secoya call mother's brothers *kwï*. These maternal uncles are not members of ego's patrilineage.

The Siona terminology of "older father" and "younger father" recognizes that father's brothers are fellow sib members of the parental generation, and that they often provide social and economic support in a paternal fashion. Secoya paternal uncles (pïkï yohe) behave similarly. Given this volume's emphasis on partible paternity, it must be emphasized that these "older fathers," "younger fathers," and pïkï yohe do *not* normally enjoy sexual access to ego's mother. Such behavior, should it occur in Siona and Secoya society, would be viewed as deviant and undesirable because it would severely damage family relationships and unity. Among the Siona and Secoya the extended family is an extremely important social and economic unit and is the ultimate supporter of children's welfare.

Conclusion

The data and interpretations presented in this chapter suggest that Siona-Secoya sexual expression is comparatively restrained due to cultural beliefs about reproduction and the dangers of female menstruation and excessive intercourse. In part, Siona-Secoya concerns focus on the hardships women endure during pregnancy and childbirth. But men are equally concerned about the perceived "hazards" female sexuality and menstruation pose to their health and ability to experience spirituality through yahé. All these considerations are reflected in their ideals and generally normative patterns of premarital cloistering of girls, arranged marriages, monogamy, marital fidelity, and their numerous taboos on sexual activity. As in all cultures, there are deviations from these ideals and norms, but these are negatively sanctioned through backbiting and ostracism. By modern Western standards, the Siona and Secoya appear to be as sexually repressed as late-nineteenth-century Victorians, perhaps more so.

Certainly, the Siona-Secoya do not recognize multiple biological or "secondary" fathers, which Beckerman et al. (1998, 164) see as "particularly common" in lowland South American Indian societies. As Marvin Harris (1980, 11) has noted, a negative case does not disprove a theory and the challenge for a naysayer is to provide a better theory to explain the observed phenomena. I accept this challenge and present my interpretation of paternity certainty and uncertainty below.

The Siona-Secoya practice of recognizing one genitor is consistent with the biology of human sexual reproduction, although they deny the reproductive contribution of the mother (via her ovum and nurturing of the fetus). Needless to say, medical science has demonstrated that in about 98.9% of all pregnancies a single fetus results from the fertilization of one ovum of one female (the biological mother) by one spermatozoon from a single male (the biological father) (Clayman 1989, 815, 1016). About 1.1% of pregnancies are "multiple pregnancies" involving twins, which may be either monozygotic (identical) or dizygotic (fraternal). Monozygotic twins result when a single fertilized ovum divides at an early stage of development. Dizygotic twins occur when the female produces two ova that are fertilized by two separate spermatozoa. Triplets, quadruplets, and quintuplets are statistically quite rare.

Further, the male who typically has the greatest frequency of sexual intercourse with the biological mother is the mother's socially recognized "husband." Hence, Siona-Secoya beliefs and practices concerning paternity reflect the statistical probabilities of correct paternity identification and support the materialist theoretical argument that cultural beliefs and behaviors are predominantly influenced by infrastructural factors such as the "modes of production and reproduction" (Harris 1980).

The Siona-Secoya case is also consistent with the theory of evolutionary ecology (also known as sociobiology) since this theory allows for various reproductive decisions and strategies. Borgerhoff Mulder notes in a recent review of our current knowledge on human reproductive decisions:

> Fisher (1958) first called attention to how natural selection might adjust the allocation of an organism's limited resources between growth and maintenance (collectively called somatic effort) and reproduction (reproductive effort). Resources allocated to reproduction can be subdivided (Alexander and Borgia 1979) into parental effort (the provisioning and rearing of offspring) and mating effort (the pursuit of mating opportunities). These patterns of allocation differ among individuals, both within and between species, and are called an individual's life history. . . .
>
> Since Fisher's time, and particularly since the 1960s, there has been a massive growth in studies that examine how different patterns of allocation are adapted to the socioecological conditions an individual can expect to experience in its lifetime. (1992, 340)

One of the allocation decisions people can make is "offspring quantity" versus "offspring quality" (Lessels 1991). The data presented in this chapter concerning Siona-Secoya reproductive decisions clearly suggest they have chosen parental effort over mating effort, and offspring quality over offspring quantity. Ostensibly this is because their parental investment improves their children's survival rates and reproductive chances, thus enhancing the representation of the parents' genes in succeeding generations. Certainly both Siona-Secoya fathers and mothers invest greatly in the welfare of their children by providing food, shelter, clothing, education, protection, and other basic needs (Malinowski 1922).

Edward O. Wilson's argument (1979, 129–30) that the optimal human male reproductive strategy is to maximize one's genes in succeeding generations by copulating with as many females as possible is severely limited by the norms and beliefs of Siona-Secoya society. The venerable nineteenth-century anthropologist Lewis Henry Morgan (1877) hypothesized that such a condition obtained in the "ethnical period" of "lower savagery" as the first humans evolved from lower animals and prior to the institution of incest rules. He termed the social organization of this hypothetical period the "promiscuous horde." However, there is no ethnographic evidence for such a pattern of unrestricted sexual access in any known society of *Homo sapiens*. Wilson himself observed: "A particularly severe form of aggressiveness should be reserved for actual or suspected adultery. In many human societies, where sexual bonding is close and personal knowledge of the behavior of others detailed, adulterers are harshly treated. The sin is regarded to be even worse when offspring are produced. Although fighting is uncommon in hunter-gatherer peoples such as the Eskimos, Australian aborigines, and !Kung Bushmen, murder or fatal fighting appears to be frequent in these groups in comparison with other societies and is usually a result of retaliation for actual or suspected adultery" (1975, 327).

The fact that some lowland South American societies recognize multiple fathers must derive from the reproductive decisions and patterns of sexual intercourse that are normative in these societies. That is, the members of these societies tolerate or permit married females to have sexual relations with multiple males as a fairly common practice. Under such conditions it is understandable that a pregnancy might be viewed as the product of more than one male genitor, especially if the culture is an indigenous one that has little knowledge of modern biological science and its findings on human reproduction.

A more important question is whether such a belief in partible paternity confers any adaptive advantages. As suggested earlier, if there is paternity uncertainty because the mother has multiple sex partners, it would make sense for her male consorts to contribute to the welfare of her child since they have a statistical chance of being the biological father and having their genes passed on to the next generation. Again, any male's exact chance of being the biological father would depend on the number of males who had intercourse with the mother, their relative frequency of intercourse with her, and the timing of that intercourse.

However, each "secondary father" also bears the risk that he is not the biological father of the child. Due to this risk he would be foolish to invest all of his efforts in a child of uncertain paternity. Thus I predict that such secondary fathers would extend their support activities to a number of children with whose mothers they had sexual intercourse, and most particularly to those whose mothers had fewer sex partners. Finally, such men should invest most of their support in the children of their wives, since these children would have a greater probability of carrying their genes (assuming that the husband is the most frequent sex partner of his wife).

Finally, individual children might well benefit from the support of "multiple fathers" as suggested by several of the chapters in this volume. Siona children also enjoy "multiple fathers" according to their kinship terminology and the social and economic organization of their extended families, which are based on patrilocal residence and patrilineal descent groups. This is a common pattern in unilineal descent systems around the world. Of course, unilineal kinship systems do embody a concept of family and shared descent from common ancestors, even when partible paternity is not recognized. Hence child support by larger groups of "parents" is often based on kinship principles rather than a literal belief in multiple biological fathers.

Author's note: I thank Steve Beckerman and Paul Valentine, whose organization of the 1997 symposium on partible paternity at the 49th International Congress of Americanists in Quito got me started on this project. Through the years my research among the Siona and Secoya has been supported by an NDEA Title IV Fellowship (1972), the Henry L. and Grace Doherty Charitable Foundation (1973–74), the National Institute of Mental Health (1975–76), the Florida International University Foundation (1979, 1984), Cultural Survival (1980), the National Endowment for the Humanities (1985–86), the School of American Research (1985–86), the Fulbright Scholar program (1994), the Institute for Science and Interdisciplinary Studies (1997, 1998), and the Latin American and Caribbean Center and College of Arts and Sciences of Florida International

University (1980, 1984). Affiliations with Ecuadorian institutions have been provided by the Instituto Nacional de Antropología e Historia, the Instituto Nacional de Colonización de la Región Amazónica Ecuatoriana, the Facultad Latinoamericana de Ciencias Sociales, and the Pontificia Universidad Católica of Quito. I also thank all the Siona and Secoya people who have made my fieldwork both possible and enjoyable.

Bibliography

Abelove, Joan M.

1978   "Pre-Verbal Learning of Kinship Behavior among Shipibo Infants of Eastern Peru." Ph.D. dissertation, City University of New York.

Adams, Kathleen, and David Price, eds.

1994   *The Demography of Small-Scale Societies: Case Studies from Lowland South America.* South American Indian Studies, no. 4. Bennington, Vt.: Bennington College.

Adams, P.

1962   "Textos Kulina." *Folklore americano* 10: 93–222.

1963   "Some Notes on the Material Culture of the Kulina Indians." *Antropológica* 12: 27–44.

1976   "Ceramica Kulina." *Peru indígena* 10 (24–25): 82–87.

Agerkpop, Terry

1983   *Piaroa, Venezuela.* Caracas: Instituto Interamericano de Etnomusicología y Folklore.

Alès, Catherine

1984   "Violence et ordre social dans une société amazonienne: Les Yanomamï du Venezuela." *Études rurales* 95–96: 89–114.

1990   "Chroniques des temps ordinaires: Corésidence et fission Yanomami." *L'homme* 30: 73–101.

1998   "Pourquoi les Yanomamï ont-ils des filles?" In *La production du corps: Approches anthropologiques et historiques,* ed. M. Godelier and M. Panoff, 281–315. Paris: Éditions des Archives Contemporaines.

2000   "Anger as a Marker of Love: The Ethic of Conviviality among the Yanomami." In *The Anthropology of Love and Anger: The Aesthetics of Conviviality in Native Amazonia,* ed. J. Overing and A. Passes, 133–51. London and New York: Routledge.

2001a "Ethnologie ou Discours-écrans? Fragments du discours amoureux yanomami." In *Pour une anthropologie de l'interlocution: Les rhétoriques du quotidien*, ed. B. Masquelier and J. L. Siran, 211–46. Paris: L'Harmattan.

2001b "L'Aigle et le chien sylvestre: La Distinction de sexe dans les rites et la parenté yanomami." In *Sexe relatif ou sexe absolu? De la distinction de sexe dans les sociétés*, ed. C. Alès amd C. Barraud, 169–215. Paris: Editions de la Maison des Sciences de L'Homme.

Alexander, R. D., and G. Borgia

1979 "On the Origin and Basis of the Male-Female Phenomenon." In *Sexual Selection and Reproductive Competition in Insects*, ed. M. F. Blum and N. Blum, 413–40. New York: Academic Press.

Alexander, R. D., and K. Noonan

1979 "Concealment of Ovulation, Parental Care, and Human Social Evolution." In *Evolutionary Biology and Human Social Behavior: An Evolutionary Perspective*, ed. N. Chagnon and W. Irons, 436–53. North Scituate, Mass.: Duxbury Press.

Alexiades, Miguel

1999 "Ethnobotany of the Ese Eja: Plants, Health, and Change in an Amazonian Society." Ph.D. dissertation, City University of New York.

Anduze, Pablo J.

1974 *Dearuwa: Los dueños de la selva.* Caracas: Academia de Ciencias Físicas, Matemáticas y Naturales.

Århem, Kaj

1981 *Makuna Social Organization: A Study in Descent, Alliance and the Formation of Corporate Groups in the North-Western Amazon.* Acta Universitatis Upsaliensis, Uppsala Studies in Cultural Anthropology, no. 4. Uppsala: Academiae Upsaliensis.

1989 "The Maku, the Makuna, and the Guiana System: Transformations of Social Structure in Northern Lowland South America." *Ethnos* (1–2): 5–22.

Aristotle

1942 *Generation of Animals.* Trans. A. L. Peck. Loeb Classical Library, no. 366. Cambridge, Mass.: Harvard University Press.

1992 *Aristotle's De partibus animalium I and De generatione animalium I (with Passages from II.1–3).* Trans. D. M. Balme. Oxford: Clarendon Press.

Arvelo-Jiménez, Nelly

1971 *Political Relations in a Tribal Society: A Study of the Ye'cuana Indians of Venezuela.* Ann Arbor: University Microfilms International.

1974 *Relaciones políticas en una sociedad tribal: Estudio de los Ye'cuana, indígenas del amazonas venezolana.* Mexico City: Instituto Indigenista Interamericano.

Bai, Jie
1999 "Methods for Correlated Binary Responses with Application in Anthropology." M.A. thesis, Pennsylvania State University.

Bamberger, Joan
1967 "Environment and Cultural Classification: A Study of the Northern Kayapó." Ph.D. dissertation, Harvard University.
1974 "The Myth of Matriarchy: Why Men Rule in Primitive Society." In *Women, Culture, and Society*, ed. Michelle Rosaldo and Louise Lamphere, 263–80. Stanford: Stanford University Press.

Barral, Basilio de
1979 *Diccionario Warao-Castellano, Castellano-Warao.* Caracas: Universidad Católica "Andrés Bello."

Basso, Ellen B.
1970 "Xingu Carib Kinship Terminology and Marriage: Another View." *Southwestern Journal of Anthropology* 26: 402–16.
1973 *The Kalapalo Indians of Central Brazil.* New York: Holt, Rinehart and Winston.
1975 "Kalapalo Affinity: Its Cultural and Social Contexts." *American Ethnologist* 2 (2): 207–28.

Beckerman, Stephen
1977 "The Use of Palm Trees by the Barí Indians of the Maracaibo Basin." *Principes* 21 (4): 143–54.
1983 "Optimal Foraging Group Size for a Human Population: The Case of Barí Fishing." *American Zoologist* 23 (2): 283–90.
1991 "Barí Spear Fishing: Advantages to Group Formation." *Human Ecology* 19 (4): 529–54.
1997a "The Barí Partible Paternity Project: Preliminary Results." Manuscript.
1997b "Partible Paternity among the Barí of Venezuela." Paper presented to the 49th International Congress of Americanists, Quito, June 7–11.

Beckerman, Stephen, and Roberto Lizarralde
1995 "State-Tribal Warfare and Male Biased Casualties among the Barí." *Current Anthropology* 36 (3): 497–500.
n.d. "Paternidad compartida entre los Bari." In *Caminos cruzados: Ensayos en antropológia social, etno-ecología, y etno-educación*, ed. C. Alès and J. Chiappino. Caracas: Ediciones Monte Avila/IRD, in press.

Beckerman, S., R. Lizarralde, C. Ballew, S. Schroeder, C. Fingelton, A. Garrison, and H. Smith
1998 "The Barí Partible Paternity Project: Preliminary Results." *Current Anthropology* 39 (1): 164–67.

Bishop, M.W.H., and A. Walton
1960 "Spermatogenesis and the Structure of Mammalian Spermatozoa." In *Marshall's Physiology of Reproduction*, 3d ed., ed. A. S. Parkes, 1: 1–129. London: Longmans Green.

Boglár, Lajos
1971 "Chieftainship and the Religious Leader: A Venezuelan Example." *Acta etnográfica* 20 (3–4): 331–37.
1978 "Cuentos y mitos de los Piaroa." *Montalbán* 6: 221–311.

Borgerhoff Mulder, Monique
1992 "Reproductive Decisions." In *Evolutionary Ecology and Human Behavior*, ed. Eric Alden Smith and Bruce Winterhalder, 339–74. New York: Aldine de Gruyter.

Bourdieu, Pierre
1977 *Outline of a Theory of Practice*. Cambridge: Cambridge University Press.

Boyd, R., and Silk, J.
1997 *How Humans Evolved*. New York: Norton.

Briggs, Charles L.
1996 "Conflict, Language Ideologies, and Privileged Arenas of Discursive Authority in Warao Dispute Mediation." In *Disorderly Discourse: Narrative, Conflict, and Inequality*, ed. Charles L. Briggs, 204–41. New York: Oxford University Press.

Butt, Audrey
1975 "Birth Customs of the Akawaio." In *Studies in Social Anthropology: Essays in Memory of E. Evans-Pritchard*, ed. J.H.M. Beattie and R. G. Lienhardt, 285–310. Oxford: Oxford University Press.

Camargo, Eliane
1999 "La découverte de l'amour par Hidi Xinu: Récit caxinauá." *Bulletin de l'Institut Français d'Études Andines* 28 (2): 249–70.

Carneiro, Robert
n.d. "The Concept of Multiple Paternity among the Kuikuru: A Step toward the New Study of Ethnoembryology." Manuscript.

CEDI
1982 "Matis: Gripe reduz população quase a metade." *Povos indígenas no Brasil* (São Paulo), no. 2.

Chagnon, Napoleon
1968 *Yąnomamö: The Fierce People*. New York: Holt, Rinehart and Winston.
1988 "Life Histories, Blood Revenge, and Warfare in a Tribal Population." *Science* 239: 985–92.

Chantre y Herrera, José
1901 *Historia de las misiones de la Compañía de Jesús en el Marañón español*. Madrid: Imprenta de A. Avrial.

Chernela, Janet

1985 "Indigenous Fishing in the Neotropics: The Tukano Uanano of the Blackwater Uaupes River Basin in Brazil and Colombia." *Interciencia* 10 (2): 78–86.

1988a "Gender, Language, and Placement in Uanano Songs and Litanies." *Journal of Latin American Lore* 14 (2): 193–206.

1988b "Righting History in the Northwest Amazon: Myth, Structure and History in an Arapaço Narrative." In *Rethinking History and Myth: Indigenous South American Perspectives on the Past,* ed. J. Hill, 35–49. Urbana: University of Illinois Press.

1988c "Some Considerations of Myth and Gender in a Northwest Amazon Society." In *Dialectics and Gender: Papers in Honor of Robert F. and Yolanda Murphy,* ed. Richard Randolph, David Schneider, and May N. Diaz, 67–79. Boulder, Colo.: Westview.

1989 "Marriage, Language, and History among Eastern Tukanoan Speaking Peoples of the Northwest Amazon." *Latin American Anthropology Review* 1 (2): 36–42.

1991 "Symbolic Inaction in Rituals of Gender and Procreation among the Garifuna (Black Caribs) of Honduras." *Ethos* 19 (1): 52–67.

1993 *The Wanano Indians of the Brazilian Amazon: A Sense of Space.* Austin: University of Texas Press.

1997 "Ideal Speech Moments: A Woman's Narrative Performance in the Northwest Amazon." *Feminist Studies* 23(1): 73–96.

Cipolletti, María Susana

1988 *Aipë koka, la palabra de los antiguos: Tradición oral secoya.* Quito: Ediciones Abya-Yala; Rome: MLAL.

Civrieux, Marc de

1970 *Watunna: Mitología Makiritare.* Caracas: Monte Avila.

Clark, Kathleen E.

1982 "Subsistence Fishing at San Carlos de Río Negro, Venezuela." Paper presented to the Symposium on the Structure and Function of Amazonian Forest Ecosystems of the Upper Río Negro, Instituto Venezolano de Investigaciones Científicas, Caracas.

Clayman, Charles B., ed.

1989 *The American Medical Association Encyclopedia of Medicine.* New York: Random House.

Codazzi, Agustín

1940 *Resumen de la geografía de Venezuela.* Caracas: Taller de Artes Gráficas.

Conklin, Beth A.

1996 "Reflections on Amazonian Anthropologies of the Body." *Medical Anthropology Quarterly* 10 (3): 373–75.

Coppens, Walter
1971   "Las relaciones comerciales de los Yekuana del Caura-Paragua." *Antropológica* 30: 28–59.

Counts, D.E.A., and D. R. Counts
1983   "Father's Water Equals Mother's Milk: The Conception of Parentage in Kaliai, West New Guinea." *Mankind* 14 (1): 45–56.

Crocker, William H.
1984   "Canela Marriage: Factors in Change." In *Marriage Practices in Lowland South America*, ed. Kenneth M. Kensinger, 63–98. Illinois Studies in Anthropology, no. 14. Urbana: University of Illinois Press.

1990   *The Canela (Eastern Timbira), I: An Ethnographic Introduction.* Smithsonian Contributions to Anthropology, no. 33. Washington, D.C.: Smithsonian Institution Press.

1997   "Other Fathers among the Canela of Brazil." Paper presented to the 49th International Congress of Americanists, Quito, June 7–11.

n.d.   "The Canela Extramarital Sex System and Its Decline." In *An Anthology on South American Indians*, ed. P. Lyon. Prospect Heights, Ill.: Waveland Press, in press.

Crocker, William H., and Jean Crocker
1994   *The Canela: Bonding through Kinship, Ritual, and Sex.* Fort Worth, Texas: Harcourt Brace.

Da Matta, Roberto
1976   *Um mundo dividido: A estrutura social dos indios Apinayé.* Petrópolis, Rio de Janeiro: Editora Vozes.

Darwin, Charles
1868   *The Variation of Animals and Plants under Domestication.* 2 vols. London: Murray.

Dean, Bartholomew
1998   "Forbidden Fruit: Infidelity, Affinity and Brideservice among the Urarina of Peruvian Amazonia." *Journal of the Royal Anthropological Institute*, n.s., 1: 87–110.

Delaney, Carol
1986   "The Meaning of Paternity and the Virgin Birth Debate." *Man.* n.s., 21: 494–513.

DeMallie, Raymond J.
1994   "Kinship and Biology in Sioux Culture." In *North American Indian Anthropology: Essays on Society and Culture*, ed. R. J. DeMallie and Alfonso Ortiz, 125–46. Norman: University of Oklahoma Press.

Descola, Philippe
1986   *La nature domestique: Symbolisme et praxis dans l'écologie des Achuar.* Paris: Éditions de la Maison des Sciences de l'Homme.

Dole, Gertrude E.
1979 "Pattern and Variation in Amahuaca Kin Terminology." In *Social Correlates of Kin Terminology*, ed. David J. Thomas, 13–36. Working Papers on South American Indians, no. 1. Bennington, Vt.: Bennington College.
1984 "The Structure of Kuikuru Marriage." In *Marriage Practices in Lowland South America*, ed. Kenneth M. Kensinger, 45–62. Illinois Studies in Anthropology, no. 14. Urbana: University of Illinois Press.

Draper, Patricia, and Jennie Keith
1992 "Cultural Contexts of Care: Family Caregiving for the Elderly in America and Africa." *Journal of Aging Studies* 6 (2): 113–33.

Dreyfus, Simone
1963 *Les Kayapo du nord*. Paris: Mouton.

Duby, G.
1995 *Dames du douzième siècle*. Vol. 2, *Le souvenir des aïeules*. Bibliothèque des histoires. Paris: Gallimard.

Dufour, Darna L.
1983 "Nutrition in the Northwest Amazon: Household Dietary Intake and Time-Energy Expenditure." In *Adaptive Responses of Native Amazonians*, ed. R. B. Hames and W. T. Vickers, 329–55. New York: Academic Press.
1989 "Effectiveness of Cassava Detoxification Techniques Used by Indigenous Peoples in Northwest Amazonia." *Interciencia* 14 (2): 88–91.
1992 "Nutritional Ecology in the Tropical Rain Forests of Amazonia." *American Journal of Human Biology* 4: 197–207.
1994 "Diet and Nutritional Status of Amazonian Peoples." In *Amazonian Indians from Prehistory to the Present: Anthropological Perspectives*, ed. Anna Roosevelt, 151–76 . Tucson: University of Arizona Press.

Eakin, Lucille, Erwin H. Lauriault, and Harry Boonstra
1980 *Bosquejo etnográfico de los Shipibo-conibo del Ucayali*. Lima: Prado Pastor.

Erikson, Philippe
1988 "Choix des proies, choix des armes, et gestion du gibier chez les Matis et d'autres Amérindiens d'Amazonie." In *L'animal dans l'alimentation humaine: Les critères de choix*, ed. L. Bodson, 211–20. Liège: *Anthropozoologica*, 2d special number.
1990 "Near Beer of the Amazon." *Natural History* 8 (90): 52–61.
1993 "A onomástica matis é amazônica?" In *Amazônia: Etnologia e história indígena*, ed. Eduardo Viveiros de Castro and Manuela Carneiro da Cunha, 323–38. São Paulo: Nucléo de História Indígena et do Indigenismo, USP/FAPESP.
1996 *La griffe des aïeux: Marquage du corps et démarquages ethniques chez les Matis d'Amazonie*. Louvain: Peeters; Paris: SELAF. Spanish translation: *El sello de los antepasados: Marcado del cuerpo y demarcación étnica entre los Matis de la Amazonía*. Lima: IFEA; Quito: Abya-Yala.
n.d. "Reflexos de si, ecos de outrem: Efeitos do contato sobre a auto-representação

matis." In *Imagens do Branco na história indígena: Simbolica do contato e resistencia cultural no norte da Amazônia,* ed. Bruce Albert and Alcida Ramos. São Paulo: Editora da USP, in press.

Evans-Pritchard, E. E.

1951 [1992] *Kinship and Marriage among the Nuer.* Oxford: Clarendon Press.

Farb, Peter, and George Armelagos

1983 *Consuming Passions: The Anthropology of Eating.* New York: Washington Square Press.

Fields, Harriet, and William R. Merrifield

1980 "Mayoruna (Panoan) Kinship." *Ethnology* 19 (1): 1–28.

Fisher, R. A.

1958 *The Genetical Theory of Natural Selection.* 2d ed. New York: Dover.

Fortes, Meyer

1950 "Kinship and Marriage among the Ashanti." In *African Systems of Kinship and Marriage,* ed. A. R. Radcliffe-Brown and D. Forde, 252–84. Oxford: Oxford University Press.

García Castro, Alvaro, and H. Dieter Heinen

1999 "El impacto ecológico del cierre del caño Manamo (Delta del Orinoco, Estados Delta Amacuro y Monagas)." *Antropológica* 91: 31–56.

Geertz, Hildred

1961 *The Javanese Family.* Glencoe, Ill.: Free Press.

Gilij, Padre Felipe Salvador, S.J.

1965 *Ensayo de historia americana.* Traducción y estudio preliminar de Antonio Tovar. Fuentes para la historia colonial de Venezuela, nos. 71–73. Caracas: Biblioteca de la Academia National de Historia. (Originally written between 1773 and 1782; originally published in 1782.)

Godelier, Maurice, T. R. Trautmann, and F. Tjon Sie Fat

1998 Introduction to *Transformations of Kinship,* ed. M. Godelier, T. R. Trautmann, and F. Tjon Sie Fat, 1–26. Washington, D.C.: Smithsonian Institution Press.

Goldman, Irving

1957 "Variations in Polynesian Social Organization." *Journal of the Polynesian Society* 66 (4): 374–90.

1963 *The Cubeo: Indians of the Northwest Amazon.* Illinois Studies in Anthropology, no. 2. Urbana: University of Illinois Press.

Goodenough, Ward H.

1970 "Transactions in Parenthood in Hawaii." In *Adoption in Eastern Oceania,* ed. Vern Carroll. Honolulu: University of Hawaii Press.

Goody, Jack
1956 "A Comparative Approach to Incest and Adultery." *British Journal of Sociology* 7: 286–305.

Gow, Peter
1989 "The Perverse Child: Desire in a Native Amazonian Subsistence Economy." *Man*, n.s., 24: 299–314.
1991 *Of Mixed Blood: Kinship and History in Peruvian Amazonia.* Oxford: Clarendon Press.

Gregor, Thomas
1977 *Mehinaku: The Drama of Daily Life in a Brazilian Indian Village.* Chicago: University of Chicago Press.
1985 *Anxious Pleasures: The Sexual Lives of an Amazonian People.* Chicago: University of Chicago Press.
1990 "Male Dominance and Sexual Coercion." In *Cultural Psychology: Essays on Comparative Human Development*, ed. James W. Stigler, Richard A. Shweder, and Gilbert Herdt, 477–95. Cambridge: Cambridge University Press.

Grelier, Joseph
1957 "Les indiens Piaroa et le curare." *L'ethnographie*, n.s., 52: 78–86.

Harvey, Paul
1986 "Roman Code." Translation. Manuscript.

Harris, Marvin
1980 *Cultural Materialism: The Struggle for a Science of Culture.* New York: Vintage Books.

Hartung, John
1985 "Matrilineal Inheritance: New Theory and Analysis." *Behavioral and Brain Sciences* 8: 661–70; comments, 670–81; reply, 681–88.

Hedeker, D.
1998 "MIXNO: A Computer Program for Mixed-Effects Nominal Logistic Regression." <http://www.uic.edu/~hedeker/mix.html>

Heinen, H. Dieter
1972 "Residence Rules and Household Cycles in a Warao Subtribe: The Case of the Winikina." *Antropológica* 31: 21–86.
1988 "Los Warao." In *Los aborígenes de Venezuela.* Vol. 3, *Etnología contemporánea*, ed. Walter Coppens and Bernarda Escalante, 585–689. Caracas: Fundación La Salle de Ciencias Naturales/Monte Avila Editores.

Heinen, H. Dieter, George Salas, and Miguel Layrisse
1980 "Migration and Cultural Distance: A Comparative Study of Five Warao Subtribes." In *Demographic and Biological Studies of the Warao Indians*, ed.

Johannes Wilbert and Miguel Layrisse, 48–59. UCLA Latin American Studies, vol. 45. Los Angeles: UCLA Latin American Center Publications, University of California.

Heinen, H. Dieter, Werner Wilbert, and Tirso Rivero

1998 *Idamo kabuka imasibukomoni: Vida y dichos de Don Antonio Lorenzano Pacheco, indígena Waraowitu de las Bocas del Orinoco.* Caracas: Fundación La Salle de Ciencias Naturales.

Hemming, John

1978 *Red Gold: The Conquest of the Brazilian Indians.* Cambridge, Mass.: Harvard University Press.

1987 *Amazon Frontier: The Defeat of the Brazilian Indians.* Cambridge, Mass.: Harvard University Press.

Henry, Jules

1941 *Jungle People: A Kaingáng Tribe of the Highlands of Brazil.* New York: J. J. Augustin.

Héritier, Françoise

1981 *L'exercice de la parenté.* Paris: Gallimard.

1996 *Masculin/féminin: La pensée de la différence.* Paris: Éditions Odile Jacob.

Hill, Jonathan D.

1983 "Wakuenai Society: A Processual-Structural Analysis of Indigenous Cultural Life in the Upper Rio Negro Region of Venezuela." Ph.D. dissertation, Indiana University.

1993 *Keepers of the Sacred Chants: The Poetics of Ritual Power in an Amazon Society.* Tucson: University of Arizona Press.

Hill, Kim, and Magdalena Hurtado

1996 *Aché Life History: The Ecology and Demography of a Foraging People.* New York: Aldine de Gruyter.

Hill, Kim, and H. Kaplan

1988 "Tradeoffs in Male and Female Reproductive Strategies among the Aché: Part 2." In *Human Reproductive Behavior: A Darwinian Perspective,* ed. L. Betzig, M. Borgerhoff Mulder, and P. Turke, 291–305. Cambridge: Cambridge University Press.

Hippocrates

1978 "The Seed." Translated by I. M. Lonie. In *Hippocratic Writings,* ed. G.E.R. Lloyd. London: Penguin.

Hitchcock, Charles B.

1948 "La región Orinoco-Ventuari, Venezuela." *Boletín de la Sociedad de Ciencias Naturales* 11 (72): 131–79.

Hobcraft, J. N., J. W. McDonald, and S. O. Rutstein

1983   "Child-Spacing Effects on Infant and Early Child Mortality." *Population Index* 49: 585–618.

Holmes, Rebecca

1981   "Estado nutricional en cuatro aldeas de la selva amazónica, Venezuela: Un estudio de adaptación y aculturación." M.A. thesis, Instituto Venezolano de Investigaciones Científicas, Caracas.

1985   "Nutritional Status and Cultural Change in Venezuela's Amazon Territory." In *Change in the Amazon Basin*, ed. J. Hemming, 237–55. Manchester: University of Manchester.

Hopper, Janice

1967   *Indians of Brazil in the Twentieth Century.* Washington, D.C.: Institute for Cultural Research.

Houseman, Michael, and Douglas White

1998   "Taking Sides: Marriage Networks and Dravidian Kinship in Lowland South America." In *Transformations of Kinship*, ed. M. Godelier, T. R. Trautmann, and F. Tjon Sie Fat, 214–43. Washington, D.C.: Smithsonian Institution Press.

Hugh-Jones, Christine

1979   *From the Milk River: Spatial and Temporal Processes in Northwest Amazonia.* Cambridge: Cambridge University Press.

Hugh-Jones, Stephen

1979   *The Palm and the Pleiades: Initiation and Cosmology in Northwest Amazonia.* Cambridge: Cambridge University Press.

1993   "Clear Descent or Ambiguous Houses? A Re-examination of Tukanoan Social Organisation." *L'homme* 33 (2–4): 95–120.

Hurault, Jean

1965   *La vie matérielle des noirs réfugiés Boni et des Indiens Wayana du Haut-Maroni (Guyane française): Agriculture, économie, et habitat.* Paris: Office de la Recherche Scientifique et Technique Outre-Mer.

Jackson, Jean E.

1974   "Language Identity of the Colombia Vaupes Indians." In *Explorations in the Ethnography of Speaking*, ed. R. Bauman and J. Sherzer. Cambridge: Cambridge University Press.

1976   "Vaupés Marriage: A Network System in an Undifferentiated Lowland Area of South America." In *Regional Analysis*, vol. 2: *Social Systems*, ed. C. Smith, 65–93. New York: Academic Press.

1983   *The Fish People: Linguistic Exogamy and Tukanoan Identity in Northwestern Ama-*

ʒonia. Cambridge Studies in Social Anthropology. Cambridge: Cambridge University Press.

Jones, Nicholas Blurton, and R. Sibley

1978 "Testing Adaptiveness of Culturally Determined Behaviour: Do Bushmen Women Maximize Their Reproductive Success by Spacing Births Widely and Foraging Seldom?" In *Human Behaviour and Adaptation,* ed. Nicholas Blurton Jones and Vernon Reynolds, 135–58. Symposia of the Society for the Study of Human Biology, vol. 18. London: Taylor and Francis.

Journet, Nicolas

1995 *La paix des jardins: Structures sociales des Indiens curripaco du haut Rio Negro (Colombie).* Paris: Institut d'ethnologie.

Kalka, Claudia

1995 *Eine Tochter ist ein Haus, ein Boot, und ein Garten: Frauen und Geschlechtersymmetrie bei den Warao-Indianern Venezuelas.* Ethnologische Studien, 25. Münster: LIT Verlag.

Kensinger, Kenneth

1995 *How Real People Ought to Live: The Cashinahua of Eastern Peru.* Prospect Heights, Ill.: Waveland Press.

Kimura, Hideo

1983 "Ese Eja Relationship Terminology." *Shakai jinruigaku nenp'o* (Tokyo-K'obund'o) 9: 53–81.

Knodel, J.

1978 "Natural Fertility in Preindustrial Germany." *Population Studies* 32: 481–510.

Krisólogo, Pedro J.

1976 *Manual glotológico del idioma wo'tiheh.* Caracas: Universidad Católica "Andrés Bello."

Krute, Laurence Dana

1988 "Piaroa Nominal Morphosemantics." Ph.D. dissertation, Columbia University.

Layrisse, Miguel, George Salas, and H. Dieter Heinen

1980 "Vital Statistics of Five Warao Subtribes." In *Demographic and Biological Studies of the Warao Indians,* ed. Johannes Wilbert and Miguel Layrisse, 60–69. UCLA Latin American Studies, vol. 45. Los Angeles: UCLA Latin American Center Publications, University of California.

Lea, Vanessa

1984 "Brazil's Kayapó, Cursed by Gold." *National Geographic* 165 (5): 674–94.

1992 "Mẽbengokre (Kayapó) Personal Names: Total Social Facts in Central Brazil." *Man,* n.s., 27: 129–53.

1995a "The Houses of the Mẽbengokre (Kayapó) of Central Brazil: A New Door to Their Social Organization." In *About the House: Lévi-Strauss and Beyond,* ed.

Janet Carsten and Stephen Hugh-Jones, 206–25. Cambridge: Cambridge University Press.

1995b "Casa-se do outro lado: Um modelo simulado da aliança Mẽbengokre (Jê)." In *Antropologia do Parentesco: Estudos Ameríndios*, ed. E. Viveiros de Castro, 321–59. Rio de Janeiro: Universidade Federal do Rio de Janeiro.

2001 "The Composition of Mẽbengokre (Kayapó) households in Central Brazil." In *Beyond the Visible and the Material: The Amerindianization of Society in the Work of Peter Rivière*, ed. Laura Rival and Neil Whitehead. Oxford: Oxford University Press, in press.

Lessels, C. M.

1991 "The Evolution of Life Histories." In *Behavioural Ecology*, ed. J. R. Krebs and N. B. Davies, 32–68. 3d ed. Oxford: Blackwell Scientific Publications.

Lévi-Strauss, Claude

1949 *Les Structures élémentaires de la parenté*. Paris: Presses Universitaires de France.

1991 *Histoire de Lynx*. Paris: Plon.

Lizarralde, Manuel

1997 "Secondary Fathers after the Death of the Primary Father among the Barí." Paper presented to the 49th International Congress of Americanists, Quito, June 7–11.

Lizarralde, Manuel, and Roberto Lizarralde

1991 "Barí Exogamy among Their Territorial Groups: Choice and/or Necessity." *Human Ecology* 19 (4): 453–68.

Lizarralde, Roberto

1991 "Barí Settlement Patterns." *Human Ecology* 19 (4): 437–52.

1997 "Territorial Differences in Secondary Fatherhood among the Barí." Paper presented to the 49th International Congress of Americanists, Quito, June 7–11.

Lizarralde, Roberto, and Stephen Beckerman

1982 "Historia contemporánea de los Barí." *Antropológica* 58: 3–52.

Lorrain, Claire

2000 "Cosmic Reproduction, Economics and Politics among the Kulina of Southwest Amazonia." *Journal of the Royal Anthropological Institute*, n.s., 6: 293–310.

Lounsbury, Floyd G.

1964 "A Formal Account of the Crow- and Omaha-Type Kinship Terminologies." In *Explorations in Cultural Anthropology*, ed. Ward H. Goodenough, 351–93. New York: McGraw-Hill.

MAG/ORSTOM

1980 *Mapa morfo-edafológico provisional, nor-oriente, hoja no. 2*. Quito: Ministerio de Agricultura y Ganadería/Office de la Recherche Scientifique et Technique Outre-Mer.

Malinowski, Bronislaw

1922 *Argonauts of the Western Pacific.* New York: E. P. Dutton.

1927 *Sex and Repression in Savage Society.* London: Routledge and Kegan Paul.

1929 *The Sexual Life of Savages in North Western Melanesia.* London: Routledge and Kegan Paul. Reprint, 1982.

1930a "Kinship." *Man* 30 (2): 19–29.

1930b "Parenthood: The Basis of Social Structure." In *The New Generation: The Intimate Problems of Modern Parents and Children,* ed. V. F. Calverton and S. D. Schmalhausen, 112–68. New York: Macaulay.

Mansutti Rodríguez, Alexander

1986 "Hierro, barro cocido, curare y cerbatanas: El comercio intra e interétnico entre los Uwotjuja." *Antropológica* 65: 3–75.

1988a "Fundos, comunidades, y pueblos: Los patrones de asentamiento Uwotjuja." *Antropológica* 69: 3–35.

1988b "Investigaciones socio-antropológicas, Proyecto APS-Piaroa." Progress report, Office de la Recherche Scientifique et Technique Outre-Mer, Puerto Ayacucho.

1988c "La pesca entre los Piaroa (Uwotjuja) del Orinoco y la cuenca del Sipapo." *Memoria de la Sociedad de Ciencias Naturales La Salle* 47 (130): 3–39.

1990 *Los Piaroa y su territorio.* Cuadernos de trabajo del CEVIAP, no. 8, Caracas.

1991 *Sans guerriers il n'y a pas de guerre: Étude sur la violence che{ les Piaroa du Vene{uela.* DEA report, École des Hautes Études en Sciences Sociales, Paris.

1993a "Una mirada al futuro de los indígenas en Guayana." *Boletín antropológico* 29: 51–67.

1993b *Los Piaroa: El censo indígena de Vene{uela.* Vol. 1. Caracas: OCEI.

Mansutti Rodríguez, Alexander, and C. Briceño-Fustec

1993 "Edad, generación, y matrimonio entre los Piaroa de la cuenca de Sipapo (Venezuela)." *Boletín antropológico* 27: 51–64.

Marcano, Gaspar

1971 *Etnografía precolombina de Vene{uela.* Caracas: Universidad Central de Venezuela.

Matos Arvelo, Martín

1912 *Vida indiana.* Barcelona: Casa Editorial Maucci.

Mauss, M., and H. Beuchat

1950 "Essai sur les variations saisonnières des sociétés eskimos." In *Sociologie et anthropologie,* ed. M. Mauss. Paris: Presses Universitaires de France.

Maybury-Lewis, David

1967 *Akwẽ-Shavante Society.* Oxford: Clarendon Press.

Mayr, E.

1982 *The Growth of Biological Thought: Diversity, Evolution, and Inheritance.* Cambridge, Mass.: Harvard University Press.

McCallum, Cecilia

1994 "Ritual and the Origin of Sexuality in the Alto Xingu." In *Sex and Violence: Issues in Representation and Experience,* ed. Penelope Harvey and Peter Gow, 90–114. London: Routledge.

1996 "The Body That Knows: From Cashinahua Epistemology to a Medical Anthropology of Lowland South America." *Medical Anthropology Quarterly* 10 (3): 347–72.

Mead, Margaret

1935 *Sex and Temperament in Three Primitive Societies.* New York: Morrow.

Meggers, Betty J.

1975 "Application of the Biological Model of Diversification to Cultural Distributions in Lowland South America." *Biotropica* 7 (3): 141–61.

Melatti, J. C.

1979 "The Relationship System of the Krahó." In *Dialectical Societies,* ed. D. Maybury-Lewis, 46–79. Cambridge, Mass.: Harvard University Press.

Menget, Patrick

1984 "Delights and Danger: Notes on Sexuality in the Upper Xingu." In *Sexual Ideologies in Lowland South America,* ed. Kenneth Kensinger, 4–11. Working Papers on South American Indians, no. 4, Bennington, Vt.: Bennington College.

Monod, Jean

1987 *Wora: La déesse cachée.* Paris: Éditeurs Evidant.

Morales, Severiano, Jesus Caballero, Laureano Castillo, and Aléxander Mansutti

1984 "Así somos los Uhuottoj'a: Manual de cultura bilingüe, 1er. Nivel." Caracas: Ministerio de Educación/ Fundación La Salle de Ciencias Naturales. Manuscript.

Moran, Emilio F.

1990 *A ecologia humana das populações da Amazônia.* Petrópolis, Rio de Janeiro: Editora Vozes.

1991 "Human Adaptive Strategies in Amazonian Blackwater Ecosystems." *American Anthropologist* 93 (2): 361–82.

1995 "Disaggregating Amazonia: A Strategy for Understanding Biological and Cultural Diversity." In *Indigenous Peoples and the Future of Amazonia: An Ecological Anthropology of an Endangered World,* ed. L. E. Sponsel, 71–96. Tucson: University of Arizona Press.

Morgan, Lewis Henry

1877 *Ancient Society.* New York: Holt, Rinehart and Winston.

Moya, Ruth

1992 *Requiem por los espejos y los tigres: Una aproximación a la literatura y lengua secoya.* Quito: Ediciones Abya-Yala/ Oficina Regional de Cultura para América Latina y el Caribe.

Murphy, Yolanda, and Robert F. Murphy
1974 *Women of the Forest*. New York: Columbia University Press.

Musallam, B. F.
1983 *Sex and Society in Islam*. Cambridge: Cambridge University Press.

Nahoum-Grappe, Véronique
1996 "L'usage politique de la cruauté: L'épuration ethnique (ex-Yougoslavie, 1991–1995)." In *De la violence*, ed. Françoise Héritier, 273–323. Paris: Éditions Odile Jacob.

Nimuendajú, Curt
1946 *The Eastern Timbira*. Ed. and trans. Robert Lowie. Berkeley: University of California Press.

Oldham, Paul
1998 "Cosmología, shamanismo, y práctica medicinal." In *Del microscopio a la maraca*, ed. J. Chiappino and C. Alès, 225–49. Caracas: Ex Libris.

Overing, Joanna
1972 "Cognition, Endogamy, and Teknonymy: The Piaroa Example." *Southwestern Journal of Anthropology* 28: 282–97.

1973 "Endogamy and the Marriage Alliance: A Note on Continuity in Kindred-Based Groups." *Man* 8 (4): 555–70.

1975 *The Piaroa, a People of the Orinoco Basin: A Study in Kinship and Marriage*. Oxford: Clarendon Press.

1986 "Men Control Women? The Catch 22 in the Analysis of Gender." *International Journal of Moral and Social Studies* 1 (2): 135–56.

Overing, Joanna, and M. R. Kaplan
1988 "Los Wóthuha (Piaroa)." In *Los aborígenes de Venezuela*. Vol. 3, *Etnología contemporánea*, ed. Walter Coppens and Bernarda Escalante, 307–411. Caracas: Fundación La Salle de Ciencias Naturales/Monte Avila Editores.

Pereira, Levi Marques
1999 "Parentesco e organização social kaiowá." M.A. thesis, Universidade Estadual de Campinas.

Piaguaje, Celestino
1990 *Ecorasa: Autobiografía de un secoya*. Shushufindi, Ecuador: Ediciones CICAME.

Pinker, Steven
1997 *How the Mind Works*. New York: Norton.

Pollock, Donald
1993 "Death and Afterdeath among the Kulina." *Latin American Anthropology Review* 5 (2): 61–64.

1996 "Personhood and Illness among the Kulina." *Medical Anthropology Quarterly* 10 (3): 319–41.

1998 "Food and Gender among the Kulina." In *Food and Gender: Identity and Power,* ed. Carole Counihan and Steven Kaplan, 11–28. Amsterdam: Harwood Academic.

Radcliffe-Brown, R.
1950 Introduction to *African Systems of Kinship and Marriage,* ed. A. R. Radcliffe-Brown and D. Forde, 1–85. Oxford: Oxford University Press.

Ramos, A., and B. Albert
1977 "Yanomama Descent and Affinity: The Sanumá/Yanomam Contrast." In *Actes du XLII Congrès International des Américanistes* 2: 71–90. Paris: Fondation Singer-Polignac.

Rattray, R. S.
1923 *Ashanti.* Oxford: Clarendon Press.

Rival, Laura
1998 "Androgynous Parents and Guest Children: The Huaorani Couvade." *Journal of the Royal Anthropological Institute* 4: 619–42.

Rivière, Peter
1969 *Marriage among the Trio.* Oxford: Clarendon Press.
1974 "The Couvade: A Problem Reborn." *Man,* n.s., 9: 423–35.
1984 *Individual and Society in Guiana: A Comparative Study of Amerindian Social Organization.* New York: Cambridge University Press.

Rüf, Isabelle
1972 "Le 'dutsee tui' chez les Indiens Kulina du Perou." *Bulletin de la Société Suisse de Américanistes* 36: 73–80.

SAS Institute
1998 SAS/STAT User's Guide. Version 7. Statistical Analysis Software/Statistics. Cary, N.C.: SAS Institute.

Scheffler, Harold W., and Floyd G. Lounsbury
1971 *A Study in Structural Semantics: The Siriono System Kinship.* Englewood Cliffs, N.J.: Prentice-Hall, Inc.

Schneider, D. M.
1968 *American Kinship: A Cultural Account.* Englewood Cliffs, N. J.: Prentice-Hall.
1984 *A Critique of the Study of Kinship.* Ann Arbor: University of Michigan Press.

Schultes, Richard Evans, and Albert Hofmann
1980 *The Botany and Chemistry of Hallucinogens.* 2d ed. Springfield, Ill.: Charles C. Thomas.

Seeger, Anthony, Roberto Da Matta, and Eduardo Viveiros de Castro
1979 "A construção da pessoa nas sociedades indígenas brasileiras." *Boletim do Museu Nacional* (Rio de Janeiro) 32: 2–19.

Shapiro, Judith
1974 "Alliance or Descent: Some Amazonian Contrasts." *Man* 9 (2): 305–6.

Silva Monterrey, Nalúa Rosa

1992 "La constitution du groupe local: Relations génealogiques et territoriales: Le cas de Jyüwütüña." DEA report, École des Hautes Études en Sciences Sociales, Paris.

Simson, Alfred

1879 "Notes on the Piojes of the Putumayo." *Journal of the Anthropological Institute of Great Britain and Ireland* 7: 210–22.

1886 *Travels in the Wilds of Ecuador and the Exploration of the Putumayo River.* London: Sampson Low, Marston, Searle, and Rivington.

Siskind, Janet

1973 *To Hunt in the Morning.* Oxford: Oxford University Press.

Sorensen, Arthur

1967 "Multilingualism in the Northwest Amazon." *American Anthropologist* 69 (6): 670–84.

Stack, Carol B.

1974 *All Our Kin: Strategies for Survival in a Black Community.* New York: Harper and Row.

Steward, Julian H.

1949 "The Native Population of South America." In *Handbook of South American Indians,* vol. 5, *The Comparative Ethnology of South American Indians,* ed. Julian H. Steward, 655–68. Bureau of American Ethnology Bulletin no. 143. Washington, D.C.: U.S. Government Printing Office.

Stolze Lima, Tânia

1995 "A parte do Cauim, etnografia Juruna." Ph.D. dissertation, Universidade Federal do Rio de Janeiro/Museu Nacional.

Strathern, Marilyn

1995a "Bisogno di padri, bisogno di madri: Le 'madri vergini' in Inghilterra." In *Madri: Storia di un ruolo sociale,* ed. G. Fiume. Venice: Marsilio Editori.

1995b "Necessidade de pais, necessidade de mães." *Estudos feministas* 3: 303–29.

Suárez, María M.

1968 *Los Warao: Indígenas del Delta del Orinoco.* Caracas: Instituto Venezolano de Investigaciones Científicas.

Taylor, Douglas

1941 "Columbus Saw Them First." *Natural History* 48: 40–49.

Teixeira Pinto, Márnio

1997 *Ieipari: Sacrifício e vida social entre los índios Arara.* São Paulo: Hucitec, Anpocs.

Terray, Emmanuel

1996 "Le mariage de la science et du crime." *L'homme* 139: 137 ff.

Tessmann, Günter

1930 *Die Indianer nordost-Perus: Grundlegende Forschungen für eine systematische Kulturkunde.* Hamburg: Friederichsen, de Gruyter.

Thiel, Barbara

1994 "Further Thoughts on Why Men Share Meat." *Current Anthropology* 35: 440–41.

Thomas, David

1982 *Order without Government: The Society of the Pemon Indians of Venezuela.* Illinois Studies in Anthropology, no. 13. Urbana: University of Illinois Press.

Townsend, Patricia, and P. Adams

1978 "Estructura y conflicto en el matrimonio de los indios kulina de la amazonia peruana: Communidades y Culturas Peruanas." Lima: El Instituto Lingüistico de Verano.

Turner, Terence

1966 "Social Structure and Political Organization among the Northern Kayapó." Ph.D. dissertation, Harvard University.

1979 "Kinship, Household, and Community Structure among the Kayapó." In *Dialectical Societies: The Gê and Bororo of Central Brazil,* ed. D. Maybury-Lewis, 179–214. Cambridge, Mass.: Harvard University Press.

1993 "Imagens desafiantes: A apropriação Kaiapó do vídeo." *Revista de antropología* 36.

Uhl, Christopher

1980 "Studies of Forest, Agricultural, and Successional Environments in the Upper Rio Negro Region of the Amazon Basin." Ph.D. dissertation, Michigan State University.

Valentine, Paul

1991 "Curripaco Social Organization: A Study in History, Kinship, and Marriage in the Upper Rio Negro Valley." Ph.D. dissertation, Pennsylvania State University.

Veiga, Juracilda

1994 "Organização social e cosmovisão Kaingang: Uma introdução ao parentesco, casamento, e nominação em uma sociedade Jê Meridional." M.A. thesis, Universidade Estadual de Campinas.

2000 "Cosmologia e práticas rituais Kaingang." Ph.D. dissertation, Universidade Estadual de Campinas.

Venezuela, República de

1993 *Censo Indigena de Venezuela.* Vol. 1. Caracas: Oficina Central de Estadística e Informática.

Vickers, William T.

1976 "Cultural Adaptation to Amazonian Habitats: The Siona-Secoya of Eastern Ecuador." Ph.D. dissertation, University of Florida.

1983 "The Territorial Dimensions of Siona-Secoya and Encabellado Adaptation." In *Adaptive Responses of Native Amazonians,* ed. Raymond B. Hames and William T. Vickers, 451–78. New York: Academic Press.

1989a "Patterns of Foraging and Gardening in a Semi-Sedentary Amazonian Community." In *Farmers as Hunters: The Implications of Sedentism*, ed. Susan Kent, 46–59. Cambridge: Cambridge University Press.

1989b *Los sionas y secoyas: Su adaptación al ambiente amazónico.* Quito: Ediciones Abya-Yala; Rome: MLAL.

1991 "Hunting Yields and Game Composition over Ten Years in an Amazon Indian Community." In *Neotropical Wildlife Use and Conservation*, ed. John G. Robinson and Kent H. Redford, 53–81. Chicago: University of Chicago Press.

1994 "The Health Significance of Wild Plants for the Siona and Secoya." In *Eating on the Wild Side: The Pharmacologic, Ecologic, and Social Implications of Using Noncultigens*, ed. Nina L. Etkin, 143–65. Tucson: University of Arizona Press.

Vickers, William T., and Timothy Plowman

1984 *Useful Plants of the Siona and Secoya Indians of Eastern Ecuador.* Fieldiana Botany, no. 15. Chicago: Field Museum of Natural History.

Viveiros de Castro, Eduardo

1986 *Araweté: Os deuses canibais.* Rio de Janeiro: J. Zahar/ANPOCS.

1987 "A frabricação do corpo na sociedade Xinguana." In *Sociedades indígenas e indigenismo no Brasil*, ed. J. Pacheco de Oliveira Filho, 112–34. Rio de Janeiro: Editor Marco Zero.

1992 *From the Enemy's Point of View: Humanity and Divinity in an Amazonian Society.* Chicago: University of Chicago Press.

1993 "Alguns Aspectos de Afinidad do Dravidianato Amazônico." In *Amazônia: Etnologia e historia indígena*, ed. E. Viveiros de Castro and M. Carneiro da Cunha, 149–210. São Paulo: NHII/USP.

Wagley, Charles

1977 *Welcome of Tears: The Tapirapé Indians of Central Brazil.* New York: Oxford University Press.

Washburn, S., and C. Lancaster

1968 "The Evolution of Hunting." In *Man the Hunter*, ed. Richard Lee and Irven DeVore, 293–303. Chicago: Aldine.

Wilbert, Johannes

1958 "Die soziale und politische Organisation der Warrau." *Kölner Zeitschrift für Soziologie und Sozialpsychologie* 10: 272–91.

1980 "Genesis and Demography of a Warao Subtribe: The Winikina." In *Demographic and Biological Studies of the Warao Indians*, ed. Johannes Wilbert and Miguel Layrisse, 13–47. Latin American Studies, vol. 45. Los Angeles: ULCA Latin American Studies Publications, University of California.

1985 "The House of the Swallow-Tailed Kite: Warao Myth and the Art of Thinking in Images." In *Animal Myths and Metaphors in South America*, ed. Gary Urton, 145–82. Salt Lake City: University of Utah Press.

Wilbert, Werner

n.d. "Warao Spiritual Ecology." In *Indigenous Religions and Ecology*, ed. L. Sullivan and John Grim. Cambridge, Mass.: Harvard University Center for the Study of World Religions, in press.

Wilson, Edward O.

1975 *Sociobiology: The New Synthesis.* Cambridge, Mass.: Belknap Press of Harvard University Press.

1979 *On Human Nature.* New York: Bantam Books.

1998 *Consilience: The Unity of Knowledge.* New York: Knopf.

Wright, Robin M.

1981 "History and Religion of the Baniwa Peoples of the Upper Rio Negro Valley." Ph.D. dissertation, Stanford University.

Wyckoff, Gerald J., Wen Wang, and Chung-I Wu

2000 "Rapid Evolution of Male Reproductive Genes in the Descent of Man." *Nature* 403: 304–9.

Zaldívar, María Eugenia, Roberto Lizarralde, and Stephen Beckerman

1991 "Unbiased Sex Ratios among the Barí: An Evolutionary Interpretation." *Human Ecology* 19 (4): 469–98.

Zent, Stanford Rhode

1992 "Historical and Ethnographic Ecology of the Upper Cuao River Wothiha: Clues for an Interpretation of Native Guianese Social Organization." Ph.D. dissertation, Columbia University.

Contributors

Catherine Alès is Chargée de Recherche at the Centre National de la Recherche Scientifique, Paris. She has worked for twenty-six years with the Yanomami of Venezuela and has published widely on war, sociopolitical systems, discourses, and gender. She is coeditor of *Sexe relatif ou sexe absolu? De la distinction de sexe dans les sociétés* (in press).

Stephen Beckerman began fieldwork with the Barí in 1970. He has taught at Pennsylvania State University since 1981.

James Boster is professor of anthropology at the University of Connecticut, Storrs. A cognitive anthropologist, he specializes in the study of patterns of cultural variation.

Janet Chernela teaches at Florida International University and has worked among the Tukanoan speakers in the Amazon basin of Brazil since 1978. Besides publishing academic articles, she is author of *The Wanano Indians of the Brazilian Amazon: A Sense of Space* (1993) and coeditor of "Healing and the Body Politic" (special edition of *Anthropology Quarterly*, 1996). She is also a contributing editor of *Hemisphere*, the publication of the Latin American and Caribbean Center.

William H. Crocker has been a curator for South American ethnology at the Department of Anthropology, Smithsonian Institution, since 1962, retiring in 1993. Since 1957 he has completed seventy-one months of research in the Canela villages of Maranhão, Brazil. His basic monograph is *The Canela (East-*

ern Timbira): 1, An Ethnographic Introduction (1990) and his case study for students (written with his wife, Jean) is *The Canela: Bonding through Kinship, Ritual, and Sex* (1994).

Philippe Erikson is professor of anthropology at the University of Paris X, Nanterre. He has done fieldwork among the Matis (in Brazil) and the Chacobo (in Bolivia), both of the Panoan linguistic family. He is the author of *La griffe des aïeux: Marquage du corps et démarquages ethniques che₂ les Matis d'Ama₂onie* (1996; Spanish translation, 1999) and has coedited (with A. Monod-Becquelin) a multilingual volume on Amerindian dialogues, *Les rituels du dialogue: Promenades ethnolinguistiques en terres amérindiennes.*

Dieter Heinen studied economics and sociology in Germany, France, and Spain and did extensive fieldwork in the Venezuelan and Brazilian Guianas, mostly on comparative economic systems and applied anthropology. Currently he is Investigador Titular at the Instituto Venezolano de Investigaciones Científicas and head of the Ethnology Lab.

Kenneth M. Kensinger is professor emeritus at Bennington College. He lived with the Cashinahua for eighty-four months between 1955 and 1968, returning for an additional nine months of study in 1993–94 and for three more months in 1997. He edited *Working Papers on South American Indians* (7 vols.) and *South American Indian Studies* (5 vols.) and organized and hosted the South American Indian Conference at Bennington College for twenty years. His collection of essays, *How Real People Ought to Live,* appeared in 1995.

Vanessa Lea has been a lecturer at UNICAMP University, São Paulo, since 1983. In 1978 she began fieldwork with the Mẽbengokre, the subject of her doctorate at the Museu Nacional, Rio de Janeiro. Publications in English include an article in *Man* on names (1992) and a chapter in a book on house-based societies (1995). Publications in Portuguese include articles on female gender, chapters of books on social organization and kinship, and expert-witness studies of land issues concerning the indigenous population of central Brazil.

Alexánder Mansutti Rodríguez is an ethnologist currently finishing his dissertation on Piaroa at the École des Hautes Études en Sciences Sociales, Paris. He has publications on Andean farmers and on the Piaroa, Akawaio, and Kari'ña and has written about Indian policy in Venezuela.

Daniela Peluso is a graduate student in the Department of Anthropology at Columbia University. She specializes in Amazonia, gender theory, and medical anthropology.

Donald Pollock teaches anthropology and medicine at the State University of New York, Buffalo. His book on Kulina ethnomedicine, *Violent Delights*, is forthcoming.

Nalúa Silva Monterrey has published articles on the Ye'kwana and participated in the mapping project of the Ye'kwana and Sanema territories. She has also presented papers at the International Congress of Americanists in 1997 and 2000. Currently she is research professor at the Universidad Nacional Experimental de Guayana, Venezuela.

Paul Valentine began his fieldwork with the Curripaco in 1980. He is a senior lecturer in anthropology at the University of East London.

William T. Vickers is professor of anthropology at Florida International University. He has conducted ethnological fieldwork in Ecuador, Peru, and Mexico, focusing primarily on the human ecology of Native American communities and their land and civil rights. His books and monographs include *Los Sionas y Secoyas: Su adaptación al ambiente amazónico* (1989); *Useful Plants of the Siona and Secoya Indians* (coauthored with Timothy Plowman, 1984); and *Adaptive Responses of Native Amazonians* (coedited with Raymond B. Hames, 1983).

Werner Wilbert is associate research professor in the Department of Anthropology of the Instituto Venezolano de Investigaciones Científicas in Caracas, Venezuela. Since 1980, he has been conducting longitudinal fieldwork among the Warao of the Orinoco delta, specializing in ethnoecology, ethnomedicine, and shamanism of lowland South America. He is coeditor of the scientific journal *Antropológica* and author of *Fitoterapia warao: Una teoría pneumica de la salud, enfermedad, y su tratamiento* (1996). He has in press a bilingual volume (Warao-Spanish) designed to promote phytotherapy among Warao children attending the rural schools in their territory.

Index

abstentions, 172. *See also* couvade; restrictions, sexual
Aché, 5, 7–8, 84, 145
Adams, P., 49, 52
adolescence, 47, 49, 110, 118, 157, 216, 234. *See also* puberty
adoption, 72–73, 137, 138, 141–44, 148–49, 150, 156, 158, 185–87. *See also* orphans
adultery. *See* affairs/trysts
affairs/trysts
    Canela, 100, 94, 97
    Cashinahua, 17–18, 19, 21–22
    Curripaco, 190–91
    Ese Eja, 138–40, 144–49, 155, 157
    Kulina, 53
    Mẽbengokre, 110, 115
    public, 129, 138, 148, 169, 222
    secret/discreet, 14, 17, 19, 24, 102, 103, 138, 144, 169–70, 190
    Siona-Secoya, 222, 239–40
    Wanano, 13, 169–70, 174
    See also extramarital affairs
affinal relations
    Barí, 30–31
    Canela, 91–93, 96–97, 100
    Cashinahua, 15–19, 21, 24, 26
    Curripaco, 181–84, 187–91
    Ese Eja, 138, 145, 148–49
    Kulina, 44–53, 59
    Matis, 124, 129–30
    Matses, 136

    Mẽbengokre, 106, 109, 117–18
    Mehinaku, 4
    Piaroa, 198
    Siona-Secoya, 234
    Wanano, 165, 168–69, 175
    Warao, 212–13, 216, 220
    Ye'kwana, 200, 204
affinity, 11, 51, 52, 55, 59, 60, 105, 117, 118, 158
age class, 98, 104, 127
agnates, 164, 168
agriculture, 87, 95. *See also* farming; settled agriculturists; slash-and-burn agriculture; subsistence patterns
Aguarico River, 223–29
Amazon basin, 123, 135, 177, 179, 192, 225
Amazon northwest, 160–77, 178–91
Amazon River, 86
anaconda, ancestral, 164, 195
ancestors
    Canela, 94
    Curripaco, 181–82
    Ese Eja, 139
    Mẽbengokre, 115
    Siona-Secoya, 223
    Trobriand, 112
    Wanano, 161–66, 169, 172, 175, 177
    Warao, 214
    Yanomami, 63, 79–80
Andes, 28
Anduze, Pablo J., 207

animals
  behavior of, 232
  fertilization in, 2
  as food item, 28–30, 43–44, 54, 57–58, 60,
    206, 225, 228. *See also* dietary intake;
    food; nutrition; subsistence patterns
  and food restrictions, 54, 66, 89, 201
  hunted, 23, 43–44, 66, 97, 139, 179, 226–
    29. *See also* game animals; hunting
  and parental care, 3, 54
  See also ecological conditions; fauna;
    totemic ancestors; totemic souls
anthropology, 8, 10, 161, 162, 176
Apanyekra, 96
Apinayé, 113
Arara, 126
Arawak, 4, 178
Araweté, 5, 7, 126
Aristotle, 1, 62, 83
Arvelo-Jiménez, Nelly, 202–3, 207, 209

backlanders, 95–96, 102–3
Barasana, 127
Barí, 7, 8, 10, 11, 12, 27–41, 42, 43, 56–57, 59,
  84, 98, 144, 178, 191, 206, 221
Barí Partible Paternity Project (BPPP), 27–
  41, 42, 221
Basso, Ellen B., 45–49
beer, manioc, 130, 136
Beckerman, Stephen, 42, 43, 56, 58, 133–34,
  140, 221, 241
biological fathers. *See* fathers, biological
Bixa orellana, 216
blood, 238
  and fetal development, 63–64, 83, 89, 127,
    185, 187, 202–3, 209, 214, 219
  clotted/coagulated, 185, 214
  and food prohibitions, 187, 201, 233, 235.
    See also restrictions, on food
  integrity, 214
  and kinship, 46–48, 85, 89, 187, 189, 216
  menstrual, 5, 17, 52, 63–65, 83, 84, 201,
    202, 214, 216, 233–36, 240–41. *See also*
    menstruation

  and vitality, 201, 213, 214
Bolivia, 137, 150
Borgerhoff Mulder, Monique, 222, 239, 242
boys
  adolescent, 48, 157, 234
  and adoption, 136, 143. *See also* adoption;
    orphans
  naming of, 19. *See also* names
  as preferred sex, 17, 136
  relations of, with father, 24, 117–18, 205
  and sexual abstinence, 232–23
  See also kindred; kinship; sons
Brazil, 4–5, 42–61, 86, 95, 103, 105–22, 123–
  36, 160–77, 199
breast-feeding. *See* breast milk
breast milk, 21, 28, 47–48, 53, 54, 55, 66, 75,
  84–85, 136, 143. *See also* nursing
bride service, 220
bridewealth, 113
brotherhood, 118, 164, 167. *See also* brothers
brothers
  and childcare, 13, 55–56, 69, 71, 73, 81,
    173, 189
  competition between, 173, 189
  as fathers, 71, 73, 78, 79, 80–81, 85, 145,
    149, 169, 174, 205, 215, 219
  and marriage, 50–51, 55–56, 73, 146, 149,
    166, 173–74
  as providers/protectors, 73, 81, 173, 189
  as sexual partners, 17, 47, 55–56, 68–69,
    146, 166, 215, 219
  and wife-sharing, 81, 128, 189, 215, 219
  See also brotherhood; kinship terminolo-
    gies; siblings

Canela, 7, 10, 11, 13, 84, 86–104, 116, 121,
  144, 145, 158, 178, 185, 191
Carneiro, Robert, 13
Cashinahua, 10, 11, 12, 14–26, 157, 161
census, 35, 106, 123, 176
ceremony. *See* rituals
cerrados/closed savannahs, 86
Chacobo, 128
Chagnon, Napoleon, 85, 133

Chernela, Janet M., 59
Chibchan, 7, 28, 211
childbirth, 22, 90, 93, 210, 214, 233, 235, 238, 241. *See also* couvade
child care, 5, 12
    Canela, 98–99
    Cashinahua, 17, 20
    Curripaco, 190–91
    Ese Eja, 139, 141–43, 158
    Kulina, 56–58
    Mẽbengokre, 106–9
    Piaroa, 194, 199, 206
    Siona-Secoya, 221, 244
    Wanano, 162, 167, 175
    Warao, 212, 215
    Yanomami, 70–71, 73–74, 82–83
    Ye'kwana, 202, 204–6
    See also nursing; parents
childlessness, 110. *See also* adoption; infertility
children
    Barí, 27, 32, 35–41
    Canela, 88, 101
    Cashinahua, 14–26
    Curripaco, 191
    Ese Eja, 140–48
    Kulina, 42, 54, 56
    legitimate, 1–2, 8, 185
    Matis, 133–34
    Mẽbengokre, 110–11
    of multiple mothers, 53–54, 67, 142
    Piaroa, 206–7
    provisioning of, 3, 20–21, 33, 41, 58, 66, 81, 114, 134, 170, 173
    relationship of, with adults, 90, 141, 153–54, 172
    of several fathers, 1, 5–9, 12, 27, 32, 35–41, 42, 54, 56, 69, 72, 76–80, 88, 101, 110–11, 133–34, 140–48, 191, 206–7, 215, 217, 222, 244. *See also* fathers, secondary; partible paternity
    of single fathers, 1, 2, 7–9, 56, 62, 67, 202, 242
    Siona-Secoya, 242, 244
    social identity of, 19, 167, 188, 191

Warao, 215, 217
Yanomami, 62, 67, 69, 72, 76–80
Ye'kwana, 206–7
    See also boys; girls; infants
Christianity, influence of, 139, 207
Cipolletti, María Susana, 224
clan brothers, 178–91
clans, 8, 161–76, 178–91
clusters. *See* households, clusters of
co-fathers, 18–23, 70–85, 134–35, 157, 160. *See also* fathers, secondary; partible paternity
co-genitors. *See* genitor, multiple
coitus, 62, 63, 65, 202, 206. *See also* copulation
collective hunting. *See* hunting
Colombia, 27–41, 160–77, 179–91, 192, 223, 226
communal ceremonies, 200, 222, 232. *See also* rituals
communal dwellings, 28–29, 81. *See also* longhouse
communal marriage, 162
communal meals, 29, 125, 180–81, 188, 200
competition
    between brothers, 173, 189
    between local descent groups, 170
    between men and women, 11
conception
    Canela, 87
    Curripaco, 179, 185, 191
    Ese Eja, 140–42
    Kulina, 42, 47, 59
    Matis, 126–28, 133, 136
    Mẽbengokre, 109–10
    moment of, 2, 10, 52, 110, 202
    Piaroa, 192
    polyandrous, 123–36. *See also* partible paternity
    Wanano, 163, 171, 175–75
    Warao, 210, 214, 219
    Siona-Secoya, 236–37
    Yanomami, 63–64, 69–70, 73, 83
    Ye'kwana, 202

conflict, 19, 68, 82, 84, 121, 131, 243
  between males, 11, 169
  marital, 52, 72
consanguinuity
  Barí, 30
  Canela, 96
  Cashinahua, 16, 26
  Kulina, 48, 59
  Mẽbengokre, 118
  Wanano, 168, 176
  Yanomami, 67, 80
  See also kindred
cooperation
  in child production, 5, 69, 140. See also
    partible paternity
  with domestic groups/kinsmen, 16, 23,
    53, 98, 138, 200, 205
  economic, 16, 138, 200, 205, 228
co-paternity, 19, 21, 63, 69–81. See also
  partible paternity; paternity, shared
co-procreation, 78. See also partible paternity
co-progenitors, 70, 77, 79. See also fathers,
  secondary; genitor; partible paternity
copulation, 10, 62, 65, 74, 129, 185. See also
  coitus; sexual relations
coresident, 17, 23, 54. See also domestic
  groups; villages
courtship, 3, 234
couvade
  Canela, 86, 90, 101
  Curripaco, 179, 188
  Matis, 135
  Mẽbengokre, 112
  Mehinaku, 4
  Siona-Secoya, 222, 238, 240
  Wanano, 171
  Warao, 215
  Ye'kwana, 204
  See also childbirth; restrictions, postpar-
    tum
criollo, 199, 203, 209
Crocker, William H., 86–104, 121
cross-cousin marriage
  Amazonian, 119, 163

Curripaco, 183–84
  Ese Eja, 149, 154
  Kulina, 51
  Piaroa, 197
  Wanano, 166, 168, 173
  Ye'kwana, 200, 220
  See also kinship terminologies
cross-cousin sexual relations
  Ese Eja, 149, 154
  Matis, 51, 128–29, 131
  Wanano, 168, 169
  See also kinship terminologies
Crow kinship terminology, 96, 119
cultivation, 157, 225, 227
Curripaco, 7, 10, 12, 13, 59, 178–91

dancing, 170, 203, 215
daughters
  and marriage, 24–25, 29, 92, 99, 146, 212–
    13, 216, 217, 234
  as preferred sex, 17, 22
  and relations with father, 19, 111, 145,
    146, 216
  See also children; girls; kinship terminol-
    ogies
Dearua. See Piaroa
death
  of child, 1, 11–12, 34 , 36–40, 54, 57, 90,
    101, 106, 111–12, 133, 146, 186, 199, 218
  of father, 31, 73–74, 82, 84, 98, 116, 149,
    167, 175, 213
  of mother, 31, 98–99, 133, 213, 220
  rate of, 31–32, 35–40
  of spouse, 11–12, 31, 73–74, 107, 163,
    167, 180, 184, 189, 191, 213, 230
  See also ancestors; illness; mortality;
    orphans; survivorship
DeMallie, Raymond J., 132–33
demography, 87, 114
Desana, 161, 168, 169
descent
  double, 117, 118
  matrilineal. See matrilineal descent
    groups

patrilineal. *See* patrilineal descent groups
  unilineal, 85, 163, 244
descent groups, 29, 161, 164–67, 170, 172,
  174–76, 177, 181–84, *See also* clans;
  descent; kinship
dietary intake, 9, 28–29, 32, 143, 171, 180,
  188, 214, 229–30. *See also* food; nutrition
disputes, 165, 227. *See also* conflict; feud
division of labor. *See* sexual division of
  labor
divorce
  Barí, 20
  Canela, 100, 102
  and childcare, 72, 107, 190
  Curripaco, 190
  Ese Eja, 156
  Mẽbengokre, 107
  Piaroa, 207
  rate of, 107, 235
  Siona-Secoya, 235, 236, 239
  Yanomami, 67, 72, 80
  Ye'kwana, 207
domestic groups, 51, 87, 98
  composition of, 97, 111, 114, 123, 138,
    205, 212–13, 219. *See also* kinship
    terminologies
  cooperation within, 16, 23, 53, 130, 138,
    194, 200, 205
  See also hearth groups; households;
    kindred; villages
Dravidian kinship terminology, 30, 44, 69–
  70, 81–82, 117, 138, 183–84, 197, 205
Dreyfus, Simone, 110
dwellings, 115, 200
  cluster, 213, 227
  communal, 28–29, 81. *See also* longhouse
  See also households

ecological conditions
  Barí, 28
  Canela, 86, 94–96
  Curripaco, 179
  Kulina, 43
  Mẽbengokre, 119–20

Piaroa, 192–93
Siona-Secoya, 224–45
Wanano, 161–62
Warao, 210–11
economic unit, 29, 139, 162, 172, 181, 226, 241
economy
  of the Canela, 99
  of the household, 18, 30, 230
  See also subsistence patterns
Ecuador, 221–45
elder father, 69–73
elder generation, 123, 129, 200
elder males, 118, 181, 193, 200
elder relatives, 106
emic/etic models, 87–88, 131, 135, 160
Encabellado, 223, 224, 226
endogamy
  local group, 31, 44, 46, 51, 119, 212. *See*
    also madiha
  territorial group, 31
  See also marriage patterns
Erikson, Philippe, 187
Ese Eja, 10, 11, 12, 137–59
ethnobiology, 42, 52–60, 87–90, 103, 202
Evans-Pritchard, E. E., 113
evolutionary ecology, 221–22, 242–43. *See*
  also sociobiology
exchange, 140, 162, 207
  of gifts for sex, 18, 53, 109, 116
  of names, 166
  of raw food for cooked, 43
  restricted, 167
  of spouses, 9, 15, 51, 156–57, 167
  See also trade
exogamy
  Curripaco, 181, 184
  Ese Eja, 138
  linguistic, 177
  Mẽbengokre, 105
  Shavante, 97
  Wanano, 163–64
  Warao, 212
  See also marriage patterns
extended family. *See* family, extended

extramarital affairs, 11
  Barí, 32
  Canela, 92, 94, 100, 103–4
  Cashinahua, 14–26
  Curripaco, 190–91
  Ese Eja, 137–38, 141, 144–48, 150, 152,
    154–55
  Kulina, 53, 55, 59
  Matis, 128–31
  Mẽbengokre, 110, 115–21
  Mehikaku, 4
  Piaroa, 197
  Siona-Secoya, 222, 231, 239–40, 243
  Wanano, 169–71, 174
  Yanomami, 70–79
  See also affairs/trysts
extramarital sexual relations. See extramarital
  affairs; sexual relations

fagi (Kuikuru), 5
family, 23, 70–74, 168, 180, 189, 202–8, 219,
  230, 244
  adoptive, 141–43, 148–50
  extended, 8, 16–17, 29, 87, 98, 150, 200,
    226–27, 231, 241
  immediate/primary, 11, 21, 141, 240
  nuclear/conjugal, 16, 29, 94, 98, 161–63,
    172, 175–76, 190, 194, 205, 220, 226,
    231
  See also kindred; kinship; kinship
    terminologies
farming, 95, 162. See also agriculture;
  subsistence patterns
father-child relations, 172
father-daughter relations, 19, 111, 145, 146,
  216
fatherhood, 7, 27, 32, 39, 42, 75–76, 83, 87,
  130–31, 135, 137, 156, 163, 167, 172–76,
  185, 189, 219–20
  public recognition of, 10–11, 14, 19–22,
    54–55, 71, 144–46, 174, 188
fathers
  Barí, 27, 31–41

biological, 1–4, 6, 9, 27, 42, 68, 71, 72, 87–
  88, 90, 98, 113, 128, 131, 134–35, 140,
  169, 173–74, 178, 221, 242, 244. See also
  genitor
  Canela, 86–90
  Cashinahua, 14, 19–20, 24–25
  Curripaco, 178, 186, 188, 191
  death of, 31, 73–74, 82, 84, 98, 116, 149,
    167, 175, 213
  Ese Eja, 139–49, 153, 156–57
  identity of, 14, 67, 72, 171
  language of, 167, 174
  Kulina, 42, 52, 54–60, 62
  Matis, 128, 131, 133–36
  Mẽbengokre, 106, 110–13, 116
  multiple, 7, 52, 54, 78, 83, 133, 206. See
    also co-fathers; partible paternity;
    paternity, shared
  "other," 55–60, 86–88. See also co-fathers;
    partible paternity; paternity, shared
  provisioning by, 3, 8, 20, 37–38, 134, 230,
    242
  putative, 4
  role of, 8–9, 19, 24–25, 68, 72, 82, 88, 106,
    110–13, 163, 172, 175, 186, 188, 219
  single, 1, 2, 7–9, 56, 62, 67, 202, 242
  Siona Secoya, 221–22, 230, 242, 244
  social, 7, 9, 13, 68, 71, 72, 74, 77, 79, 131,
    163, 191
  Wanano, 163, 167, 169, 171–75
  Warao, 213, 219
  Yanomami, 67–69, 71–75, 77–79, 82–84
  Ye'kwana, 202, 206
  See also fatherhood; paternity
—secondary, 10–12
  Aché, 7–8
  Barí, 8, 27, 32–41
  Canela, 7, 88
  Cashinahua, 20
  Curripaco, 186, 188, 191
  Ese Eja, 139–49, 153, 156–57
  Matis, 128, 134, 136
  Siona-Secoya, 221–22, 244

Yanomami, 69, 71, 75, 77–79
  See also paternity; partible paternity
father's milk, 47, 75. *See also* semen
father-son relations, 24, 117–18, 205
fauna, 225, 227. *See also* ecological conditions
fertility
  and adoption, 142
  ceremony, 215
  female, 63
  and food prohibitions, 66. *See also*
    restrictions, on food
  male, 63, 215
  See also infertility
festivals, 63, 103, 130, 131, 190, 200
fetal wastage, 38, 39, 41
fetus
  composition of, 5, 24, 47, 65–66, 84, 88, 127
  conception of, 10, 47, 52, 70, 73, 219
—formation and development of, 2, 4–5, 10
  Barí, 32
  Canela, 86–89, 101–3
  Cashinahua, 14, 24
  Curripaco, 185, 187
  Ese Eja, 140
  Kulina, 47, 52
  Mẽbengokre, 106, 109–15
  Piaroa, 196, 206
  Siona-Secoya, 222, 236–37
  Warao, 214–15, 219
  Yanomami, 64–68, 71, 73, 82
feud, 170, 182. *See also* conflict; disputes
fighting. *See* conflict
fire, 31, 95. *See also* hearths
firstborn, 129, 217
fish
  as gifts/provisioning, 33, 38–39, 41, 109,
    138, 145, 170, 173, 189, 205, 213, 230–31
  as part of diet, 8, 9, 29–30, 38–39, 43,
    105–6, 114, 157, 162, 172, 180, 187–88,
    221, 225, 228
  success of catches, 28, 96, 225, 228
fishing
  as method of subsistence, 9, 16, 23, 28, 43,

  66, 95–97, 114, 119, 130, 139, 157, 162,
    182, 211, 227–29, 234
  techniques of, 28, 139, 173, 180, 194
flirtation, 169, 186
flora, 214, 227. *See also* ecological conditions
food
  distribution of, 12, 29, 94, 97–98, 114–15,
    124, 133–34, 139, 158, 173, 193–94, 199,
    206–8
  preparation of, 17, 173, 193, 200, 226, 231
  and provisioning, 8, 29, 39, 58, 68, 74, 80–
    81, 97, 99, 102, 109–10, 113, 116, 134–
    35, 163, 173, 188–89, 243
  restrictions on, 14, 19, 24, 47, 55, 61, 66,
    88–89, 101, 106, 111, 143, 145, 171–72,
    187–88, 204–5, 235, 237. *See also*
    couvade
  sharing of, 2, 3, 29, 45, 87, 145, 173, 180–
    81, 226, 231
  taboos on, 9, 237. *See also* food,
    restrictions on
  See also dietary intake
forests
  destruction of, 119
  mangrove, 211
  rain, 28, 32, 86, 178, 225
  spirits of the, 183
friends
  as co-fathers, 70–72, 76–79
  formal, 91, 92, 96–97, 106, 111, 116–17,
    118, 121–22
  as sexual partners, 69
FUNAI (National Foundation of Indians),
    103, 121, 124
funeral practices. *See* death

game animals
  as food provisioning, 3, 8, 33, 38–41, 114–
    16, 145, 189, 221, 231
  as part of diet, 28–30, 43,58, 66, 95–97,
    105, 114–16, 119, 124, 157, 179–80, 187,
    211, 225, 228–29
  See also hunting

gardens, 23, 95, 157, 162, 169, 179. *See also* cultivation; horticulture

gathering
  as female subsistence activity, 17, 139
  as male subsistence activity, 116
  as subsistence activity, 66, 95, 157, 211
  See also hunter-gatherer; subsistence patterns

Gê, 4, 86, 132, 215

gender
  of fetus, 67
  relations between, 43, 192, 196. *See also* sexual division of labor
  specific terminology of, 54, 165

genealogy, reckoning of, 131

genitor, 55
  donor, 215–16
  multiple, 5, 13, 106–16, 135, 202, 204–5, 214, 219, 242–43
  unique, 5, 27, 135, 198, 222, 236
  See also fathers, biological; partible paternity

genitrix, 53, 112

gestation, beliefs about, 10
  Kulina, 52, 55, 59
  Piaroa, 192, 195–96, 199, 208
  Warao, 213–15, 217, 219
  Ye'kwana, 192, 206, 208
  See also pregnancy

gift-giving
  Barí, 33, 39, 41
  Canela, 102
  Cashinahua, 18, 20, 23
  Curripaco, 190
  Ese Eja, 138, 145
  Siona-Secoya, 231
  Wanano, 173
  Warao, 215–16, 220

girls
  adolescent, 49, 216
  childless, 110
  and first menstruation, 216, 234
  and marriage, 113, 129, 234–35, 241
  and ritual sex, 94, 110

  sexual education of, 129
  See also children; daughters

godparents, 216

Goodenough, Ward, 158, 160

Gow, Peter, 109, 113

grandparents, 15, 19–20, 89, 90, 94, 107, 138, 145, 199

Guayana region, 192–209, 210–20

habi sanuka ceremony (Piaroan), 215, 219

half siblings, 83, 213, 217. *See also* kindred

Harris, Marvin, 241, 242

Hawaiian kinship terminology, 212

hearth groups, 29–31, 97–98

hearths, 29, 81, 97–98, 172, 179, 180–81, 183, 226, 231

Hill, Kim, 5, 7, 8

Hippocrates, 62, 83

Homo erectus, 3

Homo sapiens, 2, 27, 243

horticulture
  Barí, 28
  Canela, 86, 95, 103
  Cashinahua, 16–17, 23–24
  Curripaco, 179–80
  Ese Eja, 139–40
  Kulina, 43
  Mẽbengokre, 114
  Siona-Secoya, 227–30, 234
  Wanano, 162, 173
  Warao, 220
  Yanomami, 66
  See also farming; subsistence patterns

households
  adjacent, 81, 92, 95, 181, 182, 183, 210, 227
  Canela, 92, 94–95, 97
  Cashinahua, 16–17, 19, 24
  clusters of, 16, 56, 140, 142, 212, 220, 227, 231
  Curripaco, 181–83
  economy of, 18, 94, 114, 139, 173, 200, 228
  Ese Eja, 138–39, 140, 142

Kulina, 49–51, 56–57
Mẽbengokre, 114
nonadjacent, 92
Siona-Secoya, 226–28, 231
Wanano, 172–73
Warao, 210, 210, 220
Ye'kwana, 200
    See also dwellings
human evolution, 2–3
hunter-gatherers, 7, 86–87, 116, 243. *See also*
    subsistence patterns
hunting
    collective, 30, 53, 115, 124, 173, 194
    as male subsistence activity, 16, 23, 28–30,
        43, 53, 66, 96–97, 109, 114–16, 130,
        139, 180, 182, 228–32
    parties, 30, 53, 97, 200
    restrictions concerning, 21, 89, 171, 204,
        233
    returns on, 179
    as source of protein, 9, 28, 43, 66, 114,
        145, 179, 228–29. *See also* dietary
        intake; food; nutrition
    success of, 19, 89, 232, 235
    techniques of, 30, 97, 119, 139, 226–29
    women's participation in, 28, 139
    See also subsistence patterns
Hurtado, Magdalena, 5, 7, 8
husbands
    absence of, 205
    adulterous, 18, 22, 72, 155, 190
    and childcare, 142, 167, 175, 191, 202, 215
    death of, 33, 73, 163, 167, 180, 184
    as fathers, 2, 5, 19–20, 42, 50, 68–71, 77–
        80, 140, 142, 144, 172–73, 176, 219, 242
    female choice of, 11–12, 201
    former, 156
    future/potential, 99, 198
    "other," 90, 97
    and provisioning, 8, 11, 16, 23, 66, 73, 94,
        97, 109, 113–15, 188, 189, 230–31
    relations of, with wife, 49–50, 115, 152–
        54, 170, 183, 187, 203–4, 213, 226, 230,
        235–38

second, 81, 189
    and sexual jealousy, 3, 18, 32, 110, 170,
        174, 219
    as sexual partner, 4, 55, 111, 129, 244
    See also spouse

identity
    of father, 14, 67, 72, 171
    of secondary father, 10–12, 34, 144–46,
        148
    social, 15–16, 19–20, 24–25, 44, 80, 137,
        147, 163, 167, 174–75, 182, 188–89, 191
ideology
    of conception and fetal development, 5,
        9, 127, 191
    of partible paternity, 6, 11, 42, 176
    of sexual restraint, 12
    uterine, 105
illness, 139, 183, 193, 214–15, 232
    and pollutants, 89, 233
    and restrictions, 106, 111, 113, 184, 187,
        237
incest, 70, 81, 92, 124, 128, 194
    Barí, 30–31
    Ese Eja, 139, 146, 148–50, 153
    Wanano, 168
    See also restrictions
    onomastic, 115
    rules of, 165, 173, 243. *See also* kindred
    as taboo, 30, 31, 139, 146, 148, 149, 150,
        153, 168
infants
    birth of, 174, 216, 237
    development of, 4, 47, 55, 140, 171–72,
        174, 217, 237
    mortality among, 57–58, 106, 194
    nursing of, 32, 54, 84
    provisioning of, 69, 71
    See also children
infertility
    female, 236
    male, 111, 215–16, 219
    rate of, 158
    See also fertility

infidelity
  female, 201, 215
  male, 204
  marital, 14, 18, 19, 119, 128–31, 170, 197,
    207
  See also affairs/trysts
initiation, menstrual. See menarche;
  menstruation; puberty
in-laws. See affinal relations
in-marrying, 46, 49, 161, 166–68. See also
  marriage
intermarriage, 81, 138, 224. See also marriage

Jê, 105–22
jealousy
  paternal, 134
  sexual, 11, 12, 103, 104

Kaingang, 127. See also Xocleng
Kalapalo, 45–50
Kariera kinship terminology, 124, 128–31
Kashinaua, 43
Kayapó, 86, 88, 105–22. See also Mẽbengokre
Kensinger, Kenneth M., 160
kindred, 13, 45, 114, 161
  affinal. See affinal relations
  Barí, 29–30
  Canela, 89–94, 96–98
  Cashinahua, 16–19, 21, 25, 26
  consanguineal, 11, 16, 26, 30, 48, 59, 67,
    80, 96, 118, 168, 176. See also
    consanguinuity
  Curripaco, 182–84, 188–91
  Ese Eja, 137–39, 142–43, 146, 148–50,
    153–54
  half siblings, 83, 213, 217
  Kulina, 44–52, 54–56, 59
  maternal, 15, 20, 89, 90, 94, 107, 129, 213,
    218, 241
  Matis, 124, 127–29, 131–32
  Mẽbengokre, 115, 118–19, 120
  paternal, 89–90, 94, 167, 212, 241
  Piaroa, 193–97, 207
  Siona-Secoya, 230–31, 241

  Wanano, 165–69, 173, 176
  Warao, 212–13, 215, 219
  Yanomami, 69–71, 73, 78–81, 83
  Ye'kwana, 205–7
  See also kindred; kinship; kinship
    terminologies
kinship
  Barí, 29–31
  Canela, 87, 89–93, 96
  Cashinahua, 15–16
  Curripaco, 179, 183
  Ese Eja, 137–38, 141, 144–45, 149–50,
    153–54, 156, 157
  Kulina, 42, 44–45, 52, 59
  Matis, 123–24, 127–29, 131–34
  Mẽbengokre, 113, 118–19, 120
  phratric, 165
  Piaroa, 192, 194, 197–98, 206–8
  ritual, 216
  sex-free definition of, 131, 132
  Siona-Secoya, 227, 240, 244
  theory, 8–9
  Wanano, 162, 165, 177
  Warao, 216
  Yanomami, 67–68, 70–71, 83
  Ye'kwana, 192, 204, 206–8
  See also kinship terminologies, kindred
kinship terminologies, 8–9
  Barí, 30
  Canela, 93, 96
  Cashinahua, 15
  Crow, 96, 119
  Curripaco, 183–84
  Dravidian, 30, 44, 69–70, 81–82, 117, 138,
    183–84, 197, 205
  Ese Eja, 138
  Hawaiian, 212
  Kariera, 124, 128–31
  Kulina, 44–47, 55–56
  Matis, 123–24, 127–28
  Mẽbengokre, 118–19
  Omaha, 118–19, 240
  Piaroa, 197–99
  Samo, 118

Siona, 240–41, 244
Warao, 212–13
Yanomami, 68–70, 81–83
Ye'kwana, 205
kintype, 128
Kuikuru, 5
Kulina, 10, 11, 12, 42–61, 191

lactation. *See* breast milk; nursing
languages
Arawak, 4, 178, 188
Aruan, 43
Carib, 5
Chibchan, 7, 28, 211
Gê, 4, 86, 132, 215
Ese Eja, 137
Panoan, 123
Piaroan, 206
Portuguese, 45
Tukanoan, 161, 163, 168, 174, 233
Tupi-Guaraní, 5
Wanano, 167
Yanomami, 5
Ye'kwana, 201, 206
legitimacy, 171, 175, 176
of children, 1–2, 8
of husband, 72, 79–81
paternal, 74, 171, 175–76
of partner, 124
of sexual relations, 129–30
Lévi-Strauss, Claude, 9, 133
liaisons, sexual. *See* affairs/trysts; extramarital affairs
lineages
Canela, 97
Curripaco, 181–84, 186–87, 191
Ese Eja, 138
Shavante, 97
Tukanoan, 177
Wanano, 177
Yanomami, 80
See also clans; descent groups; kinship
local groups, 30, 119, 213
logistic regression, 7, 33, 36–37

longhouse, 28–32, 56, 92, 94, 124, 130, 134, 172, 180, 226, 231
Lounsbury, Floyd G., 90
lovers, 4–5
Barí, 27, 32, 38–39
Canela, 86–87, 94, 98, 100
Cashinahua, 18, 20–23, 27
Curripaco, 186, 190–91
Ese Eja, 155
Kulina, 44, 49, 56
Matis, 133–34
Mẽbengokre, 106–14, 121
Piaroa, 194
Siona-Secoya, 231, 239
Wanano, 168–70, 174
Lusi, 6

madiha, 44–52, 60–61
Maionkong. *See* Ye'kwana
Makiritares. *See* Ye'kwana
Malinowski, Bronislaw
on the family, 162–3, 172, 175–76
on parenthood, 8–9, 42, 171
on pregnancy, 65
malnutrition, 28, 44. *See also* dietary intake; nutrition
maloca. See longhouse
manioc
drink, 130, 173, 180, 230
as gifts/provisioning, 33
harvesting of, as female activity, 23, 43, 98, 162, 173, 179, 228, 234
as staple crop, 9, 28–29, 43–44, 54, 66, 86, 95, 115, 162, 179, 211, 228
See also dietary intake; food
Mapachica, 189
Maracaibo Basin, 28
marriage
arranged, 51, 234
Barí, 31
Canela, 91–92, 96–97, 99
Cashinahua, 15, 17–20, 23–26
communal, 162
consummation of, 113

marriage—*continued*
   Curripaco, 178, 184, 186–89, 191
   definitions of, 161
   Ese Eja, 137, 138–40, 146, 150, 154–56
   Kulina, 44–51, 55–56, 59
   Matis, 123, 128–29
   Mēbengokre, 106–9, 116–19
   patterns of. *See* marriage patterns
   Piaroa, 194, 197–99
   restrictions on. *See* incest; marriage,
     restrictions on
   rites of, 49, 216
   rules of, 92, 96–97, 149, 166, 178, 97–99,
     212–13
   sections. *See* marriage sections
   of siblings, 44–51, 55–56, 73, 82
   Siona-Secoya, 224, 228, 231, 233–26, 240
   and social life, 11, 23, 188
   theories of, 9, 162
   Tukanoan, 163, 176
   Wanano, 166, 174
   Warao, 212–13, 217, 220
   Ye'kwana, 200, 203, 208
   See also cross-cousin marriage; divorce;
     kinship terminologies; remarriage
marriage patterns
   Canela, 91–92, 96–97
   Cashinahua, 15
   Curripaco, 183
   endogamous 31, 46, 60, 96, 119, 212. *See*
     also endogamy
   Ese Eja, 138–40, 146, 150
   exogamous, 48, 163, 184, 212. *See also*
     exogamy
   Kulina, 51
   Matis, 123, 128
   Mēbengokre, 107–9, 117
   Piaroa, 197–99
   Siona-Secoya, 233–36
   Tukanoan, 194
   Wanano, 163, 166
   Warao, 213–13
   Ye'kwana, 203

   See also marriage; polyandry; polygamy;
     polygyny
marriage sections, 15, 17, 19–20, 24–26
maternal contribution to fetal development, 47
maternal grandparents, 15, 20, 89, 90, 94, 107,
   138, 199
maternal home, 115, 118. *See also* kindred,
   maternal
maternal milk. *See* breast milk
maternity, 112, 137, 156, 215
   multiple, 43, 54, 55, 59
   Matis, 7, 10, 11, 12, 123–36, 157, 191
matri-house, 105, 113–18
matrilaterality, 183
matrilineal descent groups, 9, 31, 90–94, 118,
   121, 142, 156, 161
matrilocality
   Barí, 31
   Cashinahua, 16–17, 24
   Canela, 90–93
   Ese Eja, 138, 142, 146, 157
   Kulina, 54
   Matis, 127, 135
   Mēbengokre, 106
   Piaroa, 12, 193, 197
   Warao, 12, 212
   Ye'kwana, 205
   See also matri-uxorilocality; uxorilocality
matri-uxorilocality, 107, 197
Mayongon. *See* Ye'kwana
Mead, Margaret, 127
meals, 23, 29, 30, 39, 124, 125, 173, 180–81,
   188, 200, 230, 231. *See also* food;
   provisioning
Mēbengokre, 10, 11, 12, 105–22
Mehinaku, 4, 7, 57, 133, 144, 154
Melatti, J. C., 115
menarche, 23, 216, 234
Mendel, Gregor, 2
menopause, 142, 236
menses. *See* menarche; menstruation
menstruation. *See* blood, menstrual;
   menarche

mestizo, 147, 148
milk
 father's, 47, 75. *See also* semen
 mother's. *See* breast milk
miscarriage, 34, 38
missionaries, among the Siona-Secoya, 227, 236, 240
moieties, 15, 19, 20, 24–26, 104, 137–38, 143, 146, 156–58
Morgan, Lewis Henry, 162, 243
mortality
 adult, 32, 107
 age-specific, 7
 infant, 57, 58, 194, 219, 239
 preadolescent, 219
 rate of, 57, 58, 107
 See also death
motherhood, 137, 143, 146. *See also* maternity; mothers
mothers
 and childcare, 53–54, 66, 80, 99, 143, 163, 202. *See also* child care
 contribution of, to infant development, 2, 24, 47, 53, 65–66, 127, 140, 171, 187, 201–2, 206, 209, 214, 236, 242
 death of, 34, 39, 98–99
 identity of, 14, 129, 148
 language of, 167–68
 multiple. *See* maternity, multiple
 original territory of, 36, 38, 40
 "other," 55, 58, 136
 and sexual relations, 4, 7, 13, 17, 27, 58, 67, 68–69, 71–72, 81, 88, 102, 106, 114, 131, 135, 140–41, 144, 146, 148, 169, 185, 214, 221, 242, 244. *See also* affairs/trysts; extramarital affairs
 unmarried, 110–11
 See also kinship terminologies; maternity; parents
mother's milk. *See* breast milk
multiple maternity. *See* maternity, multiple
multiple paternity. *See* paternity, multiple
multiple semen acquisition. *See* semen

names, ceremonies for giving of, 115, 121, 131, 166
neoliberalism, 120
Nimuendajú, Curt, 95, 102
nonkin, 168. *See also* affinal relations
nonmarital sexual relations. *See* extramarital affairs
nuclear family. *See* family, nuclear/conjugal
Nuer, 113, 161
nursing, 21, 32, 44, 53–54, 127, 187. *See also* breast milk
nutrition, 28, 41, 66. *See also* dietary intake; food

okjibara (Barí), 30–32. *See also* affinal relations
Omaha kinship terminology, 118–19, 240
One Sperm, One Fertilization Doctrine, 2, 3
organization, social. *See* social organizations
Orinoco River, 193
 Alto/Upper, 81, 199, 206, 207
 delta, 210, 211, 214, 220
orphans, 31, 87, 99, 114, 125, 136, 212, 213. *See also* adoption
"other" fathers, 55–60, 86–88. *See also* fathers, secondary; partible paternity
"other" mothers, 54, 58, 136. *See also* maternity, multiple; mothers
out-marriage, 163. *See also* marriage
Overing, Joanna, 45–48, 52, 208–9

parallel cousins, 59, 118, 139, 150, 181, 182, 220
parenthood, 70, 137, 143, 162, 171, 202. *See also* fathers; kindred; mothers; parents
parents
 adoptive, 158
 contribution of, to fetal development, 112
 living with, 28, 57, 227
 multiple, 202
 relationship of, with children, 90, 141, 153
 See also parenthood

partible paternity, 1–13
  Aché, 5, 7–8
  Araweté, 5, 7
  Barí, 7, 27–41
  Canela, 7, 86–104
  Curripaco, 7, 178–91
  Ese Eja, 137–59
  Kuikuru, 5–6
  Kulina, 42–61
  Lusi, 6
  Matis, 7, 125–26, 133, 135
  Mehinaku, 4, 7
  Sanumá, 5
  Siona-Secoya, 241, 243–44
  Tapirapé, 5
  Warao, 214
  Xocleng, 4
  Ye'kwana, 10
  See also co-paternity; fathers, secondary;
    paternity, shared; polyandrous
    conception
partition, 175, 237
pater, 7, 9, 87, 131, 163, 169, 175–76, 197, 215,
  219. *See also* fathers
paternal contribution to fetal development,
  47, 63, 66
paternal grandparents. *See* grandparents
paternal investment, 3, 6, 58, 71, 175, 205
paternal recognition, 7, 71, 113, 171, 199. *See*
  also fathers; kindred, paternal
paternity
  certainty of, 2–3, 11, 27, 189, 241
  multiple, 7, 33, 80, 82, 83, 105–22, 157,
    185, 219
  See also partible paternity
—shared
  Cashinahua, 15, 18–20, 24
  Curripaco, 191
  Piaroa, 192, 196–99, 206–8
  Wanano, 160, 174
  Yanomami, 63, 68, 70
  Ye'kwana, 192, 202, 204, 206–8
  See also fathers, secondary

patriclans, 59, 161, 163–67, 181, 184
patrikin, 189. *See also* fathers; kindred,
  paternal
patrilaterality, 193
patrilineal descent groups, 9, 11–12, 79, 81,
  85, 117, 118, 163, 171, 175, 177, 181, 197,
  244
  Barí, 31
  Canela, 97
  Curripaco, 181–84, 188–89
  Ese Eja, 137, 146
  Kaingang, 107
  Kulina, 58
  Piaroa, 207–8
  Siona-Secoya, 240–41, 244
  Tukanoan, 161, 163–5, 167, 172, 174–75
  Yanomami, 79
  Ye'kwana, 207–8
patrilocality, 166–67, 226–27, 244. *See also*
  residence rules
peppers, 124, 171, 173, 184
Peru, 14, 43, 137, 223, 226, 235
philanderers, 18, 22, 24–25, 200. *See also*
  affairs/trysts
Phratries, 165. *See also* kinship
Piaroa, 12, 13, 45, 48, 50, 52, 192–209
Pike, Kenneth, 160
Pinker, Steven, 3–4
Piro, 113
political relationships
  among Wanano, 167
  among Yanomami, 81–82
Pollock, Donald, 11
pollution, 47, 89–90, 234, 235, 240
polyandrous conception, 126–28, 134–35. *See*
  also partible paternity
polyandry, 80–81, 126–28, 133–35
polygamy, 59, 80–81, 85, 203
polygyny, 31, 128, 141, 158, 212, 217
population
  composition of, 114, 160, 193, 212, 223
  density of, 9, 75, 96, 105, 120, 123, 160–
    61, 179, 193, 198, 199, 212, 223

distribution of, 192
movement of, 43
population-averaged effect, 36–39
postmarital residence, 17, 31, 157, 167, 193, 197, 198. *See also* residence rules
postpartum restrictions. *See* restrictions, postpartum
postpartum rites. *See* rites, postpartum
postpartum seclusion, 88, 90, 112, 171
postpartum taboos. *See* couvade; taboos, postpartum
pregnancy, 10
    Aché, 5
    Barí, 27, 28, 32–35, 38–41
    Canela, 86–90, 100–102
    Cashinahua, 14, 17–18, 22, 24
    Curripaco, 185–87
    Ese Eja, 140, 144–46
    Kulina, 47, 49, 52–53
    and malnutrition, 28, 32
    Mẽbengokre, 105–6, 110–12
    Piaroa, 196, 206
    prayers for, 196
    premarital, 49
    Sanumá, 5
    Siona-Secoya, 235, 241, 243
    Tapirapé, 5
    Warao, 214–19
    Yanomami, 63–66, 74
    Ye'kwana, 201–2, 206
    See also gestation, beliefs about
premarital cloistering of girls, 241
premarital sexual relations, 14, 15, 18, 22, 203
procreation, beliefs about, 62–85, 127, 132, 158, 162. *See also* sexual reproduction
production
    economic, 138–39, 172–3, 192, 226–28
    of food, 29, 66, 194, 203, 228
    See also subsistence patterns
promiscuity, 22, 23–24, 133, 217, 233, 243
provisioning, 13, 229
    by descent group, 173, 176, 205
    by males, 3, 230, 242

by secondary fathers, 8, 20, 37–38, 134
puberty
    female, 32, 113, 129, 233–34, 240
    male, 172
    rites of, 32, 172, 233–34, 240
    See also adolescence
public recognition
    of affairs, 14, 18, 53, 130, 169–70
    of fatherhood, 10–11, 14, 19–22, 54–55, 71, 144–46, 174, 188
    of sexual activity, 130, 169–70, 203
pudali ceremonies (Curripaco), 190–91
Purus River, 43, 57, 61
putative relative
    ancestor, 161, 163–64, 175, 177, 182
    child, 221–22
    father, 4

Radcliffe-Brown, R., 9, 113
rain forest. *See* forests
ranchers, 95, 102
rape, 110, 133
Rawlins, Nikole, 27–41
remarriage, 31, 107, 143. *See also* marriage
reproduction
    collective, 130–31
    sexual. *See* sexual reproduction
    See also coitus; conception; gestation; semen
reproductive rights, 7, 175, 203
residence rules, 12, 19
    Barí, 31
    Canela, 90–91, 93
    Cashinahua, 19
    Curripaco, 183–84, 190
    endogamous, 31, 46, 60, 119, 212. *See also* endogamy; marriage patterns
    Ese Eja, 142, 146, 157
    exogamous, 163, 184. *See also* exogamy; marriage patterns
    Piaroa, 193, 197
    postmarital, 17, 31, 157, 167, 193, 197, 198
    Siona-Secoya, 226–27, 244
    Wanano, 166

residential/household clusters. *See* households, clusters
restrictions
on food, 14, 19, 24, 47, 55, 61, 66, 88–89,
101, 106, 111, 143, 145, 171–72, 187–88,
204–5, 235, 237
on hunting, 21
on marriage, 168, 184
postpartum, 19, 24, 88, 100, 128, 171–72,
238
sexual, 21, 89, 101, 128, 145, 232–33
See also couvade
Rio Curanja, 14
Rio Negro, 160
rites
of birth, 118, 160
of passage, 116, 216
of paternity, 160
postpartum, 90, 101
of pregnancy, 90
of puverty. *See* puberty, rites of
shamanic, 197
of vengeance, 204
rituals
activities pertaining to, 16, 25, 124, 133,
182, 203
of bathing, 233–34
and blood, 63
of death, 73
of female puberty, 233–34, 240
of foreplay, 130
of the hunt, 61
of kinship, 216
of meat-sharing, 116
and objects, 181
paternal, 115, 171–74, 188–89, 233. *See
also* couvade
of sexual intercourse, 53, 103, 110, 130–31
shamanic, 195, 203, 233
of wife-sharing, 219
roles
ceremonial, 94
of fathers, 8–9, 19, 24–25, 68, 72, 82, 88,

106, 110–13, 163, 172, 175, 186, 188,
219
of female in child development, 53, 62,
65–66, 111, 136, 187
of male in fetal development, 10, 62, 66,
84, 196, 201
parenting, 5, 116, 158, 162, 212–13
sexual, 27–29. *See also* sexual division of
labor
social, 56, 87

sagdojira (Barí), 30–31. *See also* kindred,
consanguineal
sanctions, 11, 138, 194, 239
Sanumá, 5
seclusion, 32, 133, 172–74. *See also* couvade
secondary fathers. *See* fathers, secondary
secrecy, 11, 101–2, 144, 180, 186, 189–90. *See
also* affairs/trysts
section system, Cashinahua, 15–25. *See also*
marriage sections
semen, 101
and kin relations, 47–48
and menstruation, 133
of multiple males, 7, 24, 52, 69, 87–88,
215, 219
See also sperm
—accumulation of, in the womb, 7, 10
Cashinahua, 24
Ese Eja, 140
Kulina, 47, 52
Mẽbengokre, 110
Piaroa, 194–96
Wanano, 171
Yanomami, 64, 74, 81–82
Ye'kwana, 202, 206
—contribution of, to formation of infant, 4,
5, 10
Canela, 87
Cashinahua, 14, 24
Ese Eja, 140, 146
Kulina, 47, 52–53
Mẽbengokre, 110–11, 115

Piaroa, 196
Siona-Secoya, 236
Wanano, 171
Warao, 213–15, 219
Yanomami, 63–65, 73
Ye'kwana, 201–3, 206
sequential sex, 88, 94, 100, 110
settled agriculturalists, 86, 87
settlement patterns
Canela, 87, 93–94
Cashinahua, 16
Curripaco, 180–84
Kulina, 43, 56
Mẽbengokre, 105
Piaroa, 193
Siona-Secoya, 226–27
Wanano, 161
Warao, 212
Ye'kwana, 199–200
sex
ceremonial, 110–11, 121
sequential, 88, 94, 100, 110
sexual abstinence. See restrictions,
sexual
sexual behavior, 7, 11, 14. See also sexual
relations
sexual division of labor, 2, 28, 43, 139, 162
sexual favors, 18, 41, 126
sexual intercourse. See coitus
sexual liaisons. See affairs/trysts; extramari-
tal affairs
sexual receptivity, 3
sexual relations
Barí, 27, 32
Canela, 86–89, 91–92, 100–104
Cashinahua, 14–15, 17–18, 21–22, 24–25
Curripaco, 178, 184–86, 189–90
Ese Eja, 139–40, 142, 144–46, 149–50,
154–56, 159
Kulina, 43, 47–49, 52–53, 55–56, 59
Matis, 129–31, 135
Mẽbengokre, 109–10, 113, 116, 121
Piaroa, 195–96, 206–7

Siona-Secoya, 221–22, 231, 233, 235–36,
238, 240–44
Wanano, 169
Warao, 213–16, 219
Yanomami, 63–65, 67, 77, 85, 71, 74
Ye'kwana, 201, 206–7
sexual reproduction, 8, 11
Curripaco, 182
Ese Eja, 137
Kulina, 42, 45, 59–60
Siona-Secoya, 222, 231, 240–43
Wanano, 162, 166, 175
Warao, 214
Yanomami, 63, 65, 66, 68, 81–82, 85
See also sexual relations
sexuality, 26, 64, 65, 127, 168, 171, 222, 231–
33, 241
shamanism, 118, 124, 172, 183–84, 194–96,
201, 209, 217, 224, 232–36, 240
Shapiro, Judith, 11, 59
shared paternity. See paternity, shared
sharing
of childcare, 141, 158
of food, 226, 231
of meat, 30, 116, 134, 231
of a name, 131–33
of resources, 162, 181
of a spouse, 3, 138, 186, 190, 219
Shavante, 86, 88, 97
Shipibo, 127
Siawani, 212, 220
siblinghood, 127, 166
siblings, 28, 56, 89, 109, 168
conflict among, 189
and marriage, 44–49, 73, 82
sexual relations with, 59, 82
survivorship of, 39–41
See also kindred; kinship; siblingship
siblingship, 11, 42, 45–52, 55, 59–60, 67, 90–
91, 115, 141. See also kinship; siblings
sibs, 161, 241. See also clans
Siona-Secoya, 12, 13, 58, 59, 221–45
worldview of, 232, 233, 240

Siskind, Janet, 109
sisters
    and childcare, 31, 54–55, 58, 74, 99, 187
    classificatory. *See* kinship terminologies
    exchange of, 9, 51
    provisioning of, 24, 115
    sexual relations with, 17, 47, 139, 146, 166,
        194, 198. *See also* incest
    See also kindred; kinship; siblings
slash-and-burn agriculture, 21, 23, 43, 95, 227
social networks, 80, 137, 156
social organizations, 29, 48, 49, 52, 55, 56,
    118, 135, 164, 193, 243
social unit, 68, 82, 87, 139, 161, 165, 169, 177,
    212, 241
sociobiology, 8, 58, 60, 85, 242. *See also*
    evolutionary ecology
sociogeography, 44, 46
solidarity, 45, 59, 67, 74, 82, 130, 164, 167, 173
son-in-law. *See* affinal relations
sons
    Canela, 101
    Cashinahua, 16, 17, 19, 22
    Curripaco, 182–83
    Ese Eja, 138, 143, 146
    Matis, 129, 131, 133–34
    "true," 67–68
    Wanano, 165–66, 169
    Warao, 217–18
    Yanomami, 67–68, 73, 82
    Ye'kwana, 205
    See also boys; children; kindred
sorcery, 109, 148, 170, 173, 182–83, 189–91,
    209, 224, 227
sperm, 1, 63–68, 79, 83–84, 127, 140–41, 196,
    206. *See also* semen
spirits, 5, 196, 232
    ancestral, 60, 112, 157, 165
    forest, 183
spouse
    acquisition/selection, 28, 44, 77, 97. *See
        also* marriage
    exchange of, 155–56, 159. *See also* wife-
        sharing

infidelity of, 18, 25, 110, 138, 169, 190. *See
    also* affairs/trysts
"other," 97
violence against, 72, 78
See also husbands; wives
Standard Model of Human Evolution, 3–4
staple crops, 9, 28, 43, 157, 179
staple diet, 28, 230
status
    of child, 191
    inherited, 164
    marital, 75, 77
    social, 138, 147–50, 186, 213, 215, 219, 232
stepparents, 31, 98, 141, 143, 191, 213
stepsisters, 118
sterility, 145, 215. *See also* infertility
stillbirth, 38, 214
Strathern, Marilyn, 112
subpopulation, 38
subsistence patterns
    Barí, 28
    Canela, 87, 95
    Curripaco, 189
    Ese Eja, 157–58
    Siona-Secoya, 225, 227
    Wanano, 162
    Warao, 211
    See also fishing; hunting; trade
survivorship, 7, 27, 33, 34, 36–41, 221–22, 239

taboos
    incestual. *See* incest
    postpartum, 17, 21, 24–25, 111–12, 135, 171
teknonyms, 48, 50
terra firma, 211, 220
territorial groups, Barí, 30
Timbira, 86, 93, 94, 96, 97
Tocantins River, 86
totemic ancestors, 163–64
totemic souls, 181–83, 188
Townsend, Patricia, 49, 52
trade, 16, 18, 21, 23, 96–97, 119, 138, 192, 211,
    212, 231
trickster, 181

Trobriand, 42, 161, 175
Tukano, 160–77, 193, 215
Tupi, 5, 7, 107, 215
Turner, Terence, 110, 117, 121

Uaupés River, 160–61, 164, 176–77, 183, 193
Uraricoera River, 199
uxorilocality, 11–12, 16–17, 25, 93, 142, 146.
    See also matrilocality

vagina, 48, 67, 75, 80, 181
Vaupés River. *See* Uaupés River
Venezuela, 7, 27–41, 75, 160, 178, 192–209,
    210, 221
Ventuari River, 193, 199, 206–7
villages
    Canela, 87, 92–95
    Cashinahua, 16, 17, 19, 21–23
    Curripaco, 180–91
    Kulina, 43–46, 48, 53, 55–56, 59–60
    Mẽbengokre, 105–6, 112, 114–15, 122
    Piaroa, 193–94
    Siona-Secoya, 227–29, 231, 234–39
    Wanano, 161–62
    Warao, 212–13, 216
    Ye'kwana, 199–200
    See also settlement patterns
violence, 30, 32, 78, 148, 165, 179, 191, 194
virginity, 113
virilocality, 11, 90, 128, 167, 190

Wanano, 10, 12, 13, 59, 160–77
Warao, 12, 13, 130, 210–20
warfare
    Canela, 94–95
    Curripaco, 183
    Matis, 138
    Mẽbengokre, 116, 118
    Yanomami, 82, 86–87
Warime ceremony (Ye'kwana), 194, 196
Wayana, 5
weaning, 54
Western beliefs about reproduction, 1–2, 110,
    185, 207

Western goods, as payment for sexual
    relations, 115
Western notions of paternity, 3, 106, 110,
    113, 121, 185, 207
widows, 24, 31, 73, 111, 167, 175, 180, 191,
    213, 217, 218, 219
wife, second, 20, 213, 220. *See also* wives,
    multiple
wife-sharing, 126, 130, 189, 219
Wilbert, Werner, 130
Wilson, Edward O., 3, 243
Winikina, 210, 213, 217
wives
    Barí, 29, 32
    Canela, 91–94, 97, 99, 102–3
    Cashinahua, 16–20, 22, 24–25
    Curripaco, 178, 180, 183–91
    Ese Eja, 139–43, 146, 152, 154, 159
    Kulina, 46, 49–51, 55–58
    male choice of, 11–12, 73, 212, 234
    Matis, 126, 128–31, 133, 135
    Mẽbengokre, 106–11, 113–15, 120
    multiple, 19–20, 22, 92, 97, 135, 213, 220, 235
    "other, 97
    Piaroa, 193, 198–99, 206
    provisioning of, 17, 20, 58, 69, 81, 94, 114–
        15, 135, 170, 173, 180, 189, 220, 230
    "real," 131
    sharing of. *See* wife-sharing
    Siona-Secoya, 226, 228, 230–38, 244
    Wanano, 166–68, 170–76
    Warao, 212–13, 215–20
    Yanomami, 66, 68–70, 72–73, 76–77, 84
    Ye'kwana, 200–201, 203–4, 206
    See also kinship terminologies; mothers;
        parents; spouse
Wothuja. *See* Piaroa

Xocleng, 4, 107

yahé ceremony (Siona-Secoya), 233
Yanomami, 10, 12, 62–85, 127
Yapima, 167
Ye'kwana, 199